Book Organization

A spread is the pair of pages seen when the book is laid open. *The A.T. Guide* contains trail data and services in alternating spreads; a spread containing trail data is followed by a spread detailing services available to hikers within that section. Occasionally the information is not distributed evenly and there are back-to-back spreads of data or services.

Data Spread

Data Spreads contain a table of landmarks, mileages and elevations. Every spread covers approximately 44 miles of trail (22 miles per page). An elevation profile is "watermarked" on the data. The lines of text that describe the landmarks are spaced so that they intersect the profile map at the approximate location of each landmark. Small triangular pointers below the profile line identify shelter locations. The vertical exaggeration of the profile maps is 5.6.

Services Spread

The Services Spreads contain information about stops along the AT where hikers can regroup and resupply. These mostly cover towns that the trail passes through or near. This book presents a limited view of trail towns. Businesses are selectively included, and maps may only show a portion of town closest to the trail.

When a map is provided, information presented in the map is not repeated in the text unless more elaboration about the service is needed. Three features of the maps help in estimating distance around town: 1) the maps are proportionally scaled, 2) the width of the mapped area is at the bottom of the map, and 3) horizontal and vertical gridlines cross the map every one-half mile. There are a few exceptions where gridlines mark one mile intervals on larger maps. Keep in mind that places of business that appear to be adjacent may be separated by one or more unspecified buildings or roads.

Prices are listed as given in fall of 2009. **No establishment is obliged to maintain these prices.** Lodging prices are particularly volatile, but most facilities listed will do their best for hikers. Let them know if you are thru-hiking; there may be a "thru-hiker rate."

Elevation in feet for profile & for this location.

Elev

(12) 5920

Cables.

6000
5000
4000
3000
2000
1000

Miles from Katahdin *Miles from Springer* *Elevation in feet for profile & for this location.*

SoBo NoBo

1958.0 220.3 **Tri-Corner Knob Shelter** . . . . 20.1◄12.6◄5.2◄►7.7►14.8►25.3

The next 3 shelters to the north are 7.7, 14.8 and 25.3 miles from this shelter. (5.2, 12.6, and 20.1 to the south).

There is a privy, water source, and shelter (capacity 12) at this location.

Elevation profile

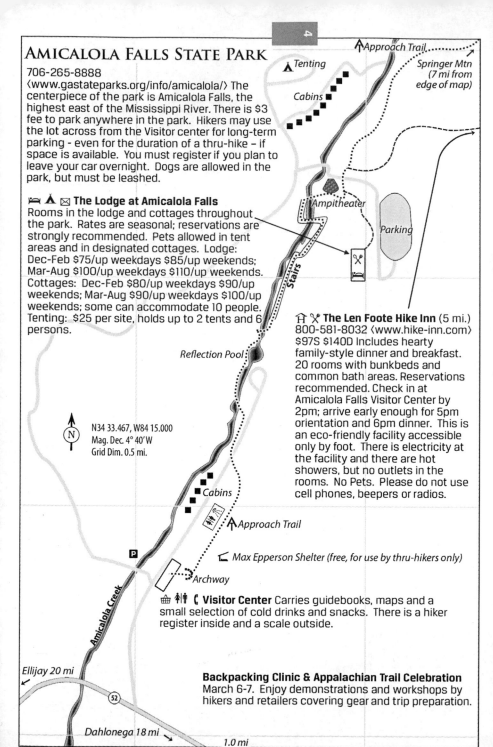

Amicalola Falls State Park

706-265-8888
⟨www.gastateparks.org/info/amicalola/⟩ The centerpiece of the park is Amicalola Falls, the highest east of the Mississippi River. There is $3 fee to park anywhere in the park. Hikers may use the lot across from the Visitor center for long-term parking - even for the duration of a thru-hike – if space is available. You must register if you plan to leave your car overnight. Dogs are allowed in the park, but must be leashed.

⊨ ⚊ ⊠ The Lodge at Amicalola Falls
Rooms in the lodge and cottages throughout the park. Rates are seasonal; reservations are strongly recommended. Pets allowed in tent areas and in designated cottages. Lodge: Dec-Feb $75/up weekdays $85/up weekends; Mar-Aug $100/up weekdays $110/up weekends. Cottages: Dec-Feb $80/up weekdays $90/up weekends; Mar-Aug $90/up weekdays $100/up weekends; some can accommodate 10 people. Tenting: $25 per site, holds up to 2 tents and 6 persons.

Reflection Pool

N34 33.467, W84 15.000
Mag. Dec. 4° 40′W
Grid Dim. 0.5 mi.

Cabins

Approach Trail

⟁ *Tenting*

Cabins

Ampitheater

Parking

Stairs

⌂ ✗ The Len Foote Hike Inn (5 mi.)
800-581-8032 ⟨www.hike-inn.com⟩ $97S $140D Includes hearty family-style dinner and breakfast. 20 rooms with bunkbeds and common bath areas. Reservations recommended. Check in at Amicalola Falls Visitor Center by 2pm; arrive early enough for 5pm orientation and 6pm dinner. This is an eco-friendly facility accessible only by foot. There is electricity at the facility and there are hot showers, but no outlets in the rooms. No Pets. Please do not use cell phones, beepers or radios.

⊏ *Max Epperson Shelter (free, for use by thru-hikers only)*

Archway

⌂ ♣ (Visitor Center
Carries guidebooks, maps and a small selection of cold drinks and snacks. There is a hiker register inside and a scale outside.

Ellijay 20 mi

Amicalola Creek

(52)

Dahlonega 18 mi

1.0 mi

Backpacking Clinic & Appalachian Trail Celebration
March 6-7. Enjoy demonstrations and workshops by hikers and retailers covering gear and trip preparation.

Springer Mtn (7 mi from edge of map)

Symbols and Notations

- Any source of drinking water
- ⌣ AT Shelter
- ⚠ Camping, Tentsite
- ⌂ Hostel
- Hotel, Cabin or B&B
- Outfitter
- Shuttle, Bus or Taxi
- ✕ Any place that serves food
- Long term resupply
- Short Term Resupply
- Hardware store
- $ Bank or ATM
- + Intersection
- **P** Parking. Most trailhead parking areas are preceded by coordinates in GPS format. Hikers or persons meeting them can use their vehicle's GPS to navigate to the trailhead. Coordinates are approximate, but should get you within sight of the lot. GPS systems are not always able to plot a course to remote locations.

- Post Office
- ⊃ Privy
- Public restroom
- Pay Phone
- Laundry
- ⓘ Info center
- Train Station
- Pharmacy
- ✚ First Aid
- Vet or kennel
- ✂ Barber
- Lounge

- Shower - Shown when available without stay
- ✉ Maildrop: Any place that will hold mail.
- Internet: Listed if computer is available (not just WiFi).
- ★ Could not be contacted for 2010 updates. It is probable that the business is still in operation, but details, particularly prices, may have changed.

- ■ Service not categorized by other symbols; only on maps.
- **(x.xE)** Distance and direction (E or W) from the trail, rounded to the nearest tenth of a mile (0.1mi=176 yards). East (E) is always right for a northbound hiker and left for a southbounder. Due to bends in the trail, "E" or "W" may not correspond to a compass reading.
- **(pg.xx)** More information on page xx
- **B/L/D** Breakfast/Lunch/Dinner
- **$nnS, $nnD, $nnPP, $nnEAP:** Room prices: single, double, per-person, each additional person.

Contents

The A.T. Guide

Copyright © 2010 by David Miller

2010 Northbound Edition

ISBN 978-0-9797081-5-2

Edited by David "Awol" Miller

Contributors:

Jim Austin (Skyline), Tripp Clark, Ernest Engman (SGT Rock), Steve Huntress (Pilgrim), Rodney Ketterman (Rodman), Dave Levy (Survivor Dave), David Martinage (Arrow), James Maute (Trail Bug), Juli Miller, Raymond Myers (Rain Man), Edmond Obrien (Irish Eddy), Linda Patton (eArThworm), Jeff Phillips (Chaco Taco), Bill Van Horn

Jerelyn Press
Titusville, FL
www.jerelyn.com

Be aware of trail conditions before heading out, and tune in to advice from outfitters and other hikers. The trail gets re-routed, springs dry up, streams alter their course. Businesses come and go and prices change. Be prepared to deal with changes, particularly with respect to water sources. Never plan to carry just enough water to reach the next spring.

Visit the Website: www.theATguide.com

The website contains the most recent updates, additions and corrections to the information contained in this book. Please let us know if there is anything we can do to improve the material or its presentation.

Maildrop Guidelines

▼ Use your real name (not a trail name), and include an ETA.
▼ FedEx and UPS packages cannot be addressed to PO boxes.
▼ Be prepared to show an ID when you retrieve your mail.
▼ Only send "General Delivery" mail to a Post office.
▼ The "C/O" name is essential when mailing to a business's PO Box; without it, they may not be able to retrieve your mail.
▼ Do not send maildrops to a lodging facility unless you plan to stay with them. If your plans change, offer to pay for the service of holding your mail.

Packages sent to post offices:

John Doe
C/O General Delivery
Trail Town, VA 12345

Please hold for AT hiker
ETA May 16, 2010

Packages sent to businesses:

John Doe
C/O Hiker Hostel
2176 Appalachian Way
Trail Town, VA 12345
Please hold for AT hiker
ETA May 16, 2010

Getting to Springer Mountain

The southern terminus of the trail is atop Springer Mountain, and is accessible only by foot. The 8.8-mile Approach Trail, originating at the Visitor Center in Amicalola State Park, is one means of getting there. An alternative is to drive to Big Stamp Gap via USFS 42, a dirt road passable by most vehicles. From the gap, hike one mile south to Springer Mountain. Your hike would begin by retracing your steps back to Big Stamp Gap.

The closest major city is Atlanta, GA, 82 miles south. If you fly or take AMTRAK into Atlanta, take the MARTA rail system to the North Springs Station, and one of the shuttle services will pick up from there. There is also Greyhound bus service to Gainesville, GA, 38 miles from the park.

Hiker Hostel (see page 9)
Survivor Dave's Trail Shuttle 678-469-0978 〈www.atsurvivordave.com〉 Shuttle service to/ from Atlanta Airport, Gainesville Bus/AMTRAK Terminal, and North Springs MARTA Station to Amicalola, Springer, Woody Gap, Neels Gap, Unicoi Gap, Dick's Creek Gap and as far as Fontana Dam. Will stop at the outfitter and/or supermarket for supplies (time permitting). Reasonable rates. 24 hours notice please. Will respond promptly to phone messages.
Wes Wisson 706-747-2671 〈dwisson@alltel.net〉 Suches, GA. Will shuttle year-round, up to four hikers. MARTA to Amicalola or to Big Stamp Gap.
Ron Brown Home: 706-636-2825, Cell: 706-669-0919 Shuttle range Atlanta to Hiawassee.

Sobo	Nobo	The Approach Trail		Elev
8.8	0.0	**Amicalola Falls State Park**	♦ 🏛 ♙♟	1700
		Approach Trail starts at archway behind Visitor Center.		
8.7	0.1	**Max Epperson Shelter**	♦♙♟ ⌂ ⌐ (12)	1720
		Shelter for thru-hiker use only. Restroom to north of shelter has a shower and is open later than those at the Visitor Center.		
8.4	0.4	Reflection Pond at base of falls		1680
8.1	0.7	Staircase - 604 steps to the top of the Falls		1720
7.9	0.9	Top of the Falls		2550
7.7	1.1	Parking, side trail to Lodge	♙♟	2570
7.5	1.3	Trail to **Len Foote Hike Inn** (5.0E)		2570
		Connects with AT at mile 5.4		
7.4	1.4	Footbridge	♦	2560
7.3	1.5	USFS Road 46, steps on north side		2585
5.6	3.2	High Shoals Road		2760
4.0	4.8	Frosty Mountain	♦	3384
		Spring (0.2E) is unreliable		
3.7	5.1	Frosty Mountain Road, USFS Road 46		2560
3.4	5.4	Trail to **Len Foote Hike Inn** (1.0E)		3250
		Lime-green blazed trail.		
3.1	5.7	Woody Knob		3406
2.8	6.0	Nimblewill Gap, USFS Road 28		3100
2.6	6.2	Spring (left of trail), unreliable	♦	3220
1.8	7.0	Black Mountain		3605
1.5	7.3	**Black Gap Shelter** (0.1W)	⊃♦ ⛺ ⌐ (8)	3300
		Spring is on opposite side of the Approach Trail (0.1E).		
0.0	8.8	Springer Mountain		3782

SoBo	NoBo		Elev
		GA 6 1000 2000 3000 4000 5000 6000	
2179.1	**0.0**	Springer Mountain southern terminus	3782
2178.9	**0.2**	**Springer Mountain Shelter** (0.2E) . . . . 🌙💧⛺🏕(12)	3730
		0.0◄0.0◄0.0◄►2.6►7.6►14.9 Cables. Benton MacKaye Trail tp east.	
2178.1	**1.0**	Big Stamp Gap, USFS 42 . . . . N34 38.257 W84 11.725 🅿	3350
2177.8	**1.3**	Benton MacKaye Trail to east.	3200
2177.2	**1.9**	Benton MacKaye / Duncan RidgeTrail to east	3300
2176.4	**2.7**	Stover Creek, multiple crossings from here north to Three Forks . . . . 💧	3100
2176.3	**2.8**	**Stover Creek Shelter** (0.1E) . . . . 🌙💧⛺🏕(10)	2900
		0.0◄0.0◄2.6◄►5.0►12.3►24.2 Water 90 yards right of shelter.	
2175.3	**3.8**	Stover Creek . . . . 💧	2660
2174.9	**4.2**	Benton MacKaye / Duncan Ridge Trail to east	2580
2174.8	**4.3**	Three Forks, USFS 58, side trail to Long Creek Falls. . . . . . 💧	2530
2174.0	**5.1**	Benton MacKaye / Duncan Ridge Trail to west	2800
2173.1	**6.0**	Logging road	3100
2171.4	**7.7**	Stream . . . . 💧	3224
2171.3	**7.8**	**Hawk Mountain Shelter** (0.2W) . . . . 🌙💧🏕(12)	3200
		0.0◄7.6◄5.0◄►7.3►19.2►20.5 Water 0.1 mile	
		behind shelter. Next water source is 6 miles north.	
2170.8	**8.3**	Hightower Gap, junction USFS 42 & 69. . . . . . N34 39.809 W84 7.779 🅿	2854
2168.9	**10.2**	Horse Gap.	2673
2167.9	**11.2**	Sassafras Mountain	3320
2167.3	**11.8**	Cooper Gap, USFS 15, 42 & 80 . . . . . . N34 39.1686 W84 5.0789 🅿	2800
2166.7	**12.4**	Justus Mountain	3224
2165.4	**13.7**	Logging road	2557
2165.3	**13.8**	Justus Creek, footbridge, campsites uphill. . . . . 💧🏕	2550
2164.6	**14.5**	Blackwell Creek . . . . 💧	2600
2164.0	**15.1**	**Gooch Mountain Shelter** (0.1W) . . . . 🌙💧🏕🏕(14)	3000
		14.9◄12.3◄7.3◄►11.9►13.2►21.8 Cables.	
		Water 100 yards behind shelter.	
2162.9	**16.2**	Spring . . . . 💧	2835
2162.6	**16.5**	Gooch Gap, USFS 42 . . . . N34 39.1256 W84 1.9402 🅿💧🏕	2784
		Suches, GA (2.7W) (see town info on page 9)	
2161.1	**18.0**	Liss Gap	2952
2160.4	**18.7**	Ramrock Mountain . . . . no bunk space	3260
2159.0	**20.1**	Woody Gap, GA 60 . . . . N34 40.659 W84 0.000 🅿💧🚻 (pg.9)	3150
		Suches, GA (2.0W); Hostel (6.0E); spring behind parking area.	
2158.9	**20.2**	Spring . . . . 💧	3200
2158.0	**21.1**	Big Cedar Mountain, rock ledges and views.	3737
2157.5	**21.6**	Small spring on west side of trail. . . . . 💧	3598

SoBo	NoBo		Elev
2156.8	22.3	Small stream .... ♦	3455
2156.7	22.4	Dan Gap	3300
2156.1	23.0	Miller Gap, Dockery Lake Trail	3250
2155.8	23.3	Lance Creek 3|1.6|10 ?............... ♦▲	3050
2155.0	24.1	Henry Gap is 70 yards west on side trail........... 🅿	3120
		unpaved road to GA 180	
2153.9	25.2	Burnett Field Mountain	3480
2153.4	25.7	Jarrard Gap .... ♦ (0.3W) **(pg.9)**	3250
2152.4	26.7	Turkey Stamp Mountain	3770
2152.1	27.0	**Woods Hole Shelter** (0.4W) 24.2◄19.2◄11.9◄►1.3►9.9►14.5 . ☽ ♦ ⊏ (7)	3600
2152.0	27.1	Bird Gap, Freeman Trail .... ▲	3650
2151.6	27.5	Slaughter Creek Campsite, stream unreliable ...... ♦▲	3800
2151.5	27.6	Duncan Ridge Trail, Coosa Trail	3895
2150.8	28.3	**Blood Mountain Shelter** (1934) .... ☽⊏ (8)	4461
		20.5◄13.2◄1.3◄►8.6►13.2►20.4 Privy 50 yards north on east side of AT.	
		No fires. Stream on trail to Slaughter Creek (0.8S)	
2149.4	29.7	Flatrock Gap .... ♦ (0.2W)	3450
2149.3	29.8	Balance Rock	3440
2148.4	30.7	Neels Gap, US 19 .... N34 44.464 W83 55.237 🅿 **(pg.9)**	3125
2147.3	31.8	Bull Gap, spring 0.1W .... ♦▲	3690
2146.9	32.2	Levelland Mountain	3942
2146.3	32.8	Swaim Gap	3470
2145.6	33.5	Rock Spring Top, spring to west of trail .... ♦	3520
2145.1	34.0	Corbin Horse Stamp	3620
2145.0	34.1	Wolf Laurel Top, campsite with views to east. .... ▲	3766
2144.2	34.9	Baggs Creek Gap .... ♦▲	3800
2143.7	35.4	Cowrock Mountain	3842
2142.9	36.2	Tesnatee Gap, GA 348, Russell Hwy ...... N34 43.5708 W83 50.8453 🅿	3138
2142.4	36.7	Wildcat Mountain	3420
2142.2	36.9	**Whitley Gap Shelter** (1.2E) 21.8◄9.9◄8.6◄►4.6►11.8►19.6 . ☽ ♦ ⊏ (6)	3370
		Spring 0.3 miles behind shelter.	
2142.0	37.1	Hogpen Gap, GA 348 .... N34 43.551 W83 50.395 🅿 ♦	3450
2141.1	38.0	White Oak Stamp	3470
2140.1	39.0	Poor Mountain	3620
2139.5	39.6	Wide Gap	3150
2138.4	40.7	Sheep Rock Top	3600
2137.6	41.5	**Low Gap Shelter** .... ☽ ♦ ▲ ⊏ (7)	3050
		14.5◄13.2◄4.6◄►7.2►15.0►22.5 Cables. Water 30 yards in front of shelter.	
2137.2	41.9	Stream, cascade .... ♦	3080
2136.2	42.9	Poplar Stamp Gap .... ♦▲	3334
		spring 0.1E down old railroad bed.	
2135.7	43.4	Stream .... ♦	3650

Trail Etiquette

The AT is probably better without rigid rules of behavior, and definitely better without hikers who harangue others with such rules. Act as a civil person would in any public place. For more on etiquette, visit backpacking websites.

Avoid using a cell phone anywhere within the trail corridor, especially in shelters or within earshot of other hikers.

When hikers approach one another on the trail, the uphill hiker has the right-of-way, but the rule is irrelevant. If a hiker is approaching, look for an opportunity to step aside, regardless of your position, doing your best not to trample the last living patch of rock gnome lichen. Be aware of hikers approaching from behind, and step aside so that they may pass.

Take only as much shelter space as you need to sleep. Shelter spaces cannot be reserved for friends who have yet to arrive. If you bring alcohol to a shelter or campsite, do so discreetly. Soon after dark is bedtime for most hikers.

The AT is liberating, and outlandish behavior is part of AT lore. Be considerate; boisterous and erratic behavior may be unsettling to strangers stuck in the woods with you. Conversely, hikers seeking a serene experience should be aware that AT hiking is, for many, a social experience. Be tolerant. Stay flexible and be prepared to move on rather than trying to convince others to conform to your expectations.

Town Etiquette

Ask permission before bringing a pack into a place of business.

Don't expect generosity, and show appreciation when it is offered. If you are granted work-for-stay, strive to provide service equal to the value of your stay.

Assume that alcohol is not permitted in hostels & campsites until told otherwise.

Respect hotel room capacities; hotel owners should know how many people intend to stay in a room. Try to leave hotel rooms as clean as a car traveler would. If a shower is available, use it.

leave no trace

1. Plan Ahead and Prepare
2. Travel and Camp on Durable Surfaces
3. Dispose of Waste Properly
4. Leave What You Find
5. Minimize Campfire Impacts
6. Respect Wildlife
7. Be Considerate of Other Visitors

This copyrighted information has been reprinted with permission from the Leave No Trace Center for Outdoor Ethics: ⟨www.LNT.org⟩

20.1 GA 60 - Woody Gap

Hiker Hostel 770-312-7342 (6.0E) <www.hikerhostel.com> hikerhostel@yahoo.com Available mid-February through late May. Bunks $16PP, private room for 2. All overnight stays include breakfast, sheets & towel for shower. SPECIAL: $70 pick up from Atlanta North Springs Station or Gainesville, overnight stay, shuttle to Amicalola or Springer, 8oz of white gas or alcohol. Pickups 5pm daily at Woody Gap from late February to mid-April. Shuttles from Atlanta to Dick's Creek Gap. Maildrops: (UPS/FedEx) 7693 Hwy 19N, (USPS) PO Box 802, Dahlonega, GA 30533.

Suches, GA 30572 (2.0W)

Suches General Store M-F 7:30-11:30, 1-4:30, Sa 7:30-11:30, 706-747-2611

High Valley Resort (0.6W) of Post Office, 706-747-2037 <www.highvalleyresort.com> Camping $15PP, bunkhouse $45PP, Tenters and bunkhouse have access to bathhouse, showers and lodge with satellite TV. Winter special (until Apr 1): cabins $100/night, some sleep 4, some sleep up to 8 persons.

Two Wheels Only 706-747-5151 Camping (hiker rate) $7PP, Hot showers. Grill serves breakfast 7 days, B/L/D on weekends.

Wes Wisson 706-747-2671

Big Rock Clinic 706-747-1421, M-Tu, Th-F 8-3, walk-ins 9-10.

25.7 Jarrard Gap

(1.0W) **Lake Winfield Scott Recreation Area** tent sites $14, showers & bathrooms, leash dogs.

(2.0W) **Lenny's Grill** F-Sa 4-9, Su 10:30-3.

30.7 US 19 & 129 Neels Gap

Mountain Crossings 706-745-6095 <www.mountaincrossings.com> A full-service outfitter and gift shop operated by Winton Porter, bunk $15PP with towel and shower, sleeps 16. Shower without stay $3.50. No pets in hostel, kennels available. Denatured alcohol/oz. UPS/USPS Maildrops held for two weeks with $1 fee at pick up: 9710 Gainesville Hwy, Blairsville, GA 30512. Mar-Oct hours Su-Sa 8:30-6, Nov-Feb hours Su-Sa 9-5, call for cabin rates (available by reservation) Ask about shuttles.

(0.3E) **Blood Mountain Cabins** 800-284-6866 <www.bloodmountain.com> Thru-hiker rate $60. Cabin with kitchen and CATV holds up to 4 adults & 2 children under the age of 13. Laundry free w/stay, no pets.

(3W) **Vogel State Park** 706-745-2628 <www.gastateparks.org> Tent sites with shower $12, cabins for 2 to 10 persons $85-$140, $2 shower w/o stay. Long term parking $5.

(3.5W) **Goose Creek Cabins** 706-745-5111 <www.goosecreekcabins.com> goosecreek@alltel.net. $25PP and up, tent sites $10PP, shower/towel without stay $2, laundry $5 per load, pets allowed, includes lodge with game room, CATV, and shuttles from/to trail. Parking for section hikers free with stay. $5 for shuttle to AYCE restaurant in Blairsville, $25 for shuttle to Hogpen Gap. Trout fishing on-site. UPS Maildrops: Goose Creek Cabins, 29 Goose Creek, Blairsville, GA 30512.

Blairsville, GA (14W) All major services.

Dahlonega, GA (17E) All major services.

SoBo	NoBo		Elev
2133.8	**45.3**	Cold Springs Gap	3300
2132.6	**46.5**	Chattahoochee Gap, Jacks Knob Trail. . . . . ♦	3500
		east 0.5 to spring	
2132.0	**47.1**	Red Clay Gap	3485
2131.3	**47.8**	Site of former Rocky Knob Shelter . . . . ▲	3600
2131.1	**48.0**	Spring west of trail down slope . . . . ♦	3500
2130.6	**48.5**	Spring on west side of trail . . . . ♦	3960
2130.4	**48.7**	**Blue Mountain Shelter** . . . . ▷ 》 ♦ ⊏ (7)	3900
		20.4◄11.8◄7.2◄▸7.8▸15.3▸23.3 Spring on AT (0.1S)	
2129.6	**49.5**	Blue Mountain	4025
2128.2	**50.9**	Unicoi Gap, GA 75, ...N34 48.101 W83 44.578 🅿 **(pg.12)**	2949
		Helen, GA (9.0E)	
2127.6	**51.5**	Stream . . . . ♦	3300
2126.9	**52.2**	Rocky Mountain . . . . ▲	4017
2125.6	**53.5**	Indian Grave Gap, USFS 283. . . . . N34 47.563 W83 42.855 🅿	3113
2124.9	**54.2**	Tray Mountain Rd, USFS 79 . . . . ♦	3500
2124.6	**54.5**	Cheese factory site, water (0.1W) on blue-blazed trail . . . . ♦▲	3590
2123.8	**55.3**	Tray Gap, Tray Mountain Rd, USFS 79 . . . . . N34 47.959 W83 41.461 🅿▲	3847
2123.0	**56.1**	Tray Mountain, Fontana Lake sometimes visible 3/19 5:22 PM . . .	4430
2122.6	**56.5**	**Tray Mountain Shelter** (0.2W) . . . . ▷ 》 ♦ ⊏ (7)	4200
		19.6◄15.0◄7.8◄▸7.5▸15.5▸22.8	
		Cables. Spring 0.1 mile behind shelter.	
2121.4	**57.7**	Wolfpen Gap	3550
2120.9	**58.2**	Steeltrap Gap . . . . ♦	3500
2120.4	**58.7**	Young Lick Knob	3800
2119.0	**60.1**	Swag of the Blue Ridge	3400
2118.3	**60.8**	Round Top	3960
2117.8	**61.3**	Sassafras Gap, spring 0.1 downhill to east . . . . ♦▲	3500
2117.0	**62.1**	Addis Gap,. . . . . ♦ ▲ (0.5E)	3304
		Campsite 0.5E down old fire road, stream to right of campsite.	
2116.0	**63.1**	Kelly Knob. . . . . ♦	4276
		Water (0.1E) down steep trail. Summit 0.2W.	
2115.1	**64.0**	**Deep Gap Shelter** (0.3E) . . . . 》♦⊏ (12)	3350
		22.5◄15.3◄7.5◄▸8.0▸15.3▸20.2 Water (0.1) before shelter.	
2114.2	**64.9**	"Vista" blue-blaze leads (0.1E) to campsite . . . . ▲	3550
2113.8	**65.3**	Powell Mountain	3850

SoBo	NoBo		Elev
2112.8	66.3	Moreland Gap	3200
2112.2	66.9	Streams . . . . ♦	2650
2111.6	67.5	Dicks Creek Gap, US 76 . . . . N34 54.728 W83 37.130 🅿 ♦ **(pg.12-13)**	2675
		Water, picnic tables t the gap, **Hiawassee, GA** (11.0W) *3/20-21 pizza/beer*	
2111.2	67.9	Little Bald Knob	3440
2110.5	68.6	Camping, water (0.1E) down steep blue-blazed trail . . . . . . ♦ �	3150
2110.2	68.9	Stream . . . . ♦ ⚑	3060
2109.8	69.3	Cowart Gap . . . . ♦ ⚑	2900
2108.6	70.5	Buzzard Knob	3760
2108.3	70.8	Bull Gap	3531
2107.1	72.0	**Plumorchard Gap Shelter** (0.2E) . . . . ☽ ♦ ⚑(14)	3013
		23.3◄15.5◄8.0◄►7.3►12.2►19.8 Privy 0.2 mile down steep blue-blazed trail. Creek on trail to shelter and spring (0.1W) of AT.	
2106.4	72.7	As Knob	3460
2105.8	73.3	Blue Ridge Gap	3020
2105.2	73.9	Wheeler Knob	3560
2104.8	74.3	Campsite . . . . ♦ ⚑	3500
2104.6	74.5	Rich Cove Gap	3390
2102.7	76.4	**GA-NC** border	3825
2102.6	76.5	Bly Gap, spring west 30 yards . . . . ♦ ⚑	3840
		Old and twisted tree often photographed.	
2100.7	78.4	Sassafras Gap	4300
2100.1	79.0	Stream . . . . ♦	4351
2099.8	79.3	**Muskrat Creek Shelter** . . . . ☽ ♦ ⚑ ⚑ (8)	4600
		22.8◄15.3◄7.3◄►4.9►12.5►19.3	
2099.0	80.1	Whiteoak Stamp	4620
2098.8	80.3	Chunky Gal Trail	4700
2097.9	81.2	Wateroak Gap	4490
2095.8	83.3	Deep Gap, USFS 71 . . . . N35 2.3756 W83 33.1812 🅿 ♦	4341
		Kimsey Creek Tr. 3.7E to **Standing Indian Campground,** see mi 104.0.	
2094.9	84.2	**Standing Indian Shelter** . . . . ☽ ♦ ⚑ (8)	4760
		20.2◄12.2◄4.9◄►7.6►14.4►19.7 Creek 70 yards downhill.	
2093.4	85.7	Lower Ridge Trail . . . . ♦ ⚑ (0.2W)	5498
		Standing Indian Mountain, Camping at summit.	

50.9   GA 75 (Unicoi Gap)

Helen, GA 30545 (9E)

🏪 M-F 9-5, Sa 9-12, 706-878-2422 Tourist town with many hotels, restaurants, gift shops, ice cream shops, river rafting and tubing rentals. Visitor Center on Bruckenstrasse (near the PO) has information about places to stay and a free phone for making reservations.

🏨 ⛺ ⌂ **Helendorf River Inn** 800-445-2271 Prices are for 1 or 2 persons Su-Th; weekends are more: Dec-Mar $34, Apr-May $54, Jun-Sep $74, $5EAP, pets $10. Includes cont B. Visa/MC accepted.

🏨 **Super 8 Motel** 706-878-2191, ask for hiker room $45, no pets.

🏨 **Econo Lodge** 800-443-6488   Weekdays $60, higher on weekends. Pets under 20 pounds allowed with $20 fee.

🏨 ⌂ **Best Western Motel** 800-435-3642, $69 weekdays, $99 weekends.

🛒 **Betty's Country Store** 706-878-2943 open 7 days 7am-9pm.
⛺ **laundromat**

67.5   US 76 (Dick's Creek Gap)

🏠 ▲ ⛺ ⊠ (W3.4) **Blueberry Patch Hostel** 706-896-4893 Christian ministry in its 18th season operated by Gary and Lennie Poteat. Gary is a 1991 thru-hiker. Open mid-February until the end of April. Bunks and tentsites; donations accepted. Please check in between 10am and 6pm. Shower, laundry, breakfast and 9:30 shuttle back to Dick's Creek Gap. No pets; no alcohol or drugs. Maildrops: 5038 Hwy 76 East, Hiawassee, GA 30546.

Hiawassee, GA (11W) *(more services on map)*

🏨 ⊠ ⊠ **Mull's Motel** 706-896-4195, $45 and up, no pets, shuttles can be arranged, maildrops for guests only 213 N. Main St., Hiawassee, GA 30546.

🏨 ⛺ ⊠ **Hiawassee Inn** 706-896-4121 $35S, $5EAP, pets $10, laundry $3.   Accepts Visa/MC.   Continental breakfast included. Maildrops: 193 East Main Street, Hiawassee, GA 30546.

🏨 ⛺ ⊠ **Holiday Inn Express** 706-896-8884 ⟨www.hiexpress.com/hiawasseega⟩ Seasonally discounted rates, accepts all major credit cards. Full hot breakfast included, free use of bicycles, indoor pool and hot tub, no pets. Maildrops: 300 Big Sky Drive, Hiawassee, GA 30546.

🏠 **Bill's Wheels of Georgia** 706-994-3431 (Cell) BillsWheelsOfGeorgia@yahoo.com Shuttles to/from airports, bus & train stations and trailheads from Atlanta to NOC in Wesser, NC. Available 365 days a year at any hour, however extremely early or extremely late shuttles are price-adjusted accordingly. Advance notice appreciated.

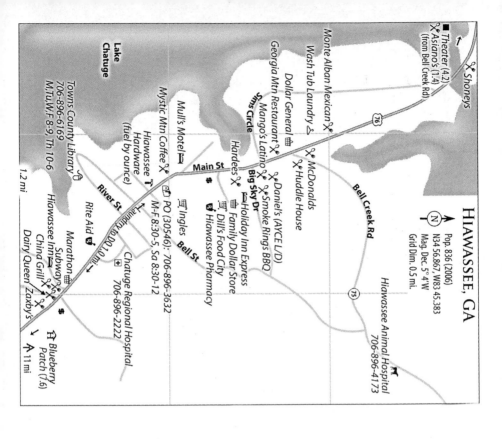

HIAWASSEE, GA

(N) Pop. 836 (2006)
N34 56.867, W83 45.383
Mag. Dec. 5° 4' W
Grid Dim. 0.5 mi.

Shoneys

■ Theater (4.2)
✗ Asiano's (1.4)
(from Bell Creek Rd)

Monte Alban Mexican ✗

Wash Tub Laundry △

Dollar General 盦
Georgia Mtn Restaurant 盦

Mystic Mtn Coffee ✗

Mull's Motel ⊨

Sims Circle

Mango's Latino ✗
Smoke Rings BBQ ✗

McDonalds ✗
Huddle House ✗

Hardees ✗
Main St

Daniel's (AYCE L/D) ✗
Big Sky Dr

⊨ Holiday Inn Express
盦 Family Dollar Store
⌁ Dill's Food City
⊕ Hiawassee Pharmacy

**Lake
Chatuge**

Towns County Library ⌂
706-896-6169
M,Tu,W,F 8-9, Th. 10-6

Hiawassee
Hardware
(fuel by ounce)

River St

Rite Aid ⊕

Ingles ⌁
Bell St

Chatuge Regional Hospital
⊕ 706-896-2222

⊡ PO (30546): 706-896-3632
M-F 8:30-5, Sa 8:30-12

Marathon 盦
Subway ✗
China Grill ✗
Dairy Queen ✗ Zaxby's ✗

1.2 mi

11 mi ↑

⚥ Blueberry
Patch (7.6)

Bell Creek Rd

(76)

(75)

Hiawassee Animal Hospital
706-896-4173

At most post offices, postal workers are present
before and after the window closes, and may retrieve
a package for you. Doing so is a courtesy not an
obligation. Do not impose on them unnecessarily.

SoBo	NoBo	Description	Elev
2090.5	**88.6**	Beech Gap Tenting area with water. . . . . ♦🛆	4460
2090.0	**89.1**	Stream . . . . ♦	4450
2089.7	**89.4**	Stream . . . . ♦	4500
2088.7	**90.4**	Coleman Gap.	4300
2087.7	**91.4**	Timber Ridge Trail	4700
2087.3	**91.8**	**Carter Gap Shelters** . . . . ☽♦🛆⌐ (14)	4540

19.8◄12.5◄7.6◄►6.8►12.1►19.6
Spring 100 yards downhill behind old shelter.

White blazes on the north side of trees are
identical to the blazes on the south side. Make
sure you are headed in the right direction,
especially when sleepily leaving shelters in the morning.

SoBo	NoBo	Description	Elev
2083.6	**95.5**	Betty Creek Gap . . . . ♦🛆	4300
2082.7	**96.4**	Mooney Gap, USFS 83	4400
2082.5	**96.6**	Spring . . . . ♦	4500
2082.4	**96.7**	Big Butt Mountain.	4600
2081.4	**97.7**	USFS 67, Albert Mtn bypass west on road reconnects 0.4 north	4790
2081.1	**98.0**	Albert Mountain, fire tower	5250
2081.0	**98.1**	USFS 67, Albert Mountain bypass	5050
2080.5	**98.6**	**Big Spring Shelter** . . . . ☽♦⌐ (8)	4940

19.3◄14.4◄6.8◄►5.3►12.8►20.1
Cables. Spring behind and to left of shelter.

SoBo	NoBo	Description	Elev
2078.5	**100.6**	Spring . . . . ♦	4930
2077.7	**101.4**	Glassmine Gap, Long Branch Trail 2.0W to USFS 67	4160
2075.7	**103.4**	Spring (seasonal) . . . . ♦	4130
2075.2	**103.9**	**Rock Gap Shelter** . . . . ☽♦⌐ (8)	3760

19.7◄12.1◄5.3◄►7.5►14.8►19.6 Cables.

SoBo	NoBo	Description	Elev
2075.1	**104.0**	Rock Gap . . . . N35 5.6402 W83 31.3555 **P** 🚰🚻 (🛆	3750

Standing Indian Campground (1.5W) $16, Easter-Thanksgiving.

SoBo	NoBo	Description	Elev
2074.5	**104.6**	Wallace Gap, Old US 64	3738
2074.4	**104.7**	Stream . . . . ♦	3805
2072.1	**107.0**	Stream . . . . ♦	4250
2071.4	**107.7**	Winding Stair Gap, US 64 . . . . N35 7.178 W83 32.878 **P** ♦ **(pg.16-17)**	3850

pipe spring east of steps, **Franklin, NC** (10.0E)

SoBo	NoBo	Description	Elev
2071.1	**108.0**	Stream by waterfall . . . . ♦	3850
2070.5	**108.6**	Camping, stream . . . . ♦🛆	3970
2070.3	**108.8**	Swinging Lick Gap . . . . ♦	4100
2069.4	**109.7**	Panther Gap	4480

2067.7	111.4	**Siler Bald Shelter** (0.5E)	☽ ◦ ⌐ (8)	4600
		19.6◄12.8◄7.5◄►7.3►12.1►17.9		
2067.3	111.8	Siler Bald.	◦	4950
2066.0	113.1	Pipe spring	◦	4500
2065.6	113.5	Wayah Crest Picnic Area . . . . N35 9.237 W83 34.844 **P**		4170
2065.5	113.6	Wayah Gap, NC 1310		4180
2064.2	114.9	Wilson Lick Trail Junction		4650
2063.7	115.4	USFS 69, piped stream to east	◦	4900
2063.3	115.8	Bartram Trail		5290
2063.2	115.9	Wine Spring	◦ ⋀	5290
		Water on west side of the AT		
2061.6	117.5	Wine Spring Rd		5320
2061.4	117.7	Latrines and parking . . . . N35 10.509 W83 34.845 **P** ⋔		5313
2061.3	117.8	Wayah Bald, Stone tower and paved footpath		5342
2060.9	118.2	Camping, spring to west of trail	◦ ⋀	5200
2060.4	118.7	**Wayah Shelter,** east to shelter, west 0.2 to water.	☽ ◦ ⋀ ⌐ (8)	4810
		20.1◄14.8◄7.3◄►4.8►10.6►15.5		
2059.1	120.0	Licklog Gap . . . . ◦ ⋀ (0.5W)		4440
2057.2	121.9	Stream	◦	4600
2056.8	122.3	Burningtown Gap, NC 1397		4236
2055.6	123.5	**Cold Spring Shelter** . . . . ☽ ◦ ⋀ ⌐ (6)		4920
		19.6◄12.1◄4.8◄►5.8►10.7►18.4 Trail to tentsites 0.1N on AT.		
2054.9	124.2	Copper Ridge Bald Lookout		5080
2053.7	125.4	Side trail to Rocky Bald Lookout		5030
2053.4	125.7	Spring	◦	4900
2052.0	127.1	Tellico Gap, NC 1365 . . . . N35 16.082 W83 34.353 **P**		3850
2050.6	128.5	Wesser Bald, east 40 yards to observation tower, panoramic views		4627
2049.9	129.2	Spring-fed stone cistern on blue-blazed trail (0.1E)	◦	4100
2049.8	129.3	**Wesser Bald Shelter** (0.1W) . . . . ☽ ⋀ ⌐ (8)		4115
		17.9◄10.6◄5.8◄►4.9►12.6►21.7 Cables.		
		Spring 0.1 mi. south on AT (at switchback).		
2048.2	130.9	Jumpup Lookout		4000

| SoBo | NoBo | | NC 15 | 1000 | 2000 | 3000 | 4000 | 5000 | 6000 | Elev |

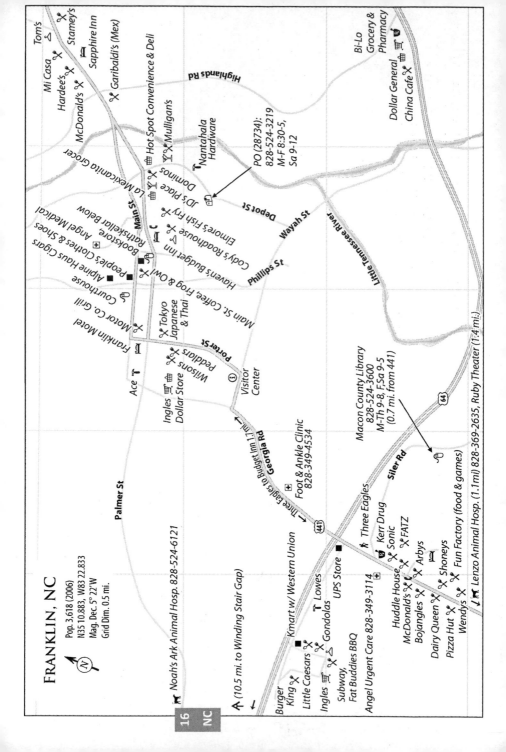

FRANKLIN, NC

Pop. 3,618 (2006)
N35 10.883, W83 22.833
Mag. Dec. 5° 22'W
Grid Dim. 0.5 mi.

Noah's Ark Animal Hosp. 828-524-6121

Palmer St

↑ (10.5 mi. to Winding Stair Gap)

Franklin Motor Co. Grill
Courthouse
Alpine Haus Cigars
People's Clothes & Shoes
Bookstore, Angel Medical
Rathskellar Below
Haven's Budget Inn
Ace

Tom's
Stamey's
Sapphire Inn
Mi Casa
Hardee's
McDonald's
Garibaldi's (Mex)

Highlands Rd

Hot Spot Convenience & Deli
Mulligan's
Dominos
La Mexicanita Grocer
JD's Place
Nantahala Hardware

PO (28734):
828-524-3219
M-F 8:30-5,
Sa 9-12

Depot St

Wayah St

Main St
Elmore's Fish Fry
Cody's Roadhouse
Phillips St
Main St. Coffee, Frog & Owl

Tokyo Japanese & Thai
Wilsons Peddlers
Ingles Dollar Store

Porter St

Visitor Center

Budget Inn
Georgia Rd

Three Eagles

Foot & Ankle Clinic
828-349-4534

Macon County Library
828-524-3600
M-Th 9-8, F,Sa 9-5
(0.7 mi. from 441)

Siler Rd

64

Little Tennessee River

Bi-Lo
Grocery &
Pharmacy

Dollar General
China Cafe

Kmart w/ Western Union
Lowes
Gondolas
UPS Store

Burger King
Little Caesars
Ingles
Subway,
Fat Buddies BBQ

Angel Urgent Care 828-349-3114

Kerr Drug
Sonic
FATZ
Huddle House
McDonald's
Bojangles
Arbys
Dairy Queen
Shoneys
Pizza Hut
Wendys
Fun Factory (food & games)

Lenzo Animal Hosp. (1.1mi) 828-369-2635, Ruby Theater (1.4 mi.)

Franklin, NC (10E) *(more services on map)*

"Franklin Appalachian 100 Mile Event (FAME)" April 2-3 downtown.

▣ Ron Haven, owner of Budget Inn, Sapphire Inn and Franklin Motel, makes three trips every morning Mar-Apr, and picks up at Rock Gap, Wallace Gap and Winding Stair Gap.

⌂△♨▣ ✉ **Haven's Budget Inn** 828-524-4403 (www.havensbudgetinn.com) $39.99S, $5EAP, $50 pet deposit, shuttles back to trail and around town. Internet and laundry on-site. Maildrops: 433 East Palmer Street, Franklin, NC 28734.

⌂♨ ✉ **Sapphire Inn** 828-524-4406, $39.99S + $5EAP Maildrops: 761 E. Main St. Bus 441, Franklin, NC 28734.

⌂△♨▣ ✉ **Franklin Motel** 800-433-5507 (www.thefranklinmotel.com) King bed rooms $45 $5EAP, Maildrops: 17 West Palmer Street, Franklin, NC 28734.

⌂♨ ✉ **Microtel Inn & Suites** 888-403-1700 $45.95S, $62.95D, pets $20. Includes continental breakfast. Maildrops: 81 Allman Dr., Franklin, NC 28734

⌂ **Oak Hill Country Inn** 828-524-7907 (www.oakhillcountryinn.com) $100/up includes breakfast.

✕ ✉ **Three Eagles Outfitters** 828-524-9061 Open M-Sa 10-6, Su12-4. Full-service outfitter, fuel/oz. Maildrops: 78 Siler Road, Franklin, NC 28734.

🍴 **Ace Hardware** Coleman/alcohol/oz

▣ **City Taxi** 828-369-5042, until 6 pm.

▣ **Roadrunner Driving Services** 706-201-7719 where2@mac.com Shuttle anywhere from Atlanta to Damascus.

✚ **Angel Urgent Care** 828-349-3114 M-F 8-6, Sa 8-2, Su 10-2

🐾 **Lenzo Animal Hospital** 828-369-2625

ⓘ **Visitor Center** (Chamber of Commerce) 828-524-3161, M-F 9-5. Also open Sa 9-5 May-Oct. List of hiker services, including shuttles.

UPS Store 828-524-9800, M-F 8-6, Sa 10-3.

Appalachian Trail Conservancy (ATC)

The ATC works with the National Park Service, 30 volunteer maintaining clubs, and multiple other partners to engage the public in conserving this essential American resource.

Their website, www.AppalachianTrail.org, contains information about trail history and protection, hike planning, and trail conditions. If you hike all of the AT, you may complete a "2,000-miler" application and receive a certificate and patch from the ATC. You will also be added to their registry of 2,000-milers and your name will be printed in the May/June issue of ATC's member magazine, *AT Journeys*. The application is available from the website.

The ATC provided the bulk of the mileage data that appears in this book, and a portion of every book sold is donated to the organization. We encourage all AT hikers, particularly hikers who intend to hike all of the AT, to join or donate to the ATC.

SoBo	NoBo		Elev
2044.9	**134.2**	**A. Rufus Morgan Shelter** . . . . ✦ ⌐ (6)	2300
		15.5◄10.7◄4.9◄►7.7►16.8►22.9 Stream on opposite side of AT.	
2044.1	**135.0**	US 19 & 74, ... N35 19.873 W83 35.529 🅿 **(pg.20)**	1723
		Nantahala Outdoor Center	
2042.5	**136.6**	Wright Gap	2390
2041.8	**137.3**	Tyre Top	2800
2041.6	**137.5**	Camping (0.1W) . . . . ✦▲	2880
2041.0	**138.1**	Grassy Gap . . . . ✦	3050
2040.6	**138.5**	Grassy Top.	3250
2038.8	**140.3**	The Jump up	4034
2038.1	**141.0**	Swim Bald . . . . ✦	4720
2037.2	**141.9**	**Sassafras Gap Shelter** (0.1E) . . . . ☽✦⌐ (14)	4330
		18.4◄12.6◄7.7◄►9.1►15.2►21.8	
		Reliable spring front-right of shelter.	
2036.0	**143.1**	Cheoah Bald . . . . ✦▲	5062
		Camping at top of Cheoah Bald. Spring (0.1W) down mountain.	
2033.6	**145.5**	Locust Cove Gap. . . . . ✦▲	3625
2032.6	**146.5**	Simp Gap	3700
2030.5	**148.6**	Stecoah Gap, NC 143 . . . . N35 21.494 W83 43.076 🅿 ✦(pg.20)	3165
		Sweetwater Creek Rd (paved) 100 yards	
		west to spring and picnic tables.	
2029.5	**149.6**	Sweetwater Gap.	3270
2028.7	**150.4**	Cliffs, west 20 yards to view.	3910
2028.1	**151.0**	**Brown Fork Gap Shelter** . . . . ☽✦⌐ (6)	3800
		21.7◄16.8◄9.1◄►6.1►12.7►24.0 Reliable spring to right of shelter.	
2027.9	**151.2**	Brown Fork Gap . . . . ✦	3600
2027.2	**151.9**	Knob	3910
2026.1	**153.0**	Hogback Gap.	3540
2025.3	**153.8**	Cody Gap, water 0..2W . . . . ✦▲	3600

3/25

SoBo	NoBo		Elev

2023.3 | **155.8** Stream . . . . ◆ 3100
2022.9 | **156.2** Yellow Creek Gap, NC 1242, Yellow Creek Mountain Rd 2980

2022.0 | **157.1** **Cable Gap Shelter**. ☽ ◆ ▲ ⊏ (6) 2880
22.9◄15.2◄6.1◄►6.6►17.9►20.4 Stream in front of shelter.
2020.9 | **158.2** High Tops 3680
2020.6 | **158.5** Black Gum Gap. 3490

2019.8 | **159.3** Summit 3721
2019.2 | **159.9** Walker Gap 3450
2019.0 | **160.1** Camping . . . . ◆▲ 3200
2018.8 | **160.3** Stream . . . . ◆ 2950

3/28 - 29

2016.5 | **162.6** NC 28, **Fontana 28 AT Crossing**. . . N35 26.485 W83 47.806 ▣**(pg.20-21)** 1810
Fontana Dam, NC (2.0W)
2015.4 | **163.7** **Fontana Dam Shelter** . . . . 🚻 🚿 ◆ ⊏ (20) 1775
21.8◄12.7◄6.6◄►11.3►13.8►16.7 Shelter east of AT.
2015.1 | **164.0** **Dam Visitor Center** . . . . N35 27.118 W83 48.079 ▣ ⓘ **(pg.20-21)** 1700
2014.9 | **164.2** Center of Fontana Dam (NC 1245) Little Tennessee River 1800
2014.7 | **164.4** Great Smoky Mountains National Park southern boundary 1800
2013.8 | **165.3** Spring (seasonal) . . . . ◆ 1956

The Benton MacKaye Trail intersects with the AT at Sassafras Gap and at Davenport Gap in the Smokies. The AT is 67.3 miles between the two crossings, and stays high along the ridge. The BMT section is 102 miles and explores the NC side of the park, including many rich cove forests. The high point of the BMT in the Smokies is 5843' and there is only one shelter.

2010.7 | **168.4** Shuckstack Mountain, fire tower 0.1E 3800
2010.4 | **168.7** Sassafras Gap, Benton MacKaye Trail (BMT) 3650
2009.8 | **169.3** Red Ridge Gap 3500
2009.5 | **169.6** Birch Spring Gap . . . . ◆▲ 3680
Campsite west 100 yards down slope.
Cables and tent pads. Spring unreliable.
2008.7 | **170.4** Spring 100 yards down west slope . . . . ◆ 3760

2007.2 | **171.9** Doe Knob 4520

2006.8 | **172.3** Mud Gap 4260

2005.8 | **173.3** Ekaneetlee Gap . . . . ◆ 3842

2004.1 | **175.0** **Mollies Ridge Shelter** . . . . ◆ ⊏ (12) 4570
24.0◄17.9◄11.3◄►2.5►5.4►11.7 Nearby spring unreliable.
2003.8 | **175.3** Devils Tater Patch 4775

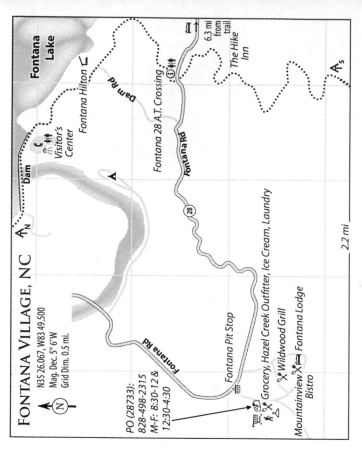

FONTANA VILLAGE, NC

N35 26.067, W83 49.500
Mag. Dec. 5°6′ W
Grid Dim. 0.5 mi.

Fontana Lake

Dam

Fontana Hilton

Visitor's Center

Dam Rd

Fontana 28 A.T. Crossing

Fontana Rd

6.3 mi from trail

The Hike Inn

$\hat{A}_N$

$\hat{A}_s$

Fontana Rd

Fontana Pit Stop

Grocery, Hazel Creek Outfitter, Ice Cream, Laundry

Wildwood Grill

Mountainview *Fontana Lodge Bistro*

PO (28733):
828-498-2315
M-F: 8:30-12 & 12:30-4:30

2.2 mi

135.0 US 19
Nantahala Outdoor Center
888-905-7238 ⟨www.noc.com⟩ Large complex at the intersection of the AT and the Nantahala River has bunkrooms, motel rooms, restaurants, outfitter, laundry, whitewater rafting and a general store. Coin operated showers available to non-guests.

Base Camp (hostel) $17 includes shower. Check in at general store.

There are 6 "cabin motel" rooms on-site for $54 and up. More rooms, at a higher rate, are available at their **Nantahala Inn** 1.5 miles away.

River's End Restaurant (B/L/D); **Joe's Cafe** (Lunch); **Relia's Garden** (Dinner); **Pourover Pub** Live music.

NOC Outfitters Full service outfitter, fuel/oz. Maildrops: dated & marked "Hold for AT Hiker", 13077 Hwy 19W, Bryson City, NC 28713.

148.6 Stecoah Gap, NC 143
The Cabin in the Woods
Phil Capper 828-735-3368
⟨www.thecabininthewoods.com⟩ Cabin and Hostel; both include a ride to/from the trail up to 15 mi. each way. Cabin is often booked so reserve early. The hostel can only accommodate 2 hikers. $30PP includes ride, shower, bathroom, and a continental breakfast. Shuttles Georgia through Davenport Gap; longer shuttles can be arranged for 50 cents per mile round trip (subject to change).

162.6 NC 28
Fontana 28 AT Crossing Has bathrooms, vending machines, GSMNP maps for $1, and a house phone that can be used to call a $3 shuttle from Fontana Village. The phone cannot be used for other calls; a pay phone is further north at the Visitor Center. Northbound hikers can fill out a backcountry permit here or at the Visitor Center.

Fontana Village, NC (2.0W) *(more services on map)*
Contact for all facilities: 800-849-2258 <www.fontanavillage.com>

Fontana Lodge $60 room, no pets. Rates available from 02/01/09 - 04/19/09. Subject to availability outside of these dates.

General Store / Hazel Creek Outfitter Small grocery store, seasonal ice cream shop, Coleman/alcohol/oz, a small selection of major gear items (packs, tents, sleeping bags). 10% discount for thru-hikers. In winter (Nov 1 - March 1) the store is only open Friday, Saturday and Sunday.

Getting prepared meals is problematic. The **Mountainview Bistro** is pricey; the **Wildwood Grill** does not open until May 1; the **Fontana Pit Stop offers** only hot dogs, nachos and microwave fare.

Laundromat 7 days

164.0 Fontana Dam Visitor Center
A small store sells sodas, snacks, and camera supplies, free showers. Northbound hikers should fill out a Great Smoky Mountain National Park self-registration permit, open 9am-7pm daily May-Nov.

(6.3E) **The Hike Inn** 828-479-3677 <www.thehikeinn.com> <hikeinn@graham.main.nc.us> A hikers only service open Feb 15 - Jul 10 and Sep 1 - Dec 1, other dates by reservation only. 5 rooms with max 2 per room. Thru-hiker/long distance hiker package: reservations required, (check in by 4pm, check out by 9am firm) $60S, $75D rate includes shuttle to and from dam, 1 load laundry, evening (5-7pm) shuttle to Robbinsville for dinner and supplies. For pick-up call from pay phone at Fontana Dam Visitors Center. Section/day hikers $40S/D (room only). Mail accepted for guests only c/o Hike Inn 3204 Fontana Rd, Fontana Dam, NC 28733 ($30 service charge for non-guests includes delivery to dam area only.) NO credit cards or pets. Coleman/alcohol/oz, shuttles, slack-packs, internet at Robbinsville public library.

Great Smoky Mountains National Park (GSMNP)

Backcountry Information: 865-436-1297

Reservations: 865-436-1231

A permit is required - There is no cost. NoBos can get one at 28 AT Crossing or Dam Visitor Center. SoBos get permit from Bluff Mountain Outfitters in Hot Springs, at Standing Bear Farm, or at Big Creek Ranger station.

Limited campsites - The only near-trail campsite is Birch Spring. Otherwise AT hikers must overnight at the shelters. Section hikers must make reservations. Four spaces are set aside at each shelter for thru-hikers. When those spaces are taken, additional thru-hikers may tent in the vicinity of the shelter. Thru-hikers who want to ensure shelter space may reserve them. All hikers must use the bear cables to secure their food.

No pets - Dogs are not permitted inside the park. Below are options for kenneling:

Standing Bear Farm (see page 30)

Rippling Water Kennels 828-488-2091 <www.ripplingwaterkennel.com> Will pickup and kennel your dog for up to one week for $245 and a $50 deposit. Reservations required. Owners David and Peggy Roderick.

Loving Care Kennels 865-453-2028, 3779 Tinker Hollow Rd, Pigeon Forge, TN 37863. Pick up your dog at Fontana Dam and return him/her to Davenport Gap. $300 for one dog, $350 for two, $400 for three. Will also hold maildrops and deliver at time of pickup or return. It is recommended that you call at least 2 days in advance.

SoBo	NoBo		Elev
2002.4	**176.7**	Little Abrams Gap	4120
2002.2	**176.9**	Big Abrams Gap	4080
2001.6	**177.5**	**Russell Field Shelter**, Spring 0.1W . . . . ♦ ⌐ (14)	4360
		20.4◄13.8◄2.5◄►2.9►9.2►14.7	
1998.7	**180.4**	**Spence Field Shelter** (0.2E) on Eagle Creek Trail . . . . ☽ ♦ ⌐ (12)	4915
		16.7◄5.4◄2.9◄►6.3►11.8►13.5 Bote Mountain Trail to west.	
1998.3	**180.8**	Jenkins Ridge trail.	5015
1997.5	**181.6**	Rocky Top	5440
1996.9	**182.2**	Thunderhead east peak	5527
1996.6	**182.5**	Beechnut Gap 25 yards west to piped spring. . . . . ♦	4920
1995.9	**183.2**	Mineral Gap.	5030
1995.1	**184.0**	Brier Knob	5215
1993.5	**185.6**	Sugar Tree Gap	4435
1992.7	**186.4**	Chestnut Bald	4950
1992.4	**186.7**	**Derrick Knob Shelter** . . . . ♦ ⌂ ⌐ (12)	4880
		11.7◄9.2◄6.3◄►5.5►7.2►13.5 Cables. Reliable spring near shelter.	
1992.2	**186.9**	Sams Gap . . . . ♦	4995
1990.4	**188.7**	Cold Spring Knob	5240
1989.6	**189.5**	Buckeye Gap . . . . ♦	4817
1986.9	**192.2**	**Silers Bald Shelter,** . . . . ♦ ⌐ (12)	5460
		14.7◄11.8◄5.5◄►1.7►8.0►15.5 Spring 75 yard to right of shelter.	
1986.7	**192.4**	Silers Bald	5607
1986.3	**192.8**	Welch Ridge	5350
1985.7	**193.4**	Jenkins Knob	5650
1985.2	**193.9**	**Double Spring Gap Shelter** . . . . ☽ ♦ ⌐ (12)	5505
		13.5◄7.2◄1.7◄►6.3►13.8►21.2 Cables. Better water option 15 yards from crest on NC side. Water is also 35 yards down TN side.	
1984.6	**194.5**	Goshen Prong Trail	5751
1982.8	**196.3**	Mt Buckley	6582
1982.3	**196.8**	Clingmans Dome . . . . N35 33.433 W83 29.634 🅿(0.5E) ♿🚻	6643
		There are no sinks in the restrooms. Outside water fountains are turned off unitl May 1. Seven miles from parking area to Newfound Gap.	

1981.1	**198.0**	Mt Love		6446
1980.0	**199.1**	Collins Gap		5886
1979.4	**199.7**	Mt Collins		6188
1978.9	**200.2**	Sugarland Mtn Trail, **Mt Collins Shelter** (0.5W) . . . . ☽ ⬩ ⊑ (12)		5870

13.5◄8.0◄6.3◄►7.5►14.9►20.1
Cables. Small spring 0.1 mile beyond shelter on
Sugarland Mountain Trail.

| 1976.1 | **203.0** | Indian Gap, road . . . . | | 5286 |
| 1975.6 | **203.5** | Mt Mingus Ridge . . . . | | 5297 |

| 1974.4 | **204.7** | Newfound Gap, US 441 . . . . N35 36.669 W83 25.540 🅿 **(pg.24-25)** | | 5045 |

Large parking area, restrooms. There are no sinks in restrooms, and water
fountain is turned off in winter.
Gatlinburg, TN (15.0W)

1972.7	**206.4**	Sweat Heifer Creek Trail		5650
1971.7	**207.4**	Boulevard Trail to Mt LeConte		5695
1971.4	**207.7**	**Icewater Spring Shelter** . . . . ☽ ⬩ ⊑ (12)		5920

15.5◄13.8◄7.5◄►7.4►12.6►20.3 Spring 50 yards north on AT.

1970.5	**208.6**	Charlies Bunion (0.1W)		5905
1970.3	**208.8**	Dry Sluice Gap		5375
1970.2	**208.9**	Dry Sluice Gap Trail		5380

| 1968.6 | **210.5** | Porters Gap . . . . | | 5500 |

| 1966.6 | **212.5** | Woolly Tops Lead . . . . | | 5800 |

| 1965.3 | **213.8** | Bradleys View . . . . | | 5200 |

| 1964.0 | **215.1** | **Pecks Corner Shelter** (0.5E) . . . . ☽ ⬩ ⊑ (12) | | 5280 |

21.2◄14.9◄7.4◄►5.2►12.9►20.0 Water 50 yards in front of shelter. Spring
just south of shelter side trail.

| 1963.0 | **216.1** | Eagle Rocks . . . . | | 5750 |

| 1961.3 | **217.8** | Mt Sequoyah . . . . | | 6069 |

| 1960.6 | **218.5** | Mt Chapman Gap . . . . | | 5650 |

| 1959.8 | **219.3** | Mt Chapman . . . . | | 6417 |

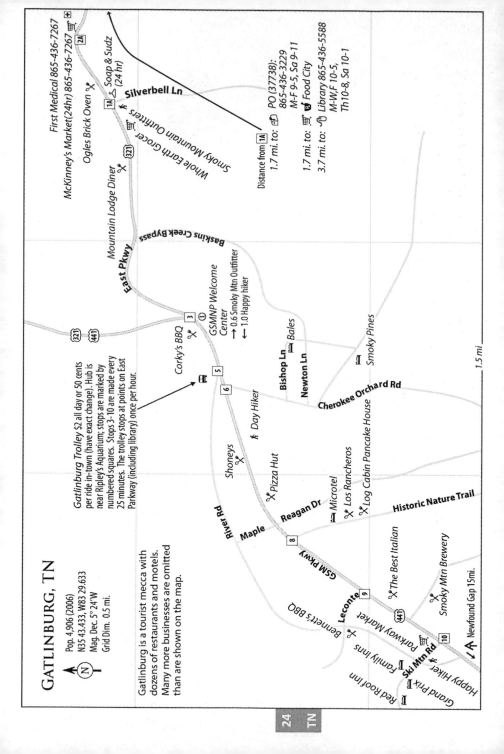

GATLINBURG, TN

Pop. 4,906 (2006)
N35 43.433, W83 29.633
Mag. Dec. 5° 24'W
Grid Dim. 0.5 mi.

Gatlinburg is a tourist mecca with dozens of restaurants and motels. Many more businesses are omitted than are shown on the map.

Gatlinburg Trolley $2 all day or 50 cents per ride in-town (have exact change). Hub is near Ripley's Aquarium; stops are marked by numbered squares. Stops 3–10 are made every 25 minutes. The trolley stops at points on East Parkway (including library) once per hour.

First Medical 865-436-7267
McKinney's Market(24hr) 865-436-7267
Ogles Brick Oven ✕
Soap & Sudz (24 hr)
Silverbell Ln
Whole Earth Grocer
Smoky Mountain Outfitters
Mountain Lodge Diner
East Pkwy
Baskins Creek Bypass

Distance from 1A:
1.7 mi. to: PO (37738):
865-436-3229
M-F 9-5, Sa 9-11
1.7 mi. to: Food City
3.7 mi. to: Library 865-436-5588
M-W-F 10-5,
Th10-8, Sa 10-1

GSMNP Welcome Center
→ 0.6 Smoky Mtn Outfitter
← 1.0 Happy hiker
Corky's BBQ ✕
Bishop Ln Bales
Newton Ln
Smoky Pines
Cherokee Orchard Rd
Day Hiker
Shoneys ✕
Pizza Hut ✕
River Rd
Maple
Reagan Dr
Microtel
Los Rancheros ✕
Log Cabin Pancake House ✕
Historic Nature Trail
GSM Pkwy
The Best Italian ✕
Smoky Mtn Brewery ✕
Leconte
Bennett's BBQ ✕
Parkway Market
Ski Mtn Rd
↙ Newfound Gap 15mi.
Newfound Gap
Red Roof Inn
Grand Prix
Happy Hiker
Family Inns

1.5 mi

Gatlinburg, TN (15.0W) *(more services on map)*

White Blaze Day Backpacking reps, music, to raise money for the AT. Held behind The Happy Hiker Outfitter. Date TBD, usually scheduled mid April.

⛺🏠📶📱 **Grand Prix Motel** 865-436-4561 $29.95/up, Shuttle up to 4 persons to Newfound Gap or Clingmans Dome for $30. Other shuttles $IPP/mile.

⛺🏠 **Smoky Pines Motel** 877-678-3041 Hiker rates: $39 double, $29 single. No pets; no smoking, 344 Baskins Creek Road. Good off-strip choice for those wanting quiet, clean rooms.

⛺📶 **Microtel Gatlinburg** 865-436-0107, $39.95, pets $10. Call ahead if you'd like to send a maildrop: 211 Historic Nature Trail, Gatlinburg, TN 37738.

⛺📶 **Family Inns** 865-436-3300 Ask for hiker rate $39.77 + tax. Includes continental breakfast. Pets $10. Maildrops: 218 Sk Mountain Rd., Gatlinburg, TN 37738.

⛺📶 **Bales Motel** 865-436-4773, $30/up, ask for hiker rate, no pets. Laundry can be done at hotel next door. Maildrops: 221 Bishop Lane, Gatlinburg, TN 37738.

⛺🏠 **Red Roof Inn** 865-436-7813 〈www.redroofgatlinburg.com〉 Trolley stops at the front door. All major CC. Heated pool, free continental breakfast. $10 pet fee. Maildrops: 309 Ownby St, Gatlinburg, TN 37738.

🥾📶 **The Happy Hiker** 865-436-6000 〈www.happyhiker.com〉 Full service outfitter, Coleman/alcohol/oz and other fuels, 10% thru-hiker discount, repair services, pack scale, open 7 days. 25 years of thru-hiker photos are on the wall; please have yours added. Maildrops (UPS): 905 River Road, Suite 5, Gatlinburg, TN 37738.

🥾📶 **Smoky Mountain Outfitters** 865-430-2267 Full service backpacking store, Coleman/alcohol/oz and other fuels, discount for thru hikers, gear repair, open 7 days, 8-6. Shuttles to all locations in the park. Maildrops: 469 Brookside Village Way, Gatlinburg, TN 37738.

🥾 **The Day Hiker** 865-430-0970 Small shop with shoes and fuel.

📶📱 **A Walk in the Woods** 865-436-8283 〈www.awalkinthewoods.com〉 GSMNP guides Vesna and Erik Plakanis are extremely professional and knowledgeable, shuttle anywhere from Springer to Damascus. Can also help with resupply and dog shuttle/kenneling while you are in the Smokies.

📶 **Cherokee Transit** 866-388-6071 〈www.cherokeetransit.com〉 Newfound Gap to Gatlinburg $7 one-way, $12 round trip; same rates to Cherokee, NC. Pickup at Happy Hiker, Welcome Center and Newfound Gap.

ⓘ **Carol Capooth** 865-640-7653 Trail angel.

📶🐾📶 **Appalachian Services** 828-507-5747 Bill (GryWolf) Johnson, Cherokee, NC 〈www.appalachianservices.com〉 24hr cell. Full service hiker support since 2001. Shuttles Amicalola Falls to Harpers Ferry, package drop and re-supply, canine shuttle/kennel and vehicle relocation. Airport, bus, train shuttles to/from most stations between Atlanta, GA and Damascus, VA. Year around, 7 days/week. No fee for transportation to urgent care facilities within 50 miles of GSMNP.

Reminder:

Visit the website to get updates, additions and corrections. Also, please let us know if you've found anything that should be added or corrected.

www.theATguide.com

SoBo	NoBo		1000	2000	3000	4000	5000	6000	Elev
1958.9	220.2	Big Cove Gap							5825
1958.8	220.3	**Tri-Corner Knob Shelter** 20.1◄12.6◄5.2◄►7.7►14.8►25.3 . . ☽ ♦ ⊏ (12)							5920
1958.6	220.5	Balsam Mountain Trail							6070
1957.6	221.5	Guyot Spur							6360
1957.0	222.1	Guyot Spring						♦	6150
1956.9	222.2	Mt Guyot Trail							6395
1955.9	223.2	Deer Creek Gap							6020
1955.3	223.8	Yellow Creek Gap							6020
1955.0	224.1	Snake Den Ridge Trail, 5.3W to Crosby Campground							5600
1953.6	225.5	Camel Hump Knob							5250
1952.6	226.5	Camel Gap, Camel Gap Trail to the east							4645
1951.7	227.4	Cosby Knob							5150
1951.1	228.0	**Cosby Knob Shelter** 100 yards east . . . . ☽ ♦ ⊏ (12)							4700
		20.3◄12.9◄7.7◄►7.1►17.6►25.8							
1950.4	228.7	Low Gap, 2.5W to Crosby Campground							4240
1949.3	229.8	Sunup Knob							5050
1948.3	230.8	Mt Cammerer Trail							5000
1947.8	231.3	Spring						♦	4300
1946.2	232.9	Spring 50 yards on side trail						♦	3700
1945.9	233.2	Lower Mt Cammerer Trail, Cosby Campground (7.8W)							3600
1945.0	234.1	Chestnut Branch Trail . . . . N35 45.558 W83 6.412 🅿 (2.0E)							2848
		Parking at Big Creek Campground.							
1944.0	235.1	**Davenport Gap Shelter** . . . . ♦ ⊏ (12)							2600
		20.0◄14.8◄7.1◄►10.5►18.7►23.6 Spring to left of shelter.							
1943.2	235.9	Great Smoky Mountains National Park northern boundary							1985
1943.1	236.0	TN 32, NC 284, **Davenport Gap, TN** (1.3E) . . . . **(pg.30)**							1975
1942.4	236.7	Power line							1873
1941.8	237.3	State Line Branch						♦ ⛺	1600
1941.6	237.5	Pigeon River							1400
1941.2	237.9	I-40							1500
1941.1	238.0	Waterville School Rd							1600
1940.7	238.4	Green Corner Rd . . . . **(pg.30)**							1800
1938.9	240.2	Painter Branch						♦ ⛺	3100
		Blue-blazed trail east across Painter Creek to campsite and spring.							
1938.4	240.7	Stream						♦	3100
1937.5	241.6	Spanish Oak Gap							3730

1936.0	**243.1**	Snowbird Mountain, road	4623
1935.5	**243.6**	Camping. . . . . ▲	4100
1935.3	**243.8**	Wildcat Spring uphill from trail . . . . ▲	4050
1934.6	**244.5**	Turkey Gap	3526
1933.5	**245.6**	**Groundhog Creek Shelter** (0.2E) . . . . ☽ ▲ ⊏ (6)	2900

245.6 25.3◄17.6◄10.5◄►8.2►13.1►23.0
Stone shelter with reliable spring to left.

1931.1	**248.0**	Spur trail to Hawks Roost	3709
1930.6	**248.5**	Brown Gap, road . . . . ▲	3500
1930.0	**249.1**	Spring 0.1 west in steep ravine . . . . ▲	3900

1927.9	**251.2**	NC 1182, Max Patch Rd . . . . N35 47.776 W82 57.762 🅿	4380
1927.8	**251.3**	Stream . . . . ▲	4175
1927.1	**252.0**	Max Patch Summit (campfires not permitted on bald)	4629
1926.6	**252.5**	Camping . . . . ▲ ▲	4285
1926.4	**252.7**	Logging road	4050
1925.7	**253.4**	Stream . . . . ▲	3725
1925.3	**253.8**	**Roaring Fork Shelter** . . . . ☽ ▲ ⊏ (10)	3950

253.8 25.8◄18.7◄8.2◄►4.9►14.8►29.0

1925.2	**253.9**	Stream . . . . ▲	3999
1924.2	**254.9**	Stream, footbridge . . . . ▲	3640
1923.6	**255.5**	Stream . . . . ▲ ▲	3678

1921.9	**257.2**	Stream . . . . ▲ ▲	3678
1921.7	**257.4**	Lemon Gap, NC 1182, TN 107	3550
1921.0	**258.1**	Streams . . . . ▲	3999
1920.4	**258.7**	**Walnut Mountain Shelter** 23.6◄13.1◄4.9◄►9.9►24.1►32.7 . ☽ ▲ ⊏ (6)	4260

Bears activite here in 2009; hang food and cook away from shelter.

1919.6	**259.5**	Kale Gap	3679
1918.7	**260.4**	Streams . . . . ▲	4350
1918.0	**261.1**	Bluff Mountain	4686
1917.2	**261.9**	Spring 50 yards west of side trail . . . . ▲	3950
1916.4	**262.7**	Big Rock Spring located in ravine . . . . ▲	3730

SoBo	NoBo			Elev

SoBo	NoBo	Feature		Elev
1915.2	**263.9**	Brook with cascades . . . . ◦		2963
1913.9	**265.2**	Garenflo Gap, road, power line . . . . .N35 51.206 W82 52.556 🅿▲		2500
1912.5	**266.6**	Stream, footbridge . . . . ◦		2640
1911.8	**267.3**	Little Bottom Branch Gap		2750
1910.5	**268.6**	**Deer Park Mountain Shelter** . . . . 🌙 ◦ ⌐ (5)		2330
		23.0◄14.8◄9.9◄▸14.2▸22.8▸29.6		
		Spring halfway between shelter and Gragg Gap.		
1907.3	**271.8**	NC 209, US 25/70 . . . . .N35 53.371 W82 49.937 🅿 (pg.30-31)		1326
		Hot Springs, NC		
1907.0	**272.1**	French Broad River, US 27/70 bridge		1320
		NoBo hikers turn east (hop rail) immediately after crossing river.		
1905.9	**273.2**	Lovers Leap Rock . . . . ◦		1820
1904.0	**275.1**	Pump Gap.		2130
1902.4	**276.7**	Camping above boxed spring and along pond. . . . . ◦▲		2490
1901.4	**277.7**	Tanyard Gap, US 25/70 overpass. . . . . N35 54.597 W82 47.461 🅿		2278
1899.1	**280.0**	Trail (0.1W) Rich Mountain Fire Tower. Camping, spring to east. . . . . ◦▲		3600
1898.8	**280.3**	Side trail to Rich Mountain		3500
1898.0	**281.1**	Hurricane Gap, road.		2900
1896.3	**282.8**	**Spring Mountain Shelter**. . . . . 🌙 ◦ ▲ ⌐ (5)		3300
		29.0◄24.1◄14.2◄▸8.6▸15.4▸21.3		
		Water 75 yards down blue-blazed trail on east side of AT.		
1894.8	**284.3**	Spring, just west of trail . . . . ◦		3000
1894.6	**284.5**	Deep Gap.		2850

Elevation scale: 1000, 2000, 3000, 4000, 5000, 6000

1892.6	**286.5**	NC 208, TN 70, Allen Gap, piped spring unreliable	. . . .	♦ 2234
1891.0	**288.1**	Log Cabin Drive	**(pg.31)** 2560
1887.7	**291.4**	**Little Laurel Shelter** . . . . ☾ ♦ ⚑ ⊏ (5) 3620

32.7◄22.8◄8.6◄►6.8►12.7►21.5
Boxed spring 100 yards down blue-blazed trail behind shelter. Campsites
west side of AT, south of shelter.

1886.4	**292.7**	Road, side trail west to Camp Creek Bald fire tower.	4750
1884.7	**294.4**	Spring, east below trail.	♦ 4390
1884.4	**294.7**	Blackstack Cliffs	4400
1883.4	**295.7**	Big Firescald Knob	4360
1880.9	**298.2**	Chestnut Log Gap, **Jerry Cabin Shelter** . . . . ☾ ♦ ⊏ (6) 4150

29.6◄15.4◄6.8◄►5.9►14.7►24.8
Water on small knoll, 100 yards up path on opposite side of AT.

1879.3	**299.8**	Dirt road	4464
1879.0	**300.1**	Big Butt Mountain . . . . ⚑ 4750
1877.7	**301.4**	Spring on blue-blazed trail 0.1W.	♦ 4480
1877.4	**301.7**	Shelton Gravesite	4520
1875.8	**303.3**	Flint Gap	3425
1875.0	**304.1**	**Flint Mountain Shelter** . . . . ☾ ♦ ⊏ (8) 3550

21.3◄12.7◄5.9◄►8.8►18.9►29.5
Water on AT north of shelter.

1874.1	**305.0**	Camping . . . . ♦ ⚑ 3400
1872.3	**306.8**	Devil Fork Gap, NC 212 . . . . N36 0.614 W82 36.524 🅿 3107
1871.8	**307.3**	Rector Laurel Rd, Boone Cove Rd	2960
1871.1	**308.0**	Stream and woods road . . . . ♦ 3168

| SoBo | NoBo | | NC/TN 29 | 1000 | 2000 | 3000 | 4000 | 5000 | 6000 | Elev |

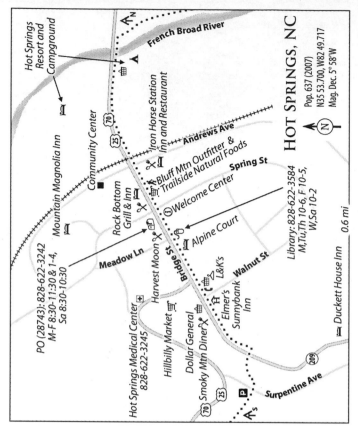

HOT SPRINGS, NC

Pop. 637 (2007)
N35 53.700, W82 49.717
Mag. Dec. 5° 58'W

French Broad River

Hot Springs Resort and Campground

Community Center

Mountain Magnolia Inn

Iron Horse Station Inn and Restaurant

Andrews Ave

Bluff Mtn Outfitter &
Trailside Natural Foods

Spring St

Rock Bottom Grill & Inn

Welcome Center

PO (28743): 828-622-3242
M-F 8:30-11:30 & 1-4,
Sa 8:30-10:30

Harvest Moon

Alpine Court

Meadow Ln

Hot Springs Medical Center
828-622-3245

Hillbilly Market

Dollar General

Smoky Mtn Diner

Elmer's Sunnybank Inn

L&K's

Walnut St

Library: 828-622-3584
M,Tu,Th 10-6, F 10-5,
W,Sa 10-2

Duckett House Inn

Surpentine Ave

0.6 mi

236.0   TN 32, NC 284 (Davenport Gap)
Great Smoky Mountain National Park
(northern boundary)

☏ (1.3E) **Big Creek Ranger Station** 828-486-5910
Self-registration backcountry permits.

▲ (2.3E) **Big Creek Campground** $14 per site, no showers. Open mid-March through October. It is 2.0 miles to AT on Chestnut Branch Trail, connecting 0.1 south of Davenport Gap Shelter.

238.4   Green Corner Road

Standing Bear Farm (0.1W) 423-487-0014
curtisvowen@gmail.com; Hostel operated by Maria and Curtis. $20PP cabin, $15 bunkhouse or tenting; cooking facilities available. $1/15min internet use. Cook your own pizza and enough resupply to get you to Hot Springs or through the Smokies. Will kennel your dog while you hike the Smokies; $15/day plus $125 for dropoff/pickup at Fontana. Directions: Green corner road is a gravel road 0.9 miles north of I-40, go west 200 yards to white farmhouse. Permits for GSMNP are available here. Maildrops: 4255 Green Corner Rd, Hartford, TN 37753.

Hot Springs, NC (more services on map)

Home to **Trailfest** on April 23-24, which includes a Friday night AYCE spaghetti dinner for a nominal fee at the Community Center. Southbound hikers can obtain permits for hiking through Smoky Mountain National Park from Bluff Mountain Outfitters.

⌂ ⊠ **Elmers Sunnybank Inn** 828-622-7206 Long-distance hikers (100 miles or more) can stay for $20PP, includes linens, towel and shower. Breakfast $6 dinner $10, gourmet organic vegetarian meals. No credit cards. Historic Sunnybank Inn has offered hospitality to AT hikers since 1947. Staffed by former thru-hikers, the Inn offers an extensive library and a well-equipped music room. Work exchange possible. Maildrops: PO Box 233, Hot Springs, NC 28743.

✗ **Iron Horse Station** 828-402-9377 $45up, $10EAP, $95 suite with jacuzzi. One pet room available. Restaurant, tavern and coffee shop. Serves L/D, offers a blue plate special and some vegetarian options.

✗ **Rock Bottom** 828-622-0001 Rooms $50 and up. Restaurant and bar on-site.

★ ⊠ **Alpine Court Motel** 828-622-3231, $44S, $66D and up, no credit cards. Maildrops: 50 Bridge St, Hot Springs, NC 28743.

✗ **Hot Springs Resort Cabins Campground & Spa** 828-622-7267 ⟨www.nchotsprings.com⟩ Tenting $10PP and camping cabins $45/up per room (sleeps 5) with common bath & hot showers. $65 camping cabin with half bath, luxury rooms starting at $145. $10 pet fee. Luxury rooms feature private Jacuzzi baths using the famous Hot Springs thermal water. The Campstore carries snacks and some supplies; grill serves B/L. Also: Mineral water spa, massage therapy. Accepts Visa/MC/Discover.

✗ **Mountain Magnolia Inn** 800-914-9306 Discount hiker rates when rooms available are $65-$130 includes AYCE breakfast. Dinner served F-M (open to all). Courtesy phone, private rooms.

★ ⊠ ⌂ **Duckett House Inn** 828-622-7621 ⟨www.ducketthouseinn.com⟩ Bed and Breakfast rooms $50PP, including full breakfast. 4 hiker bunkhouse beds available for $15, includes shower. Breakfast $12.50, laundry $4 per load. Work exchange possible. Well behaved dogs okay outside, but are not to be left unattended. Maildrops only if you have made a reservation: Duckett House Inn P.O. Box 441, Hot Springs NC 28743.

⊠ **$ Bluff Mountain Outfitters** 828-622-7162, Su-Th 9-5, F-Sa 9-6 ⟨www.bluffmountain.com⟩ Full service outfitter, fuel/oz. Natural foods grocery and other foods make this a one-stop location for complete resupply. Computer for internet access, free 30 min for hikers. ATM and scale inside. Shuttles Springer to Roanoke and to area airports. Maildrops: PO Box 114 Hot Springs, NC 28743, FedEx or UPS: 152 Bridge St. Will also ship UPS packages.

288.1   Log Cabin Drive

⊠ (0.7W) **Hemlock Hollow Farm** 423-787-0917 ⟨www.hemlockhollow.net⟩ Follow gravel Log Cabin Drive to pavec Viking Mountain Road, then turn right. Heated cabin $48D with linens, refrigerator, and microwave. Bunkhouse has kitchenette. $20 bunkroom no linens, includes shower, tent site $12 includes shower, pets $2 extra. Room prices include tax. Shower/towel (without stay) $3, camp store, cold drinks, fruit, Coleman/alcohol/canisters/esbit fuel. Guests get free return ride to trail. For-fee internet use. Shuttles as far south as Davenport Gap, north to Erwin, or to Tri-cities Airport or Asheville. Maildrops: 645 Chandler Circle, Greeneville, TN 37743, open year round. 7:30-8 during hiking season.

SoBo	NoBo								Elev
1870.5	**308.6**	Sugarloaf Gap							4000
1869.0	**310.1**	Frozen Knob/Lick Rock							4579
1868.4	**310.7**	Big Flat						◑▲	4160
1867.4	**311.7**	Rice Gap, road							3800
1866.2	**312.9**	**Hogback Ridge Shelter** (0.1E)					☽◑⌐ (6)		4255
		21.5◄14.7◄8.8◄►10.1►20.7►31.2 Spring 0.2 mile beyond shelter.							
1865.6	**313.5**	High Rock							4460
1863.8	**315.3**	Sams Gap, US 23, I-26.				N35 57.175 W82 33.636 ▣ ✕ 🏛			3800
		Little Creek Café (2.8E) B/L/possibly D.(3.1E) **Wolf Creek Market** (open 7 days) **Donna's Country Kitchen**							
1863.1	**316.0**	Spring west from survey marker						◑▲	4000
1861.5	**317.6**	Street Gap							4100
1861.4	**317.7**	Power line							4219
1860.1	**319.0**	Low Gap						◑▲	4300
1859.5	**319.6**	Spring						◑	4485
1858.1	**321.0**	Spring 100 yards west down slope						◑	4850
1857.8	**321.3**	Piped spring, camping						◑▲	4999
1857.3	**321.8**	Big Bald						▲	5516
1857.0	**322.1**	Big Stamp						◑▲ (0.3W)	5298
1856.1	**323.0**	**Bald Mountain Shelter** (0.1W)					☽◑⌐ (10)		5100
		24.8◄18.9◄10.1◄►10.6►21.1►33.9 Spring on side trail to shelter.							
1855.7	**323.4**	Campsite (0.2W) reliable spring further down trail						◑▲	4890
1854.7	**324.4**	Little Bald							5185
1852.7	**326.4**	Whistling Gap						◑▲	3650
1852.4	**326.7**	Trail to High Rocks							4100
1850.9	**328.2**	Camping						◑▲	3490
1850.4	**328.7**	Spivey Gap, US 19W.				N36 1.911 W82 25.209 ▣ (0.5W)		◑▲	3200
1850.0	**329.1**	Ogelsby Branch						◑	3800
1849.8	**329.3**	Ogelsby Branch						◑	3800
1849.1	**330.0**	Stream						◑	3579

SoBo	NoBo				Elev
1848.9	**330.2**	Old logging road and USFS 278			3539
1848.1	**331.0**	Devils Creek Gap.			3400
1845.7	**333.4**	Spring west of trail		♦	3000
1845.5	**333.6**	**No Business Knob Shelter**		⌐ (6)	3251
		29.5◄20.7◄10.6◄►10.5►23.3►32.5			
		Reliable water on AT (0.2S) of shelter.			
1843.1	**336.0**	Temple Hill Gap			2850
1839.2	**339.9**	River Rd, Unaka Springs Rd . . . . N36 6.254 W82 26.802 🅿 **(pg.34-35)**			1700
		Erwin, TN (3.8W) *Sat. 4/10/10*			
1839.0	**340.1**	Railroad tracks			1707
1838.0	**341.1**	Side trail to Nolichucky Gorge Campground		♦ **(pg.34-35)**	1836
1837.8	**341.3**	Footbridge, stream		♦	1792
1836.3	**342.8**	Campsite, AT from here south to NGC parallels/crosses		♦	2289
		stream with a least 5 footbridges.			
1835.0	**344.1**	**Curley Maple Gap Shelter**		♦ ▲ ⌐ (6)	3070
		31.2◄21.1◄10.5◄►12.8►22.0►28.4 Early 2010 renovation expected to			
		increase capacity to 14. Clearing north of shelter, water south of shelter.			
1834.5	**344.6**	Spring		♦	3213
1834.0	**345.1**	Stream		♦	3264
1833.7	**345.4**	Stream		♦	3285
1832.5	**346.6**	Campsite		▲	3101
1830.9	**348.2**	Indian Grave Gap, TN 395 . . . . N36 6.578 W82 21.696 🅿 ♦ ▲			3360
		Water 0.1E at first bend in road, campsites south on AT. (3.3W) to USFS			
		Rock Creek Recreation Area $10 tent sites, restrooms, showers.			
1830.3	**348.8**	Powerline			3812
1829.8	**349.3**	USFS 230, Gravel Road			3980
1828.6	**350.5**	Beauty Spot. . . . . N36 6.9796 W82 20.2321 🅿			4437
		Parking to west, trail parallel to USFS 230 here north to Deep Gap.			
1827.1	**352.0**	Deep Gap, piped spring & campsites 100 yrds west across USFS 230 .		♦ ▲	4100

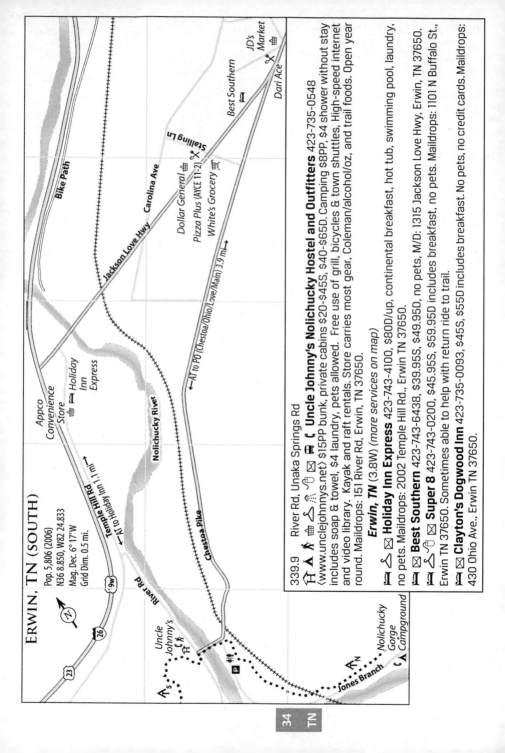

339.9 River Rd, Unaka Springs Rd

⌂ ▲ ⚲ ⛺ ⏢ 🛏 ⊠ ⚏ 🏠 🅿 (**Uncle Johnny's Nolichucky Hostel and Outfitters** 423-735-0548 (www.unclejohnnys.net) $15PP bunk, private cabins $20–$45S, $40–$65D. Camping $8PP, $4 shower without stay includes soap & towel. $4 laundry, pets allowed. Free use of grill, bicycles & town shuttles, High-speed internet and video library. Kayak and raft rentals. Store carries most gear, Coleman/alcohol/oz, and trail foods. Open year round. Maildrops: 151 River Rd, Erwin, TN 37650.

Erwin, TN (3.8W) *(more services on map)*

🍴 ⚲ ⊠ **Holiday Inn Express** 423-743-4100, $80D/up, continental breakfast, hot tub, swimming pool, laundry, no pets. Maildrops: 2002 Temple Hill Rd., Erwin TN 37650.

🍴 ⊠ **Best Southern** 423-743-6438, $39.95S, $49.95D, no pets, M/D: 1315 Jackson Love Hwy, Erwin, TN 37650.

🍴 ⚲ ⛶ ⊠ **Super 8** 423-743-0200, $45.95S, $59.95D includes breakfast, no pets. Maildrops: 1101 N Buffalo St., Erwin TN 37650. Sometimes able to help with return ride to trail.

🍴 ⊠ **Clayton's Dogwood Inn** 423-735-0093, $45S, $55D includes breakfast. No pets, no credit cards. Maildrops: 430 Ohio Ave., Erwin TN 37650.

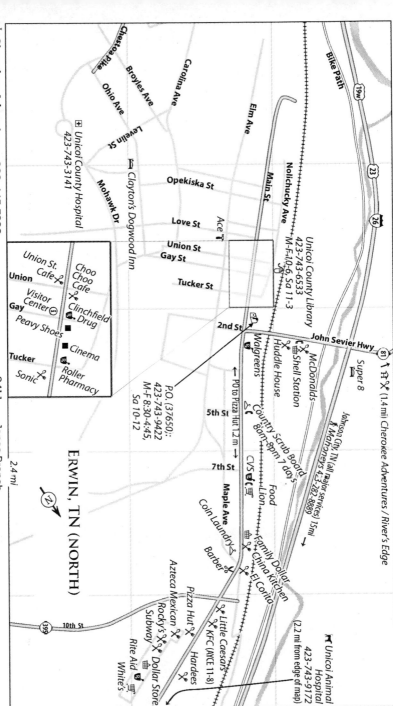

▲ **Cherokee Adventures** 800-445-7238 ⟨www.cherokeeadventures.com⟩ $8PP bunkhouse, $5PP camping. Call ahead; rides sometimes available.

✕ **Azteca** (north end of town), **River's Edge Restaurant** (west of town) are only restaurants in town that serve beer.

341.1   Jones Branch

▲ ⊆ **Nolichucky Gorge Campground** 423-743-8876, ⟨www.nolichucky.com⟩ Tent site $10, cabin $80 and up, primarily caters to river recreation.

ERWIN, TN (NORTH)

N

2.4 mi

P.O. (37650):
423-743-9422
M-F 8:30-4:45,
Sa 10-12

PO to Pizza Hut 1.2 m →

Union St. Café
Choo Choo Cafe
Visitor Center
Clinchfield Drug
Peavy Shoes
Cinema
Sonic
Roller Pharmacy

Union
Gay
Tucker

⊞ Unicoi County Hospital
423-743-3141

✝ Clayton's Dogwood Inn

Mohawk Dr
Ohio Ave
Levelin St
Broyles Ave
Carolina Ave
Chestoa Pike
Elm Ave
Opekiska St
Love St
Union St
Gay St
Tucker St
Main St
Nolichucky Ave
Bike Path

Unicoi County Library
423-743-6533
M-F 10-6, Sa 11-3

Ace

2nd St

Walgreens
McDonalds
Shell Station
Huddle House
Country Scrub Board
Food Lion 8am-8pm 7 days
CVS
5th St
7th St
Maple Ave
Coin Laundry
Barber
China Kitchen
Family Dollar
El Corito
Azteca Mexican
Pizza Hut
Little Caesars
Rocky's
KFC (AYCE 11-8)
Subway
Hardees
Dollar Store
Rite Aid
White's
10th St

John Sevier Hwy

Super 8

Johnson City, TN (all major services) 15mi
Mahoney's 423-282-8889

⛺ Unicoi Animal Hospital
423-743-9172
(2.2 mi from edge of map)

(1.4 mi) Cherokee Adventures / River's Edge

19w
23
26
81
107
399

35
TN

SoBo	NoBo		1000	2000	3000	4000	5000	6000	Elev

1826.5 **352.6** USFS 230 4660

1825.5 **353.6** Unaka Mountain. 5180

1823.6 **355.5** Low Gap, campsite weak stream 0.1W . . . . ♦ 3970
1822.8 **356.3** Footbrigde, stream . . . . ♦ 4154
1822.6 **356.5** **Cherry Gap Shelter**. . . . . ♦ ⌐ (6) 4062
33.9◄23.3◄12.8◄▶9.2▶15.6▶20.6
Spring 120 yards on blue-blazed trail behind shelter to the left.
1822.2 **356.9** Unmarked trail crossing 3900
1821.0 **358.1** Little Bald Knob 4336
1820.6 **358.5** Stream . . . . ♦ 4197

1819.1 **360.0** Iron Mountain Gap, TN 107, NC 226. . . . . N36 8.600 W82 13.990 🅿 3723

1817.9 **361.2** South end of clearing 4095
1817.8 **361.3** Campsite, water 0.1W from signpost near north end of clearing . . . . ♦ ▲ 4040
1817.0 **362.1** Rock pillar. 4182

1814.9 **364.2** Greasy Creek Gap, campsite at gap, water 0.2W, hostel 0.6E. . . . . .**(pg.38)** 4034

1814.0 **365.1** Camping, weak spring 0.1W . . . . ♦ ▲ 4127

1813.0 **366.1** **Clyde Smith Shelter** (1976) (0.1W) . . . . ♦ ⌐ (10) 4400
32.5◄22.0◄9.2◄▶6.4▶11.4▶13.1 Water 0.1 left of shelter.
1812.1 **367.0** Little Rock Knob, vistas to west, south of summit 4918

1811.1 **368.0** Stream . . . . ♦ 4400
From here north to Roan parking area, northbound trail is due south;
trail east (right for NOBO hikers) is compass west.
1809.9 **369.2** Hughes Gap, TN 1330 Hughes Gap Road . . . . N36 8.206 W82 8.457 🅿 ▲ 4040
1809.7 **369.4** Campsite 30 yards west . . . . ▲ 4317

1808.1 **371.0** Ash Gap, camping at gap, water 0.1E . . . . ♦ ▲ 5350

1807.3 **371.8** Trail junction,saddle between Roan. . . . . . N36 6.238 W82 7.984 🅿 🚻♦ 6200
High Bluff & Knob, 0.1E to parking, picnic area, restrooms and trash cans.
1807.1 **372.0** Chimney (remnant) 6192
1806.6 **372.5** **Roan High Knob Shelter** (0.1E) . . . . ♦ ▲ ⌐ (15) 6275
28.4◄15.6◄6.4◄▶5.0▶6.7▶15.4 Piped spring, highest shelter on the AT.
1805.4 **373.7** Northbounders, watch for AT turning west, leaving wide treadway . . . 5677
1805.2 **373.9** Several footbridges, stream crossings. . . . . ♦ 5535

SoBo	NoBo		Elev
1805.1	**374.0**	Carvers Gap, TN 143, NC 261 . . . . .N36 6.406 W82 6.633 **P** 🌢 ⚲	5512
1804.4	**374.7**	Round Top	5826
1803.7	**375.4**	Jane Bald, views back to Roan Mtn	5807
1803.2	**375.9**	Trail junction, west on AT, east to Grassy Ridge . . . . 🌢 ▲	5770
		Reliable water NE side of Grassy Ridge 100 yards down side trail.	
1801.6	**377.5**	**Stan Murray Shelter** . . . . 🌢 ⌐ (6)	5050
		20.6◄11.4◄5.0◄►1.7►10.4►19.7	
		Spring on blue-blazed trail opposite shelter.	
1799.9	**379.2**	**Overmountain Shelter** (0.3E) Yellow Mountain Gap . . . . ☽ 🌢 ▲ ⌐ (20)	4550
		13.1◄6.7◄1.7◄►8.7►18.0►27.6 Shelter is converted barn.	
		Water on way to shelter.	
1798.3	**380.8**	Little Hump Mountain, summit near north end of clearing . . . . ▲	5459
1797.7	**381.4**	Piped spring to east, campsites to north and south. . . . . 🌢 ▲	5149
1797.0	**382.1**	Bradley Gap, Spring east 100 yards . . . . 🌢 ▲	4960
1796.1	**383.0**	Hump Mountain (NOBOs have several false summits)	5587
1794.5	**384.6**	Spring . . . . 🌢	5200
1793.7	**385.4**	Doll Flats (unmarked), **NC-TN** border . . . . 🌢 ▲	4600
1793.3	**385.8**	Stone steps, overlook	4250
1793.1	**386.0**	Massive stone wall to west	4100
1793.2	**385.9**	Spring west of trail . . . . 🌢	4050
1791.3	**387.8**	Spring, seasonal . . . . 🌢	3060
1791.2	**387.9**	**Apple House Shelter** 15.4◄10.4◄8.7◄►9.3►18.9►26.8 . . . . . . 🌢 ⌐ (6)	3000
1790.7	**388.4**	US 19E **Elk Park, NC** (2.5E) **Roan Mtn, TN** (3.4W) . . . . **(pg.38-39)**	2895
1790.5	**388.6**	Bear Branch Rd. .N36 10.765 W02 0.767	2902
1790.4	**388.7**	Footbridge, stream . . . . 🌢	2877
1789.7	**389.4**	AT joins Jeep Path	3164
1789.3	**389.8**	North end of AT and Jeep Path	3409
1788.5	**390.6**	Open ridge with views to east and west	3718
1788.0	**391.1**	Cemetery	3549
1787.4	**391.7**	Buck Mountain Rd, water at church 0.1E . . . . . . N36 12.240 W81 59.847🌢	3393
1787.1	**392.0**	Campbell Hollow Rd	3369
1785.8	**393.3**	Side trail to Jones Falls . . . . 🌢 ▲	3100
1784.3	**394.8**	Campsite . . . . 🌢 ▲	2675

ROAN MOUNTAIN, TN

Pop. 1,208 (2007)
N36 10.640, W82 00.700 (trailhead)
Mag. Dec. 6° 34'W

Mountain Harbour

AT to PO 3.7

19E

3.7 mi.

Frank & Marty's Pizza

Roan Mtn Animal
Hospital 423-772-4124

Buck Mtn Rd

Blondie's Hair & Massage

Highlander BBQ

Subway

Bob's Dairyland

Cloudland Dr

Roan Mtn Market

Mad Martha's

(143)

↓ 7.5 mi. to Hughes Gap

Roan Mtn Pharmacy

Cloudland Market

PO (37687):
423-772-3014
M-F 8-12 & 1-4,
Sa 7:30-9:30

Roan Mtn B&B
(0.5 mi.)

38

TN

364.2   Greasy Creek Gap

🏠⛺🅿🍴♿✉🚿🐾 (0.6E) **Greasy Creek Friendly**

828-688-9948, atrailagc@yahoo.com, All room prices include tax: $10PP bunkhouse, $15PP indoor accommodations, $7.50PP tenting includes shower. Shower without stay $3. Pets outside. Kitchen privileges, vegetarian meals. Well-stocked store: Coleman/alcohol/oz. Shuttles Erwin to Damascus. Directions: take old jeep trail east, then take first left. You should be going gradually downhill all the way. Walk around metal gate. Don't be concerned with barking dogs to the left; they're fenced. Hostel is first house to your right. Maildrops: 1827 Greasy Creek Rd, Bakersville, NC 28705.

388.4   US 19E

Roan Mountain, TN 37687 (more services on map)

🏠⛺🍴♿🅿🚿✉ (0.3W) **Mountain Harbour B&B/Hostel**

866-772-9494 〈www.mountainharbour.net〉 Hostel over barn overlooking creek $18PP, semi private king bed $35, includes linens, shower, towels, full kitchen, wood burning stove and video library. Tenting with shower $8, shower only $3 with towels, laundry $5 with soap, telephone w/ calling card, fuel/oz, town shuttle $5 during stay. Breakfast $9 available during peak season when there are at least 4 persons dining. B&B rooms include AC, refrigerator, cable TV/DVD, and breakfast, $80 double, $90 king, shared bath. Suite $135 w/ 2P jacuzzi tub, separate shower & fireplace. Slack pack/long distance shuttles by arrangement. Secured parking $5/day or $2/day with shuttle. Open year round. Maildrops free for guests, $5 non-guest: 9151 Hwy 19E, Roan Mountain, TN 37687.

Roan Mountain B&B 423-772-3207 〈www.roanmountainbedandbreakfast.com〉 $65-95 includes full breakfast, free pickup/return to trail at Hwy 19E, pets free, shuttles 30 miles for $20.

✗ **Bob's Dairyland** 423-772-3641, closed Su.

✗ **Frank & Mary's Pizza** 423-772-3083

✗ **Snack Shack** 423-772-4466 L/D M-Sa.

🏬 **Roan Mountain Supermarket** 423-772-3121 M-Sa 8-9, Su 9-9

🏬 **Cloudland Market** 423-772-3201

Elk Park, NC 28622 (more services on map)

✗ (0.7E) **King of the Road Restaurant** 423-772-4968, B/L/D, Th-Sa 4-9, Su 11-8, Su buffet 11-2.

✗ **Times Square Diner** 828-733-6791, B/L/D 7 days. Buffets: Friday dinner, Saturday breakfast, Sunday lunch.

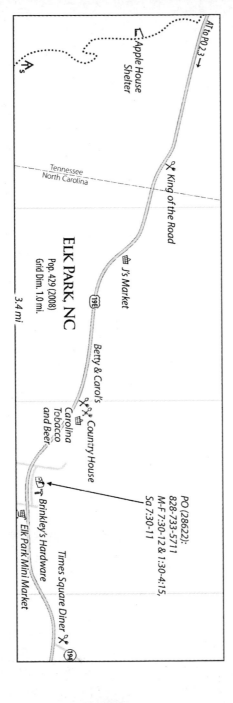

AT to PO 2.3 →

🏕 **Apple House Shelter**

Aₛ

Tennessee / North Carolina

✗ *King of the Road*

🏛 *J's Market*

ELK PARK, NC
Pop. 429 (2008)
Grid Dim. 1.0 mi.

(19E)

Betty & Carol's

✗ ✗ *Country House*
Carolina Tobacco and Beer 🏛

PO (28622):
828-733-5711
M-F 7:30-12 & 1:30-4:15,
Sa 7:30-11

📮 *Brinkley's Hardware*

Times Square Diner ✗

🏬 *Elk Park Mini Market*

(194)

3.4 mi

1782.1	397.0	Stream below waterfall, campsite west on blue-blazed trail. . . . . ⚫️🏕	3240
1781.9	397.2	**Mountaineer Shelter** . . . . ⚫️ ⌐ (14)	3470
		19.7◄18.0◄9.3◄►9.6►17.5►26.3 Water 70 yards from shelter.	
1781.1	398.0	Slide Hollow Stream . . . . ⚫️🏕	3300
1780.3	398.8	Walnut Mountain Rd	3583
1779.1	400.0	Stream . . . . ⚫️	3400
1778.6	400.5	Vista, bench, side trail to hostel . . . . **(pg.42)**	3350
1778.1	401.0	Upper Laurel Fork, Two tent spots next to small waterfall . . . . . 🏕 **(pg.42)**	3290
		Side trail to hostel.	
1774.2	404.9	Camping . . . . ⚫️🏕	3410
1772.3	406.8	**Moreland Gap Shelter** . . . . ⚫️ ⌐ (6)	3815
		27.6◄18.9◄9.6◄►7.9►16.7►23.8	
		Water source long way downhill across from shelter.	
1771.0	408.1	White Rocks Mountain	4206
1770.2	408.9	Campsite . . . . ⚫️🏕	4000
1768.0	411.1	Trail to Coon Den Falls	2660
1766.3	412.8	Dennis Cove, USFS 50 . . . . N36 15.858 W82 7.402 🅿 **(pg.42)**	2550
1765.1	414.0	Laurel Fork Falls . . . . ⚫️	2120
1764.4	414.7	**Laurel Fork Shelter** . . . . ⚫️ ⌐ (8)	2400
		26.8◄17.5◄7.9◄►8.8►15.9►22.7	
1764.1	415.0	Waycaster Spring . . . . ⚫️	1900
1763.6	415.5	Side trail to **Hampton, TN** US 321 (1.0W) . . . . **(pg.42-43)**	1900
		Hampton is west on 321.	

1760.6	**418.5**	Pond Flats . . . . ♦ ▲ 3780

1757.4	**421.7**	US 321 . . . . N36 18.123 W82 7.661 🅿 🛉🛉 ♦ **(pg.42-43)** 1990

On AT: **Shook Branch Recreation Area**, Picnic area, sandy beach
Hampton, TN (2.6W)

1756.1	**423.0**	Griffith Branch . . . . ♦ ▲ 2100
1755.6	**423.5**	**Watauga Lake Shelter** . . . . ▶ . . . . ♦ ⊏ (6) 2100

26.3◀16.7◀8.8◀▶7.1▶13.9▶21.5
Water south of shelter on AT.

1754.5	**424.6**	Watauga Dam north end 1915

1753.2	**425.9**	Wilbur Dam Rd. . . . . N36 19.726 W82 6.690 🅿 2250

1750.2	**428.9**	Spring . . . . ♦ 3360

1748.5	**430.6**	**Vandeventer Shelter** . . . . ▶ . . . . ♦ ⊏ (6) 3510

23.8◀15.9◀7.1◀▶6.8▶14.4▶22.7
Water 0.3 mile down steep blue-blazed
trail south of shelter.

1744.7	**434.4**	Spring 100 yards to east beyond bog. ♦ ▲ 3900

camping 0.1 north.

1743.3	**435.8**	Turkeypen Gap. 3970

1742.4	**436.7**	Power line. 4113
1741.9	**437.2**	Spring . . . . ♦ 4000
1741.7	**437.4**	**Iron Mountain Shelter** . . . . ▲ ⊏ (6) 4125

22.7◀13.9◀6.8◀▶7.6▶15.9▶35.5 Spring (0.3S) on AT.

1740.4	**438.7**	Nick Grindstaff Monument 4090
1740.3	**438.8**	Spring on blue-blazed side trail 0.1 west. . . . . ♦ 4131

400.5 (0.3W) Side trail to hostel
401.0 (0.4W) Upper Laurel Fork

⌂ ⚑ ⌂ ✉ (0.2W) Vango & Abby's Memorial Hostel

Rustic, no indoor toilet, two outhouses. Pets okay. Electric heated bunkroom w/stove & sink, internet, trail library, sleeps 6 and is always open. Available when caretaker present: shower $3, wash $3, dryer $3, misc. hiker-food resupply & beverages. Suggested donation $5/ night w/o heat, $10 using heat. Quiet hours 10pm - 8am. Shuttles $1.50/mi; secure parking $1/day. Directions for northbound hikers: 2 miles north of Walnut Mtn Rd, on AT there is a vista and bench. 200 ft farther, take trail at green/white AT sign downhill (SW & SE) under powerline 0.3 mi to hostel. Southbounders: take blue-blazed trail from just before hand-railed Laurel Fork bridge (requires fording creek), along mostly level ground 0.4 mi. Do not walk driveway (private property and mean dogs) Contact info: scott_vandam@ hotmail.com, 256-783-5060, PO Box 185, Roan Mtn, TN 37687 (No maildrops.)

412.8 USFS 50 (Dennis Cove Rd)

⌂ ⛺ ⌂ ⚑ ✉ ((0.2W) Kincora Hiking Hostel

423-725-4409 Cooking facilities, laundry, $4 per night suggested donation, Coleman/alcohol/oz, owner Bob Peoples will hold packages for hikers mailed to 1278 Dennis Cove Rd., Hampton, TN 37658.

★⌂ ⌂ ✉ ((0.3E) Laurel Fork Lodge 423-725-5988

<www.laurelforklodge.com> (2009 prices) Bunkhouse $10, private cabin $30/up. Hot shower included with any stay. Coleman/alcohol/ oz, snacks & sodas. Laundry $3 per load. Call ahead because groups sometimes occupy the entire facility. Maildrops ($5 for non-guests): Laurel Creek Lodge, 1511 Dennis Cove Rd., Hampton, TN 37658.

415.5 Side trail to Hampton (1.0W)
421.7 US 321 (2.6W)

Hampton, TN 37658 (more services on map)

⌂ M-F 7:30-11:30 & 12:30-4, Sa 8-10, 423-725-2177

⌂ ⚑ ✉ Brown's Grocery & Braemar Castle Hostel

423-725-2411, 423-725-2262. Both operated by Sutton Brown; check in at grocery to stay at the hostel or for shuttles. $15 bunkhouse, $20 private room with linens, $40D, common area and kitchen. Coleman/alcohol/oz, Maildrops (USPS and UPS) are received at the grocery store: 613 Hwy. 321, Hampton, TN 37658, M-Sa 8-6, closed Sunday.

✗ Quarterbacks BBQ 423-725-4227
✗ Copper Kettle 423-725-4498, 7-3, 7 days,
✗ Pizza Plus Has lunch buffet.
✗ Ice House Restaurant & bar burned down late in 2009 but is expected to rebuild.

⚑ Hampton Trails Bicycle Shop 423-725-5000 <www.hamptontrails.com> hamptontrails@embarqmail.com.

⌂ Meme's Laundry 423-725-3878 Limited hours, no longer has internet service.

⌂ ⚑ ⌂ ✉ Iron Mountain Inn 423-768-2446, 888-781-2399

<www.mountainlakevacation.com> 10 miles out of town, but you can call from Hampton for pickup, fee for pickup/return. $40PP and up. Log cabin with hot tub under the stars. Free laundry. Shuttles from Watauga Lake to Damascus. Maildrops: c/o Woods, 138 Moreland Dr, Butler, TN 37640.

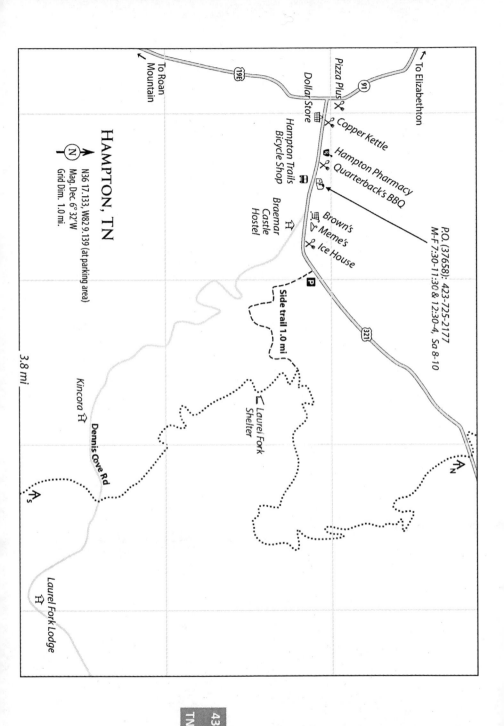

HAMPTON, TN

N36 17.133, W82 9.139 (at parking area)
Mag. Dec 6°32'W
Grid Dim. 1.0 mi.

To Roan Mountain

To Elizabethton

19E

91

Pizza Plus

Dollar Store

Copper Kettle

Hampton Pharmacy
Quarterback's BBQ

Hampton Trails
Bicycle Shop

P.O. (37658): 423-725-2177
M-F 7:30-11:30 & 12:30-4, Sa 8-10

Brown's
Meme's
Ice House

Braemar
Castle
Hostel

321

P

Side trail 1.0 mi

Laurel Fork
Shelter

Kincora

Dennis Cove Rd

3.8 mi

Laurel Fork Lodge

43

TN

SoBo	NoBo	Description	Elev
1737.9	**441.2**	Stream . . . . ♦	3505
1737.1	**442.0**	TN 91 . . . . .N36 28.883 W81 57.619 **P** (pg.46)	3450
		Shady Valley, TN (3.5E) South end of handicap-accessible trail.	
1736.6	**442.5**	North end of handicap-accessible trail	3500
1735.0	**444.1**	Spring in swampy area, camping east of the trail . . . . ♦ ⚠	3990
1734.1	**445.0**	**Double Springs Shelter,** Holston Mountain Trail . . . . ♦ ⊏ (6)	4080
		21.5◄14.4◄7.6◄►8.3►27.9►34.3 Spring 100 yards beyond shelter.	
1733.6	**445.5**	Locust Knob	4020
1731.6	**447.5**	Campsite to west . . . . ⚠	3598
1730.6	**448.5**	Low Gap, US 421 . . . . N36 32.316 W81 56.933 **P** ♦ (pg.46)	3378
		piped spring on south side of road	
		Shady Valley, TN (2.7E)	
1729.2	**449.9**	Low stone wall on east side of AT	3609
1728.7	**450.4**	Double Spring Gap, water unreliable . . . . ♦	3530
1728.2	**450.9**	Weak, muddy spring east side of AT. . . . . ♦	3654
1727.3	**451.8**	McQueens Knob, survey marker	3896
1727.2	**451.9**	McQueens Knob Shelter (disused).	3867
1726.9	**452.2**	McQueens Gap, USFS 69 . . . . .N36 34.460 W81 55.921	3680
1725.8	**453.3**	**Abingdon Gap Shelter** . . . . ♦ ⊏ (5)	3780
		22.7◄15.9◄8.3◄► 19.6►26.0►38.2	
		Piped spring 0.2 mile behind shelter	
		on blue-blazed trail.	
1721.7	**457.4**	Campsite at gap . . . . ⚠	3599
1720.4	**458.7**	Backbone Rock Trail leads 2.3E to USFS recreation area.	3460
1719.3	**459.8**	**TN-VA** border	3200
1717.9	**461.2**	Spring 0.1E on blue-blazed trail . . . . ♦	2600

SoBo	NoBo			Elev
1715.6	**463.5**	US 58, **Damascus, VA** . . . . N36 38.162 W81 47.378 🅿 **(pg.46-47)**		1928
1714.5	**464.6**	US 58, Virginia Creeper Trail		1928
1712.1	**467.0**	Feathercamp Ridge, Iron Mountain Trail		2850
1710.7	**468.4**	Beech Grove Trail		2500
1710.0	**469.1**	US 58, VA 91, Feathercamp Branch . . . . . . N36 38.694 W81 44.197 🅿 ♦		2250
1708.7	**470.4**	Stream . . . . ♦		2490
1708.0	**471.1**	Taylors Valley Trail		2850
1706.5	**472.6**	Straight Mountain		3500
1706.2	**472.9**	**Saunders Shelter** (0.2W) . . . . ☽ ♦ ⌐ (8)		3310
		35.5◄27.9◄19.6◄►6.4►18.6►23.7		
		Reliable spring on right behind shelter and down road.		
1705.1	**474.0**	Stream . . . . ♦		3150
1704.0	**475.1**	Beartree Gap Trail, (3.0W) to Beartree Recreation Area		3050
1703.8	**475.3**	Pond, campsite. . . . . ♦ ⛺		3020
1702.2	**476.9**	VA 728, picnic tables . . . . N36 38.965 W81 40.345 🅿 ⛊		2700
		Junction with Creeper Trail		
1702.0	**477.1**	Junction with Whitetop Creek and Green Cove Creek . . . . ♦		2720
1701.6	**477.5**	Virginia Creeper Trail, Whitetop Laurel Creek		2690
1701.0	**478.1**	VA 859, Grassy Creek Rd		2900
1700.8	**478.3**	Spring		3200
1699.8	**479.3**	**Lost Mountain Shelter** . . . . ☽ ♦ ⛺ ⌐ (8)		3400
		34.3◄26.0◄6.4◄►12.2►17.3►23.2		
		Water source on trail to left of shelter.		
1698.7	**480.4**	US 58. . . . . N36 38.389 W81 39.926 ♦		3160
1698.4	**480.7**	Campsites, streams . . . . ♦ ⛺		3200
1697.5	**481.6**	VA 601, Beech Mountain Rd. . . . . N36 38.235 W81 38.425 🅿 ♦		3600
1695.0	**484.1**	Buzzard Rock		5080

SoBo NoBo VA 45 1000 2000 3000 4000 5000 6000 Elev

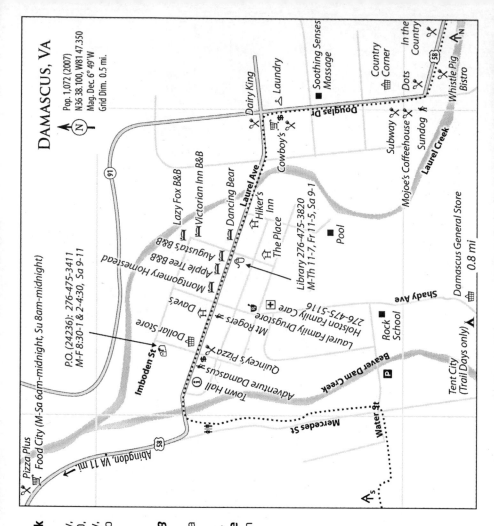

DAMASCUS, VA

Pop. 1,072 (2007)
N36 38.100, W81 47.350
Mag. Dec. 6° 49'W
Grid Dim. 0.5 mi.

442.0 TN 91
Switchback Creek Campground 407-484-3388
570 Wallace Rd., Shady Valley, TN 37688. 2-person cabin $40, campsite $12+tax. Showers, laundry, call for ride. 1.5 miles further east to TN 421 and Shady Valley (below).

448.5 US 421
Shady Valley, TN 37688
(2.7E)
M-F 7:30-11:00 & 12-3:30, Sa 7:30-9:30, 423-739-2173
S&S General Store, open daily.
Shady Valley Country Store and Deli M-Sa 6am-9pm. Coleman fuel.

Raceway Restaurant

463.5   US 58/ *Damascus, VA* (*more services on map*)

Trail Days <www.traildays.us> (May 14-16) is the largest event on the AT. Hiker reunion and talent show, presentations, music, contra dancing, and hiker parade. Many gear reps & retailers on-hand.

Dave's Place $10PP, shower without stay $3, no alcohol. Check in at Mount Rogers Outfitters.

Hikers Inn 276-475-3788, $25 bunks, hostel private room $35S, $45D. Rooms in house $65; $55/night for multi-night stays. Laundry $3, no smoking, dogs allowed in hostel, cash or travelers check.

The Place 276-475-3441, Methodist Church-run bunkrooms and tenting. Please help to keep the bunkroom clean; there is no housekeeper. No pets, no alcohol, 2 night max unless sick/injured. Funded by donations. Do not leave your gear unattended.

Dancing Bear Inn 276-475-5900 <www.dancingbearrentals.com> $65/night. Run by hikers Bob & Diane Smith. No smoking, no pets, cash or check.

Apple Tree B&B 276-475-5261 $85D-$105D, includes full breakfast. Can mend torn packs and clothing, sells beef jerky. Free long distance calls within U.S. Laundry $4, no smoking on property. Call before sending maildrops.

Augusta's Appalachian Inn 276-475-3565 <www.augustasappalachianinn.com> $90 to $125. Full breakfast with stay. Free long distance calls, internet use, and one load of laundry. No credit cards, no pets. Guest maildrops: PO Box 160, 125 East Laurel Avenue, Damascus, VA 24236.

Montgomery Homestead B&B 276-475-3053, $65 and up. No smoking, no alcohol, no pets. Guest maildrops: (FedEx, UPS) 103 Laurel Ave. (USPS) P.O. Box 12, Damascus, VA 24236.

Victorian Inn B&B 276-475-5059, $75-$85+tax, includes breakfast. Also, 2 bedroom cottage $110/night up to 4 (does not include breakfast), $20 EAP. No pets.

Lazy Fox B&B 276-475-5838, $65/up+tax. Kennel for dogs. Maildrops: PO Box 757, 133 Imboden St, Damascus, VA 24236.

Food City (0.5W) 276-475-3653, US 58, 7 days.

Mt. Rogers Outfitters 276-475-5416 <www.mtrogersoutfitters.com> Full service backpacking store, fuel/oz. Shuttle service for the Appalachian Trail, parking for section hikers $2/day. Shower only $3. Maildrops: PO Box 546, 110 W Laurel Ave, Damascus, VA 24236.

Adventure Damascus 888-595-2453 or 276-475-6262 <www.AdventureDamascus.com> Catering to thru-hikers with backpacking gear, a hiker-food section, denatured alcohol and Coleman/oz, other fuels, bike rentals, shuttles to area trailheads by arrangement, $2 showers ($4 includes a towel), open 7 days year-round. USPS and UPS Maildrops: PO Box 1113, 128 W. Laurel Ave. Damascus, VA 24236.

Sundog Outfitter 276-475-6252 <www.sundogoutfitter.com> Backpacking gear and clothing, repairs, hiker food, Coleman/alcohol/oz, other fuels, shuttles to area trailheads by arrangement, open 7 days a week. USPS & UPS Maildrops: PO Box 1113, 331 Douglas Dr. Damascus, VA 24236.

Damascus General Store Until May: F,Sa 10am-10pm, Su 12-6. After May 1, will also be open Tu-Th 10-6. Sandwiches, Candy, specialty sodas and groceries. Live music Fri and Sat nights.

Whistle Pig Bistro (formerly Fatties) Breakfast and lunch Wednesday-Sunday.

Library 276-475-3820, M-Th 11-7, F 11-5, Sa 9-1, internet 1 hr.

SoBo	NoBo		Elev
1694.5	484.6	Piped spring on east side of trail . . . . ♦	5100
1694.3	484.8	Whitetop Mountain Rd, USFS 89 . . . . N36 37.921 W81 36.112 🅿 ♦ 🛆	5150
1693.3	485.8	Brook . . . . ♦	4800
1691.8	487.3	VA 600 . . . . N36 38.769 W81 34.992 🅿	4434
1689.8	489.3	Deep Gap, water on blue-blazed side trail east 0.2 . . . . ♦	4900
1688.0	491.1	Side trail to Mt Rogers, Virginia's highest peak at 5,729 ft.	5490
1687.6	491.5	**Thomas Knob Shelter** . . . .☽ ♦ ⊏ (16)	5400
		38.2◄18.6◄12.2◄►5.1►11.0►16.0	
		Water in gated area behind shelter.	
1686.8	492.3	Rhododendron Gap	5440
1686.2	492.9	Fatman Squeeze.	5200
1685.3	493.8	Grayson Highlands State Park (south end), fence . . . . **(pg.52)**	4900
1684.7	494.4	Massie Gap, (0.2W) to parking area . . . . 🅿	4800
1682.5	496.6	**Wise Shelter** . . . . ☽ ♦ ⊏ (8)	4415
		23.7◄17.3◄5.1◄►5.9►10.9►20.0 Reliable spring south of shelter on trail	
		east of AT. No tenting near shelters in state park.	
1682.2	496.9	East fork of Big Wilson Creek, camping . . . . ♦ 🛆	4470
1681.2	497.9	Spring on east side of trail. . . . . ♦	4700
1680.0	499.1	Stone Mountain	4800
1679.7	499.4	The Scales. . . . . N36 40.182 W81 29.229 🅿	4632
1678.9	500.2	Small stream . . . . ♦	4840
1678.3	500.8	Pine Mountain	4960
1676.6	502.5	**Old Orchard Shelter** . . . . ☽ ♦ ⊏ (6)	4050
		23.2◄11.0◄5.9◄►5.0►14.1►24.7 Water 100 yards on blue-blazed trail to	
		right of shelter. Privy 50 yards to left behind shelter.	
1675.1	504.0	Small stream . . . . ♦	3503
1674.9	504.2	Fox Creek, VA 603 . . . . .N36 41.795 W81 30.398 🅿 ☽ ♦ 🛆	3480
		100 yards east to parking and porta-potty .	

| 1672.6 | **506.5** | Chestnut Flats, Hurricane Mountain Trail to west . . . . | 4322 |

1671.6	**507.5**	**Hurricane Mtn Shelter** (0.1W) . . . . 🌙 ♦ ⛺ ⊏ (8)	3858
		16.0◄10.9◄5.0◄►9.1►19.7►26.8	
		Creek and tentsites opposite side of trail.	

| 1670.2 | **508.9** | Stream . . . . ♦ | 3167 |

1668.5	**510.6**	**USFS Hurricane Campground** (0.5W) 276-783-5196. . . . . 🚻 ☂ ⛺	3150
		Tent site $12, shower $2. Open mid Apr-Oct.	
		Restroom & shower open Memorial Day-Labor Day.	

| 1667.6 | **511.5** | Comers Creek (drinking not advised) . . . . | 3100 |

1666.4	**512.7**	Dickey Gap, VA 16 (Sugar Grove Hwy) & 650, ... 🚻 **(pg.52)**	3313
		Troutdale, VA (2.6E) on Sugar Grove Hwy	
1664.9	**514.2**	Campsite. Spring on blue-blazed trail (0.2E). . . . . ♦ ⛺	3570

| 1664.3 | **514.8** | High Point, on blue-blazed trail 0.1 . . . . | 3700 |

1662.5	**516.6**	**Trimpi Shelter** . . . . 🌙 ♦ ⊏ (8)	2900
		20.0◄14.1◄9.1◄►10.6►17.7►36.2	
1661.5	**517.6**	Cattle graze in this area, close gates behind you.	2662

| 1661.0 | **518.1** | Route 672 . . . . | 2621 |

1660.0	**519.1**	Stream, seasonal. . . . . ♦	2500
1659.7	**519.4**	Route 670, South Fork Holston River . . . . . . N36 45.784 W81 29.634 🅿	2450
1658.7	**520.4**	Campsite on west side of trail . . . . ♦ (0.1S)	2730

| 1658.2 | **520.9** | Stream, intermittent . . . . ♦ | 2805 |

| 1655.9 | **523.2** | Route 601, limited parking. . . . . N36 47.963 W81 27.448 🅿 | 3194 |

| 1654.3 | **524.8** | Power line. . . . . | 3299 |

1651.9	**527.2**	**Partnership Shelter,** Showers . . . . 🌙 ☂ ♦ ⛺ ⊏ (16)	3256
		24.7◄19.7◄10.6◄►7.1►25.6►34.6 Can call for pizza from Visitor Center.	
1651.7	**527.4**	VA 16, Mt Rogers Visitor Center . .N36 48.682 W81 25.224 🅿 ℂ ⓘ **(pg.52)**	3220
		Sugar Grove, VA, 24375 (3.2E), **Marion, VA** 24354 (5.9W)	

SoBo	NoBo		VA 50	1000	2000	3000	4000	5000	6000	Elev
1651.1	**528.0**	VA 622								3258
1650.6	**528.5**	Brushy Mountain								3700
1648.1	**531.0**	Locust Mountain								3900
1647.7	**531.4**	USFS 86 . . . . ♦ N36 50.089 W81 22.246 🅿								3530
1646.8	**532.3**	Glade Mountain								3900
1644.8	**534.3**	**Chatfield Shelter** . . . . ☽ ♦ ⌐ (6)								3150
		26.8◄17.7◄7.1◄►18.5►27.5►37.5 Creek in front of shelter.									
1644.5	**534.6**	USFS 644								3050
1643.0	**536.1**	VA 615 . . . . N36 52.246 W81 21.461 🅿								2590
		Settlers Museum, parking available at the farm.									
1642.5	**536.6**	VA 729								2600
1641.2	**537.9**	Middle Fork of the Holston River. . . . . ♦								2425
1640.3	**538.8**	VA 683, US 11, I-81, **Atkins, VA** . . . . (pg.53)								2420
1639.2	**539.9**	VA 617 . . . . N36 53.840 W81 22.146 🅿								2520
1638.5	**540.6**	Spring (0.1E) on side trail. . . . . ♦								2800
1637.6	**541.5**	Davis Path Campsite								2840
1635.1	**544.0**	Gullion Mountain/Little Brushy Mountain								3300
1634.0	**545.1**	Crawfish Valley, campsites trail and to the east . . . . ♦ ⛺								2600
1632.3	**546.8**	Tilson Gap, Big Walker Mountain								3500
1630.9	**548.2**	VA 610								2700
1629.5	**549.6**	North Fork of the Holston River, VA 742 . . . . ♦								2500
1629.3	**549.8**	Pipe spring, reliable . . . . ♦								2581

| 1628.5 | **550.6** | VA 42 . . . . N36 58.995 W81 24.385 🅿 | 2600 |

1627.6	**551.5**	Brushy Mountain	3200
1626.3	**552.8**	**Knot Maul Branch Shelter** . . . . ☽ ◗ ⌐ (8)	2880
		36.2◄25.6◄18.5◄►9.0►19.0►33.0 Water (0.1N) on AT.	
1626.2	**552.9**	Spring . . . . ◗ ▲	2854
1625.2	**553.9**	Lynn Camp Creek . . . . ◗	2400

| 1624.4 | **554.7** | Lynn Camp Mountain . . . . | 3000 |

| 1621.0 | **558.1** | USFS 222 . . . . N37 1.358 W81 25.569 🅿 | 2300 |

| 1619.1 | **560.0** | Spring fed pond . . . . ◗ | 3800 |

1617.3	**561.8**	**Chestnut Knob Shelter** . . . . ☽ ⌐ (8)	4410
		34.6◄27.5◄9.0◄►10.0►24.0►33.8 Unreliable water (0.2S) on AT.	
		Concrete block shelter, fully enclosed with door.	
1616.0	**563.1**	Walker Gap . . . . N37 3.265 W81 22.731 🅿 ◗	3520

| 1611.1 | **568.0** | VA 623, Garden Mountain . . . . N37 4.622 W81 18.425 🅿 | 3880 |
| 1610.3 | **568.8** | Davis Farm Campsite . . . . ◗ ▲ (0.5W) | 3600 |

1608.0	**571.1**	Stream (unreliable) . . . . ◗	2812
1607.3	**571.8**	**Jenkins Shelter** Stream 100 yards north on blue-blazed trail. ☽ ◗ ⌐ (8)	2470
		37.5◄19.0◄10.0◄►14.0►23.8►38.0	

| SoBo | NoBo | | VA 51 | 1000 2000 3000 4000 5000 6000 | Elev |

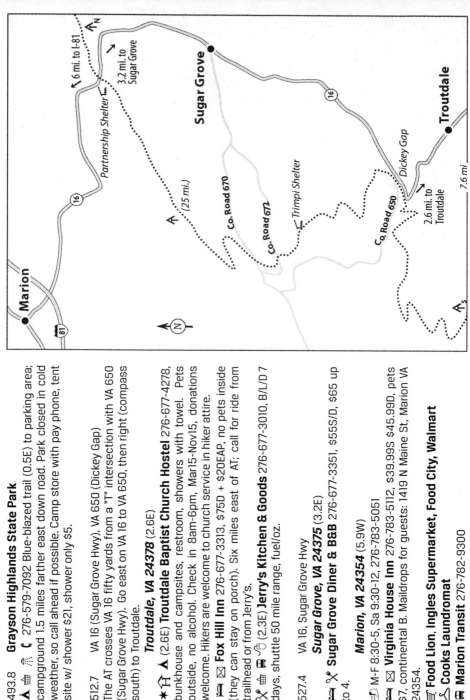

493.8 Grayson Highlands State Park

⚠ ⛺ 🚿 📞 276-579-7092 Blue-blazed trail (0.5E) to parking area; campground 1.5 miles farther east down road. Park closed in cold weather, so call ahead if possible. Camp store with pay phone, tent site w/ shower $21, shower only $5.

512.7   VA 16 (Sugar Grove Hwy). VA 650 (Dickey Gap)
The AT crosses VA 16 fifty yards from a "T" intersection with VA 650 (Sugar Grove Hwy). Go east on VA 16 to VA 650, then right (compass south) to Troutdale.

Troutdale, VA 24378 (2.6E)

★ 🏠 ⚠ (2.6E) **Troutdale Baptist Church Hostel** 276-677-4278, bunkhouse and campsites, restroom, showers with towel. Pets outside, no alcohol. Check in 8am-6pm, Mar15-Nov15, donations welcome. Hikers are welcome to church service in hiker attire.

🏠 ✉ **Fox Hill Inn** 276-677-3313, $75D + $20EAP, no pets inside (they can stay on porch). Six miles east of AT; call for ride from trailhead or from Jerry's.

🍴 ⛺ 🏠 ⛽ (2.3E) **Jerry's Kitchen & Goods** 276-677-3010, B/L/D 7 days, shuttle 50 mile range, fuel/oz.

527.4   VA 16, Sugar Grove Hwy

Sugar Grove, VA 24375 (3.2E)

🏠 🍴 **Sugar Grove Diner & B&B** 276-677-3351, $55S/D, $65 up to 4.

Marion, VA 24354 (5.9W)

🏪 M-F 8:30-5, Sa 9:30-12, $39.99S $45.99D, pets $7, continental B. Maildrops for guests: 1419 N Maine St, Marion VA 24354.

🏠 ✉ **Virginia House Inn** 276-783-5112, $39.99S $45.99D, pets $7, continental B. Maildrops for guests: 1419 N Maine St, Marion VA 24354.

🛒 **Food Lion, Ingles Supermarket, Food City, Walmart**

⚲ **Cooks Laundromat**

🚌 **Marion Transit** 276-782-9300

538.8   VA 683, US 11, I-81
Atkins, VA 24311

Upon reaching US 11, you are in Rural Retreat at the northwest edge of Atkins. There is little more than the motel, restaurant and convenience store catering to hikers and traffic exiting from nearby interstate 81. The post office, grocery and laundry are 3 miles west. There is another hotel, service station and restaurants 3.7 west near another interstate 81 interchange.

ℝ ⌂ ⊠ **Relax Inn** 276-783-5811 $40S $45D, EAP extra, pets $5. Maildrops: Relax Inn, 7253 Lee Hwy, Rural Retreat, VA 24368. $5 maildrop fee for non-guests. Shuttles when available from Damascus to Bland.

✗ **The Barn Restaurant** 276-686-6222

🏦 **$ ⟮ Shell Convenience Store** 24hr, Phone and ATM inside.

Ħ ⌂ 🛏 🄿 ⊠ **Happy Hiker Hollow** 276-783-3754 Rambunny and Aqua with 10,000 miles on the AT. All you can eat home cooking B/D, shuttle to town, showers, free long distance phone calls, high speed internet, fuel, hiker box. We do your laundry. Beds not bunks, private rooms available. Community room with cable, movies, games. Long term safe free parking for sectioners with shuttle or stay. MUST CALL AHEAD TO RESERVE YOUR SPOT. Shuttling and slackpacking available with prior arrangement. Sorry no tenting, no dogs. Will hold boxes for our guests: 484 Phillipi Hollow Road, Atkins VA 24311.

3.0 west on US 11:

⚒ **Atkins Grocery** 276-784-5267

⌂ **Laundry**

3.7 west on US 11:

ℝ ⊠ **Comfort Inn** 276-783-2144 $54/up. For best price, get coupon from hotel discount book stand at Exxon station. Maildrops: 5558 Lee Hwy, Atkins, VA 24311.

🏦 ⟮ **Exxon Convenience Store**
✗ **Atkins Diner, Subway, Pizza Plus** 276-781-2006

Atkins
8/24

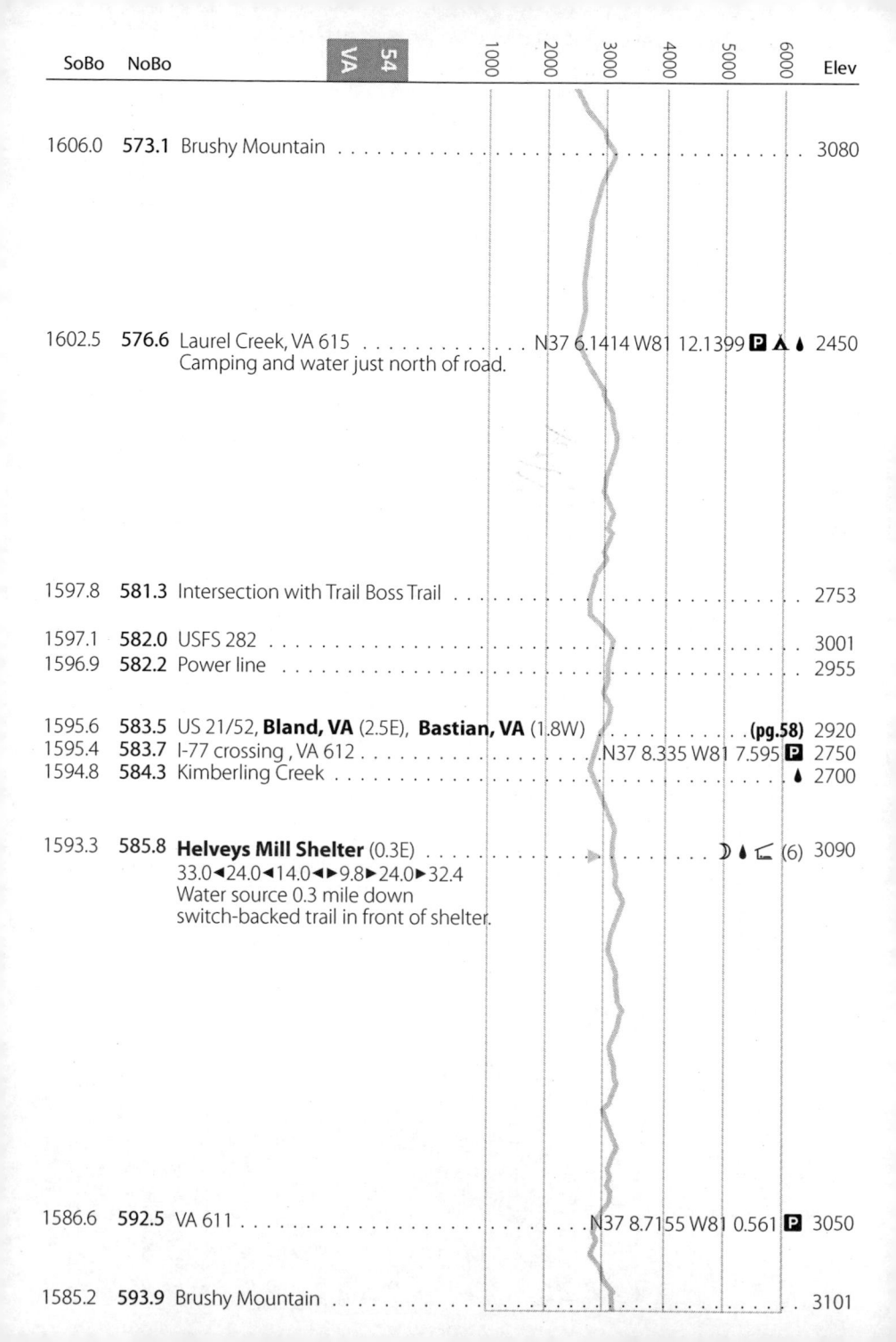

SoBo	NoBo		VA 54	1000	2000	3000	4000	5000	6000	Elev
1606.0	**573.1**	Brushy Mountain								3080
1602.5	**576.6**	Laurel Creek, VA 615 . . . . N37 6.1414 W81 12.1399 🅿 ⛺ ♦								2450
		Camping and water just north of road.								
1597.8	**581.3**	Intersection with Trail Boss Trail								2753
1597.1	**582.0**	USFS 282								3001
1596.9	**582.2**	Power line								2955
1595.6	**583.5**	US 21/52, **Bland, VA** (2.5E), **Bastian, VA** (1.8W) . . . . **(pg.58)**								2920
1595.4	**583.7**	I-77 crossing , VA 612 . . . . N37 8.335 W81 7.595 🅿								2750
1594.8	**584.3**	Kimberling Creek . . . . ♦								2700
1593.3	**585.8**	**Helveys Mill Shelter** (0.3E) . . . . ☽ ♦ ⌂ (6)								3090
		33.0◄24.0◄14.0◄►9.8►24.0►32.4								
		Water source 0.3 mile down								
		switch-backed trail in front of shelter.								
1586.6	**592.5**	VA 611 . . . . N37 8.7155 W81 0.561 🅿								3050
1585.2	**593.9**	Brushy Mountain								3101

| 1584.2 | 594.9 | Northern crest of Brushy Mountain . . . . | | 2920 |
| 1583.5 | 595.6 | **Jenny Knob Shelter** . . . . ☽ ◑ ⊏ (6) | 2800 |

33.8◄23.8◄9.8◄►14.2►22.6►37.6Table. Spring near shelter.

| 1582.3 | 596.8 | Lickskillet Hollow, VA 608 . . . . N37 9.415 W80 57.682 **P** | 2200 |
| 1582.2 | 596.9 | Stream, intermittent . . . . ◑ | 2180 |

| 1581.0 | 598.1 | Brushy Mountain (south end). . . . . | 2900 |

| 1577.1 | 602.0 | Kimberling Creek . . . . ◑ | 2095 |
| 1577.0 | 602.1 | VA 606 . . . . **(pg.58)** | 2100 |

| 1575.1 | 604.0 | Dismal Creek Falls Trail, 0.2W to overlook. . . . . ▲ | 2095 |

| 1574.2 | 604.9 | White Pine Horse Campground . . . . ◑▲ (0.5W) | 2429 |
| | | Ribble Trail south junction | |

| 1573.1 | 606.0 | Dismal Creek . . . . ◑ | 2500 |

| 1570.8 | 608.3 | Stream . . . . ◑ | 2500 |

| 1569.3 | 609.8 | **Wapiti Shelter** . . . . ☽ ◑ ⊏ (8) | 2600 |

38.0◄24.0◄14.2◄►8.4►23.4►35.9

| 1568.8 | 610.3 | Upper branch of Dismal Creek . . . . ◑ | 2694 |

| 1567.0 | 612.1 | Outcrop on crest of Sugar Run Mountain . . . . | 3870 |

| 1564.8 | 614.3 | Ribble Trail north junction . . . . ◑ | 3704 |
| 1564.7 | 614.4 | Big Horse Gap, USFS 103 . . . . | 3759 |

| 1563.5 | 615.6 | Nobusiness Creek Rd . . . . | 3711 |

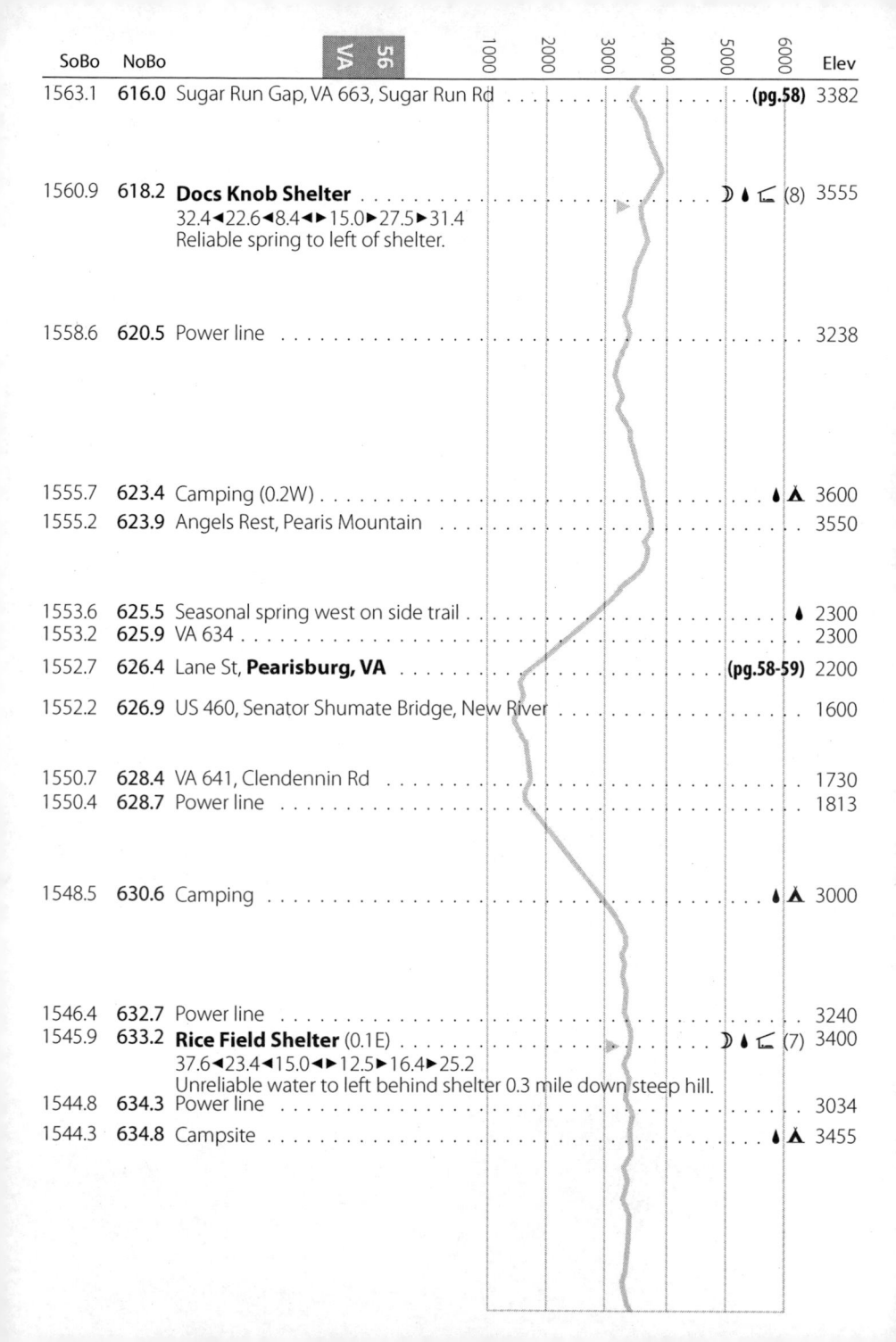

SoBo	NoBo		Elev
1563.1	616.0	Sugar Run Gap, VA 663, Sugar Run Rd . . . . **(pg.58)**	3382
1560.9	618.2	**Docs Knob Shelter** . . . . ☽ ♦ ⌐ (8)	3555
		32.4◄22.6◄8.4◄▶15.0▶27.5▶31.4	
		Reliable spring to left of shelter.	
1558.6	620.5	Power line	3238
1555.7	623.4	Camping (0.2W) . . . . ♦ ▲	3600
1555.2	623.9	Angels Rest, Pearis Mountain	3550
1553.6	625.5	Seasonal spring west on side trail . . . . ♦	2300
1553.2	625.9	VA 634	2300
1552.7	626.4	Lane St, **Pearisburg, VA** . . . . **(pg.58-59)**	2200
1552.2	626.9	US 460, Senator Shumate Bridge, New River	1600
1550.7	628.4	VA 641, Clendennin Rd	1730
1550.4	628.7	Power line	1813
1548.5	630.6	Camping . . . . ♦ ▲	3000
1546.4	632.7	Power line	3240
1545.9	633.2	**Rice Field Shelter** (0.1E) . . . . ☽ ♦ ⌐ (7)	3400
		37.6◄23.4◄15.0◄▶12.5▶16.4▶25.2	
		Unreliable water to left behind shelter 0.3 mile down steep hill.	
1544.8	634.3	Power line	3034
1544.3	634.8	Campsite . . . . ♦ ▲	3455

SoBo	NoBo			Elev

1540.8 **638.3** Symms Gap Meadow . . . . ▲ 3400

1539.8 **639.3** Groundhog Trail 3400

1538.3 **640.8** Dickinson Gap 3300

1536.1 **643.0** Peters Mountain 3860
1535.9 **643.2** Allegheny Trail 3700

1533.4 **645.7 Pine Swamp Branch Shelter** . . . . ☽ ♦ ⊏ (8) 2530
35.9◄27.5◄12.5◄►3.9►12.7►18.5
1533.1 **646.0** VA 635, Stony Creek Valley. . . . . N37 25.146 W80 36.274 🅿 2450
1532.6 **646.5** Camping at "The Captain's" place 30 yards east . . . . ♦ ▲ (pg.59) 2366
1532.0 **647.1** Dismal Branch . . . . ♦ 2420

1531.0 **648.1** VA 635, Stony Creek. 2450

1529.7 **649.4** Spring . . . . ♦ 3405
1529.5 **649.6 Bailey Gap Shelter** . . . . ☽ ♦ ⊏ (6) 3525
31.4◄16.4◄3.9◄►8.8►14.6►21.0
Water (0.2S) on AT, then east down blue-blazed trail.

1525.8 **653.3** VA 613, Salt Sulphur Turnpike. 4100
1525.6 **653.5** Wind Rock. 4100

1524.4 **654.7** Camping. . . . . ♦ ▲ 4000

1523.8 **655.3** Salt Pond Mountain. 4042

1522.7 **656.4** War Branch Trail 3720

1520.7 **658.4 War Spur Shelter** . . . . ☽ ♦ ⊏ (6) 2340
25.2◄12.7◄8.8◄►5.8►12.2►18.2
1519.9 **659.2** USFS 156/632, Johns Creek Valley . . . . ♦ 2080
1519.4 **659.7** USFS 10721 2583

583.5   US 21/52

Bland, VA 24315 (2.5E)

🛏️ M-F 8-11:30 & 12-4, Sa 9 -11, 276-688-3751

🛏️ ⊠ **Big Walker Motel** 276-688-3331, $53.95, 57.95 up to 4, pets allowed, Visa/MC. Maildrops: 70 Skyview Lane, Bland, VA 24315.

✗ **Subway, Dairy Queen**

🛒 (**Bruce's Market** 276-688-4461, M-Sa 7-10, Su 8-9 ATM at bank next door.

🏛️ **Bland Square** 276-688-3851 groceries, fuel, **Dollar General**

✚ **Mountain Medical Clinic** 276-688-4800, M-W 9-5, Th 9-12, 144 Seddon Street.

🏛️ **Bland County Library** 276-688-3737, M,W,F,Sa 9:30-4:30, T,Th 9:30-8, 697 Main St, about 0.1 mile past Bruce's Market.

Bastian, VA 24314 (1.8W)

🛏️ M-F 8-12 & 12:30-4, Sa 8-10:30, 276-688-4631

✗ **Pizza Plus** 276-688-3332

🏧 **$ Kangaroo Express** ATM

✚ **Medical Clinic** 276-688-4331, M, W, F 9-5, Tu, Th 9-8

🏛️🚌 **Greyhound Bus Lines** 304-325-9442, Bluefield, WV, 18 miles north west of Bastian on US 52.

602.1   VA 606

🏠 **Woods Hole Hostel** ⟨www.woodsholehostel.com⟩

🏚️ 🔥 (🛏️ 🥬 ✗ 🥾 **Trent's Grocery** (0.4W) 276-928-1349 Open 7-7, 540-921-3444 An 1880's chestnut-log cabin & bunkhouse on 100 acres, discovered by Roy & Tillie Wood. They opened the hostel in 1986, and it was run by Tillie for 21 years after Roy passed. Tillie passed in 2007 and her granddaughter, Neville continues the legacy with her husband, Michael. Hikers say it's "A slice of heaven, not to be missed." Directions: Going north, at Sugar Run Gap, turn right on dirt road, bear left at fork, and go 0.5 mi. down road to hostel on right; Going south at Sugar Run Gap, turn Left. Downhill 0.5 mi. Watch for signs. Travelers welcome year round. Offers massage, healing arts, & retreats. Loft bunkhouse has mattresses, electricity, and solar shower, $10 PP suggested donation. Two indoor rooms: $35S/$45D long distance hiker rate, $55S/$65D Reg Rate. Family style dinner $12, authentic southern breakfast $6.50. Yoga at 5pm. Shuttles. WiFi internet, telephone, laundry, pizza, smoothies, snacks and drinks, Coleman/alcohol/oz, fuel canisters. Pet friendly. Maildrops: Woods Hole Hostel, 3696 Sugar Run Rd. Pearisburg, VA 24134.

616.0   Sugar Run Gap

626.4   Lane Street, US 460

Pearisburg, VA (more services on map)

🛏️ 🏠 🥾 ⊠ **Rendezous Motel** 540-921-2636, $39S $47D Pets okay, free long distance for guests, Coleman/alcohol/oz & isobutane canisters. Maildrops: 795 North Main Street, Pearisburg, VA 24134.

🛏️ 🥾 🍽️ ⊠ **Plaza Motel** 540-921-2591, $40S $50D plus tax, no pets, all credit cards except Disc. Maildrops: 415 Main Street, Pearisburg, VA 24134.

🛏️ ⊠ 🍽️ **Holiday Motor Lodge** 540-921-1551, $29.71/up, hikers 15% off, pets ok. Maildrops: 401 N Main Street, Pearisburg, VA 24134.

🏠 🥾 **Holy Family Hostel** 540-921-3547 Open mid-Apr until mid-Oct, depending on end and start of cold weather. If you need to call, please do so only between 8am-6pm. 9 bunks; tenting in designated areas, toilet, hot shower, refrigerator, 2 microwaves, indoor and outdoor grill. Please arrive during daylight hours; keep hostel clean and noise down (church in residential area). Suggested donation $10PP per night, 2 night max. No pets or alcohol.

🛒 **Food Lion** 24hr, **Save-A-Lot**

⚕️ **Rite Aid Pharmacy** 540-921-1284

🏛️ **Tom Hoffman** 540-921-1184 ⟨gopullman@aol.com⟩ mid-range shuttles centered in Pearisburg.

Also: Old Towne Shoe Repair Warner Baker 540-230-6357

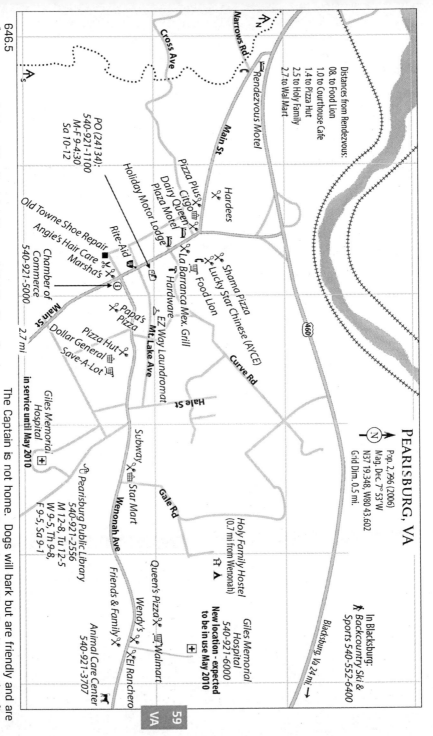

646.5

▲ Camping available at "The Captain's" house 4464 Big Stony Creek Road. Use the zip line to cross the creek at 6441. This location is about 30 yards from trail and unmarked. You may camp even when

The Captain is not home. Dogs will bark but are friendly and are contained by an invisible electric fence. Hiker Feed two weeks after Trail Days.

PEARISBURG, VA

Pop. 2,796 (2006)
Mag. Dec 7° 53'W
N37 19.348, W80 43.602
Grid Dim. 0.5 mi.

In Blacksburg:
Backcountry Ski & Sports 540-552-6400

Blacksburg Va 24 mi.

Distances from Rendezvous:
08. to Food Lion
1.0 to Courthouse Cafe
1.4 to Pizza Hut
2.5 to Holy Family
2.7 to Wal Mart

Rendezvous Motel

Narrows Rd.

Cross Ave

Main St

Pizza Plus
Citgo
Dairy Queen
Plaza Motel
Holiday Motor Lodge

Hardees

PO (24134):
540-921-1100
M-F 9-4:30
Sa 10-12

Old Towne Shoe Repair
Angie's Hair Care
Marsha's
Chamber of Commerce
540-921-5000

Rite-Aid

La Barranca Mex. Grill
Hardware
Food Lion

Shama Pizza
Lucky Star Chinese (AYCE)

Papa's Pizza

EZ Way Laundromat
Mt. Lake Ave

Pizza Hut
Dollar General
Save-A-Lot

Main St   2.7 mi.

Hale St

460

Curve Rd

Giles Memorial Hospital
540-921-6000
in service until May 2010

The Captain is not home. Dogs will bark but are friendly and are contained by an invisible electric fence. Hiker Feed two weeks after Trail Days.

Subway
Star Mart

Gale Rd

Holy Family Hostel
(0.7 mi from Wenonah)

Giles Memorial Hospital
540-921-6000
New location - expected to be in use May 2010

Queen's Pizza
Wendy's
El Ranchero

Wenonah Ave

Friends & Family

Pearisburg Public Library
540-921-2556
M 12-8, Tu 12-5
W 9-5, Th 9-8
F 9-5, Sa 9-1

Animal Care Center
540-921-3707

Walmart

59
VA

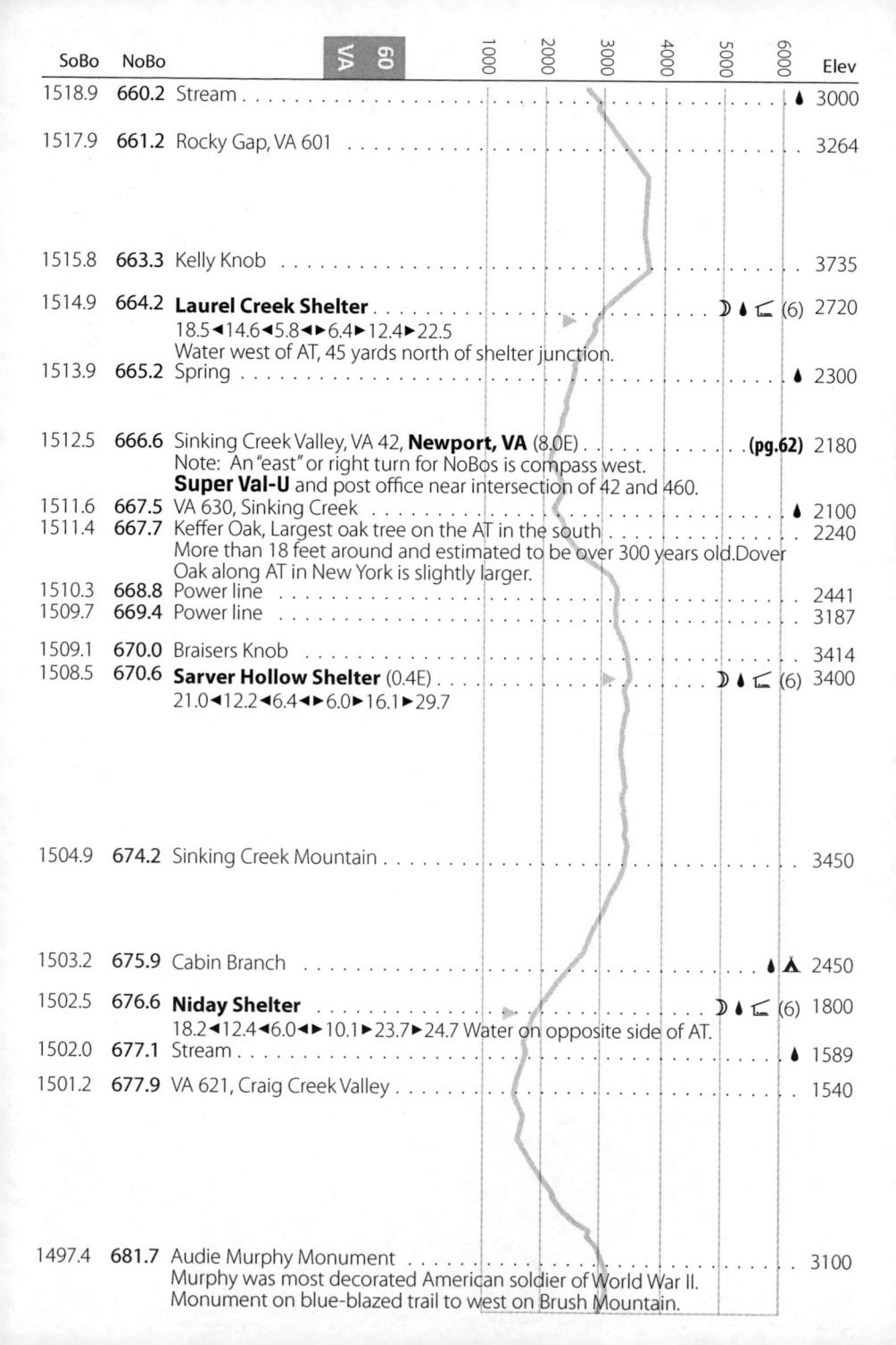

SoBo	NoBo		VA 60	1000	2000	3000	4000	5000	6000	Elev

SoBo	NoBo		Elev
1518.9	**660.2**	Stream . . . . ♦	3000
1517.9	**661.2**	Rocky Gap, VA 601	3264
1515.8	**663.3**	Kelly Knob	3735
1514.9	**664.2**	**Laurel Creek Shelter** . . . . ☽ ♦ ⊏ (6)	2720
		18.5◄14.6◄5.8◄►6.4►12.4►22.5	
		Water west of AT, 45 yards north of shelter junction.	
1513.9	**665.2**	Spring . . . . ♦	2300
1512.5	**666.6**	Sinking Creek Valley, VA 42, **Newport, VA** (8.0E) . . . . **(pg.62)**	2180
		Note: An "east" or right turn for NoBos is compass west.	
		Super Val-U and post office near intersection of 42 and 460.	
1511.6	**667.5**	VA 630, Sinking Creek . . . . ♦	2100
1511.4	**667.7**	Keffer Oak, Largest oak tree on the AT in the south	2240
		More than 18 feet around and estimated to be over 300 years old.Dover	
		Oak along AT in New York is slightly larger.	
1510.3	**668.8**	Power line	2441
1509.7	**669.4**	Power line	3187
1509.1	**670.0**	Braisers Knob	3414
1508.5	**670.6**	**Sarver Hollow Shelter** (0.4E) . . . . ☽ ♦ ⊏ (6)	3400
		21.0◄12.2◄6.4◄►6.0►16.1►29.7	
1504.9	**674.2**	Sinking Creek Mountain	3450
1503.2	**675.9**	Cabin Branch . . . . ♦ Λ	2450
1502.5	**676.6**	**Niday Shelter** . . . . ☽ ♦ ⊏ (6)	1800
		18.2◄12.4◄6.0◄►10.1►23.7►24.7 Water on opposite side of AT.	
1502.0	**677.1**	Stream . . . . ♦	1589
1501.2	**677.9**	VA 621, Craig Creek Valley	1540
1497.4	**681.7**	Audie Murphy Monument	3100
		Murphy was most decorated American soldier of World War II.	
		Monument on blue-blazed trail to west on Brush Mountain.	

1493.6	**685.5**	VA 620, Trout Creek		1525
1493.2	**685.9**	Power line		1705
1492.4	**686.7**	**Pickle Branch Shelter** (0.3E)	☽ ◑ ▲ ⌐ (6)	1845

22.5◀16.1◀10.1◀▶13.6▶14.6▶17.0
Tenting along trail to shelter.

1488.2	**690.9**	Cove Mountain		3020
		Trail to Dragons Tooth (stone monolith), views (0.1E)		
1487.2	**691.9**	Lost Spectacles Gap		2650
1486.7	**692.4**	Rawies Rest		2300
1485.7	**693.4**	VA 624, Newport Road	**(pg.62)**	1790
1484.8	**694.3**	Stream	◑	1832
1484.1	**695.0**	VA 785		1790
1484.0	**695.1**	Catawba Creek	◑	1755
1479.8	**699.3**	VA 311, **Catawba, VA** (1.0W) . . . . N37 22.808 W80 5.386 🅿 **(pg.62)**		2000
1478.8	**700.3**	**Johns Spring Shelter**	☽ ◑ ⌐ (6)	1980

29.7◀23.7◀13.6◀▶1.0▶3.4▶9.4 Unreliable spring 25 yards to left front of
shelter. Next water (0.9N), just before Catawba Mountain Shelter.

1477.8	**701.3**	**Catawba Mountain Shelter**	☽ ◑ ⌐ (6)	2145

24.7◀14.6◀1.0◀▶2.4▶8.4▶22.8 Piped spring just south on AT.

1477.1	**702.0**	Power line		2451
1476.1	**703.0**	McAfee Knob; excellent views, no camping		3197
1475.5	**703.6**	Pig Farm Campsite	◑ ▲	2661
1475.4	**703.7**	**Campbell Shelter** Water behind shelter	☽ ◑ ▲ ⌐ (6)	2580

17.0◀3.4◀2.4◀▶6.0▶20.4▶26.6

SoBo	NoBo				1000	2000	3000	4000	5000	6000	Elev

VA 61

666.6   Sinking Creek Valley, VA 42,
Note: An "east" or right turn for NoBos is compass west. Store and post office (and little else) is near intersection of 42 and 460.

Newport, VA 24128 (8.0E)

🏤 M-F 7:30-12 & 1-5, Sa 8-10:30, 540-384-6011

🛒 **Super Val-U**

693.4   VA 624 (Newport Rd)

🛒 ✗ **(Catawba Grocery** 540-384-8080
West 0.3 mile to VA 311 and then left 0.1 mile to store, B/L/D, open M-Th 5-10, F-Sa 5-11, Su 6-10. Keeps list of shuttlers.

699.3   VA 311 (Catawba Valley Dr)

Catawba, VA 24070 (1W)
Grocery PO 1.0 mi. west on 311, Homeplace 0.4mi farther.

🏤 M-F 7:30-12 & 1-5, Sa 8-10:30, 540-384-6011

🏛 ✗ ⛺ **Catawba Valley General Store & Deli** 540-384-7455,
M-F 6-8, Sa 7-8 offers sandwiches and pizzas, fuel/oz and canister.
$3 tenting near store or under roof in building behind store.

✗ **Homeplace Restaurant** 540-384-7252 Th-Fr 4-8, Sa 3-8,
Su 11-6, AYCE family-style meals including drink, dessert, and tax; $13 (2 meats) $14 (3 meats), closed June 28-July 7 and during Thanksgiving.

Equipment Manufacturers and Retailers

Adventurelite	570-429-2578	Granite Gear	218-834-6157	Platypus	800-531-9531
Arc Teryx	866-458-2473	Gregory	800-477-3420	Primus	307-857-4660
Asolo/Lowe Alpine	603-448-8827	Hi-Tec	800-521-1698	Princeton Tec	800-257-9080
Back Country	800-953-5499	Jacks R Better	757-253-8437	PUR	800-755-6701
Big Agnes	877-554-8975	JanSport	800-426-9227	REI	800-426-4840
Campmor	800-526-4784	Katadyn	800-755-6701	Royal Robbins	800-587-9044
Camp Trail	800-572-8822	Kelty	866-349-7225	Salomon	800-654-2668
Camelbak	800-767-8725	Leki	800-255-9582	Sierra Designs	800-736-8551
Cascade Designs	800-531-9531	LL Bean	800-341-4341	Six Moons	503-430-2303
Cedar Tree (Packa)	770-983-1456	Lowe Alpine	603-448-8827	Slumberjack	800-233-6283
Columbia	800-547-8066	Marmont	888-357-3252	Speer Hammocks	828-724-4444
Dana Designs	888-357-3262	Merrell	800-789-8536	Suunto	800-543-9124
Danner	800-345-0430	Mount Bell	877-666-2355	Sweetwater	800-531-9531
Eagle Creek	800-874-9925	Mountain Hardwear	800-953-8398	Henry Shires/Tarp tents	650-587-1548
Eastern Mountain Sports	888-463-6367	Montrail	206-621-9303	Tecnica	800-258-3897
Eureka!	800-572-8822	MSR	800-953-9677	Teva	800-367-8382
Ex Officio	800-644-7303	Mountainsmith	800-426-4075	The Underwear Guys	570-573-0209
Feathered Friends	206-292-6292	North Face	800-447-2333	Thermarest	800-531-9531
First Need	800-441-8166	Osprey	970-564-5900	ULA	435-753-5191
Frogg Toggs	800-349-1835	Outdoor Research	800-421-2421	Vasque	800-224-4453
Garmin	800-800-1020	Patagonia	800-523-9597	Western Mountaineering	408-287-8944
Garmont	800-943-4453	Peak 1/Coleman	800-835-3278	Zip Stove	800-594-9046
GoLite	888-546-5483	Petzl	877-807-3805		
Gossamer Gear	760-720-0500	Photon	877-584-6898		

SoBo	NoBo	Description	Elev
1472.3	**706.8**	Brickeys Gap	2200
1470.5	**708.6**	Tinker Cliffs, 0.5 mile cliff walk, Views back to McAfee Knob	3000
1470.0	**709.1**	Scorched Earth Gap, Andy Layne Trail	2360
1469.4	**709.7**	**Lamberts Meadow Shelter** . . . . ▸ . . . . ☽ ◐ ⊏ (6)	2080
		9.4◄8.4◄6.0◄▸14.4▸20.6▸27.9	
1469.1	**710.0**	Lamberts Meadow Campsite, Sawmill Run . . . . ◐ ▲	2040
1465.1	**714.0**	Angels Gap	1700
1464.0	**715.1**	Hay Rock, Tinker Ridge	1900
1462.8	**716.3**	Power line	1880
1461.2	**717.9**	Power lines	1373
1460.5	**718.6**	Tinker Creek	1165
1460.0	**719.1**	US 220, **Daleville, VA** . . . . **(pg.66-67)**	1300
1458.8	**720.3**	I-81, trail passes under on VA 779	1450
1458.5	**720.6**	US 11, railway. . . . . N37 24.269 W79 53.369 **P** **(pg.66-67)**	1390
		Troutville, VA (0.8W).	
1457.9	**721.2**	VA 652	1520
1455.0	**724.1**	**Fullhardt Knob Shelter** . . . . ▸ . . . . ☽ ◐ ⊏ (6)	2676
		22.8◄20.4◄14.4◄▸6.2▸13.5▸20.0 Treat water from cistern.	

SoBo	NoBo			Elev
1452.2	**726.9**	USFS 191, Salt Pond Rd		2250
1451.4	**727.7**	Curry Creek	💧	1700
1449.5	**729.6**	Wilson Creek	💧	1700
1448.8	**730.3**	**Wilson Creek Shelter** 26.6◄20.6◄6.2◄►7.3►13.8►20.8 Reliable stream 0.3 mile downhill in front of shelter.	☽ 💧 ⛺ ⌂ (6)	1830
1448.4	**730.7**	Spring	💧	2089
1446.4	**732.7**	Black Horse Gap, Old Fincastle Rd, USFS 186 Blue Ridge Parkway mile 97.7		2402
1445.6	**733.5**	BRP 97.0, Taylors Mountain Overlook		2365
1444.5	**734.6**	BRP 95.9, Montvale Overlook		2330
1443.9	**735.2**	BRP 95.3, Harveys Knob Overlook		2530
1442.3	**736.8**	Hammond Hollow Trail.		2295
1441.5	**737.6**	**Bobblets Gap Shelter** (0.2W) 27.9◄13.5◄7.3◄►6.5►13.5►18.4 If spring to left of shelter dry, look farther downstream.	☽ 💧 ⌂ (6)	1920
1440.8	**738.3**	BRP 92.5, Sharp Top Overlook.		2240
1440.1	**739.0**	BRP 91.8, Mills Gap Overlook		2435
1438.4	**740.7**	BRP 90.9, Bearwallow Gap, VA 43. **Buchanan, VA** (5.0W).	**(pg.67)**	2228
1436.8	**742.3**	Cove Mountain		2720
1436.4	**742.7**	Little Cove Mountain Trail		2560
1435.0	**744.1**	**Cove Mountain Shelter** 20.0◄13.8◄6.5◄►6.9►11.9►17.2	☽ ⛺ ⌂ (6)	1925
1433.3	**745.8**	Buchanan Trail		1780
1431.8	**747.3**	Jennings Creek, VA 614.	N37 31.745 W79 37.350 🅿 **(pg.67)**	951

1000 2000 3000 4000 5000 6000

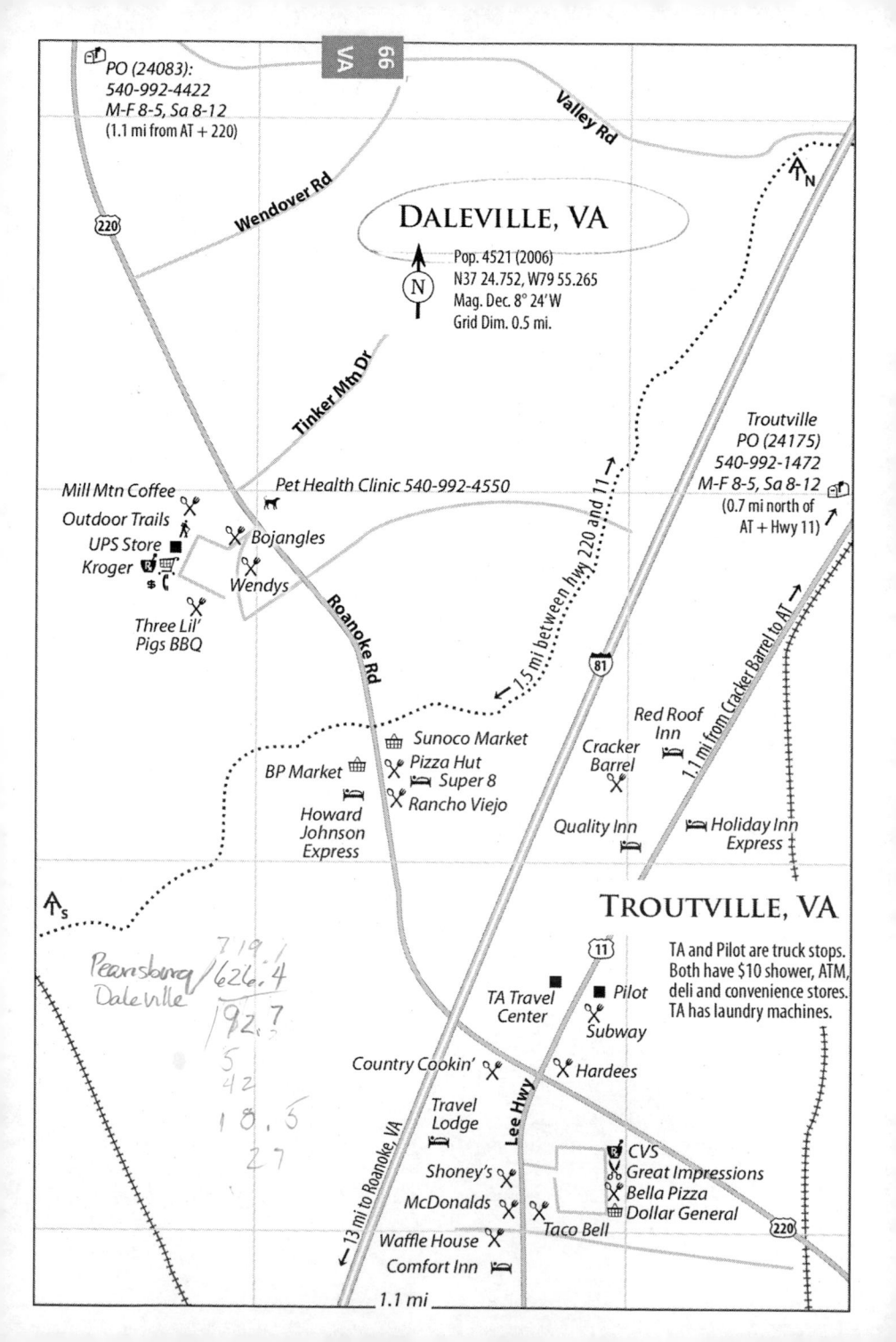

PO (24083):
540-992-4422
M-F 8-5, Sa 8-12
(1.1 mi from AT + 220)

VA 66

Valley Rd

Wendover Rd

220

DALEVILLE, VA

Pop. 4521 (2006)
N37 24.752, W79 55.265
Mag. Dec. 8° 24'W
Grid Dim. 0.5 mi.

N

Tinker Mtn Dr

Troutville
PO (24175)
540-992-1472
M-F 8-5, Sa 8-12
(0.7 mi north of
AT + Hwy 11)

N

Pet Health Clinic 540-992-4550

Mill Mtn Coffee
Outdoor Trails
UPS Store
Kroger

Bojangles

Wendys

Three Lil'
Pigs BBQ

Roanoke Rd

1.5 mi between hwy. 220 and 11

1.1 mi from Cracker Barrel to AT

81

Red Roof
Inn

Cracker
Barrel

Sunoco Market
Pizza Hut
Super 8
Rancho Viejo

BP Market

Howard
Johnson
Express

Quality Inn

Holiday Inn
Express

S

TROUTVILLE, VA

TA and Pilot are truck stops.
Both have $10 shower, ATM,
deli and convenience stores.
TA has laundry machines.

11

TA Travel
Center

Pilot

Subway

Country Cookin'

Hardees

Travel
Lodge

Lee Hwy

13 mi to Roanoke, VA

CVS
Great Impressions
Bella Pizza
Dollar General

Shoney's

McDonalds

Taco Bell

220

Waffle House

Comfort Inn

1.1 mi

Pearisburg
Daleville

719
626.4
192.7
5
42
18.5
27

Daleville, VA, Troutville, VA (more services on map)

Mountain Sports.

The adjoining towns of Daleville and Troutville have indistinct borders near the intersection of highways 220 and 11 and interstate 81, which is a major hub for truckers. The intersection is broad, busy and not at all pedestrian-friendly, which makes it a challenge to walk to services east of 81. The safer, but longer, route to these businesses is from the highway 11 trail crossing.

🛏 ⊠ **$ Howard Johnson Express** 540-992-1234, $49.95 hikerrate, includes full hot breakfast. Pool table and pool. Maildrops: 437 Roanoke Road, Daleville, VA 24083.

🛏 🍴 **Super 8** 540-992-3000, $53.08S, higher during special events, includes continental breakfast, pool, accepts major credit cards.

🛏 **Travel Lodge** 540-992-6700 $45 $6EAP.

🛏 **Comfort Inn** 540-992-5600, $94.95D-110.95D, $5EAP, includes continental breakfast.

🛏 ⊠ **Red Roof Inn** 540-992-5055, $50.99 + tax, pets allowed. Maildrops: 3231 Lee Hwy, Troutville, VA 24175.

🛏 ⊠ **Holiday Inn Express** 540-966-4444, $99-119. Maildrops: 3200 Lee Hwy, Troutville, VA 24175.

🛏 ⊠ **Quality Inn** 540-992-5335 $75/up, no pets.

🛒 🍴 **Kroger Grocery Store and Pharmacy** 540-992-4920, 24hr, pharmacy M-F 8-9, Sa 9-6, Su 12-6.

🥾 ⊠ 🍴 **Outdoor Trails** 540-992-5850, full service outfitter, fuel/ oz, ask about shuttles. Maildrops: Botetourt Commons, 28 Kingston Dr, Daleville, Virginia 24083.

🅿🚌 **Del Schechterly** 540-529-6028, shuttles from Pearisburg to Waynesboro.

Roanoke, VA (13E)

A large city with an airport. Although the center of town is approximately 13 miles away, the town extends north. There are services at the next I-81 exit, 4 miles south, most notably Gander Mountain Sports.

🥾 **Gander Mountain** 540-362-3658

740.7   Blue Ridge Parkway (Bearwallow Gap), Mile 90.9

🏕 🍴 🚌 (4.4E) **Peaks of Otter Lodge** 540-586-1081, 800-542-5927 ⟨www.peaksofotter.com⟩ $85 and up, Sa-Su breakfast buffet $12.99, B/L/D served daily May-Oct.

Buchanan, VA 24066 (5W) on VA 43 Town extends along the I-81 corridor. Services more easily accessible from VA 614 are listed below as "Buchanan (I-81 exit 168)."

🍴 M-F 8:30-1, 1:30-4:50, Sa 10-12, 540-254-2178

🍴 **Burger King, Old Buchanan Restaurant, Carini's Italian Restaurant, Subway** west of 81.

🍴 **Buchanan Supermarket** 540-254-2596, **Family Dollar**

🅖 **Ransone's Drug Store**

🏛 **Buchanan Branch Library**

VA 614/Jennings Creek ⚑ (0.3E)

🏕 🏛 ⚡ 🍴 ⊠ (1.2E) **Middle Creek Campground** 540-254-2550 ⟨www.middlecreekcampground.com⟩ cabins $65-75 $5EAP in cabin that sleeps 4-6, camping $22, showers $5, ask about shuttles, Coleman/alcohol/oz. Laundry room (around back) is always open. Can also be reached on the northern side of Fork Mountain by taking VA 714 and VA 614 east 1.4 miles. Guest maildrops: 1164 Middle Creek Road, Buchanan, VA 24066

Buchanan, VA (I-81 exit 168) (5W) on VA 614

🛏 **Wattstull Inn** 540-254-1551, $60/up, pets $10.

🍴 **Mountain View Restaurant** 540-254-1224

🏪 **Shell Convenience Store**

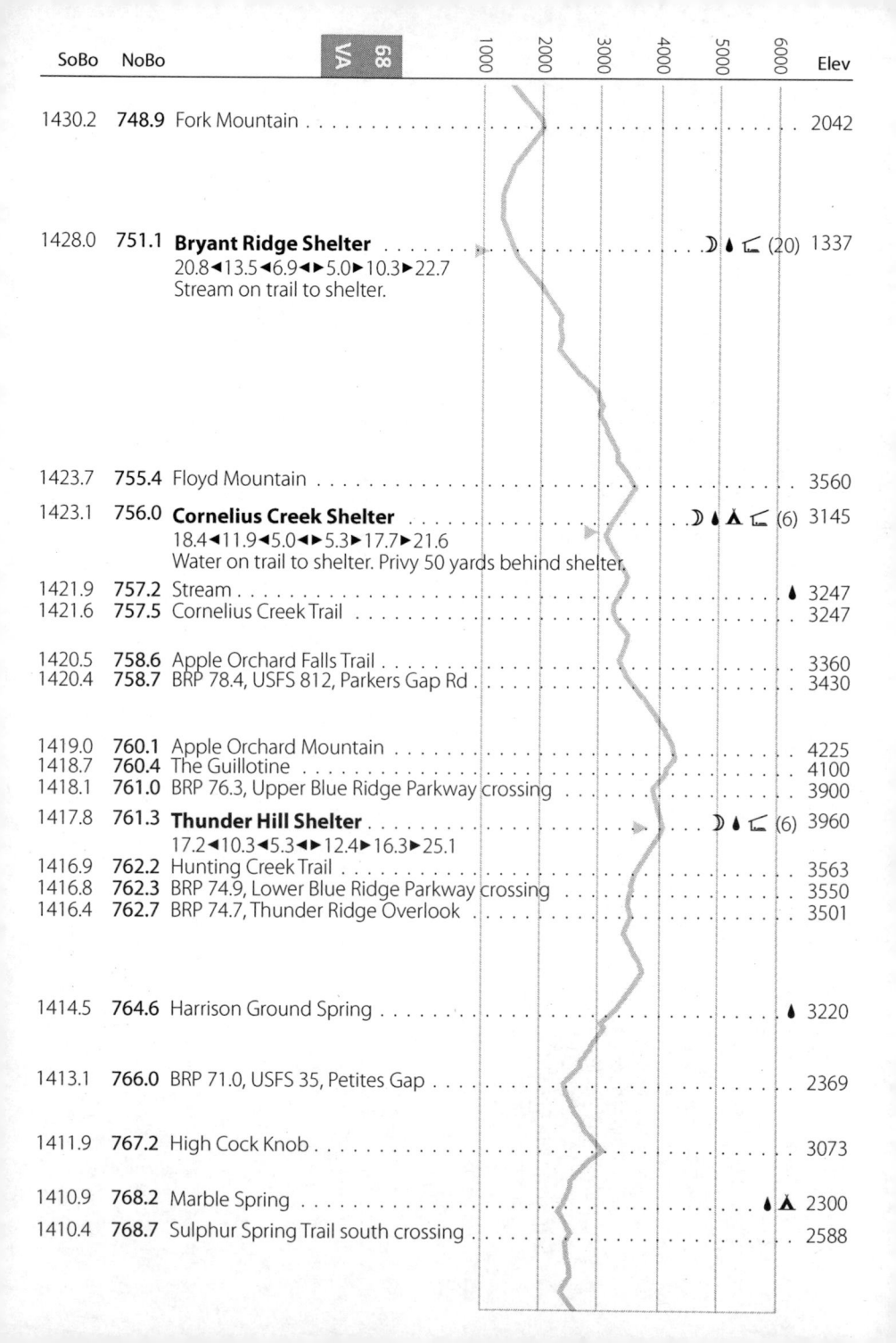

SoBo	NoBo		Elev
1430.2	**748.9**	Fork Mountain	2042
1428.0	**751.1**	**Bryant Ridge Shelter** . . . . ☽ ♦ ⌐ (20)	1337
		20.8◄13.5◄6.9◄►5.0►10.3►22.7	
		Stream on trail to shelter.	
1423.7	**755.4**	Floyd Mountain	3560
1423.1	**756.0**	**Cornelius Creek Shelter** . . . . ☽ ♦ Å ⌐ (6)	3145
		18.4◄11.9◄5.0◄►5.3►17.7►21.6	
		Water on trail to shelter. Privy 50 yards behind shelter.	
1421.9	**757.2**	Stream . . . . ♦	3247
1421.6	**757.5**	Cornelius Creek Trail	3247
1420.5	**758.6**	Apple Orchard Falls Trail	3360
1420.4	**758.7**	BRP 78.4, USFS 812, Parkers Gap Rd	3430
1419.0	**760.1**	Apple Orchard Mountain	4225
1418.7	**760.4**	The Guillotine	4100
1418.1	**761.0**	BRP 76.3, Upper Blue Ridge Parkway crossing	3900
1417.8	**761.3**	**Thunder Hill Shelter** . . . . ☽ ♦ ⌐ (6)	3960
		17.2◄10.3◄5.3◄►12.4►16.3►25.1	
1416.9	**762.2**	Hunting Creek Trail	3563
1416.8	**762.3**	BRP 74.9, Lower Blue Ridge Parkway crossing	3550
1416.4	**762.7**	BRP 74.7, Thunder Ridge Overlook	3501
1414.5	**764.6**	Harrison Ground Spring . . . . ♦	3220
1413.1	**766.0**	BRP 71.0, USFS 35, Petites Gap	2369
1411.9	**767.2**	High Cock Knob	3073
1410.9	**768.2**	Marble Spring . . . . ♦ Å	2300
1410.4	**768.7**	Sulphur Spring Trail south crossing	2588

SoBo	NoBo		Elev
1408.6	**770.5**	Hickory Stand, Belfast Trail	2650
1408.1	**771.0**	Sulphur Spring Trail north crossing	2588
1407.3	**771.8**	Big Cove Branch . . . . ♦	1855
1405.4	**773.7**	**Matts Creek Shelter** . . . . ☽♦ ⊑ (6)	835
		22.7◄17.7◄12.4◄►3.9►12.7►22.2	
1405.3	**773.8**	Matts Creek Trail	836
1404.6	**774.5**	Camping . . . . ♦ ⛺	840
1403.4	**775.7**	James River footbridge, longest foot-use-only bridge on AT.	678
1403.2	**775.9**	US 501, VA 130, **Big Island VA** (5.6E), **Glasgow VA** (5.9W) . . . . . **(pg.72)**	735
1403.1	**776.0**	Lower Rocky Row Run Bridge. . . . . ♦	760
1402.2	**776.9**	Rocky Row Run . . . . ♦ ⛺	760
1402.1	**777.0**	VA 812, USFS 36 . . . . N37 36.286 W79 23.295 🅿	830
1401.7	**777.4**	Stream . . . . ♦	919
1401.5	**777.6**	**Johns Hollow Shelter** . . . . ☽♦ ⛺ ⊑ (6)	1020
		21.6◄16.3◄3.9◄►8.8►18.3►23.9	
		Springs to left and right of shelter.	
1399.5	**779.6**	Rocky Row Trail.	2430
1399.4	**779.7**	Fullers Rocks, Little Rocky Row	2472
1398.4	**780.7**	Big Rocky Row	2992
1396.9	**782.2**	Saddle Gap, Saddle Gap Trail	2590
1395.8	**783.3**	Saltlog Gap south . . . . ♦ (0.5W)	2573
1394.3	**784.8**	Bluff Mountain, Ottie Cline Powell monument	3372
1393.2	**785.9**	Punchbowl Mountain	2870
1392.7	**786.4**	**Punchbowl Shelter** (0.2W) Spring front left of shelter. . . . . ☽♦ ⛺ ⊑ (6)	2500
		25.1◄12.7◄8.8◄►9.5►15.1►25.3	
1392.3	**786.8**	BRP 51.7 . . . . N37 40.426 W79 20.081 🅿 ♦	2170
		Punchbowl Mountain Crossing	
1392.0	**787.1**	VA 607, Robinson Gap Rd . . . . N37 40.567 W79 19.921 🅿	2150
1390.1	**789.0**	Rice Mountain	2228
1389.4	**789.7**	Spring . . . . ♦	1869
1388.2	**790.9**	USFS 39, Little Irish Creek, ... N37 40.227 W79 17.067 🅿 ♦ ⛺	1000
		Pedlar River Bridge	

1385.2	**793.9**	Pedlar Lake Rd, USFS 38								1320
1384.2	**794.9**	Brown Mountain Creek.							♦	1258
1383.2	**795.9**	**Brown Mountain Creek Shelter** . . . . ☽ ♦ ⌐ (6)								1395

22.2◄18.3◄9.5◄►5.6►15.8►22.7
In dry conditions, get water from Brown Mountain Creek, crossed by
footbridge on way to shelter. Swimming hole south of shelter.

1381.4	**797.7**	US 60, **Buena Vista, VA** (9.3W) . . . . .N37 43.405 W79 15.036 🅿 **(pg.72)**								2065
1378.6	**800.5**	Bald Knob								4059
1377.6	**801.5**	Old Hotel Trail, **Cow Camp Gap Shelter** (0.6E) . . . . . . ☽ ♦ ⌐ (8)								3428

23.9◄15.1◄5.6◄►10.2►17.1►24.6
Water source on blue-bz trail left of shelter before small stream crossing.

| 1376.4 | **802.7** | Cold Mountain . . . . | | | | | | | | 4022 |
| 1375.1 | **804.0** | Hog Camp Gap, USFS 48 . . . . ♦ ⋀ | | | | | | | | 3485 |

Grassy meadow with many campsites.
Spring is just north of the road crossing and to the east.

1374.2	**804.9**	Tar Jacket Ridge								3847
1372.9	**806.2**	Salt Log Gap north, USFS 63								3257
1371.7	**807.4**	USFS 246								3500
1371.2	**807.9**	Greasy Spring Rd . . . . ♦								3550
1369.3	**809.8**	Piney River north fork . . . . ♦ ⋀								3480
1368.7	**810.4**	Spring . . . . ♦								3505
1368.1	**811.0**	Elk Pond Branch . . . . ♦ ⋀								3650
1367.4	**811.7**	**Seeley-Woodworth Shelter** . . . . ☽ ♦ ⌐ (8)								3770

25.3◄15.8◄10.2◄►6.9►14.4►20.6
Piped spring 0.1 mile downhill to right

| 1366.3 | **812.8** | Porters Field, west 100 yards to campsite and . . . . ♦ ⋀ | | | | | | | | 3550 |

spring on second of two dirt roads.

| 1365.1 | **814.0** | Spy Rock Rd (formerly Fish Hatchery Rd) unpaved . . . . . . **(pg.73)** | | | | | | | | 3454 |

1364.6	814.5	Spy Rock (stop and climb the rock for a rewarding view) . . . . ▲	3860
1364.3	814.8	Main Top Mountain	4040
1363.5	815.6	Cash Hollow Rock	3510
1362.2	816.9	Cash Hollow Rd	3280
1361.4	817.7	VA 826, (0.5W) to Crabtree Falls Trail, leads downhill . . . . **(pg.73)**	3320

1361.4 817.7 another 2.1 miles to VA 56. This scenic trail runs alongside
waterfalls and ends near **Crabtree Falls Campground**

1360.5	818.6	**The Priest Shelter** (0.1E) 22.7◄17.1◄6.9◄►7.5►13.7►29.5. . . ☽ ♦ ⌐ (8)	3840
1360.2	818.9	Multiple paths leading west to overlook and small clearing. . . . . ▲	4047
1360.0	819.1	The Priest	4063
1357.0	822.1	Cripple Creek . . . . ♦	1780
1355.7	823.4	VA 56, Tye River . . . . N37 50.305 W79 1.387 **P (pg.73)**	970

1355.7 823.4 **Crabtree Falls Campground** (4.0W)

| 1353.0 | 826.1 | **Harpers Creek Shelter** . . . . ☽ ♦ ▲ ⌐ (6) | 1800 |

1353.0 826.1 24.6◄14.4◄7.5◄►6.2►22.0►34.0
Harpers Creek in front of shelter. Privy up hill.

1351.0	828.1	Chimney Rocks.	3100
1349.7	829.4	Three Ridges Mountain	3870
1348.8	830.3	Hanging Rock Overlook	3700
1347.2	831.9	Bee Mountain	3008
1346.8	832.3	**Maupin Field Shelter** . . . . ☽ ♦ ▲ ⌐ (6) **(pg.73)**	2720

1346.8 832.3 20.6◄13.7◄6.2◄►15.8►27.8►40.8
Piped spring behind shelter. Privy to right of shelter on unmarked path.
Mau-Har Trail to **Rusty's Hard Time Hollow**

| 1345.1 | 834.0 | BRP 13.6, VA 664, Reeds Gap . . . . N37 54.097 W78 59.115 **P (pg.73)** | 2650 |
| 1344.6 | 834.5 | BRP 13.1 . . . . N37 54.418 W78 58.771 **P** | 2620 |

1344.6 834.5 Three Ridges Parking Overlook

775.9   US 501, VA 130

▲ ♨ ⌂ ⌂ ⊠ Wildwood Campground (5.0E) 866-883-5228 (www.wildwoodcampground.com) $22 tent site, $58 and up cabins for 4, camp store. Maildrops: 6252 Elon Road, Monroe ,VA 24574.

Big Island, VA 24526 (5.6E)

🏤 M-F 8:30-12:30, 1:30-4:30, Sa 8-10, 434-299-5072

⌂ ✗ 𝄞 ⊠ H&H Food Market 434-299-5153, 7 days 5-9, B/L/D, Denatured alcohol sold by the quart. Maildrops: 11619 Lee Jackson Hwy, Big Island, VA 24526.

✚ Big Island Family Medical Center 434-299-5951

Glasgow, VA 24555 (5.9W)

🏤 M-F 8-11:30 & 12:30-4:30, Sa 8:30-10:30, 540-258-2852

⌂ ⌂ ♈ ♈ Since the closing of Howard's Motel, the town has planned to provide a hiker shelter with outdoor shower. The shelter should be available in the spring of 2010. Public restrooms are at Knick Field.

✗ Familys Inn

⌂ Glasgow Grocery Express 540-258-1818, M-Sa 6-11:30pm, Su 8-1130pm, Coleman/alcohol/oz.

⌂ CC's Stop & Go Convenience store with some hot foods.

⌂ Dollar General

⌂ Lew's Laundromat

⌖ Glasgow Public Library 540-258-2509, M, Th 10-7, T, W 10-5:30, Sa 10-1, need ID for internet.

🏥 Natural Bridge Animal Hospital 540-291-1444, 4.5W of Glasgow on VA 130.

⌂ Ken Wallace 434-609-2704 Range is Waynesboro to Daleville.

797.7   US 60

Buena Vista, VA 24416 (9.3W)

🏤 M-F 8:30-4:30, 540-261-8959

⌂ Buena Vista Motel 540-261-2138, $55.95D, first motel you come to, everything else 0.6/8 mile further into town.

⌂ ⌂ Budget Inn 540-261-2156 $45S $55D, pets $10 and must use smoking room, Sa-Su continental B, shuttles sometimes available.

▲ ⌂ Glen Maury Park Campground 540-261-7321 or 800-555-8845 $22/tent, 2 miles south of town on Beech Avenue.

✗ Domino's Pizza 540-261-1111

✗ Hardee's, Subway, Burger King

✗ Captain Tim's Galley AYCE family-style $24.95.

⌂ Food Lion 540-261-7672, 7 days

🏥 Edgewater Animal Hospital 540-261-4114
    1W of Budget Inn on US 60:

⌂ Family Dollar, Dollar General

⌂ CVS

⌂ Jim's True Value Hardware 540-261-8043

814.0 Spy Rock Road (unpaved)
1.1W to parking area, where the road is renamed to Fish Hatchery Road. It is another 1.5 to Dutch Haus; call to arrange pick up at the parking area if you plan to stay there.

🛏 🍴 ⌂ ✉ Dutch Haus B&B 540-377-2119, 800-341-9177 Price for hikers arriving on foot (or picked up at trailhead) $30 includes breakfast. Dinner extra. Free lunch is served to all thru-hikers (not just guests) during May and June from 11am - 1pm. Clearly this is exceptionally generous; please be appreciative. Maildrops: 655 Fork Mountain Lane, Montebello, VA 24464.

Montebello, VA 24464 (2.5W) West to VA 56, left 0.9
🏤 M-F 8-12 & 12:30-4:30, Sa 9-12, Su 9-12, **Montebello Camping & General Store** 540-377-2650 (www.montebellova.com) seasonal; camping $10PP and $3EAP, shower without stay $3.50, coin laundry, Coleman/alcohol/oz.

817.7 VA 826, Crabtree Falls Trail
823.4 VA 56, Tye River
🛏 🍴 ⌂ ✉ (4W) on VA 56, **Crabtree Falls Campground** 540-377-2066 ⟨www.crabtreefallscampground.com⟩ cfcg@ceva.net, cabins $50 six people, camping $22. Shower w/out camping free, Coleman by the gallon. Maildrops no bigger than a shoe box: 11039 Crabtree Falls Hwy, Tyro, VA 22976.

832.3 From Maupin Field Shelter to Rusty's:
Turn west on fire road, just north of Maupin Field Shelter, walk 1.2 miles west to the BRP, then turn left (south) 1.3 miles to Rusty's.

834.0 From Reed's Gap (VA 664) to Rusty's:
Go west a short distance to the BRP, then left (south) 3.2 to Rusty's. You may have luck hitching.
Gravel driveway at BRP 16.7 on your left has a gray, pipe gate with Rusty's name and AT stickers on one end.

⌂ Rusty's Hard Time Hollow

Since 1982 over 12,000 hikers have stayed in this unique, rustic hostel. Indescribable backwoods experience, the way it used to be. Signs are all over the property; some are for your information and some are for your amusement. You'll have to figure out which is which. There are multiple bunkhouses and tent sites, so it is never full. Phone, rainwater shower and many other forms of entertainment. Occasional rides to town for hikers who pitch in for gas. No dogs, no illegal drugs. Stay limited to one week except for medical reasons. Donations are encouraged and necessary to keep this hostel running; Rusty has no other form of income.

| 1342.4 | **836.7** | Stream . . . . ▲ | 2558 |

1340.8	**838.3**	Cedar Cliffs	2850
1340.3	**838.8**	BRP 9.6, Spring, ... N37 56.465 W78 56.214 **P** ▲	2950
		Dripping Rock Parking Area	
1339.8	**839.3**	Laurel Springs, intermittent . . . . ▲	2880

| 1337.5 | **841.6** | Humpback Mountain . . . . | 3597 |

| 1336.5 | **842.6** | Trail to Humpback Rocks . . . . | 3362 |

| 1335.0 | **844.1** | Bear Spring . . . . ▲ | 2700 |

1332.8	**846.3**	Glass Hollow Overlook	2300
1332.5	**846.6**	Side trail . . . . N37 58.150 W78 53.846 **P** ▲ ⓘ	1690
		(1.3W) to Humpback Visitors Center.	

1331.0	**848.1**	Mill Creek, **Paul C. Wolfe Shelter** . . . . ☽ ▲ ⊏ (10)	1700
		29.5◄22.0◄15.8◄►12.0►25.0►38.2	
		Mill Creek 50 yards in front of shelter.	
		Waterfall with pool 100 yards.	

| 1329.2 | **849.9** | Stream . . . . ▲ | 1874 |

| 1327.9 | **851.2** | Stream . . . . ▲ | 1748 |

1326.0	**853.1**	US 250 + Blue Ridge Pkwy. . . . N38 1.864 W78 51.545 **P** (¦ ⁂ ⓘ **(pg.76-77)**	1902
		Rockfish Gap, **Waynesboro, VA** (3.7W).	
1325.9	**853.2**	Skyline Drive, I-64 overpass	1900
1325.7	**853.4**	Skyline 105.2	1900
1325.2	**853.9**	Shenandoah National Park (SNP) . . . . **(pg.80)**	2250
		Entrance station and self-registration for overnight permits.	

| 1322.3 | **856.8** | Skyline 102.1, McCormick Gap . . . . ▲ | 2435 |

SoBo	NoBo			
1321.0	858.1	Bears Den Mountain		2885
1320.5	858.6	Skyline 99.5, Beagle Gap . . . . N38 4.373 W78 47.607 🅿		2530
1319.6	859.5	Calf Mountain		2974
1319.0	860.1	**Calf Mountain Shelter** (0.3W) . . . . ☽ ◑ (0.2W) 🛆 ⌐ (6)		2700
		34.0◀27.8◀12.0◀▶13.0▶26.2▶34.4 Bear pole. Spring on way to shelter.		
1318.4	860.7	Spring . . . . ◑		2300
1318.0	861.1	Skyline 96.9, Jarman Gap . . . . ◑		2173
1317.8	861.3	Spring . . . . ◑		2280
1316.2	862.9	Skyline 95.3, Sawmill Run Overlook		2200
1314.6	864.5	Skyline 94.1, Turk Gap. . . . . N38 7.740 W78 47.092 🅿		2625
1312.6	866.5	Skyline 92.4 . . . . N38 8.904 W78 46.477 🅿		3100
		Wildcat Ridge Trail 0.1E to parking.		
1309.6	869.5	Skyline 90.0 . . . . 🅿		2805
		Spur trail to east leads to Riprap parking area		
1309.3	869.8	Riprap Trail branches to the west		2750
1308.5	870.6	Skyline 88.9		2650
1306.7	872.4	Skyline 87.4, Black Rock Gap, Paine Run Trail . . N38 12.398 W78 44.974 🅿		2321
1306.5	872.6	Skyline 87.2		2400
1306.0	873.1	**Blackrock Hut** (0.2E) . . . . ☽ ◑ 🛆 ⌐ (6)		2645
		40.8◀25.0◀13.0◀▶13.2▶21.4▶33.8		
1305.4	873.7	Blackrock, views from summit, which is skirted by the AT		3092
1304.9	874.2	Blackrock parking area . . . . N38 13.331 W78 43.992 🅿		2917
1304.4	874.7	Skyline 84.3		2800
1304.2	874.9	Jones Run Trail Parking . . . . N38 13.805 W78 43.577 🅿		2785
1302.9	876.2	Skyline 82.9, Browns Gap . . . . N38 14.424 W78 42.653 🅿		2600
1302.0	877.1	Skyline 82.2		2820
1301.6	877.5	Skyline 81.9,. . . . . N38 14.806 W78 41.686 🅿		2900
		Doyles River Parking Overlook		
1300.7	878.4	Skyline 81.1 . . . . N38 15.254 W78 40.982 🅿 ◑		2880
		Doyles River Cabin (locked)		
1299.8	879.3	Trail to Loft Mtn ampitheater		3221
1299.4	879.7	Trail to **Loft Mtn Campground**. . . . . 🛆 (pg.81)		3436

| SoBo | NoBo | | VA 75 | 1000 | 2000 | 3000 | 4000 | 5000 | 6000 | Elev |

ROCKFISH GAP

Waynesboro 3.7mi — 250 — SNP Entrance Station — Skyline Drive — Blue Ridge Pkwy — 64 — Visitor Center — Inn at Afton

853.1   Rockfish Gap

For northbounders, the AT intersects with the Blue Ridge Parkway just south of the I-64/US 250 interchange. The Visitor Center is west of the BRP. Continuing north, the AT goes over US 250 and I-64 alongside the BRP. The BRP becomes the Skyline Drive.

ⓘ ⟨ 🅿 **Afton Mountain Visitor Center** 540-943-5187 New 2010 location is in a double-wide mobile unit uphill from US 250. Staffed by volunteers and open most days 9-5. Hiker information sheets offer the most current information about Waynesboro, town services, and trail angels. Many lodging facilities offer free pickup/return from this location. Long-term parking okay, please leave contact information and expected return date.

🛏 ✕ **Inn at Afton** 540-942-5201 $65, pets allowed, pool, located at top of hill west of I-64.

🛏 ⌂ (0.5W on 250) **Colony Motel** 540-942-4156 $54D, $10 EAP, pets $5.

Waynesboro, VA (4.5W on I-64) *(more services on map)*

A large town with all services. Home to **Hiker Fest** June 5. During Hiker Fest, there is a $5 AYCE dinner at the Grace Lutheran Church, followed by a shuttle to the movies in Staunton, VA. For more info contact Waynesboro Trail Angels, 540-942-6644.

🏠 ⌂ **Grace Hiker Hostel** 540-949-6171 Supervised hostel at the Lutheran Church next to library, open May 17-June 27, closed Sunday nights, 2-night limit. Check-in 5-8pm, check-out 9am. Closed during day, but hikers staying over may leave packs. Cots in large, downstairs air-conditioned Fellowship Hall, 2 showers, internet, big-screen DVD/VCR, kitchenette with snacks and breakfast foods in a separate hiker lounge. 15 hiker maximum. No pets, smoking, drugs or alcohol. Donations gratefully accepted. On Wednesday nights the congregation cooks a free dinner (limited to the 15 hostel guests) followed by an optional vespers service.

🅰 🛆 **YMCA** Free camping, showers, and use of YMCA facilities; donations accepted. Check-in at the front desk.

🛏 ⊠ **The Tree Streets Inn** 540-949-4484, $75S/D, includes breakfast, pool, snacks, no pets. Call from Rockfish Gap for free pickup/return to trail with stay. Maildrops for guest: 421 Walnut Avenue, Waynesboro, VA 22980

🛏 ⌂ **Belle Hearth B&B** 540-943-1910 ⟨www.bellehearth.com⟩ $75S, $95D, higher on weekends, includes breakfast, pool, pickup and return to trail, no pets, no smoking.

🛏 **Quality Inn** 540-942-1171, $45S $75D and up (seasonal), includes continental breakfast, pets $10.

🍴 ⓥ **Kroger Supermarket** 540-942-5100, 6-12

🏃 **Rockfish Gap Outfitters** 540-943-1461, full service outfitter, Coleman/alcohol/oz, other fuels, shuttle information. Located between town and the trail, so ask your ride to stop on the way.

🚌 **Lyle Kirby** 540-942-2413 Long distance shuttles. Charlottesville airport and bus station.

🪛 **Ace Hardware** Coleman/oz.

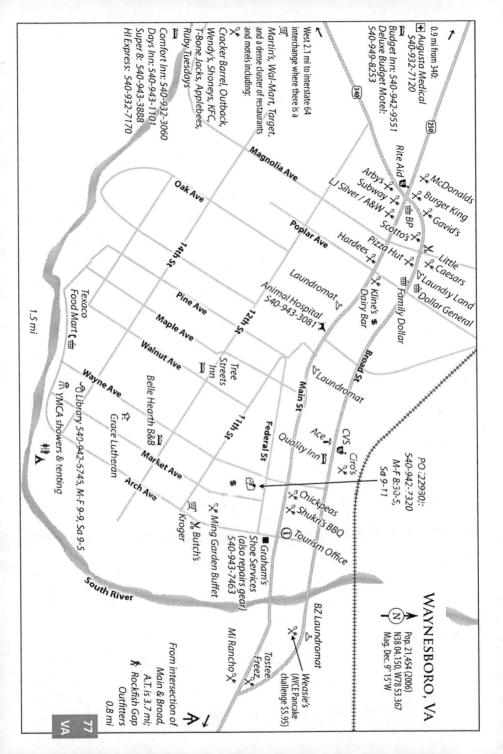

SoBo	NoBo		Elev
1298.5	**880.6**	Trail to **Loft Mtn Store** . . . . . (pg.81)	3223
1297.4	**881.7**	Frazier Discovery Trail 0.3W to **Loft Mtn Wayside**.	3321
1296.0	**883.1**	Ivy Creek. . . . . 💧	2697
1295.8	**883.3**	Cross Ivy Creek . . . . . 💧	2565
1295.1	**884.0**	View to west	2941
1294.4	**884.7**	Skyline 77.5, Ivy Creek Overlook	2837
1292.8	**886.3**	**Pinefield Hut** . . . . . ☽ 💧 ⛺ 🛖 (6) 38.2◄26.2◄13.2◄►8.2►20.6►32.1 Spring on trail to shelter and 50 yards behind. Both unreliable. Campsites uphill, beyond shelter.	2430
1292.3	**886.8**	Skyline 75.2, Pinefield Gap. . . . . N38 17.411 W78 38.511 🅿	2715
1291.8	**887.3**	Weaver Mountain	2864
1290.8	**888.3**	Skyline 73.2, Simmons Gap . . . . . 💧 Simmons Gap ranger station is on paved road 0.2E from where AT crosses Skyline. Water available at pump outside buildings.	2329
1288.0	**891.1**	View east to Powell Gap Hollow	2653
1287.5	**891.6**	Skyline 69.9, Powell Gap	2322
1285.8	**893.3**	Skyline 68.6, Smith Roach Gap	2620
1284.6	**894.5**	**Hightop Hut** (0.1W) . . . . . ☽ 💧 ⛺ (8) 🛖 (6) 34.4◄21.4◄8.2◄►12.4►23.9►34.8 Reliable spring 0.1 from shelter.	3175
1284.1	**895.0**	Spring east of AT. . . . . 💧	3496
1283.9	**895.2**	View to west from flank of Hightop Mtn	3511
1282.4	**896.7**	Skyline 66.7 . . . . . N38 20.691 W78 33.183 🅿	2640
1281.2	**897.9**	Skyline 65.5, US 33, Swift Run Gap. . . . . entrance station	2367
1279.7	**899.4**	Junction with Saddleback Mtn Trail	2987
1278.2	**900.9**	South River Picnic Area. . . . . N38 22.904 W78 31.151 🅿 (0.1W) 💧 🚻	2892

Elevation profile scale: 1000 2000 3000 4000 5000 6000

SoBo	NoBo		Elev
1276.2	**902.9**	Baldface Mountain	3600
1275.0	**904.1**	Spring, Pocosin Cabin (locked) . . . . N38 24.813 W78 29.379 🅿 ♦	3157
		Parking on Skyline.	
1274.8	**904.3**	Parking on Skyline. 🅿 ♦	3150
1274.6	**904.5**	Spring . . . . ♦	3134
1273.1	**906.0**	**Lewis Mtn Campground & Cabins** .N38 26.234 W78 28.737 🅿 (pg.81)	3376
1272.2	**906.9**	**Bearfence Mountain Hut** (0.1E) . . . . 🅿 ☽ ♦ ⚠ (6) ⌒ (6)	3110
		33.8◄20.6◄12.4◄►11.5►22.4►26.8 Unreliable spring.	
1271.4	**907.7**	Views east from Bearfence Mountain.	3496
1270.9	**908.2**	Skyline 56.4 . . . . N38 27.141 W78 28.015 🅿	3336
		Bearfence Mtn Parking area	
1269.6	**909.5**	Skyline 55.1, Bootens Gap . . . . N38 28.049 W78 27.440 🅿	3243
1268.7	**910.4**	Hazeltop.	3812
1266.8	**912.3**	Skyline 52.8, Milam Gap . . . . N38 29.928 W78 26.741 🅿	3289
1266.2	**912.9**	Stream . . . . ♦	3272
1265.9	**913.2**	Spring, No camping in Big Meadows clearing within sight of Skyline Dr ♦	3303
1265.7	**913.4**	Tanners Ridge Rd (gravel), cemetary to east	3272
1265.3	**913.8**	Lewis Spring & Road . . . . N38 27.141 W78 28.015 🅿 ♦ (pg.81)	3302
		Gravel road 0.2E to Skyline, then left 0.2 to	
		Big Meadows Wayside	
1264.2	**914.9**	Trail to **Big Meadows Lodge** . . . . (pg.81)	3569
1263.7	**915.4**	Trail to **Big Meadows Campground** . . . . (pg.81)	3579
1263.5	**915.6**	David Spring . . . . ♦	3518
1263.2	**915.9**	Stream . . . . ♦	3267
1262.6	**916.5**	Skyline 49.3, Fishers Gap.	3023
1261.3	**917.8**	Spur trail to Spitler Knoll parking, 4 cars . . . . . N38 32.892 W78 24.828 🅿	3245
1260.7	**918.4**	**Rock Spring Hut** (0.2W) . . . . ☽ ♦ ⚠ (9) ⌒ (8)	3465
		32.1◄23.9◄11.5◄►10.9►15.3►28.4 Locked cabin in front.	
1260.4	**918.7**	Side trail to Hawksbill Mountain	3700
		No camping on summit (anywhere above 3600')	
1259.4	**919.7**	Hawksbill Gap . . . . N38 33.776 W78 22.952 🅿 ♦	3312
1258.9	**920.2**	Trail to Crescent Rock Overlook, parking to east	3367
1258.1	**921.0**	Spring . . . . ♦	3258
1257.1	**922.0**	Spring . . . . ♦	3389
1256.8	**922.3**	Skyland stables, service road . . . . N38 35.201 W78 23.006 🅿	3468
1256.2	**922.9**	Trail (0.1E) to **Skyland Resort & Restaurant** . . . . 🅿 (pg.81)	3667
1256.0	**923.1**	Skyland service road north (0.2W) . . . . N38 35.557 W78 22.559 🅿	3605
1255.4	**923.7**	Trail to Stony Man Summit (0.2W)	3657

Shenandoah National Park (SNP) 540-999-3500 ⟨www.nps.gov/shen⟩

Backcountry Permits are required for overnight hikes within the park. There is no charge for the permit and there is a fine for not having one. Permits are available from self-registration sites at the south and north entrance of the AT into SNP, from any park visitor center, or by mail (see contact information above).

Concrete 4"x4" signposts are throughout the park, used to mark side trails, huts and campsites. Information is stamped into an aluminum band near the top of the post.

What is known as a "shelter" on most of the AT is called a "hut" in the Shenandoahs. Enigmatically, three-sided day-use structures called "shelters" cannot be used for overnighting. When overnighting in the park, please use the huts or designated campsites, which are usually near the huts.

If you cannot tent in a designated campsite, seek a preexisting campsite; if one cannot be found, follow LNT principles of dispersed camping. Tenting at a new location is limited to one night. Backcountry stay is limited to 14 consecutive nights; two at any one location. Campsites other than those designated must be:

- One quarter mile from any park facility (roads, campgrounds, lodges, visitor centers, and picnic areas).
- 10 yards from any water source.
- 50 yards from other camping parties, building ruins, or "no camping" signs.
- Not within designated no camping locations.

Groups are limited to 10. Campfires are only permitted at pre-constructed fire rings at the huts. Pets must be leashed. A number of lodges, camp stores and restaurants are along the

Skyline drive, many of which are readily accessible from the trail. These are operated by ARAMARK, an official concessioner. *New for 2010*: hiker discounts for lodging at Lewis Mt. Cabins, Big Meadows Lodge, and Skyland Resort are explained at www.visitshenandoah.com/mvs or by calling 1-877-778-2871. (press option 2 and ask for code SHMVS).

The Park Service operates campgrounds. Call 877-444-6777 or visit ⟨www.recreation.gov⟩ to reserve campsites. All campground campsites accommodate 2 tents and up to 6 persons. All campgrounds except Mathews Arm have coin operated laundry and showers. Many facilities are closed November-May and all are closed December-March.

Lodges and campgrounds are typically full on weekends. A small number of unreserved walk-in tentsites are available on a first-come, first-served basis at all campgrounds except Lewis Mt.

⊞ 🅿 Mountain & Valley Shuttle Service

Rodney Ketterman ("Rodman") and Jim Austin ("Skyline"), based near Luray, 1-877-789-3210, ⟨www.mvshuttle.com⟩, offers shuttles anywhere between Duncannon, PA and Daleville, VA. Also serves nearby airports, Amtrak, Greyhound. Operates fully insured, late-model vehicles, offers trail logistics, town assistance (one-day notice appreciated). Holds Commercial Use Authorization to shuttle hikers in SNP, Virginia DMV for-hire operating authority. Free limited rustic camping for shuttle clients night before or upon conclusion of hike, on-site parking at base camp (A.T.-style shelter, picnic table, BBQ grill, fire pit, hot shower, flush toilet; not a hostel). Also offers lodge-to-lodge hiking vacation package in SNP. Accepts Visa/MC/Discover (at time of phone reservation only).

879.9   Loft Mountain Campground
880.6   Loft Mountain Store

🚻 🍴 🏕 ⚷ ⛺ (**Loft Mountain Campground** Campsites $15. AT skirts the campground, and several short side trails lead to campsites and the camp store. Showers, laundry and long term resupply available from camp store.

🍴 **Loft Mountain Wayside** 1.1 miles from camp store, serves B/L/D, short-order menu, Sa-Su April early May, early May-Oct 9-5:30 7 days.

906.0   Lewis Mountain Campground

🍴 🍺 🏕 ⚷ ⛺ (**Lewis Mountain Campground and Cabins** *(see page 80 for cabin discount)* 540-999-2255, within sight of the AT, campsites $15. Reservations, 800-999-4714, Lewis Mountain Camp store, open 9-7 in summer. Open April 9 - November 7, 2010.

913.8   Lewis Spring Road

🍴 🍺 (**Big Meadows Wayside** B/L/D, soda machine. East 0.2 mi to Skyline Drive, then left another 0.2 mi. Fuel/oz available from the gas station. The wayside is also accessible from the lodge and campground area via the 0.9 mi. entrance road. Open April 1 - November 28, 2010.

914.9   Big Meadows Lodge

🍴 $ 🚻 (**Big Meadows Lodge** *(see page 80 for room discount)* Rooms include the main lodge, cabins, suites, and motel-type accommodations, reservations required. Dining room hours B: 7:30-10, L: 12-2, D: 5:30-9. Open May 20 - November 7, 2010.

915.4   Big Meadows Campground

🏕 ⚷ 🚻 (**Big Meadows Campground** Tentsites are $20 for up 2 tents and 6 persons, self-register after-hours. Coin operated laundry and showers, minimal supplies.

922.9   Side trail to Skyland

🍴 $ 🚻 (**Skyland Resort and Restaurant** 800-999-4714 *(see page 80 for room discount)* Rates seasonal and subject to change, reservation recommended. Dining room hours B: 7:30-10, L: 12-2, D: 5:30-9, nightly entertainment. Some snack foods and sodas sold at gift shop and vending machines. Open April 1 - November 28, 2010.

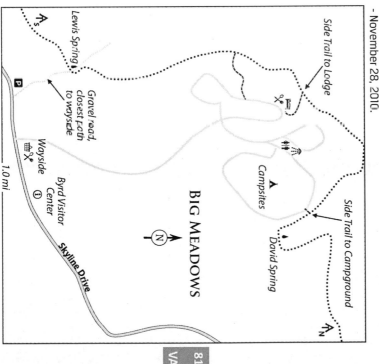

Side Trail to Lodge

Lewis Spring

Gravel road, closest path to wayside

Side Trail to Campground

Campsites

David Spring

BIG MEADOWS

Byrd Visitor Center ⓘ

Wayside

Skyline Drive

N

1.0 mi.

SoBo	NoBo	Description	Elev
1255.0	**924.1**	Overlook to the west	3483
1254.5	**924.6**	Spur trail to parking lot. . . . . N38 36.354 W78 21.983 **P**	3167
1254.0	**925.1**	Stony Man Overlook . . . . N38 36.735 W78 21.747 **P**	2999
1253.7	**925.4**	Nicholson Hollow Trail	3035
1252.9	**926.2**	Junction with Corbin Cabin Trail	3035
1252.5	**926.6**	Powerline	3200
1251.9	**927.2**	Pinnacles Picnic Area . . . . 🚻💧	3290
1251.6	**927.5**	Skyline 36.4, side trail to Jewell Hollow Overlook.	3293
1250.9	**928.2**	The Pinnacle	3730
1249.9	**929.2**	**Byrds Nest #3 Hut** . . . . 💧 🌙 🏕 ⌐ (8)	3200
		34.8◄22.4◄10.9◄►4.4►17.5►28.0 Spring 0.4E on forest road.	
1249.2	**929.9**	Meadows Spring Trail. . . . . 💧 (0.3E)	3100
1248.7	**930.4**	Overlook, Mary's Rock to west	3381
1247.6	**931.5**	Spring . . . . 💧	2865
1246.9	**932.2**	Side trail to Panorama . . . . N38 39.627 W78 19.326 **P** 💧🚻	2444
1246.7	**932.4**	US 211, Thornton Gap, **Luray, VA** (9W) . . . . (pg.86-87)	2307
1246.5	**932.6**	Skyline 31.2	2365
1245.5	**933.6**	**Pass Mountain Hut** (1939) (0.2E). . . . . 🌙 💧 🏕 ⌐ (8)	2690
		26.8◄15.3◄4.4◄►13.1►23.6►31.7 2 bear poles, 2 privies, and 8 tent sites.	
		Piped spring 15 yards behind shelter.	
1244.6	**934.5**	Pass Mountain	3052
1243.5	**935.6**	Beahms Gap Overlook, parking to east. . . . . **P**	2498
1243.1	**936.0**	Spring to west . . . . 💧	2458
1242.2	**936.9**	Neighbor Mtn Trail, Byrds Nest #4 day use picnic area . . . . . 💧 (0.5E)	2689
1241.4	**937.7**	Jeremys Run Overlook, parking to east. . . . N38 42.747 W78 19.800 **P**	2376
1238.6	**940.5**	Stream . . . . 💧	2239
1238.5	**940.6**	Jeremys Run Trail	2261
1238.1	**941.0**	**Elkwallow Wayside**, Skyline 23.9. . . . . 🍴🚻☕	2480
		Grill (B/L/D), limited groceries, vending outside, 9-7 in summer.	
1237.2	**941.9**	Range View Cabin (locked) . . . . 💧 (0.1E)	2900
1236.5	**942.6**	Skyline 21.9, Rattlesnake Point Overlook.	3105
1235.9	**943.2**	Tuscarora Trail, **Mathews Arm Campground** (0.7W) . . . . . . 🏕	3400
		Primitive campground; no services. Tent sites $14.	
1235.5	**943.6**	Skyline 21.1	3400
1235.2	**943.9**	Skyline 20.8	3400
1234.8	**944.3**	Spring . . . . 💧 (0.2E)	3420
1234.0	**945.1**	Skyline 19.7, Little Hogback Parking 50 yrds east.	2841
1233.9	**945.2**	Little Hogback Mountain	3100

SoBo	NoBo				Elev
1232.3	946.8	**Gravel Springs Hut** (0.2E) Spring en route to shelter	☾ ♦ ⚠ ⌐ (8)	2480
		28.4◄17.5◄13.1◄►10.5►18.6►24.1		
1232.1	947.0	Skyline 17.7, Gravel Springs Gap . . . . N38 46.068 W78 14.010 🅿		2666
1231.0	948.1	South Marshall Mountain		3212
1230.5	948.6	Skyline 15.9, parking to west		3090
1229.8	949.3	North Marshall Mountain		3368
1228.9	950.2	Hogwallow Flat . . . . ♦		2980
1228.3	950.8	Skyline 14.2, Hogwallow Gap . . . . N38 47.388 W78 11.319 🅿		2739
1227.4	951.7	Unnamed peak		2880
1226.6	952.5	Skyline 12.3, Jenkins Gap . . . . N38 48.389 W78 10.846 🅿		2400
1225.7	953.4	Compton Springs . . . . ♦		2550
1225.3	953.8	Compton Peak		2909
1224.5	954.6	Skyline 10.4, Compton Gap . . . . N38 49.414 W78 10.234 🅿		2415
1224.2	954.9	Indian Run Spring (unreliable) . . . . ♦ (0.3E)		2300
1222.7	956.4	Compton Gap Trail, self-registration for SNP permit . . . . **(pg. 89)**		2415
		Front Royal Hostel (0.4E).		
1222.5	956.6	SNP northern boundary, Possums Rest Overlook		2300
1221.8	957.3	**Tom Floyd Wayside** 28.0◄23.6◄10.5◄►8.1►13.6►18.1 . . ☾ ♦ ⚠ ⌐ (6)		1900
1221.6	957.5	Ginger Spring		1810
1220.3	958.8	VA 602		1100
1218.9	960.2	US 522, **Front Royal, VA** (4.0W) . . . . **(pg.88-89)**		950
1218.1	961.0	Bear Hollow Creek. . . . . ♦		1186
1215.8	963.3	Maintenance road		1801
1215.6	963.5	Tom Sealock Spring. . . . . ♦		1800
1214.7	964.4	Power line.		1700
1213.7	965.4	**Jim & Molly Denton Shelter** . . . . ☋ ☾ ♦ ⚠ ⌐ (8)		1310
		31.7◄18.6◄8.1◄►5.5►10.0►18.4 Excellent shelter with porch, chairs and		
		solar shower. Spring on AT near shelter entrance.		
1212.6	966.5	VA 638		1120

SoBo	NoBo	VA 84	1000	2000	3000	4000	5000	6000	Elev

1210.7 968.4 VA 55, Manassas Gap . . . . N38 54.550 W78 3.199 **P** 800
Linden, VA 22642 (1.2W)
🏤 M-F 8-12 & 1-5, Sa 8-12, holds packages 15 days only.
🏪 **Monterey Convenience Store**.
AT passes under I-66 on Tucker's Lane

1208.2 970.9 Manassas Gap Shelter. . . . . 🌙 ⬧ 🏕 ⌐ (6) 1655
24.1◄13.6◄5.5◄►4.5►12.9►19.8 Cables. Reliable spring downhill to right of shelter on side trail.

1206.3 972.8 Trico Tower Trail 1900

1203.7 975.4 Dicks Dome Shelter (0.2E) . . . . 🌙 ⬧ 🏕 ⌐ (4) 1230
18.1◄10.0◄4.5◄►8.4►15.3►29.4 Cables. Whiskey Hollow Creek in front of shelter (treat water). Tentsite by creek.

1202.6 976.5 Trail 0.1W to parking on Howellsville Rd. . . . . . N38 59.112 W77 59.980 **P** 1577

1201.5 977.6 Side trail (1.7E) to . . . . (⬧ 🏕 ⓘ 1840
Sky Meadows State Park Visitors Center 800-933-PARK Open W-Su, 8-5, restrooms, soda machine, 12 sites & primitive group camping, $9PP, reservation required, campers must arrive before dusk.

1200.6 978.5 View 0.4E on Ambassador Whitehouse Trail 1640

1198.9 980.2 Ashby Gap, US 50/17 900
1198.7 980.4 Side trail to parking on VA 601 . . . . N39 0.942 W77 57.718 **P** 1018

1197.4 981.7 Creek . . . . ⬧ 1255

1196.6 982.5 Trail west to Myron Glaser Cabin 1225

1195.3 983.8 Rod Hollow Shelter (0.1W) . . . . 🌙 ⬧ 🏕 ⌐ (8) 840
18.4◄12.9◄8.4◄►6.9►21.0►36.6 Piped spring just south of shelter.
1194.9 984.2 The Roller Coaster (south end) 760
13.5 miles of tightly packed ascents and descents

1193.6 985.5 Spring at Bolden Hollow 850

1192.1 987.0 Morgan Mill Stream . . . . ⬧ 766
1191.6 987.5 VA 605, Morgan Mill Rd 1100
1190.8 988.3 Stream . . . . ⬧ 942
1190.4 988.7 Spring . . . . ⬧ 1180
1189.8 989.3 Buzzard Hill 1268
1189.4 989.7 Stream . . . . ⬧ 755

SoBo	NoBo			Elev

1188.8   **990.3**   Tomblin Hill 1200

1188.4   **990.7**   **Sam Moore Shelter** (1990) .... ☽ ♦ ⚠ ⌐ (6)   990
19.8◄15.3◄6.9◄►14.1►29.7►33.8 Springs in front of shelter and to the left. Several tent sites to left of shelter.

1187.2   **991.9**   Spout Run .... ♦   789

1186.0   **993.1**   Stream .... ♦   855

1185.4   **993.7**   Bears Den Rocks, **Bears Den Hostel** (0.2E) .... **(pg. 89)** 1300

1184.8   **994.3**   Snickers Gap, VA 7 & 679, ... N39 6.919 W77 50.849 **P** **(pg.89)** 1000
Bluemont, VA (1.7E)

1184.0   **995.1**   Stream .... ♦   900

1182.3   **996.8**   **VA-WV** border... 1180
1182.2   **996.9**   Crescent Rock to east... 1300

1181.6   **997.5**   Sand Spring, good water source... ♦⚠ 1150
The Roller Coaster (north end); 13.5 miles of ascents and descents.

1181.5   **997.6**   Devils Racecourse... 1180

1178.7   **1000.4**   Wilson Gap... 1380
1177.5   **1001.6**   **Blackburn AT Center** (0.2E) .....N39 11.259 W77 47.866 **P** (♦ ⚠ ⌂ 1650
540-338-9028. Main building is home to a PATC caretaker. Small cabin near main building with wood-burning stove serves as free hiker hostel, open year-round. Solar shower on lawn, pay phone on wrap-around porch, water from hose, picnic tables.

1176.6   **1002.5**   Laurel Spring, intermittent... ♦ 1450
1176.4   **1002.7**   Campsite... ⚠ 1420

1175.6   **1003.5**   Campsite... ⚠ 1503

1174.9   **1004.2**   Buzzard Rocks... 1513

1174.3   **1004.8**   **David Lesser Memorial Shelter** (0.1E)............ ☽ ♦ ⚠ ⌐ (6) 1430
29.4◄21.0◄14.1◄►15.6►19.7►24.7 Overflow camping area below shelter. Spring 0.2 mile downhill from shelter.

1172.4   **1006.7**   Campsite... ⚠ 1048

1171.3   **1007.8**   Keys Gap, WV 9... 830
⛺ ✗ ((0.3W) **Mountaineer Mini-Mart & Torlone's Pizza**
⛺ (0.3E) **Sweet Springs Country Store**

1169.8   **1009.3**   Power line... 877

1167.4   **1011.7**   **VA-WV** border, Loudoun Heights Trail... 1200

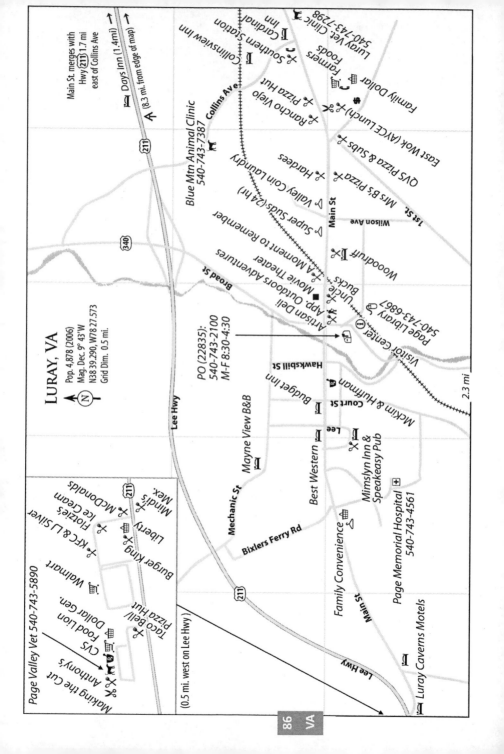

LURAY, VA

Pop. 4,878 (2006)
Mag. Dec. 9° 43'W
N38 39.290, W78 27.573
Grid Dim. 0.5 mi.

Main St. merges with Hwy 211 1.7 mi east of Collins Ave

Days Inn (1.4mi)

(8.3 mi. from edge of map)

211

340

Collins Ave

Collinsview Inn

Southern Station

Cardinal Inn

Luray Vet. Clinic 540-743-7298

Farmers Foods

Family Dollar

Rancho Viejo

Pizza Hut

East Wok (AYCE Lunch)

CVS Pizza & Subs

Mrs B's Pizza

Hardees

Blue Mtn Animal Clinic 540-743-7387

Valley Coin Laundry

Super Suds (24 hr)

A Moment to Remember

Movie Theater

APP. Outdoors Adventures

Uncle Buck's

Artisan Deli

Page Library 540-743-6867

Visitor Center

Main St

Wilson Ave

1st St

Woodruff

Broad St

Lee Hwy

PO (22835): 540-743-2100 M-F 8:30-4:30

Mayne View B&B

Mechanic St

Hawksbill St

McKim & Huffman

Court St

Budget Inn

Best Western

Lee

Mimslyn Inn & Speakeasy Pub

Family Convenience

Bixlers Ferry Rd

Main St

Page Memorial Hospital 540-743-4561

Luray Caverns Motels

Lee Hwy

211

2.3 mi

(0.5 mi. west on Lee Hwy)

Page Valley Vet 540-743-5890

Making the Cut

Anthony's

CVS

Food Lion

Dollar Gen.

Walmart

Taco Bell

Pizza Hut

Burger King

Liberty

KFC & LJ Silver

Flotzie's Ice Cream

Mindi's Mex

McDonalds

211

86 VA

932.4   Skyline 31.5, US 211 (Thornton Gap)

➟ ✗ (4.4W on US 211) to **Brookside Cabins and Restaurant** 540-743-5698 $85 and up, luxury cabins, AYCE L/D buffet daily, weekend breakfast buffet, open 7 days all year except during winter holidays.

➟ ⛺ ✗ ⛲ ⛹ (5.2W) **Yogi Bear's Jellystone Park** 540-743-4002 ⟨www.campluray.com⟩ cabins $83 and up, tent sites $48, two-night minimum on weekends.   Memorial to Labor Day snack shop serving hamburger, hot dogs, pizza on wkdays only; breakfast only on wkends. Coin laundry, campstore, pool and waterslide.

Luray, VA (9.0W) *(more services on map)*

Farmer's market held on Saturdays.

➟ **Budget Inn** 540-743-5176 $49S/UP pets $5.

➟ ⛹ **Days Inn** 540-743-6511 $84 and up, pool, no pets.

➟ **The Cardinal Inn** 888-648-4633 ⟨www.luraybestvalueinn.com⟩ $59/UP, includes breakfast, no pets.

➟ **Luray Caverns Motels** East and West Buildings 540-743-6551, 888-941-4531 ⟨www.luraycaverns.com⟩ Su-Th $72S/D, F-Sa $88S/D, $8EAP, continental breakfast, pool.

➟ **Best Western** 540-743-6511 ⟨www.bestwesternvirginia.com/luray-hotels⟩ $70-$160, pool, pet fee $25.

➟ **Cavern Inn Motel** 540-743-4575

🥾 **Appalachian Outdoors Adventure** 540-743-7400 Full-service outfitters, Coleman/alcohol/oz. (M-Sa 10am-6pm; Sun. 1-5pm).

✗ **Speakeasy at Mimslyn Inn** Dinners 4-10pm, full bar and sometimes entertainment.

American Hiking Society

Founded in 1976, American Hiking Society is the only national organization dedicated to promoting and protecting America's hiking trails, their surrounding natural areas and the hiking experience.

To learn more about American Hiking Society and our programs such as National Trail Day, National Trails Fund, and Volunteer Vacations, visit AmericanHiking.org or call (800) 972-8608.

Twi-Lite Motel

Pizza Hut

Jalisco Mexican Restaurant

Arby's

Budget Inn
Laundry

Shenandoah Ave

Skyline Restaurant

Wendy's

Warren Memorial Hospital
540-636-0300

8th St

Alberto's
Taco Bell
Papa Johns
7-11

True Value Hardware

6th St

Subway
Laundry

Virginia Ave

522

PO (22630):
540-635-8482
M-F 8:30-5,
Sa 8:30-1

3rd St

Victoria's

340

55

Eddie's

Chester St

FRONT ROYAL, VA

N

Pop. 14,561 (2006)
N38 54.650, W78 11.083
Mag. Dec. 9° 58'W
Grid Dim. 0.5 mi.

Distances from Quality Inn:
0.6 to Post office
0.3 to Outfitter
0.7 to Martin's
0.7 to CVS
1.1 to Library
1.5 to Pizza Hut

Theater

Main St

Lucky Star Lounge

Soul Mtn Cafe

Visitor's Center

Main St Mill

L-Dee's Pancake House

Weasel Creek Outfitter

Second Chance Thrift

Laundry

Blue Ridge Ave

Stokes General Store

Quality Inn

Stonewall Dr

Handi Market with Dunkin Donuts & Baskin Robbins

Anthony's Pizza
Laundry

WoodWard House B&B

Spelunker's Ice Cream

McDonald's

Burger King

Super 8

Celio's Pizza

South St

Scottish Inn

Martin's

Barber

Lester & Mowery's

Rite Aid

Blimpie

Mexico Lindo

Villa Giusseppe's

Pioneer Motel

KFC

55

Dean's Steakhouse

Criser Rd

Dollar Tree

K-Mart

CVS

Hong Kong

Food Lion

Family Dollar

Castiglia Italian

Library 540-635-3153
M-Th 10-8, F-Sa 10-5

0.9 mi

(3.1 mi)

956.4   Compton Gap Trail

⌂ ⊟ ⊠ 🚿 🍴 **Front Royal Terrapin Station Hostel** (0.4E) 540-539-0509, 504-631-0777 At the north end of SNP, there is a post labeled "Va 610/Chester Gap 0.5 miles", the AT will turn west. Go east (straight ahead for northbounders) on the AT will turn west. Trail 0.5 mile to paved road. Enter around back through marked gate (residential neighborhood, please respect noise level). Open May 2-July 10, 2010, includes bunk with mattress & sheets, shower, soap, shampoo, towels, shower clothes, laundry, free computer, free shuttle to town for groceries, P.O, etc. Fuel, snacks, sodas, ice cream & oven pizza on site. Shuttles and slackpacking available. Owned by Mike Evans (AT '95, PCT '98). ⟨gratefulgg@hotmail.com⟩ Cost: 1 day hiker-$19, 1 day couples-$34, 1 day hiking groups-$17 each 2nd and successive nights hiker-$16, couples-$30, hiking groups-$15 each. Maildrops (guests only): 304 Chester Gap Rd, Chester Gap, VA 22623.

960.2   US 522

ⓘ *Front Royal* (4.0W) *(more services on map)*

🛏 ⚹ ☏ **Visitor Center** 540-635-5788 Helpful and usually has hiker goodie bags. Restrooms, sodas.

🛏 ⛺ ⊠ **Quality Inn** 540-635-3161, $60 single or double, $10EAP (up to 4), pets $15. Pool, coin laundry, shuttle can be arranged back to trail. This is the first hotel you pass on the way into town, and may be the best choice considering location, services and price. Maildrops: 10 Commerce Avenue, Front Royal, VA 22630.

🛏 ⛺ **Scottish Inn** 540-636-6168, wkdays $45, wkends $49, pets $10.

🛏 **Super 8** 540-636-4888 10% hiker discount, pets $10.

🛏 **Pioneer Motel** 540-635-4784

🛏 **Woodward House B&B** 540-635-7010, $105D includes breakfast, pickup and return to trail.

🛏 **Blue Ridge Motel** 540-636-7200, $35S $45D, add $10 weekends, no pets.

🛍 🍴 **Weasel Creek Outfitter** 540-635-3120, Coleman/alcohol/ oz, some repairs, shuttles when available.

🍴 **Lucky Star Lounge** L/D variety, some vegetarian choices, live music.

993.7   Bears Den Rocks

⌂ ⛰ ⊟ ⚹ ⛺ ⊠ 🍴 **P** **Bears Den Hostel and Trail Center** 540-554-8708 ⟨www.bearsdencenter.org⟩ The castle-like stone lodge is ATC owned and PATC operated. Bunk $15, tent sites $10 with full house privileges which include cooking & shower. Hiker Special: Bunk, laundry, pizza, Ben and Jerry's ice cream, and a soda for $27.50 plus tax. Check in and store hours are from 5 to 9 PM, but the hiker room with lounge, internet, phone, and sodas is open 24 hours/day. Short term resupply available and fuel/oz. Short-term secured parking $3/day. Accepts credit cards. Maildrops: Bears Den Hostel, 18393 Blue Ridge Mountain Rd, Bluemont, VA 20135.

994.3   Snickers Gap, VA 7 & 679 The AT crosses VA 7 near its intersection with State Route 679. On the north of VA 7, 679 curves away on a westerly path. Take 679 west to reach the restaurants and store listed below. To reach the post office, take VA 7 0.8 mile east, the turn right on route 734 and go another 0.8 mile.

Bluemont VA 20135 (1.7E)

✉ M-F 8:30-12 & 1-5, Sa 8:30-12, 540-554-4537

🍴 (0.3W) **Horseshoe Curve Restaurant** 540-554-8291 Tu-Sa 12-9, Su 12-6, closed Monday.

🍴 💲 (0.9W) **Pine Grove Restaurant** 540-554-8126 Tu-Sa 6:30-8, Su 6:30-5, closed Monday, pub food, beer, and wine.

🏪 (1.1W) **The Village Market** 540-554-8422 7am-7pm M-Sa.

1166.7	**1012.4**	WV 32, Chestnut Hill Rd								650
1166.0	**1013.1**	US 340, Shenandoah River Bridge . .							**(pg.93)**	275
1165.7	**1013.4**	Side trail to **Appalachian Trail Conservancy** (0.2W)							**(pg.93)**	484
1165.2	**1013.9**	Jefferson Rock, view north to Potomac and Shenandoah Rivers . .								413
1165.1	**1014.0**	**Harpers Ferry, WV**, ... N39 18.989 W77 45.350 **P (pg.92-93)**								270
		Shenandoah Street								
1165.0	**1014.1**	Potomac River, Byron Memorial Footbridge, **WV-MD** border								250
1164.8	**1014.3**	C&O Canal Towpath south end (NoBos go right on towpath).								260
		No camping anywhere along the AT section of the towpath.								
1163.7	**1015.4**	Sandy Hook Bridge, US 340 high overhead							**(pg.93)**	260
1162.2	**1016.9**	C&O Canal Towpath north end								260
1162.1	**1017.0**	Keep Tryst Rd							**(pg.94)**	280
		Knoxville, MD (1.0W), **Brunswick, MD** (2.5E)								
1161.9	**1017.2**	US 340 underpass								280
1161.7	**1017.4**	Weverton Rd . . . . N39 19.977 W77 40.993 **P**								373
1160.8	**1018.3**	Trail to Weverton Cliffs								800
1158.7	**1020.4**	**Ed Garvey Shelter** . . . . ☽ ◗ Å ⌐ (12)								1150
		36.6◄29.7◄15.6◄►4.1►9.1►16.6 Water on steep 0.4 mile trail in front of shelter. 2 tent sites north & south of shelter.								
1156.7	**1022.4**	Brownsville Gap								1050
1155.0	**1024.1**	MD 572, Gapland Rd, Gathland State Park . . . . ⚦ (◗								950
		Vending machines, restroom. No camping. There are no trash cans.								
1154.6	**1024.5**	**Crampton Gap Shelter** (0.3E) . . . . ☽ ◗Å ⌐ (6)								1000
		33.8◄19.7◄4.1◄►5.0►12.5►20.7 Intermittent spring (0.1S) on AT; NoBos consider bringing water from Gathland SP in dry season.								
1152.0	**1027.1**	Spring, trail to Bear Spring Cabin (locked) . . . . ◗ (0.5E)								1480
1151.4	**1027.7**	White Rock Cliff								1650
1151.2	**1027.9**	Lambs Knoll								1723
1149.6	**1029.5**	**Rocky Run Shelter** (0.2W) . . . . ☽ ◗ Å ⌐ (16)								970
		24.7◄9.1◄5.0◄►7.5►15.7►20.6 Tent sites downhill.								
1148.6	**1030.5**	Reno Monument Rd, Fox Gap								900
1147.8	**1031.3**	**Dahlgren Backpack Campground** . . . . ⛺ ⚦ ◗ Å								990
		Large tenting area, restrooms; no fee. Note proximity to road.								
1147.6	**1031.5**	Turners Gap, US Alt 40 . . . . ⛏ ✗ **(pg.94)**								1000
		(0.1W) **Old South Mountain Inn** D Tu–Su, L on Sa; Su brunch (0.2W)								
		Boonsboro, MD (2.5W)								
1146.2	**1032.9**	Monument Rd (road passes in front of park)								1300
1146.0	**1033.1**	Washington Monument State Park . . . . ◗ (								1400
1145.6	**1033.5**	Washington Monument (0.1W)								1550
1145.3	**1033.8**	Power line								1294

SoBo	NoBo		
1143.5	**1035.6**	Boonsboro Mountain Rd.	1300
1142.8	**1036.3**	Old Wolfsville Rd.	1257
1142.7	**1036.4**	I-70 footbridge, US 40 . . . . .N39 32.115 W77 36.209 **P** (pg.94)	1225
		Parking north end of footbridge 0.1 east	
1142.1	**1037.0**	**Pine Knob Shelter** (0.1W) . . . . 🌙 ◊ ▲ ⌐ (5)	1360
		16.6◄12.5◄7.5◄►8.2►13.1►22.7 Piped spring next to shelter.	
1140.5	**1038.6**	Trail to Annapolis Rocks, campsite. . . . . 🌙 ◊ (0.2W) ▲ (13)	1730
		Caretaker on site. Tentsites near outstanding overlook.	
1139.5	**1039.6**	Black Rock Cliffs	1800
1139.1	**1040.0**	Black Rock Creek. . . . . ◊	1800
1138.9	**1040.2**	**Pogo Memorial Campsite** . . . . 🌙 ◊ ▲	1550
		Campsite east of AT, spring 30 yards west.	
1134.1	**1045.0**	MD 17, Wolfsville Rd, **Smithsburg, MD** (1.5W). . . . . (pg.94)	1400
1133.9	**1045.2**	**Ensign Cowall Shelter** . . . . 🌙 ◊ ⌐ (8)	1430
		20.7◄15.7◄8.2◄►4.9►14.5►16.9	
		Boxed spring, somewhat stagnant, south between shelter & road.	
1133.2	**1045.9**	Power line	1376
1132.6	**1046.5**	MD 77, Foxville Rd.	1450
		Smithsburg, MD (1.7W)	
1131.3	**1047.8**	Power line	1376
1130.8	**1048.3**	Warner Gap Hollow, Warner Gap Rd . . . . ◊	1200
1130.1	**1049.0**	Little Antietam Creek . . . . ◊	1113
1130.0	**1049.1**	Raven Rock Rd, MD 491	1210
1129.0	**1050.1**	**Raven Rock Shelter**. . . . . 🌙 ◊ ▲ ⌐	1480
		20.6◄13.1◄4.9◄►9.6►12.0►13.2 Replaces Devils Racecourse Shelter.	
1127.2	**1051.9**	Trail to High Rock, parking below gate . . . . . . N39 41.690 W77 31.394 **P**	1800
1124.3	**1054.8**	Pen Mar County Park . . . . .N39 42.983 W77 30.433 **P** (pg.95)	1256
		Cascade, MD (1.4E), **Waynesboro, PA** (2.1W)	
1124.1	**1055.0**	**MD-PA** border, Mason-Dixon Line	1250
1124.0	**1055.1**	Pen Mar Rd	1300
1123.4	**1055.7**	Falls Creek. . . . . ◊	928

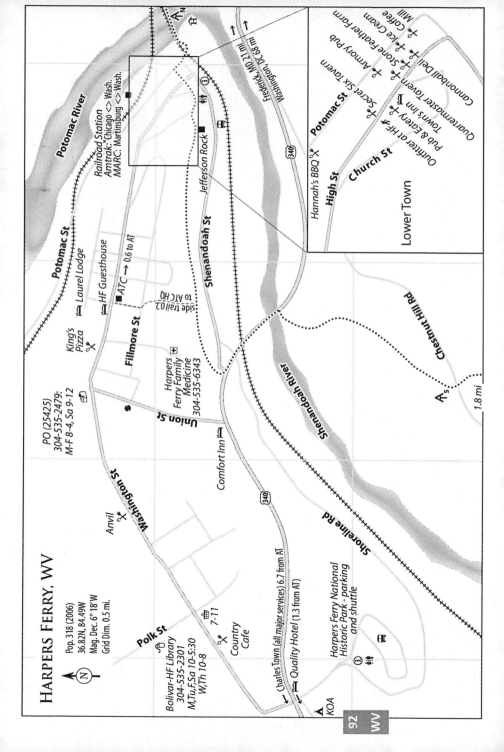

HARPERS FERRY, WV

Pop. 318 (2006)
36.8 2N, 84.49W
Mag. Dec. 6°18' W
Grid Dim. 0.5 mi.

N

PO (25425)
304-535-2479:
M-F 8-4, Sa 9-12

Bolivar-HF Library
304-535-2301
M,Tu,F,Sa 10-5:30
W,Th 10-8

Polk St

7-11

Country Cafe

Anvil

Washington St

Charles Town (all major services) 6.7 from AT

Quality Hotel (1.3 from AT)

KOA

Harpers Ferry National Historic Park - parking and shuttle

Shoreline Rd

Shenandoah River

340

Comfort Inn

Union St

Harpers Ferry Family Medicine 304-535-6343

Fillmore St

King's Pizza

Laurel Lodge

HF Guesthouse

ATC → 0.6 to AT

side trail 0.2 to ATC HQ

Potomac St

Railroad Station
Amtrak: Chicago <> Wash.
MARC: Martinsburg <> Wash.

Potomac River

N

Shenandoah St

Jefferson Rock

Washington, DC 68 mi

Frederick, MD 21 mi

340

Chestnut Hill Rd

1.8 mi

Lower Town

Hannah's BBQ

Outfitter at HF

Pub & Eatery

Quartermaster Tavern

Towns Inn

Secret Six Tavern

Armory Pub

Stone Feather Farm

Ice Cream

Coffee

Cannonball Deli

Mill

High St

Church St

Potomac St

92

WV

1013.1 US 340 (Shenandoah River Bridge) For northbounders, this is the first of three opportunities to enter Harpers Ferry (see map). Go west on 340 if you intend to stay at the Comfort Inn, Quality Hotel, KOA, or to hitch into Charles Town; east to Frederick. Stay on the AT for better access to Harpers Ferry.

╠ (**Comfort Inn** 304-535-6391, $70-$100, 10% thru-hiker discount, continental breakfast, no pets.

╠ ※ △ ≋ (1.2W) **Quality Hotel** 877-424-6423 or 304-535-6302, $85/up, 10% thru-hiker discount, pool, Vista Gourmet Restaurant.

▲ ╠ △ ㊚ (1.2W) **Harpers Ferry KOA** 304-535-6895 Hiker discount 10% on camping rates that start at $25.95. Cabins $48.95 and up. Shower only $5, coin laundry on-site.

Charles Town, WV 25414 (6.0W) All major services.

▣ ⚙ **Walmart** with grocery and pharmacy 304-728-2720

✚ **Jefferson Urgent Care** 304-728-8533.

🐾 **Jefferson Animal Hospital** 304-725-0428
Frederick, MD 21701 (20E) All major services.

1013.4 Side Trail to ATC HQ (0.2W)

ⓘ ✉ **Appalachian Trail Conservancy HQ** - 304-535-6331 ⟨www.appalachiantrail.org⟩ Open year-round, 7 days a week 9-5. Closed Thanksgiving, Christmas and New Year's Day. If you're thru-hiking or hiking the entire trail in sections, have your photo taken for the album; a postcard version of this photo may be purchased. Hiker lounge, register, scale, and cold drinks inside, along with hats, shirts, maps, all ATC publications. There is an information board with information for hikers on front porch. Maildrops: (USPS) P.O. Box 807 or (FedEx, UPS) 799 Washington St., Harpers Ferry, WV 25425.

1014.0 *Harpers Ferry, WV (more services on map)*

⌂ △ ▣ **Town's Inn** 304-702-1872 ⟨www.TheTownsInn.com⟩ In historic downtown building, this is as clean and aesthetic as any hostel on the AT. Many options (hostel, private & semi-private)

ranging $30/up, kitchen facilities with all rooms. Frozen pizza, ice cream, $5 laundry, shuttles $1/mi, no maildrops. Visa/MC accepted.

╠ **Laurel Lodge** 304-535-2886 ⟨www.laurellodge.com⟩ $95-150 for 2 includes big breakfast, view overlooking Potomac.

╠ △ **Harpers Ferry Guest House** 304-535-6955 Weekdays $100, weekends $125 plus tax, includes breakfast and laundry.

✖ 🏠 **The Outfitter at Harpers Ferry** 888-535-2087 Knowledgeable Full service outfitter with good selection of shoes and trail food. Shuttle referrals. Open daily 10-6. Also operates **Harpers Ferry General Store** where they have bike rentals.

✖ **Stone Feather Farm** New in 2010, serves Southwestern and American cuisine for B/L/D.

✚ **Foot and Ankle Care.** Dr. Warren BeVards, 304-535-3040

🅿 ⓘ **Harpers Ferry National Historical Park** $5 entrance fee, long-term parking. Free shuttle bus to lower town.

🚌 **Pan Tran** 304-263-0876 Route that goes to Charles Town departs from train station 6:45am, 9:05am, 10:40am, and 1:35pm M-Sa, no 6:45 departure on Sat. Cost $2.50.

🚌 **Amtrak.** 304-535-6346, (800) USA-RAIL, "Capitol Limited" daily from Chicago-Washington, DC Union Station. Rates vary with demand from $11 to $21. Departs for Washington at 11:25am, returns 4:05.

🚌 **Maryland Rail Commuter Service (MARC)** 410-539-5000 ⟨www.mtamaryland.com⟩. "Brunswick Line" on weekdays serves Washington and Baltimore and other regional cities. Fares $9 to $13 + $2 surcharge.

1015.4 US 340 overpass Sandy Hook Road is parallel to the towpath on the other side of the railroad tracks. About 0.1 mile north of the overpass, there are "shortcuts" to the Harpers Ferry Hostel. The paths are not blazed because crossing railroad tracks anywhere other than designated locations is not legal. Use your judgment. See Knoxville, MD services on the next page.

1017.0　Keep Tryst Road
Knoxville, MD, 21758 (1W)
Motel, grocer and restaurant are 1.0 mile west; to get to the Hostel, go west 0.9 mile, then left 0.2 mile on Sandy Hook Road.

⌂ ▲ ⌂ ♨ ⊠ **Harpers Ferry Hostel** 301-834-7652 ⟨www.harpersferryhostel.org⟩ Bunk $18+tax for members of Hostelling International, $23+tax for non-members, includes shower, kitchen privileges, internet use, free coffee & tea. Tenting $10PP, $3 for hostel amenities. Dogs on leash allowed if tenting. Laundry $4/load, $2/half load includes soap. Denatured alcohol/oz; please donate. Check in 10pm, check out noon. No drinking. Closed Nov 15-Apr 15. Maildrops: 19123 Sandy Hook Rd., Knoxville, MD 21758 (mark "Hold for AT Hiker").

🛏 **Hillside Motel** 301-834-8144, $45S, $55D & up, no pets, credit cards accepted.

Brunswick, MD 21716
🏤 M-F 8:30-1, 2-4:30, Sa 9-12, 301-834-9944 (2.5E)
🛒 **Sandy Hook Grocer,** 301-834-8353, hours approx. 3-9.
✗ **Cindy Dee's** 301-695-8181, open daily 7-9 B/L/D, uphill past Harpers Ferry Hostel to Rt.180 and go left, restaurant on right.

1031.5　Turners Gap, US Alt 40
Boonsboro, MD 21713 (2.5W)
🏤 M-F 9-1, 2-5, Sa 9-12, 301-432-6861
✗ ⌂ (**Crawfords** 301-432-2903, M-F 7-7, Sa 7-3, B/L/D, sandwiches, subs, entrees.
✗ **Vesta's Pizza** 301-432-6166, Su-Th 11-10, F-Sa 11-11.

✗ **Mountainside Deli** 301-432-6700, M-F 6-8 & Sa 8-8 B/L/D, Su 11-8 L/D. **Potomac Street Creamery** 301-432-5242. **Palettie Gourmet Bistro** 301-432-0500, W-Su 5-8, hiker special AYCE spaghetti any night $15, closed M-Tu. **Subway**
🛒 **Cronise Market place** 301-432-7377 M-F 10-7, Sa 9-7, Su 10-6.
🐾 **Boonsboro Veterinarian Hospital** 301-432-7120.
⌂ **Marcy's Laundry**
📖 **Boonsboro Free Library** 301-432-5723, M-F 10-7, Sa 10-2. **Turn the Page Book Store Café** 301-432-4588
✂ **Pete's Barber Shop**

1036.4　I-70, US 40
✗ **$ Dogpatch Tavern** 301-791-2844.
▲ ⚲ (1.4W) to **Greenbrier State Park** campsites at campground 301-791-4767, camping Apr-Oct, no pets. Camp store open May-Sep, Coleman by the gallon. Entrance fee $4PP wkdays; $6PP wkends and holidays, 62+ free entrance, tent sites with hot showers $25. Lake swimming, row boat and paddle boat rentals.

1045.0　MD 17 (Wolfsville Road)
⌂ ⌂ (⌂ ♨ ⊠ (0.3W) **The Free State Hiker Hostel**
301-824-2407 ⟨www.freestatehiker.com⟩ bunks $32, shuttles to Smithsburg when available. Open Mar 15-Nov 15, two nights only, owned by '06 thru-hiker Ken "Bone Pac" and Jennel Berry, packages sent to c/o Free State Hiker, LLC 11626 Wolfsville Road, Smithsburg, Maryland 21783. Mail drop handling fee for non-guests $2. Credit cards accepted. Pizza and Mexican delivery available. Water available from spigot in front. No alcohol and no pets.

Smithsburg, MD 21783 (1.5W)
🏤 M-F 8:30-1, 2-4:30, Sa 8:30-12, 301-824-2828
🛒 **Dollar General Store** 301-824-6940, M-Sa 8-9, Su 9-8.
🛒 **Smithsburg Market,** M-Sa 8-7, Su 9-3, **Food Lion,** daily 7-11.

1054.8 Pen Mar County Park

Open first Sunday in May to last Sunday in Oct. Vending machines and water fountains; no camping. Restrooms are locked when park is closed. Pen Mar Rd passes in front of the park, east of the AT. If you intend to walk to town, do so from the AT/Pen Mar Rd intersection 0.3 north of the park. Bobby D's and other pizza places will deliver; check for numbers near phone.

Most services are in the western edge of Waynesboro, but take note: use the Rouzerville PO which is in this part of Waynesboro. Just beyond the PO, reach Main St (PA 16), and turn left to reach all services listed below. Many more restaurants are further into town.

Waynesboro, PA (2.1W)

🏬 Walmart, Food Lion

🏪 Sheetz

✂ Cost Cutters Barber Shop

✕ Bobby D's Pizza 717-762-0388, Rita's, Blondie's, Applebee's, Old City Buffet American, Chinese, Japanese AYCE L/D.

🔧 Lowe's Hardware

Also: Olympia Sports large selection of running shoes.

2.5W of post office:

➕ Waynesboro Hospital 717-765-4000, 501 E Main St.

Wayne Heights Animal Hospital, 717-765-9636.

🛏 Days Inn 717-762-9913, (5.5W of Walmart) $50 and up with continental breakfast, $20 pet fee.

Cascade, MD (1.4E on Pen Mar/High Rock Rd)

🏬 Sanders Market M, W-F 8:30-9, Tu and Sa 8:30-8

🛁 Cascade coin 301-241-3831 (1.1 mile from PO).

✕ Rocky's Pizzeria 301-824-2066, M-F 10:30-10 Sa-Su 10:30-11. Vince's New York Pizza 301-824-3939, M-F 10:30-10 Sa-Su 10:30-11. Dixie Eatery 301-824-5334, closed M, Tu 7-2, W-F 7-8, Sa-Su 7-2. Subway 301-824-3826 (24 hrs).

➕ Smithsburg Emergency Medical 301-416-0888.

Park Circle Animal Hospital 301-824-3314.

Rite Aid pharmacy 301-824-2211, store 9-9, pharmacy 9-6

🛁 Laundry

📚 Library 301-824-7722 M-F 10a-7p, Sa 10a-2p

🔧 Ace Hardware

Waynesboro, PA (eastern edge of town)

Food Lion,
Dollar Store
■ KFC, Hardee's

■ Walmart, Sheetz,
Olympia Sports
Old City Buffet,
■ Applebees

Rita's

✕ Blondie's

✕ Brother's Pizza

Rouzerville PO (17250)
717-762-7050:
M-F 8:30-1 & 2-4:30,
Sa 8:30-11:30

Pen Mar Rd 0.1 to 191

Pen Mar Rd

PenMar Park

PO 2.0, PO 1.3

Blue Ridge Summit, PA

PO (17214)
717-794-2335;
M-F 8-4:30,
Sa 9-11:30

Cascade, MD

PO (21719)
301-241-3403:
M-F 8-1 & 2-5,
Sa 8-12

4.2 mi.

SoBo	NoBo		Elev
1123.0	**1056.1**	Buena Vista Rd . . . . ▲	1334
1121.8	**1057.3**	Old PA 16	1200
1121.5	**1057.6**	PA 16, ... N39 44.495 W77 29.422 **P** (pg.100)	1300
		Blue Ridge Summit, PA (1.2E)	
1121.3	**1057.8**	Mentzer Gap Rd, Mackie Run	1250
1120.9	**1058.2**	Rattlesnake Run Rd	1379
1120.7	**1058.4**	Bailey Spring . . . . ▲	1300
1119.4	**1059.7**	**Deer Lick Shelters** . . . . ☽ ▲ ⛺ (8)	1420
		22.7◄14.5◄9.6◄►2.4►3.6►10.2 Spring 10 yards north on AT or (0.2E) on blue-blazed trail.	
1118.1	**1061.0**	Pipeline clearing	1476
1117.0	**1062.1**	**Antietam Shelter** . . . . ☽ ⛺ (6)	890
		16.9◄12.0◄2.4◄►1.2►7.8►13.4 Water from Old Forge Park 0.1N	
1116.9	**1062.2**	Old Forge Park , Old Forge Road . . . . . . N39 48.089 W77 28.773 **P** 🚻▲	900
1115.8	**1063.3**	**Tumbling Run Shelters** . . . . ☽ ▲ ⛺ (8)	1120
		13.2◄3.6◄1.2◄►6.6►12.2►19.6 Water 100 yards right of shelter.	
1114.5	**1064.6**	Chimney Rocks	1900
1112.5	**1066.6**	Power line	1992
1111.9	**1067.2**	Snowy Mountain Rd	1562
1111.2	**1067.9**	Swamp Rd	1600
1110.9	**1068.2**	PA 233, **South Mountain, PA** 17261 (1.2E)	1600
		🏤 M–F 8–1 & 2–4:45, Sa 8–12, 717-749-5833	
		🏨 🚌 **The South Mountain Hotel** 717-749-3845	
1109.2	**1069.9**	**Rocky Mountain Shelters** (0.2E) . . . . ☽ ▲ Ⓐ ⛺ (8)	1520
		10.2◄7.8◄6.6◄►5.6►13.0►19.2 Piped spring 0.5 mile on trail to road, then right 75 yards.	
1106.2	**1072.9**	US 30, **Fayetteville, PA** (3.5W) . . . . . . N39 54.352 W77 28.714 **P** (pg.100)	960
		Nobos intending to visit Caledonia SP should stay on AT which passes close to pool. Overnight parking SW corner of US30 & Pine Grove Rd, check in at park HQ.	
1104.3	**1074.8**	Quarry Gap Rd	1380
1103.6	**1075.5**	**Quarry Gap Shelters** . . . . ☽ ▲ Ⓐ ⛺ (8)	1455
		13.4◄12.2◄5.6◄►7.4►13.6►24.5	
1103.4	**1075.7**	Stream . . . . ▲	1680
1102.1	**1077.0**	Sandy Sod Junction	1980
1101.3	**1077.8**	Power line	1837

SoBo	NoBo		Elev
1099.5	**1079.6**	Middle Ridge Rd	2050
1099.0	**1080.1**	Ridge Rd, Means Hollow Rd	1900
1098.6	**1080.5**	Milesburn Rd, PATC Milesburn Cabin (locked) . . . . ▲ 🅰	1635
		North of cabin are plenty of campsites; bring water from cabin.	
1096.8	**1082.3**	Power line	1919
1096.2	**1082.9**	**Birch Run Shelter** . . . . ☽ ♦ ⊏	1795
		19.6◄13.0◄7.4◄►6.2►17.1►25.2	
		Spring 30 yards in front of shelter.	
1094.9	**1084.2**	Shippensburg Rd, ... N39 59.834 W77 24.301 🅿	2040
		Big Flat Fire Tower Rd, limited parking.	
1093.0	**1086.1**	Side trail to Michener Cabin (locked) . . . . ♦ (0.3E)	1820
1091.1	**1088.0**	Woodrow Rd	1800
1090.0	**1089.1**	**Toms Run Shelters** . . . . ☽ ♦ ⊏ (8)	1300
		19.2◄13.6◄6.2◄►10.9►19.0►37.2 Water behind shelter.	
1089.6	**1089.5**	**AT Midpoint (1089.55)** Usually a hiker will make an improvised	1320
		midpoint marker, guessing at the location that changes nearly every year.	
1088.5	**1090.6**	Michaux Rd, ruins of WWII camp, plaque.	1328
1088.2	**1090.9**	Halfway Spring 50 yards on side trail . . . . ♦	1100
1087.9	**1091.2**	Sunset Rocks Trail . . . . 🅿	1030
1087.8	**1091.3**	Toms Run . . . . ♦	1023
1086.6	**1092.5**	PA 233	900
		NoBo follow road (0.1W), veer right on first paved road into park.	
1086.3	**1092.8**	PA 233, ... N40 01.971 W77 18.291 🅿 **(pg.100)**	820
		Pine Grove Furnace State Park, parking lot on Quarry Road	
1083.8	**1095.3**	Side trail to Pole Steeple	1300
1080.5	**1098.6**	Limekiln Rd	1080
1080.3	**1098.8**	Trail to **Mountain Creek Campground** (0.7W) . . . . 🏠 ⌂ (🏛 ▲ 🛏	987
		Open Apr-Nov, 717-486-7681, cabins $45D, $5 EAP, tent sites $25D,	
		heated pool, camp store, snack shack.	

SoBo	NoBo		Elev
1079.1	1100.0	**James Fry (Tagg Run) Shelter** (0.2E) . . . . ☽ ♦ ⚠ ⌐ (9)	805
		24.5◄17.1◄10.9◄►8.1►26.3►33.6	
		Spring uphill from shelter, and also 0.2 further east.	
1078.6	1100.5	Pine Grove Rd . . . . **(pg.100)**	671
1077.7	1101.4	PA 34, Hunters Run Rd . . . . N40 4.624 W77 11.702 🅿 (0.5S) ⛩	980
		Green Mountain Store (0.2E) 7 days	
1075.9	1103.2	PA 94, **Mt Holly Springs, PA** (2.5W) . . . . **(pg.100)**	880
1075.8	1103.3	Power line	846
1075.7	1103.4	Sheet Iron Roof Rd, trail to **Deer Run Campground** . . . △⛩ ✗⚠⇌	769
		(0.4W) 717-486-8168, tentsite $10 w/shower, cabin $62.	
1075.2	1103.9	Stream . . . . ♦	686
1074.9	1104.2	Stream . . . . ♦	667
1074.5	1104.6	Old Town Rd	727
1073.1	1106.0	Whiskey Spring Rd, reliable water from spring . . . . ♦	800
1071.1	1108.0	Little Dogwood Run . . . . ♦	880
1071.0	1108.1	**Alec Kennedy Shelter** (0.2W) ► . . . . ☽ ♦ ⌐ (7)	850
		25.2◄19.0◄8.1◄► 18.2►25.5►34.1 Unreliable spring on side trail behind	
		shelter and small stream (0.5S) of shelter.	
1070.1	1109.0	Center Point Knob	1060
1068.2	1110.9	Leidigh Dr	489
1067.6	1111.5	Backpacker's Campsite . . . . ⚠	500
1067.4	1111.7	Yellow Breeches Creek, road . . . . ⚠	500
1067.1	1112.0	PA 174 . . . . N40 8.816 W77 7.531 🅿 **(pg.101)**	500
		Boiling Springs, PA	
1065.1	1114.0	PA 74 , York Rd . . . . N40 10.385 W77 7.263 🅿	550
1064.0	1115.1	Lisburn Rd	517
1063.4	1115.7	Byers Rd	499
1063.0	1116.1	PA 641, Trindle Rd	500
1061.8	1117.3	Ridge Rd, Biddle Rd, **Pheasant Field B&B** (0.5W) . . . . ⇌ △	485
		717-258-0717, $99 and up, 10% discount, laundry free, behaved pets ok.	
		0.25W to Hickory Town Rd, left on Hickory, B&B on right.	
1061.2	1117.9	Old Stonehouse Rd	446
1060.6	1118.5	Appalachian Drive	471
1060.3	1118.8	PA Turnpike (I-76)	465
1059.1	1120.0	US 11, **Carlisle, PA** (5.0W) . . . . **(pg.102)**	465
1058.2	1120.9	I-81 crossing	485
1057.8	1121.3	Bernheisel Rd	393

SoBo	NoBo			Elev
1056.8	**1122.3**	Conodoguinet Creek . . . . N40 15.589 W77 6.221 🅿 🌙 ⬥		390

Scott Farm Trail Work Center Open May–Oct, picnic table, no camping. The AT u-turns, passes under bridge, and heads north.

1055.7	**1123.4**	Sherwood Drive		440
1054.8	**1124.3**	PA 944		480
1053.8	**1125.3**	Water where AT crosses overgrown dirt road (pipe spring) . . . . ⬥		820

Nobos planning stay at Darlington Shelter consider getting water here.

| 1052.9 | **1126.2** | Darlington Trail, Tuscarora Trail . . . . | | 1200 |
| 1052.8 | **1126.3** | **Darlington Shelter** (0.1E) . . . . 🌙 ⬥ ⌐ (5) | | 1250 |

37.2◄26.3◄18.2◄►7.3►15.9►22.6 Unreliable water on blue-blazed trail in front of shelter.

1050.9	**1128.2**	Millers Gap Rd		684
1050.5	**1128.6**	PA 850 . . . . N40 19.359 W77 4.260 🅿		650
1045.5	**1133.6**	**Cove Mountain Shelter** (0.2E) . . . . 🌙 ⬥ ⌐ (8)		1200

33.6◄25.5◄7.3◄►8.6►15.3►33.3
Spring 0.1mi on steep side trail.

1043.6	**1135.5**	Hawk Rock		1225
1042.3	**1136.8**	Sherman Creek. . . . . ⬥		335
1041.9	**1137.2**	PA 274, pass under US 11/15		350
1041.4	**1137.7**	**Duncannon, PA** . . . . **(pg.102-103)**		360
1040.4	**1138.7**	PA 849, Juniata River		390
1040.2	**1138.9**	Clarks Ferry Bridge (west side), Susquehanna River		380
1039.6	**1139.5**	US 22/322, railroad tracks . . . . N40 23.771 W77 0.482 🅿 **(pg.103)**		390
1038.6	**1140.5**	Spring 60 yards on side trail. ⬥		1199
1036.9	**1142.2**	**Clarks Ferry Shelter** (0.1E) . . . . 🌙 ⬥ ⌐ (8)		1260

34.1◄15.9◄8.6◄►6.7►24.7►38.1
Reliable piped spring just beyond shelter.

| 1036.6 | **1142.5** | Power line . . . . | | 1320 |

| SoBo | NoBo | | PA 99 | 1000 2000 3000 4000 5000 6000 | Elev |

1057.6   PA 16
Blue Ridge Summit, PA 17214 (1.2E)

🍴 M-F 8-4:30, Sa 9-11:30, 717-794-2335
✗ **Unique Bar and Grill** 717-794-2565, **Summit Plaza** 717-794-2500, open 7-8, B/L/D
△ **JJ's Laundromat**
🛠 **True Value Hardware**

1072.9   US 30
▲ ✗ 🍴 **Caledonia State Park** 717-352-2161, open end of Mar - mid Dec. Pool open 7 days mid Jun - Aug, and a few weekends before and after. Poolside snack bar 11-7. Phone and vending next to the pool and near office. Campsites with showers, $21 Su-Th, $25 F-Sa, $2 more for campsites that allow pets, $2 less for PA residents. $3.50 shower only.
✗ (1.5E) **Bobby A's Grill & Bar** 717-352-2252

Fayetteville, PA 17222 (spread out to west, distances given for each service)

(0.4W) ✗ 🍴 **Taormina's Italian Restaurant** 717-352-8503 Tu-Su 11-9, Pizza, Subs, ice cream.
(0.8W) 🛒 **Henicle's Market** deli, 7 days, M-Sa 8-9, Su 9-5.
(2.6W) 🛏 ✗ ⊠ **Scottish Inn and Suites** 717-352-2144, 800-251-1962, $55S, $69D, $15 pets. $5 for pickup, return or ride to Walmart. Maildrops for guests: 5651 Lincoln Way East, Fayetteville, PA 17222
(2.6W) ✗ **Flamingo Restaurant** excellent large breakfast.
(3.2W) △ **Squeaky Clean Laundry**
(3.2W) 🍴 M-F 8-4:30, Sa 8:30-12, 717-352-2022
(3.2W) 🧴 **Rite Aid**
(7.0W) 🛒 **Walmart**

1092.8   PA 233, Pine Grove Furnace
PA Ruck Jan 30, 31, Feb 5-7

🏛 **Pine Grove General Store,** open mid Apr-Memorial Day. Foods and cold drinks. Vending machines outside. Home of the *half gallon challenge.*

ⓘ **A.T. Museum.** Hikers are welcome to bring food to eat and relax. The museum will provide other services to hikers as well. Displays feature the Earl Shaffer Shelter, artifacts of other pioneering hikers and a children's discovery area. The museum will be open on weekends in the spring and fall and daily during the summer. Grand Opening is June 5, 2010, featuring speakers and exhibits from local hiking clubs, and group hikes ending at the opening ceremony.

🏠 △ ⊠ 🍴 🛁 **Ironmasters Mansion** 717-486-7575 Open 7:30-9:30am and 5-9 pm, thru-hikers $27 bunk bed, linen, shower, towel, kitchen use, internet access, private room $54, laundry $4, no sleeping bags, no pets. Coleman/alcohol/oz. Maildrops: Ironmasters Mansion, 1212 Pine Grove Rd., Gardners, PA 17324. Visa/ MC accepted.

▲ ✗ 🚻 **Pine Grove Furnace State park,** weekend $19 PA residents $21 nonresidents; $4 less weekdays; $2. Some dog-allowed sites. Beach/swimming area. Restrooms throughout park.

1100.5   Pine Grove Road
🛏 ▲ ✗ 🏕 🍴 △ ☕ (0.3W) **Cherokee Campground** 717-486-8000 Tent sites $25, 6 person cabin with electricity $50/up.

1103.2   PA 94
Mt. Holly Springs, PA 17065 (2.5W)

🍴 M-F 8:30-4:30, Sa 9-12, 717-486-3468
🛏 ✗ 🍴 **Holly Inn, Restaurant and Tavern** 717-486-3823 $55, Continental breakfast. Free ride to/from trailhead, when available. .
🏪 **Sheetz**
✗ **Deer Lodge Restaurant, Subway, Sicilia Pizza**
💊 **Holly Pharmacy** 717-486-5321
△ **Laundromat**

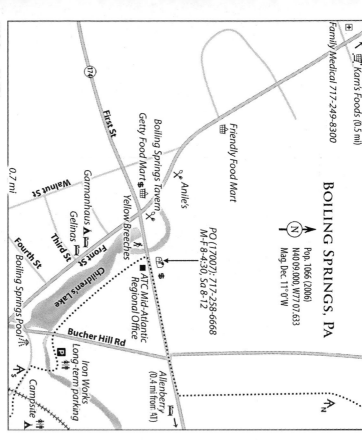

BOILING SPRINGS, PA

Pop. 1066 (2006)
N40 09.000, W77 07.633
Mag. Dec. 11°0'W

PO (17007): 717-258-6668
M-F 8-4:30, Sa 8-12

Friendly Food Mart

Boiling Springs Tavern
Getty Food Mart
Boiling Springs Tavern

Aniele's

First St

Garmanhaus
Gelinas

Walnut St
Yellow Breeches
Third St
Front St
Fourth St
Children's Lake
Boiling Springs Pool
0.7 mi

ATC Mid-Atlantic
Regional Office

Bucher Hill Rd

Iron Works
Long-term parking
Campsite

Allenberry
(0.4 mi from AT)

Family Medical 717-249-8300

Karn's Foods (0.5 mi)

1112.0   PA 174

⚡️🍴🛏️ **Boiling Springs, PA** *(more services on map)*

⚡️🍴🛏️ **Allenberry Resort Inn & Playhouse** 717-258-3211, 800-430-5468 (www.allenberry.com) $25 hiker special (this is an exceptional lodging offer) $6 breakfast buffet, $10 lunch buffet, $25 dinner theater, $3 laundry, pool, all major credit cards accepted.

⚡️🛏️✉️ **Gelinas Manor** 717-258-6584

(www.gelinasmanor.com) $79D/up, no pets. Full breakfast served 8:30. Laundry $6/load. Credit cards accepted. Computer access by request only. Maildrops (with reservation) MUST say "in care of Gelinas Manor", 219 Front Street, Boiling Springs, PA 17007.

🏠✉️🛏️ **Garmanhaus B&B** 717-258-3980 Hiker rates starting at $50S $75D wkdays, $75S $100D wkends, breakfast included. Do-it-yourself laundry privileges. Cash & checks only. Maildrops: P.O. Box 307, or 217 Front Street, Boiling Springs, PA 17007.

🛏️ Free hiker campsite with privy south of town.

🍴 **Boiling Springs Tavern** 717-258-3614, L/D 11:30-2, 5-9:30, closed Su-M. **Aniele's Ristorante & Pizzeria** 717-258-5070, L/D subs, pizza, entrees, about 0.5 miles north of Gettys. Su-Th 11-10, F-Sa 11-11.

🛒 **Karn's Quality Foods** 717-258-1458, Daily 7-10.

🏪 **Gettys Food Mart** 717-241-6163, ATM inside.

🥾 **Yellow Breeches Outfitters** 717-258-6752. Primarily a fishing outfitter; limited hiking selection.

🏊 **Boiling Springs Pool** 717-258-412, Memorial Day-Labor Day, M-Su 11-7, $10 admission, $1 hot shower.

➕ **Boiling Springs Family Medical** 717-249-8300

🐾 **Boiling Springs Family Animal Hosp.** 717-258-4575 M- 8-7:30, W-F 8-6, Sa 8-1, 1.4W on Park Dr.

ℹ️ **ATC Mid-Atlantic Regional Office** 717-258-5771 Open wkdays 8-3, possibly later. Water faucet on south side of building. Bulletin board with hiker info. Staff provides information on trail conditions, weather forecast, and water availability. Small shop with guidebooks and maps. White gas/denatured alcohol for small donation. Call for info on permit parking.

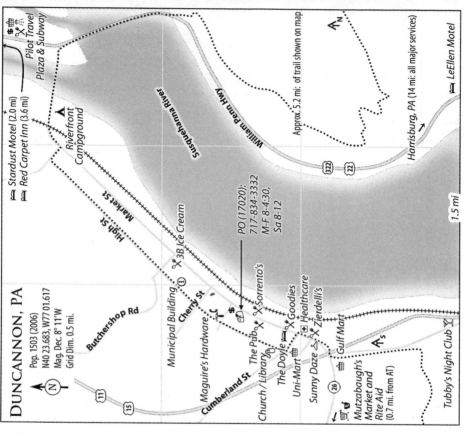

DUNCANNON, PA

(N)

Pop. 1503 (2006)
N40 23.683, W77 01.617
Mag. Dec. 8° 11'W
Grid Dim. 0.5 mi.

Butchershop Rd

Municipal Building (i)

Maguire's Hardware

Cherry St

High St

Market St

3B Ice Cream

The Pub Sorrento's

Church / Library

Cumberland St

The Doyle Goodies

Uni-Mart Healthcare

Sunny Daze Zierdelli's

Gulf Mart

26

Mutzbaugh's Market and Rite Aid (0.7 mi. from AT)

Tubby's Night Club

PO (17020): 717-834-3332 M-F 8-4:30, Sa 8-12

Susquehanna River

William Penn Hwy

322 22

Harrisburg, PA (14 mi: all major services)

LeEllen Motel

N

Approx. 5.2 mi: of trail shown on map

1.5 mi

Riverfront Campground

Pilot Travel Plaza & Subway

Stardust Motel (2.0 mi)
Red Carpet Inn (3.6 mi)

1120.0   US 11

The AT passes over the highway on a footbridge. Side trails are bushwhacked down to the road on either end. Most businesses listed below will be in view from the overpass. This is a narrow corridor bewteen large towns east (Carlisle, 5mi) and west (Mechanicsburg, 7mi), which have nearly every motel, restaurant or retail outlet one could imagine. All area hotels run short of rooms (and go up in price) every other weekend when there is a car show.

Super 8 Motel 717-249-7000, $54.99S, $59.99D, includes continental breakfast, $10 pet fee. Maildrops for guests: 1800 Harrisburg Pike, Carlisle, PA 17013.

Hotel Carlisle 717-243-1717, $64.95, $10 pet fee.

America's Best Inn 717-245-2242, $55 and up with continental breakfast, $25 pet fee. Maildrops: 1825 Harrisburg Pike, Carlisle, PA 17013.

Motel 6 717-245-2400, $39.99/up, pets $10. Maildrops: 1450 Harrisburg Pike, Carlisle, PA 17015.

Econo Lodge 717-249-7775, $49.99/up, includes continental breakfast, $10 pet fee.

Middlesex Diner serves B/L/D.

(0.4E) **Flying J Truckstop** 717-243-6659, 24hrs. Has store, diner, pizza by the slice, showers ($10) and laundry.

Mechanicsburg, PA (7.0E)

Holiday Inn 717-697-0321 Notable due to it's two sizeable sports bars (**Legends** and **Hardware Bar**) "beach" volleyball courts.

1137.7 **Duncannon, PA** (*more services on map*)

🛏🍴🛁🚿🖥📮 **Doyle Hotel** 717-834-6789, $25S, $7.50EAP + tax, bar serves L/D, pay phone inside, iso cannisters, Coleman/alcohol by oz, accepts Visa/MC. USPS and UPS maildrops: 7 North Market Street, Duncannon, PA 17020.

🛏🛁🏨 **Motel Stardust** 717-834-3191

★🛏 **Red Carpet Inn** $47.95S $60D + tax.

▲🏨 **Riverfront Campground** 717-834-5252, south of the Clarks Ferry Bridge, sites and shower $3.50PP, shuttles.

🍴 **Zeiderelli's Pizza & Subs** 717-834-3331

🍴 **Sorrento Pizza** 717-834-5167

🍴 **Goodies** B/L/D.

🍴 **Ranch House Restaurant** B/L/D, near Motel Stardust has breakfast and dinner buffet on weekends.

🍺 **Mutzabaugh's Market** 7 days, pickup/return to Doyle once daily.

💊 **Rite Aid** next door to market.

🏧🚿🍴🛁 **All American Travel Plaza**, $8 showers.

🐾 **Cove Mountain Animal Hospital** 717-834-5534

🛁 **Laundry**

🔧 **Maguire's Hardware** Denatured alcohol, Colman, and Heet.

Also: Trail Angel Mary 717-834-4706

(7.2E, compass south) on US 11

🚶 **Blue Mountain Outfitters** 717-957-2413

(1E, compass south) on US 11

✚ **Holy Spirit Hospital** 717-834-6919

1139.5   US 22/322

🛏 **Le-Ellen Motel** 717-921-8715, $35S, $40D, no pets. Can be reached by walking 1.0E alongside railroad tracks.

1033.0 **1146.1** PA 225 . . . . N40 24.711 W76 55.796 **P** 1280
1032.4 **1146.7** Power line. 1265

1031.1 **1148.0** Table Rock. 1380
1030.2 **1148.9** **Peters Mountain Shelter** . . . .🌙 ◍ ⌐ (12) 1180
22.6◄15.3◄6.7◄►18.0►31.4►35.5 ►
Weak spring 0.1mi steeply downhill from shelter.
1029.4 **1149.7** Victoria Trail. 1193

1027.4 **1151.7** Shikellimy Overlook . . . . N40 26.259 W76 49.185 **P** (0.9E) 1320

1023.9 **1155.2** Spring 100 yards on side trail. ◍ 840
1023.5 **1155.6** PA 325, Clarks Valley . . . . **P** ◍ 550
1023.4 **1155.7** Clarks Creek . . . . N40 27.092 W76 46.574 **P** ◍ 531

1020.2 **1158.9** Stony Mountain, Horse-Shoe Trail 1650

1019.6 **1159.5** Rattling Run. . . . . ◍ 1125

1016.8 **1162.3** Yellow Springs Village Site (0.1E) . . . . ◍ ▲ 1420
Clearing with trail register.

1014.5 **1164.6** Cold Spring Trail 1400

| 1012.2 | **1166.9** | **Rausch Gap Shelter** (0.3E). . . . . ☽ ◖ ⌐ (12) | 980 |

1012.2 **1166.9** **Rausch Gap Shelter** (0.3E). . . . . ☽ ◖ ⌐ (12) 980
33.3◄24.7◄18.0◄►13.4►17.5►32.6 No tenting or fires permitted.
1011.6 **1167.5** Rausch Creek. . . . . ◖ 960
1010.7 **1168.4** Haystack Creek . . . . ◖ 824

1009.9 **1169.2** Second Mountain 1362

1007.5 **1171.6** PA 443 484

1006.1 **1173.0** Swatara Gap, PA 72, **Lickdale, PA** (2.1E) . . . . **(pg.106)** 480
1005.7 **1173.4** I-81, AT passes underneath 441
1005.3 **1173.8** Woods road. 620

1000.0 **1179.1** Oil pipeline 1382

998.8 **1180.3** **William Penn Shelter** (0.1E). . . . . ☽ ◖ ⚑ ⌐ (16) 1380
38.1◄31.4◄13.4◄►4.1►19.2►33.9
Water and tent sites 0.1W on blue-blazed trail.

996.6 **1182.5** PA 645, Waggoners Gap Rd . . . . . N40 30.396 W76 22.609 🅿 **(pg.106-107)** 1300
Pine Grove, PA (3.4W)

994.8 **1184.3** PA 501 . . . . N40 30.751 W76 20.664 🅿 **(pg.106-107)** 1460
Pine Grove, PA (4.2W), **Bethel, PA** (4.5E)
994.7 **1184.4** **501 Shelter** (0.1W), Caretaker house nearby. . . . . ☽ 🏠 ◖ ⚑ ⌐ 1460
35.5◄17.5◄4.1◄►15.1►29.8►38.9 Solar shower, house faucet, no
alcohol, no smoking in shelter, pets on leash.
994.2 **1184.9** Trail to Pilger Ruh (Pilgrims Rest) . . . . ◖⚑ 1465
Spring, side trail to Applebee Campsite.

991.6 **1187.5** Round Head, Shower Steps . . . . ◖ 1600

| SoBo | NoBo | | PA 105 | 1000 | 2000 | 3000 | 4000 | 5000 | 6000 | Elev |

1173.0   PA 72, Swatara Gap

Lickdale PA (2.1E) *(more services on map)*

🛏 ⛽ ⊕ **Days Inn** 717-865-4064, $55 and up, includes continental breakfast, pets $15, jacuzzi.

🛏 ⛽ ⊕ **Quality Inn** 717-865-6600, $109.99 plus tax, includes continental breakfast, pets $10, heated pool.

🛏 ⛽ ⊕ **Best Western** 717-865-4234, $62.99 and up, hikers 10% discount, continental breakfast, indoor heated pool, no pets.

⛺ 🏠 **Lickdale Campground & General Store** 877-865-6411 Open 5-9, 7 days. $25 tentsites.

🏠 ✗ **Love's Truckstop** $9 showers, ATM

1184.3   PA 645

Pine Grove PA (3.4W) *(more services on map)*

✗ **Original Italian Pizza.** 570-345-5432 Delivers to 501 shelter.

✗ ⛽ 🏠 ⛺ $ **Gooseberry Farms** 570-345-8800, 24hr, other side of 81, Subway & DQ inside, B/L/D, shower $9.

🛒 **Bergers Market** 570-345-3663,

📧 **PA Moneypit** 570-345-1119, pamoneypit@yahoo.com, shuttles to most PA towns & airports, $1.50/mile.
4.8W near intersection of I-81

🛏 **Colony Lodge** 570-345-8095, $40-$65, Some pet rooms.

🛏 **Econo Lodge** 570-345-4099, $55S, $60D, pets $10 in smoking room.

🛏 **Comfort Inn** 570-345-8031, $60.50 with continental breakfast, hiker friendly, honors flat rate all season, pet fee $10, pool.

1184.3   PA 501

Bethel, PA (4.1E) *(more services on map)*

⊕ **Bethel Library** 717-933-4060, M-Th 10-8, F 10-5, Sa 9-4.
Pine Grove PA 17963 (4.2W)

LICKDALE, PA

N40 27.066, W76 30.822
Mag. Dec. 11° 29'W
Grid Dim. 0.5 mi.

Footbridge

Mountse Valley Rd

Rail Trail 2.5 mi

(72)

81

Godfather's Pizza / Blimpie
Wendy's
Days Inn
Quality Inn
McDonald's / Chester's Chicken
Love's Truck Stop: convenience store,
ATM & showers,

Lickdale Campground

Subway

Best Western

Dairy Queen

Fisher Ave

1.5 mi

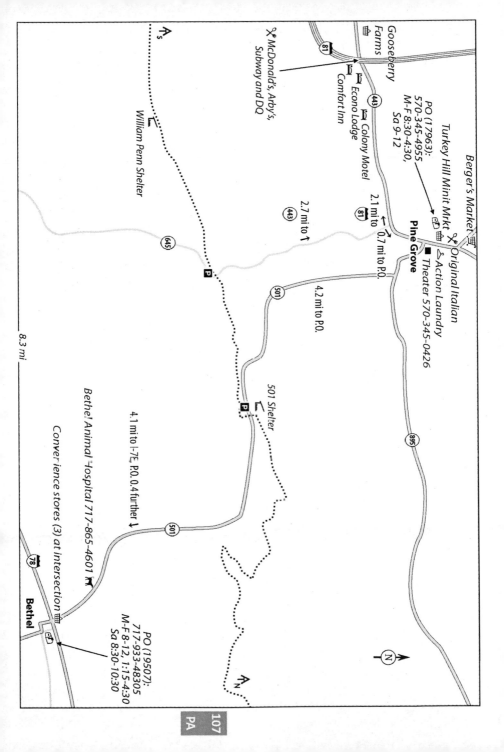

Gooseberry Farms

McDonald's, Arby's, Subway and DQ

William Penn Shelter

81

443

PO (17963):
570-345-4955
M-F 8:30-4:30,
Sa 9-12

Turkey Hill Minit Mrkt

Berger's Market

Original Italian

Action Laundry

Theater 570-345-0426

Econo Lodge
Colony Motel
Comfort Inn

443

2.7 mi to ↑

2.1 mi to
81

0.7 mi to P.O.

Pine Grove

645

501

4.2 mi to P.O.

895

501 Shelter

4.1 mi to I-7E, P.O. 0.4 further ↓

Bethel Animal Hospital 717-865-4601

501

Convenience stores (3) at intersection

78

Bethel

8.3 mi

PO (19507):
717-933-48305
M-F 8-12, 1:15-4:30
Sa 8:30-10:30

N

989.1	**1190.0**	Hertlein Campsite (between two streams) picnic table . . . . ♦ ▲	1220
989.0	**1190.1**	Shuberts Gap.	1163
988.3	**1190.8**	Oil pipeline	1508

985.7	**1193.4**	Fort Dietrich Snyder Marker. ♦ (0.2W)	1420
985.4	**1193.7**	PA 183, Rentschler Marker	1440
984.9	**1194.2**	Game Commission Administrative road . . . . N40 31.636 W76 12.888 🅿	1355
984.1	**1195.0**	Black Swatara Spring . . . . ♦ (0.3E)	1580

980.3	**1198.8**	Sand Spring Trail . . . . ♦ (0.2E)	1500
979.6	**1199.5**	**Eagles Nest Shelter** (0.3W) . . . . ☽ ♦ ⌐ (8)	1510
		32.6◄19.2◄15.1◄►14.7►23.8►31.2	
		Spring on trail to shelter.	

977.7	**1201.4**	Shartlesville-Cross Mtn Rd, ... ⛺ ✗ 🛏	1300
		Shartlesville, PA 19554 (3.6E)	
		Scottish Inn 610-488-1578, $42 and up, pets $5, ATM nearby.	
976.2	**1202.9**	State Game Land Rd	1408

| 975.0 | **1204.1** | Phillips Canyon Spring (unreliable) . . . . ♦ | 1500 |

| 973.0 | **1206.1** | State Game Land Rd . . . . | 1406 |
| 972.5 | **1206.6** | Pipeline . . . . | 1385 |

971.1	**1208.0**	Railroad bridge . . . . N40 34.774 W76 1.600 🅿	389
971.0	**1208.1**	**Port Clinton, PA** . . . . **(pg.110-111)**	400
970.3	**1208.8**	PA 61, **Hamburg, PA** (1.7E) . . . . **(pg.110-111)**	430

SoBo	NoBo		Elev
967.7	**1211.4**	Pocahontas Spring . . . . ♦⬣	1200
966.5	**1212.6**	Minnehaha Spring, frequently dry . . . . ♦	1340
965.9	**1213.2**	Stream, intermittent . . . . ♦	848
965.1	**1213.9**	Reservoir Road . . . . N40 35.374 W75 56.659 🅿 (0.3E)	800

Parking only with permission from Hamburg Borough 610-562-7821

| 964.9 | **1214.2** | **Windsor Furnace Shelter** (0.1W) . . . . ☽♦⊏ (8) | 940 |

33.9◄29.8◄14.7◄►9.1►16.5►26.5 Shelter on blue-blazed trail near
reservoir, no swimming, creek south of shelter.

963.8	**1215.3**	Trail to **Blue Rocks Campground** (1.5E) . . . . **(pg.111)**	1600
963.3	**1215.8**	Pulpit Rock	1582
961.5	**1217.6**	Trail to **Blue Rocks Campground** (1.5E) . . . . **(pg.111)**	1600
961.1	**1218.0**	The Pinnacle, panoramic view, no camping or fires	1635
959.1	**1220.0**	Gold Spring, dependable . . . . ♦	1580
957.6	**1221.5**	Panther Spring, dependable . . . . ♦	1081
956.7	**1222.4**	Parking lot on side trail (0.43) . . . . N40 37.528 W75 57.208 🅿	614
955.8	**1223.3**	**Eckville Shelter** (0.2E), Hawk Mountain Rd . . . . ⛺♦⊏ (6)	600

38.9◄23.8◄9.1◄►7.4►17.4►24.2
Open May-Sep, enclosed bunkroom, tent platforms, flush toilet, spigot at
1.6W to Hawk Mountain Sanctuary

955.5	**1223.6**	Stream . . . . ♦	513
954.1	**1225.0**	Hawk Mtn trail east	1360
953.0	**1226.1**	Dans Pulpit	1640
952.3	**1226.8**	Dans Spring (0.1E)	1510
949.7	**1229.4**	Tri-County Corner	1560
948.4	**1230.7**	**Allentown Hiking Club Shelter** . . . . ☽♦⬣⊏ (8)	1350

31.2◄16.5◄7.4◄►10.0►16.8►33.5
Spring downhill in front of shelter 0.2 mile, another 0.1 further.

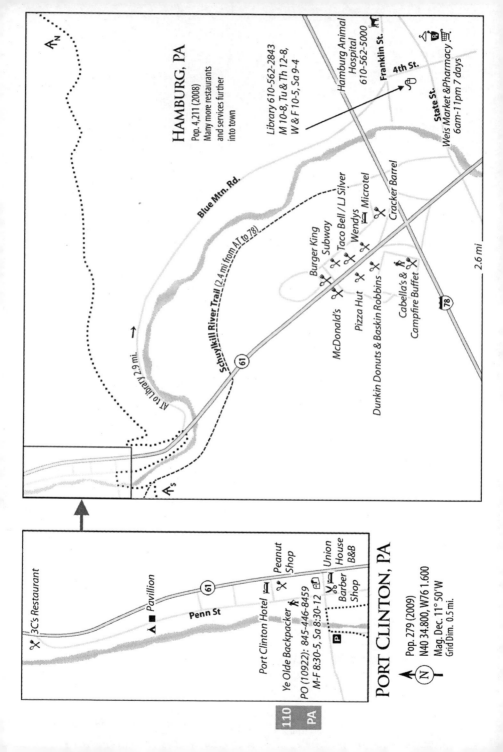

HAMBURG, PA

Pop. 4,211 (2008)
Many more restaurants
and services further
into town

Library 610-562-2843
M 10-8, Tu & Th 12-8,
W & F 10-5, Sa 9-4

Hamburg Animal
Hospital
610-562-5000

Franklin St.

4th St.

State St.

Weis Market & Pharmacy
6am-11pm 7 days

Blue Mtn. Rd.

Schuylkill River Trail (2.4 mi from AT to 78)

AT to Library 2.9 mi.

Cracker Barrel

Microtel

Wendys

Taco Bell / LJ Silver

Subway

Burger King

Pizza Hut

McDonald's

Dunkin Donuts & Baskin Robbins

Cabella's &
Campfire Buffet

61

78

2.6 mi

PORT CLINTON, PA

3C's Restaurant

Pavillion

61

Penn St

Peanut
Shop

Port Clinton Hotel

Ye Olde Backpacker
PO (10922): 845-446-8459
M-F 8:30-5, Sa 8:30-12

Union
House
B&B

Barber
Shop

N

Pop. 279 (2009)
N40 34.800, W76 1.600
Mag. Dec. 11° 50'W
Grid Dim. 0.5 mi.

1208.1 Port Clinton, PA 19549 *(more services on map)*

🛏✕⛺ **Union House Bed & Bath** ⟨www.union-house.com⟩
610-562-3155, after 5pm 610-562-4076, open F-Su, $65.35S
$87.15D includes tax, dinner restaurant, Visa/MC accepted, no pets.

🛏✕⛺ **Port Clinton Hotel** 610-562-3354, 888-562-2626
⟨www.portclintonhotel.net⟩ $49.05S, $62.13D, $10 deposit for room
key and towel, limited rooms available. Laundry, dining Tu-Th 11-9,
F-Sa 11-closing, Su 11-10, closed Monday. Please shower before use
of dining room. Visa/MC accepted.

🏠 **The Peanut Shop.** trail mixes, ATM.

✕ 🏠 ⛺ 📷 📧 **Ye Olde Backpacker** 610-562-2322 ⟨staff@
yeoldebackpacker.com⟩ M-Sa 9-8 Su 10-5, full service outfitter. Fuel/
oz, freeze-dried foods, snack foods, sodas, and ice cream. Shuttle
range 150 miles, small fee for safe long term parking. Maildrops UPS/
FedEx preferred: 45 Penn St, Port Clinton, PA 19549. Need picture ID
to claim parcels.

🔥 ⛺ **Pavillion Tenting** sign in at pavillion or with outfitter, no car
camping, no drive-ins.

1208.8 PA 61

Hamburg, PA 19526 (1.7E) *(more services on map)*

🏨 M-F 9-5, Sa 9-12, 610-562-7812

🛏⛺ **Microtel Inn** 610-562-4234 ⟨www.microtelinn.com⟩ $84.50S
$95.50D, reservations recommended, pub & lounge

✕ **Wendy's, Burger King, Cracker Barrel**

🍴 **Cabela's** 610-929-7000, M-Sa 8-9, Su 9-8

✕ **Campfire Restaurant** Inside Cabela's with AYCE B $6.99, L/D
$8.99.

🛒 **$ King's Supermarket** 610-562-3828, 6-11, 7 days.

🏠 **Turkey Hill Market**

💊 **Rite Aid** 610-562-9454, **CVS** 610-562-2454

🧺 **Hamburg Coin Laundry**

🐾 **Hamburg Animal Hospital** 610-562-5000 M-Th 9-7, Sa 9-11.

🚌 **Barta Bus Service** 610-921-0601⟨www.bartabus.com⟩

Pottsville, PA (15.0W, compass north of AT on PA 61)

🍺 **Yuengling Brewery** 570-628-4890 America's oldest brewery
has three tours daily.

1215.3   Side trail to campground

1217.6   Side trail to campground

🔥 ⛺ 🛏 **Blue Rocks Campground** 610-756-6366 Hiker rate $15
for tentsite, cabins $50-$70. Closed Nov-Apr.

SoBo	NoBo		Elev
946.5	**1232.6**	Fort Franklin Rd . . . . N40 41.655 W75 50.515 🅿	1400
944.3	**1234.8**	PA 309, Blue Mountain Summit . . . . . . N40 42.429 W75 48.516 🅿 **(pg.114)**	1360
942.6	**1236.5**	Power line.	1427
942.5	**1236.6**	New Tripoli Campsite. . . . . 🔹 🏕 (0.2W)	1400
941.5	**1237.6**	Knife Edge.	1550
940.8	**1238.3**	Bear Rocks.	1530
939.4	**1239.7**	Bake Oven Knob Rd . . . . N40 44.677 W75 44.314 🅿	1400
939.0	**1240.1**	Bake Oven Knob	1560
938.4	**1240.7**	**Bake Oven Knob Shelter** . . . . 🔹 🏕 ⌐ (6)	1380

26.5◄17.4◄10.0◄►6.8►23.5►37.3 Trail in front of shelter leads downhill to multiple water sources, more reliable farther down.

SoBo	NoBo		Elev
936.2	**1242.9**	Power line	1281
936.0	**1243.1**	Lehigh Furnace Gap, Ashfield Rd . . . . N40 46.173 W75 41.649 🅿	1320
931.6	**1247.5**	**George W. Outerbridge Shelter** . . . . 🔹 ⌐ (6)	1000

24.2◄16.8◄6.8◄►16.7►30.5►61.7 Reliable piped spring (0.1N).

SoBo	NoBo		Elev
931.0	**1248.1**	Lehigh River south bank, PA 873, **Slatington, PA** (2.0E) . . . . . . **(pg.114)**	380
930.9	**1248.2**	Lehigh River north bank, PA 145, **Walnutport, PA** (2.0E) . . . . . . **(pg.114)**	380
930.7	**1248.4**	PA 248, **Palmerton, PA** (1.5W) . . . . 🅿 **(pg.115)**	380

PA 248 is fast-moving and shoulderless, and so is not an easy hitch. Nobos intending to go into Palmerton should cross at traffic light and continue on the AT for 0.1 mile, where a clearly marked, level side trail leads 1.5 miles to town. Rocky climb from Lehigh Gap. Deforested ridge due to zinc smelting from1898-1980. Palmerton Superfund site.

SoBo	NoBo		Elev
926.7	**1252.4**	Power line	1571
925.7	**1253.4**	Little Gap . . . . N40 48.369 W75 32.077 🅿 **(pg.116)**	1100
		Danielsville, PA (1.5E)	
925.4	**1253.7**	Weathering Knob, views	1320

921.9	**1257.2**	Power line	1576
920.9	**1258.2**	Delps Trail . . . . N40 48.551 W75 27.073 **P** (0.7E)	1580
919.1	**1260.0**	Stempa Spring 0.6E . . . . ♦	1560
919.0	**1260.1**	Campsite . . . . **⅄**	1560
918.4	**1260.7**	Smith Gap Rd . . . . N40 49.327 W75 24.999 **P** (0.3E) **(pg.116)**	1550

914.9 **1264.2** **Leroy A. Smith Shelter** (0.2E). . . . .) ♦ ⅄ ⊏ (8) 1410
33.5◄23.5◄16.7◄►13.8►45.0►51.6 Water 0.2 mile down blue-blazed
trail; second source 0.2 mile further. Piped spring 0.5 mile down service
road.

913.3	**1265.8**	Pipeline	1467
911.3	**1267.8**	Hahns Lookout.	1500
910.6	**1268.5**	Power line.	1440
910.3	**1268.8**	PA 33, **Wind Gap, PA** (1.0E) . . . . . N40 51.639 W75 17.565 **P** **(pg.116-117)**	980
908.3	**1270.8**	Crest of ridge.	1640
903.3	**1275.8**	Wolf Rocks	1620

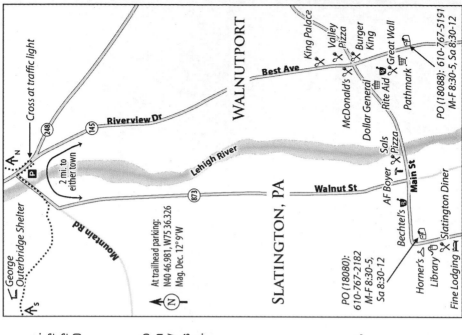

1234.8 PA 309

🛏🏕🍴⊠ **Blue Mountain Summit B&B** 570-386-2003, 877-386-2003 ⟨www.bluemountainsummit.com⟩ Just north of trail. $95-$125, no pets, ask about camping near restaurant, water at outside spigot at southwest corner of building, dining Th-Sa 11-10, Su 11-8, live music F7-10, all major credit cards accepted. Maildrops for guests: 2520 W Penn Pike, Andreas, PA 18211

1248.1 Lehigh Gap, PA 873

Slatington, PA 18080 (2.0E) *(more services on map)*

🛏🏨🛌⊠ **Fine Lodging** 610-760-0700 This is a residency hotel so call ahead. $39/up, access to microwave, $4 shower, well-behaved clean pets okay, limited computer use, alcohol in moderation. Free pickup/return from Lehigh Gap when available. Longer shuttles for donation as time permits. USPS/UPS Maildrops: 700 Main Street, Slatington, PA 18080. Please put "Fine Lodging" and ETA on packages.

🍴 **Slatington Diner** B/L

🛌 **Bechtel's Pharmacy** 610-767-4121

🛌 **Slatington Library** 610-767-6461 M,W: 9-7, Tu 9-3, F 9-5, Sa 8-2.

🔨 **AF Boyer Hardware**

1248.2 Lehigh Gap, PA 145

Walnutport, PA 18088 (2.0E) *(more services on map)*

🛒 **Pathmark Supermarket** 610-760-8008, M-Sa 6-12pm, Su 6-10.

🏬🛌 **Kmart** 610-767-1812

🍴 **King Palace Chinese Restaurant** 610-767-0151, AYCE lunch $5.75, also delivers.

🍴 **Valley Pizza Family Restaurant** 610-767-9000 L/D, delivers.

🍴 **Momma's Pizza** 610-767-5560.

➕ **St Luke's Family Practice Center** 610-760-8080

🛌 **Rite Aid Pharmacy** 610-767-9595

🐾 **Blue Ridge Veterinary Clinic** 610-767-4896 Call before coming.

1248.4   PA 248, east of Lehigh River Bridge
Palmerton, PA 18071 (1.5W)

(more services on map)

⌂ **Jail House Hostel** 610-826-2505, 443 Delaware Avenue. Spacious basement of the borough hall was never used as a jail. Hikers stay free; showers available. Check in at the borough office before 4:30pm on wkdays. Otherwise check in at police station after 4:30 and on wkends. 10pm curfew. ID is required. No vehicle assisted hikers. No pets inside, but they can be left tied outside.

✕ ⌂ **Palmerton Hotel** 610-826-5454, Caters to monthly renters but sometimes has a room available. Dining M-Th 4-10, F-Su 11-10, no pets, no smoking, all major credit cards accepted.

🛒 $ **Country Harvest Family Market** four blocks from hostel.

✕ ⌂ **Bert's Restaurant** B/L/D, close to hostel, has internet.

✕ **Tony's Pizzeria** L/D, no delivery. **Joe's Place** L/D, deli sandwiches. **Simply Something** B/L/D. **Palmerton Pizza, Hunan House Chinese Restaurant.**

✚ **Palmerton Hospital** 610-826-3141

🐾 **Little Gap Animal Hospital** 610-826-2793 Town Ordinance: Pets must be kept on leash. (3.5W) from town.

⚴ **Laundromat** across the street from hostel.

📖 **Palmerton Area Library** 610-826-3424, M 10-8, Tu-F 10-5, Sa 9-4

PO (18071):
610-826-2286
M-F 8:30-5,
Sa 8:30-12

Palmerton Hospital
✚ 610-826-3141

Library 610-826-3424
M 10-8, Tu-F 10-5, Sa 9-4

Convenient Mart/ATM
Subway
Rite Aid

Palmerton Pizza

One Ten Tavern
Gulf Quick Stop
State Rd / Red Hill Dr
Delaware Ave
Tony's Pizza
Shea's Hardware
Palmerton Hotel
Shipman's Pharmacy
Bert's Steakhouse
Towne Laundry
Jan's Barber Shop
Hunan House
Borough Hall / Jail House Hostel
Country Harvest

1st St
2nd St
3rd St
4th St
5th St
6th St

Lehigh River
(248)
↑ (1.5 mi. from PO)

1.0 mi

PALMERTON, PA

N

Pop. 5,209 (2008)
N40 47.975, W75 36.933
Mag. Dec. 12° 9' W
Grid Dim. 0.5 mi.

1253.4 Little Gap
Danielsville, PA 18038 (1.5E) on Blue Mountain Dr, then left on Mountainview Dr to PO and B&B.

 M-F 8-12 & 1-5, Sa 8-12, 610-767-6882

 Filbert B&B 610-428-3300 <www.filbertbnb.com> $75PP/up, includes full country breakfast. Will pickup at Lehigh, Little, or Smith Gaps. Call ahead for reservations, cash/checks only, owner Kathy. Maildrops: 3740 Filbert Dr, Danielsville, PA 18038.

 $ (0.8E) **Blue Mountain Restaurant & Ice Cream** 610-767-6379.

 (1.0E) **Miller's Market**

1260.7 Smith Gap Road
 (1.0W) Home of John "Mechanical Man" Stempa, eponym of the spring 0.7 miles south. The Stempas (610-381-4606) welcome you to get water from the spigot at rear of the house, to camp in their yard, and to use the outside shower. Water turned off in winter. If they are home, they will be even more accommodating. This is a safe place to park your car. If you do so please donate. For-fee shuttles ranging from 309 to Delaware Water Gap. Ask about stoves and fuel.

1268.8 PA 33
(0.1W) **Gateway Motel** 610-863-4959, $59S $65D $5EAP, $10 pet fee, sodas sold at office, free shuttle to town when available, welcome to refill water.

(4W) **Creature Comforts** 610-381-2287, 24/7 emergency animal care.

Wind Gap, PA 18091 (1.0E) *(more services on map)*

 M-F 8:30-5, Sa 8:30-12, 610-863-6206

 Travel Inn 610-863-4146, $52S $59 up to 4, pets $10.

 Giant Food Store 24hr

 K-Mart with pharmacy

 Turkey Hill Market

 Beer Stein L/D

 J&R's Smokehouse L/D

 Sal's Pizza 610-863-7565, delivers

 Hong Kong Chinese L/D buffet,

 CVS 610-863-5341

 Slate Belt Family Practice 610-863-3019

Also: Gap Theatre 610-863-3094

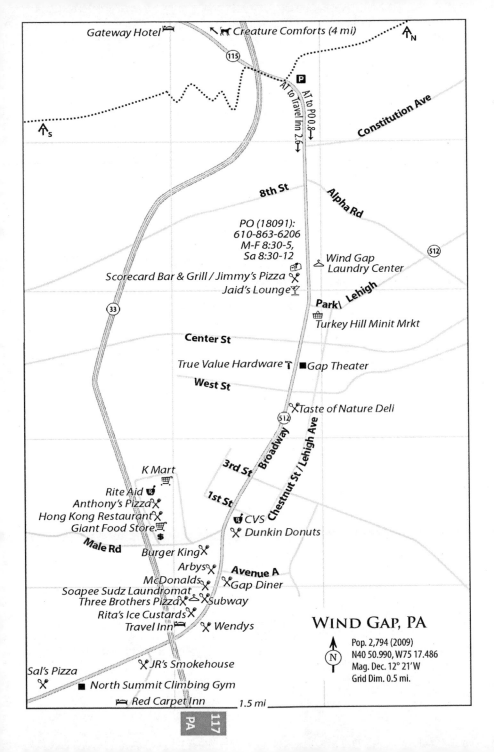

Gateway Hotel

Creature Comforts (4 mi)

115

A_N

P

AT to Travel Inn 2.6

AT to PO 0.8

A_S

Constitution Ave

8th St

Alpha Rd

512

PO (18091):
610-863-6206
M-F 8:30-5,
Sa 8:30-12

Wind Gap
Laundry Center

Scorecard Bar & Grill / Jimmy's Pizza

Jaid's Lounge

Park\ Lehigh

Turkey Hill Minit Mrkt

Center St

True Value Hardware

Gap Theater

West St

Taste of Nature Deli

512

Broadway

Chestnut St / Lehigh Ave

3rd St

K Mart

Rite Aid

Anthony's Pizza

Hong Kong Restaurant

Giant Food Store

1st St

CVS

Dunkin Donuts

Male Rd

Burger King

Arbys

Avenue A

McDonalds

Gap Diner

Soapee Sudz Laundromat

Three Brothers Pizza

Subway

Rita's Ice Custards

Travel Inn

Wendys

Sal's Pizza

JR's Smokehouse

North Summit Climbing Gym

Red Carpet Inn

1.5 mi

WIND GAP, PA

N

Pop. 2,794 (2009)
N40 50.990, W75 17.486
Mag. Dec. 12° 21'W
Grid Dim. 0.5 mi.

901.7 **1277.4** Fox Gap, PA 191 . . . . N40 56.126 W75 11.815 **P** 1320

901.1 **1278.0** **Kirkridge Shelter** . . . . **☽ ◗ ⌐** (6) 1500
37.3◄30.5◄13.8◄►31.2►37.8►43.6 Shelter on blue-blazed trail. Tap 0.1 mile to back left of shelter, off in cold months.

899.4 **1279.7** Power line. 1300
899.2 **1279.9** Totts Gap 1290

897.2 **1281.9** Mt Minsi 1461

896.2 **1282.9** Lookout Rock. 820
895.4 **1283.7** Council Rock 500
895.0 **1284.1** Hiker parking lot . . . . N40 58.788 W75 8.518 **P** 498
894.7 **1284.4** PA 611, **Delaware Water Gap, PA** . . . . **(pg.120)** 520
894.0 **1285.1** **PA-NJ** border, Delaware River Bridge west end 350

893.4 **1285.7** Kittatinny Visitor Center . . . . N40 58.219 W75 7.729 **P ◗ ⓘ** 360
Nobos cross under I-80 and turn left.
893.1 **1286.0** Parking, Water pump, For overnight parking, visitor center is preferred. ◗ 358
The sign "camping for A.T. through hikers" refers to a site 3.0N on AT.
892.8 **1286.3** Dunnfield Creek . . . . ◗ 366

891.5 **1287.6** Trail to Holly Spring . . . . ◗ (0.2E) 980

889.9 **1289.2** Backpacker Campsite-Worthington State Forest . . . . **Ａ** 1320
Pump at north end of parking lot where AT begins ascent. Camping at sites only, no fires, use bear boxes/poles, leash dogs.
888.6 **1290.5** Sunfish Pond, no camping 1382
888.5 **1290.6** Spring on side trail . . . . ◗ 1390

887.6 **1291.5** Brook . . . . ◗ 1450
887.1 **1292.0** Power line 1528

884.2 **1294.9** Camp Road (unpaved) . . . . N41 1.977 W75 0.237 **P (pg.120)** 1120
Mohican Outdoor Center (0.3W)

881.8 **1297.3** Catfish Fire Tower 1565
881.2 **1297.9** Rattlesnake Spring . . . . ◗ 1500
On dirt road about 17 yards west of AT.

SoBo	NoBo			Elev

880.8 **1298.3** Millbrook-Blairstown Rd . . . . N41 3.567 W74 57.815 🅿 🏃🏻 (1350
Millbrook Village (1.1W) historical park with picnic area.
880.2 **1298.9** Power line 1368

876.9 **1302.2** Blue Mtn Lakes Rd . . . . N41 5.357 W74 54.783 🅿 ⬥ 🏃🏻 (🚿 ⊏(16) 1350
Pump south of road and west of AT, no camping 0.5mi of road. Camp
Ken-Etiwa-Pec (0.6W), signs at road. Two screened shelters, no fee May-
Sep. Bunks open for thru-hikers before official season.

874.9 **1304.2** Crater Lake (0.5E) 1500

874.0 **1305.1** Buttermilk Falls Trail 1560

872.6 **1306.5** Stream . . . . ⬥ 1345
872.1 **1307.0** Rattlesnake Mountain 1492
871.8 **1307.3** Stream . . . . ⬥ 1260
871.3 **1307.8** Dirt road 1168

869.9 **1309.2** **Brink Road Shelter** (0.2W) . . . . ⬥ (0.2W) ⊏ (5) 1110
61.7◀45.0◀31.2◀▶6.6▶12.4▶15.3
Spring 100 yards to right. Bear box. Close to road.

868.2 **1310.9** Jacobs Ladder trail 1300

867.5 **1311.6** Viewpoint 1378

866.8 **1312.3** Power line 1300

866.3 **1312.8** US 206, Culvers Gap, **Branchville, NJ** (3.4E) . . . . **(pg.121)** 935
865.8 **1313.3** Sunrise Mountain Road . . . . N41 10.780 W74 47.277 🅿 958

864.4 **1314.7** Culvers Fire Tower 1500

863.4 **1315.7** Stony Brook . . . . ⬥ 1302
863.3 **1315.8** **Gren Anderson Shelter** (0.1W) . . . . ☽ ⬥ (0.1W) ⊏ (8) 1320
51.6◀37.8◀6.6◀▶5.8▶8.7▶13.0
Spring to left of shelter and downhill 70 yards.

860.9 **1318.2** Sunrise Mountain, no camping at pavilion 1653

860.1 **1319.0** Crigger Rd 1400

Sycamore Grill

Antelao Restaurant (upscale dining)

Edge of the Woods Outfitters 570-421-6681
Full line of gear, trail food, gear repair, Coleman/alcohol/oz. Shuttles from Little Gap to Bear Mtn. Maildrops (UPS or Fedex only): 110 Main St., Delaware Water Gap, PA 18327.

Pack Shack 570-424-8533 Gear, food, fuel/oz, shuttles and slackpacks. Leki repair and replacement.

Pocono Pony 570-893-6862 ⟨gomcta.com⟩ $1.25 each way to Stroudsburg Mall.

Martz Trailways 570-421-3040 $56.50 NYC roundtrip.

Pocono Cab 570-424-2800,

WGM Taxi 570-223-9289.

Stroudsburg, PA (3.5W)
Large town with all services, including motels, supermarket, laundry, and movie theater.

Dunkleberger's Sports 570-421-7950

Walmart 24hrs

1294.9   Camp Road (unpaved)
Mohican Outdoor Center (0.3W)
908-362-5670
⟨www.outdoors.org/lodging/lodges/mohican/⟩
$25PP in a cabin with bunk, stove, shower, and a towel. 2000-milers camp free, $2 for shower and towel. Six tent sites, each with a max four people. No campfires. Lobby with microwave open to all guests 8am-8pm. Water available at the lodge or a spigot near the garage on the right. Camp store open 9am-5pm with deli sandwiches, sodas, candy, Coleman/alcohol/oz, and limited hiker supplies. Operated by the AMC. UPS Maildrops (no USPS/FedEx): 50 Camp Road, Blairstown, NJ 07825.

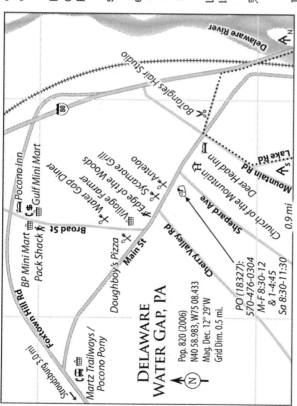

DELAWARE WATER GAP, PA

Pop. 820 (2006)
N40 58.983, W75 08.433
Mag. Dec. 12° 29'W
Grid Dim. 0.5 mi.

Martz Trailways / Pocono Pony — Stroudsburg 3.0 mi.

Foxtown Hill Rd
BP Mini Mart
Pack Shack
Broad St
Gulf Mini Mart
Pocono Inn
Water Gap Diner
Village Farmer
Edge of the Woods
Sycamore Grill
Antelao
Doughboy's Pizza
Main St
Shepard Ave
Cherry Valley Rd
Deer Head Inn
Church of the Mountain
Mountain Rd
Lake Rd
Bortongies Hall Studio
80
Delaware River
N

PO (18327):
570-476-0304
M-F 8:30-12
& 1-4:45
Sa 8:30-11:30

0.9 mi

1284.4   PA 611, *Delaware Water Gap, PA* (more services on map)

The Church of the Mountain Hostel 570-476-0345 Bunkroom with showers, overflow lean-to and tent, rides to Stroudsburg when available, donations encouraged. No drive-ins, no parking, no laundry. Phone numbers of persons who can be of assistance to hikers are posted in the hostel.

Pocono Inn 570-476-0000 $55.20. Recently remodeled, restaurant/lounge planned for 2010.

Deer Head Inn 570-424-2000 $100/up no TV. Restaurant & lounge open to all. Live music Th-Su, hiker attire okay.

Water Gap Diner B/L/D, **Doughboy's Pizza** open 7 days in summer.

Village Farmer & Bakery Hot dog and slice of pie $2.49.

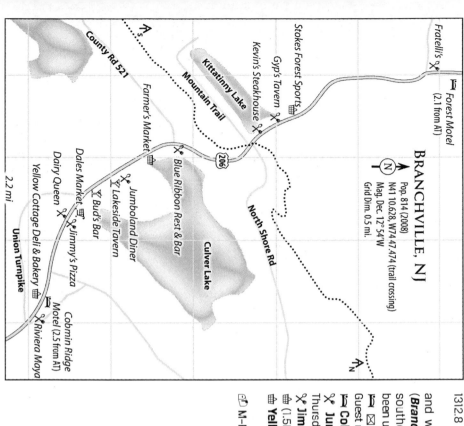

BRANCHVILLE, NJ

Pop. 814 (2008)
N41 10.628, W74 47.474 (trail crossing)
Mag. Dec. 12° 54'W
Grid Dim. 0.5 mi.

(map labels)
Fratelli's
Forest Motel (2.1 from AT)
County Rd 521
Stokes Forest Sports
Kittatinny Lake
Mountain Trail
Kevin's Steakhouse
Gyp's Tavern
206
North Shore Rd
Blue Ribbon Rest & Bar
Farmer's Market
Culver Lake
Jumboland Diner
Lakeside Tavern
Bud's Bar
Dales Market
Jimmy's Pizza
Dairy Queen
Yellow Cottage Deli & Bakery
Cobmin Ridge Motel (2.5 from AT)
Riviera Maya
Union Turnpike
2.2 mi.

1312.8 Culvers Gap, US 206 (*more services on map*) Many businesses are within 3 miles east and west from the trail crossing. The center of town (*Branchville, NJ*) and post office is about 3.4 miles to the southeast (trail east). **Joe to Go**, just west of the trail, has been unwelcoming to hikers in the past.

🛏️ ✉️ **Forest Motel** 973-948-5456, $50S $60D, pets $20. Guest maildrops: 104 US 206, Branchville, NJ 07826.

🛏️ **Cobmin Ridge Motel** 973-948-3459

✕ **Jumboland Diner** B/L/D, $2.99 breakfast special and Thursday dinner buffet.

✕ **Jimmy's Pizza & Pasta** closed M,

🏪 (1.5E) **Dale's Market** 973-948-3078

🏪 **Yellow Cottage Deli & Bakery**
Branchville, NJ 07826 (3.4E)
M-F 8:30-5, Sa 8:30-1, 973-948-3580

| 857.5 | **1321.6** | **Mashipacong Shelter** 43.6◄12.4◄5.8◄►2.9►7.2►19.6 . . . . . ☽ ⌐ (8) | 1425 |

Spring (0.6N) on red-blazed Iris Trail. Bear box.

| 857.3 | **1321.8** | Deckertown Turnpike . . . . N41 15.136 W74 41.367 🄿 | 1400 |

| 854.6 | **1324.5** | **Rutherford Shelter** (0.4E) . . . . ☽ ♦ ▲ ⌐ (6) | 1345 |

15.3◄8.7◄2.9◄►4.3►16.7►28.3 Spring 100 yards before shelter on connecting trail. Shallow, slow running stream. Bear box.

| 852.0 | **1327.1** | NJ 23 .N41 18.275 W74 40.182 🄿 ♦ (pg.124) | 1500 |

High Point State Park Headquarters

| 850.8 | **1328.3** | Side trail to High Point Monument . . . . | 1803 |
| 850.3 | **1328.8** | **High Point Shelter** (0.1E) . . . . ☽ ♦ ⌐ (8) | 1280 |

13.0◄7.2◄4.3◄►12.4►24.0►36.0 Streams on both sides of shelter. Road to privy to right of shelter. Bear box.

| 849.0 | **1330.1** | County 519 . . . . | 1180 |

848.3	**1330.8**	Streams	♦	991
848.2	**1330.9**	Courtwright Rd		859
847.6	**1331.5**	Pond	♦	900

847.0	**1332.1**	Fergerson Rd, east 120 yards on road.		859
846.5	**1332.6**	Small Brook	♦	729
846.4	**1332.7**	Gemmer Rd		740
846.1	**1333.0**	Stream, second of three footbridges	♦	695

845.4	**1333.7**	Goodrich Rd		610
845.2	**1333.9**	Pond	♦	633
845.0	**1334.1**	Trail to privately owned cabin, welcome to get water (0.2W)	♦	660
844.6	**1334.5**	Goldsmith Lane		669
844.1	**1335.0**	Unionville Rd, Country Rd 615 . . . . (pg.124)		610
843.9	**1335.2**	Quarry Rd		626
843.2	**1335.9**	Lott Rd, **Unionville, NY** (0.4W) . . . . (pg.124)		600

| 842.2 | **1336.9** | NJ 284 . . . . N41 17.631 W74 33.369 🄿 ⌂(0.4W) | 420 |

End of the Line Grocery deli, ATM, M-S 6–9, Sa–Su 6:–7

| 841.7 | **1337.4** | Lower Rd . . . . | 510 |

| 840.7 | **1338.4** | Wallkill River, Oil City Rd, State Line Rd . . . . . N41 17.005 W74 31.562 🄿 | 396 |

| 838.4 | **1340.7** | Lake Wallkill Rd, Liberty Corners Rd . . . . ♦ | 440 |
| 837.9 | **1341.2** | **Pochuck Mountain Shelter** (0.1W) . . . . ☽ ▲ ⌐ (6) | 840 |

19.6◄16.7◄12.4◄►11.6►23.6►37.9 Spigot at vacant house at foot of Pochuck Mtn. Bear box.

SoBo	NoBo			Elev
836.4	**1342.7**	Pochuck Mountain		1194
835.8	**1343.3**	Woods road, Lovemma Lane		1061
835.7	**1343.4**	Stream . . . . ♦		995
835.3	**1343.8**	Stream . . . . ♦		777
835.2	**1343.9**	County Rd 565, **Glenwood, NJ** (1.1W) . . . . ♦ **(pg.124)**		700
		Small creek west of road.		
833.7	**1345.4**	Country Rd 517 . . . . N41 14.142 W74 28.830 🅿 **(pg.124)**		410
		Glenwood, NJ (1.1W)		
833.0	**1346.1**	Pochuck Creek suspension footbridge.		380
		Boardwalk over swamp for (0.6S) and (0.2N) of footbridge.		
832.3	**1346.8**	Canal Rd . . . . N41 13.597 W74 28.137 🅿		565
832.1	**1347.0**	Bridge over Wawayanda Creek . . . . ♦		403
831.4	**1347.7**	NJ 94, **Vernon, NJ** (2.4E) . . . . N41 13.159 W74 27.313 🅿 **(pg.125)**		450
830.0	**1349.1**	Wawayanda Mountain		1340
829.2	**1349.9**	Stream, footbridge . . . . ♦		1121
828.3	**1350.8**	Barrett Rd, **New Milford, NY** (1.8W) . . . . **(pg.125)**		1240
827.6	**1351.5**	Stream, intermittent . . . . ♦		1054
827.2	**1351.9**	Iron Mountain Road Bridge		1170
826.6	**1352.5**	Wawayanda Rd		1200
826.4	**1352.7**	**Wawayanda Shelter** (0.4E) . . . . 🌙 ♦ 𝗔 ⌐ (6)		1200
		28.3◄24.0◄11.6◄►12.0►26.3►31.6 Water 0.4 east of AT.		
826.2	**1352.9**	Wawayanda State Park (0.3E) . . . . N41 11.883 W74 23.847 🅿 ♦ 🚻 🌲		1200
825.9	**1353.2**	Warwick Turnpike . . . . N41 12.088 W74 23.483 🅿		1140
825.4	**1353.7**	Brook . . . . ♦		1206
824.5	**1354.6**	Long House Rd (Brady Road) . . . . N41 11.732 W74 22.290 🅿		1200
823.4	**1355.7**	Long House Creek. . . . . ♦		1180
823.0	**1356.1**	Small stream . . . . ♦		1261
822.3	**1356.8**	**NJ-NY** border, State Line trail 1.0E to **Lakeside, NJ**		1395
		Hitchhiking is illegal in NY; camp only in designated sites;		
		fires allowed only within official campsite fire rings.		
821.9	**1357.2**	Prospect Rock, Highest point on AT in NY		1433
		Views of Greenwood Lake to east.		
820.9	**1358.2**	Furnace Brook . . . . ♦		1245
820.7	**1358.4**	Stream, seasonal . . . . ♦		1250
819.7	**1359.4**	Brook. . . . . ♦		1100
819.3	**1359.8**	Cascade Brook . . . . ♦		1102
818.9	**1360.2**	Small Brook . . . . ♦		1101
817.9	**1361.2**	Village Vista Trail		1100
817.2	**1361.9**	Brook, outlet of marsh . . . . ♦		1150
816.8	**1362.3**	Power line.		1160
816.4	**1362.7**	NY 17A, **Bellvale, NY** (1.6W) . . . . . . N41 14.658 W74 17.216 🅿 **(pg.125)**		1110
		Greenwood Lake, NY (2.0E)		
815.1	**1364.0**	Eastern Pinnacles		1294

1327.1 NJ 23

High Point State Park Headquarters 973-875-4800, Office open year-round. Water spigot outside.

2.5 mile from headquarters is campground, swim area, concession stand, grill, and hot showers. $20 night, 6 per site. No pets or alcohol. Open Apr 1 - Oct 31.

(1.5E) **High Point Country Inn** 973-702-1860 $79D, continental breakfast, laundry $7, soda available, pets okay, no room phone. Free pick-up/return to trail, local restaurants & resupply. Longer shuttles for a fee. Guest maildrops: 1328 NJ 23, Wantage, NJ 07461.

Port Jervis, NY (4.4W)

Comfort Inn 845-856-6611, wkdays $109.99, wkends $129.99, $10 EAP, continental breakfast, dog fee $20. Guest maildrops: 2247 Greenville Turnpike, Port Jervis, NY 12771.

Best Western 570-491-2400, wkdays $89, wkends $120, $10 EAP, continental breakfast, pets $10 (4 rooms only), restaurant B/L/D, sauna and heated pool.

Brookside Cottages 845-856-6548, open mid-May-Sep, $65D, laundry $5, some cottages with shower/kitchen/heat/TV, no phone, behaved pets allowed, Visa/MC accepted. Dunkin Donuts across the street with phone.

Village Pizza 973-293-3364

Little Caesars Pizza 570-491-4436

Shop Rite Markets, Price Chopper

Rite Aid, 845-856-8342, **Medicine Shoppe**, 845-858-6681

Bon Secours Community Hospital 845-858-7000

Tri-States Veterinary Medical 845-856-1914

1335.0   Unionville Road
1335.9   Lott Road

Unionville, NY 10988 (0.5W) from either road

M-F 8-11:30 & 1-5, Sa 9-12, 845-726-3535

Hikers may use **Unionville Memorial Park** to pitch a tent, has a pavilion, go to Horler's General Store to fill out permission slip.

Back Track Inn 845-726-3956, bunks at bar $3PP, sleeps 4-6, bar serves meals wkdays 2pm-12am, wkends 2pm-2am, restroom use during bar hours, cash only.

Horler's Store M-Sa 6-9, Su 7-7, open 7 days

Also: Trail angel Dick Ludwick 845-726-3894, offers laundry and shower, donations welcome.

1343.9   Country Road 565
1345.4   Country Road 517

Glenwood, NJ 07418 (1.1W from either road)

M-F 7:30-5, Sa 10-2, 973-764-2616

Apple Valley Inn 973-764-3735, $130-$160, includes country breakfast, no pets, shuttles to Country Roads 517 & 565 with stay. Guest maildrops: PO Box 302, Glenwood, NJ 07418.

Pochuck Valley Farm, deli, outside water spigot, and restroom. Open daily M-F 5-6:30, Sa-Su 5-6.

1347.7   NJ 94

⊕ (0.1W) **Heaven Hill Farm** 973-764-5144, 7 days, 9-5, ice cream and bakery.

⌂ (1.8E) **Appalachian Motel** 973-764-6070, $69-99, pets $25.

Vernon, NJ 07462 (2.4E)

⛺ ⓗ ⌂ ⅏ Located in **St. Thomas Episcopal Church,** capacity 12, stay limited to one night, no pets, towel, refrigerator, microwave, and cooking in kitchen by permission, $10PP donation. Hikers may have to share space with other groups and are expected to help with cleanup. No alcohol is permitted. Hikers not staying for Sunday services must be out by 9:30am.

✗ **Rigatoni's, Mixing Bowl, Place By the Tracks, Alpine Pizza Restaurant** 973-827-4804, **Long Spring Chinese Restaurant, Burger King**

🍴 🛒 **A&P Food Store**

⊞ **Newton Memorial Hospital** 973-383-2121, **Vernon Urgent Care** 973-209-2260, 1.1 miles beyond hostel, M-F 8-8, Sa-Su 9-5.

🐾 **Vernon Veterinary Hospital** 973-764-3630

🔧 **Rite Aid**

⚒ **K&C Washer**

📚 **Dorothy Henry Library** M/W/F 9-5, Tu/Th 9-8:30.

1350.8   Barrett Road

New Milford, NY 10959 (1.8W)

✉ M-F 8:30-12:30 & 2-4:30, Sa 9-11:30, 845-986-3557

1362.7   NY 17A

▲ (0.2W) **Bellvale Farms,** ice cream, water from hose.

Bellvale, NY 10912 (1.6W)

✉ M-F 8-11:30 1-4:30, Sa 9-12, 845-986-2880

Greenwood Lake, NY 10925 (2E)

✉ M-F 8-5, Sa 8-12, 845-477-7328

⌂ ✗ $ **Breezy Point Inn** 845-477-8100 <www.breezypointinn.com> rooms begin at $85, no pets, no smoking, L/D dining 7 days.

⌂ ✗ ⌂ 🐾 ✉ **Anton's on the Lake** 845-477-0010 800-754-8835 <www.antonsonthelake.com> thru hikers $80S/D Su-Th, all major CC, rooms with whirlpool available, no pets, no smoking, laundry small loads only, swimming, pub/restaurant B/L/D, offers free shuttles and slackpacking with stay, open year round, very hiker friendly. You can pick up a commuter bus out front for about $10 that will take you into Time Square for the day. Maildrops: PO Box 1505, Greenwood Lake, Warwick, NY 10925.

✗ **Subway, Sing Loong Kitchen, Ashley's Pizzeria & Café, Delicious Deli, Doc's Pizza & Steak**

⊕ **Country Grocery, Cumberland Farms** with deli sandwiches 24/7.

💊 **CVS Pharmacy**

📚 **Greenwood Lake Public Library** M/F 9-5, Tu-Th 9-9, Sa 10-4, Su 11-3.

🚕 **Greenwood Lake Taxi** 845-477-0314

🔧 **Greenwood True Value Hardware**

Warwick, NY 10990 (4.5W)

✉ M-F 8:30-5, Sa 9-4, 845-986-0271

✗ **Mamma's Boy Pizza** 845-986-1802, deli sandwiches, 7 days.

🍴 **Shop Rite Supermarket**

🐾 **Dr Flanigan's Veterinary** 845-988-0171, **Orchard Grove Animal Hospital** 845-983-9399

⊞ **St Anthony Community Hospital** 845-986-2276

💊 **CVS, Akin's Pharmacy, Rite Aid**

🧺 **South Street Wash & Fold, Warwick Laundry Center**

📚 **Albert Wisner Public Library** 845-986-1047, M-Th 9-8, F-Sa 9-5, Su 12-4.

814.8	**1364.3**	Brook								1038
814.6	**1364.5**	Cat Rocks								1050
814.4	**1364.7**	Stream								1065
814.3	**1364.8**	**Wildcat Shelter** (0.2W) ☽ ♦ ⛺ ⌐ (8)								1180

36.0◄23.6◄12.0◄►14.3►19.6►22.7 Water on trail to shelter.

812.8	**1366.3**	Lakes Rd								680
812.6	**1366.5**	Bridge over Trout Brook								648
812.5	**1366.6**	Fitzgerald Falls								820
812.4	**1366.7**	Trout Brook and tributary								850
810.5	**1368.6**	Mombasha High Point								1280

NYC skyline sometimes visible to the southeast.

809.3	**1369.8**	West Mombasha Rd. N41 16.159 W74 12.876 🅿								990
809.2	**1369.9**	Stream, outlet to Kloibers Pond								719
808.9	**1370.2**	Stream								1022
808.4	**1370.7**	Buchanan Mountain								1142
807.6	**1371.5**	East Mombasha Rd								796
806.9	**1372.2**	Little Dam Lake								750
806.2	**1372.9**	Orange Turnpike N41 16.167 W74 10.862 🅿 ♦ (0.5E)								800
805.5	**1373.6**	Arden Mountain								1180
804.4	**1374.7**	NY 17, **Southfields, NY** (2.1E), **Harrriman, NY** (3.7W) **(pg.128)**								550
804.2	**1374.9**	New York State Thruway 87								560
804.0	**1375.1**	Arden Valley Rd N41 15.922 W74 9.229 🅿								550
802.1	**1377.0**	Lemon Squeezer								1140
801.9	**1377.2**	Island Pond Mountain								1303
801.0	**1378.1**	Surebridge Mountain								1269
800.7	**1378.4**	Surebridge Brook								1135
800.0	**1379.1**	**Fingerboard Shelter** ♦ ⌐ (8)								1300

37.9◄26.3◄14.3◄►5.3►8.4►39.4 Spring downhill to left is unreliable. Dependable water at Lake Tiorati, (0.5E) on Hurst Trail.

| 799.4 | **1379.7** | Fingerboard Mountain | | | | | | | | 1328 |
| 798.9 | **1380.2** | Arden Valley Rd N41 16.542 W74 5.286 🅿 🚻 🚿 | | | | | | | | 1196 |

(0.3E) Lake Tiorati Circle, restrooms, showers, beach, and vending machines. Open during summer.

796.9	**1382.2**	Stream								1076
796.7	**1382.4**	Seven Lakes Drive								830
795.9	**1383.2**	Goshen Mountain								1295
794.7	**1384.4**	**William Brien Memorial Shelter** ⌐ (8)								1070

31.6◄19.6◄5.3◄►3.1►34.1►43.1 Unreliable spring-fed well 80 yards down blue-blazed trail to right of shelter.

| 793.3 | **1385.8** | Black Mountain | | | | | | | | 1160 |

SoBo	NoBo			Elev
792.6	**1386.5**	Palisades Interstate Parkway . . . . (林♦ ⓘ		680
		Visitor center (0.4W), soda & snack machines. NY City 34E.		
792.4	**1386.7**	Beechy Bottom Brook . . . . ♦		680
792.1	**1387.0**	Beechy Bottom Rd		666
791.6	**1387.5**	**West Mountain Shelter** (0.6E) . . . . ⌐ (8)		1240
		22.7◄8.4◄3.1◄►31.0►40.0►47.8		
790.0	**1389.1**	Seven Lakes Drive		650
788.4	**1390.7**	Bear Mountain, Harriman State Park. . . . . . . .N41 18.670 W74 0.434 🅿 ♦		1305
		Unreliable hand pump at summit.		
786.6	**1392.5**	**Bear Mountain, NY** . . . . **(pg.128)**		155
785.9	**1393.2**	Trailside Museum & Zoo **Fort Montgomery, NY** (1.8W) . . . . . **(pg.128)**		124
785.8	**1393.3**	Bear Mountain Bridge over Hudson River		131
785.1	**1394.0**	NY 9D		145
784.6	**1394.5**	Camp Smith Trail, 0.6E to Anthonys Nose, views		700
783.6	**1395.5**	Hemlock Springs Campsite . . . . ♦ ⋀		550
783.4	**1395.7**	South Mountain Pass (Manitou Road) . . . . . . N41 19.776 W73 57.195 🅿		460
782.3	**1396.8**	Unmarked woods road.		783
780.0	**1399.1**	US 9, **Peekskill, NY** 10566 (4.5E) . . . . **(pg.129)**		400
779.9	**1399.2**	Old Highland Turnpike		464
779.4	**1399.7**	Old West Point Rd, **Graymoor Spiritual Life Center** . . . . . **(pg.129)**		515
778.1	**1401.0**	Denning Hill		960
776.7	**1402.4**	Old Albany Post Rd, Chapman Rd		620
775.1	**1404.0**	Brook. . . . . ♦		350
775.0	**1404.1**	Canopus Hill Rd . . . . **(pg.129)**		420
774.0	**1405.1**	South Highland Rd		650
772.8	**1406.3**	Stream . . . . ♦		675
771.3	**1407.8**	Dennytown Rd. . . . . N41 25.234 W73 52.135 🅿 ♦ ⋀		830
		Water on side of pump building, open late-Apr-Oct.		
		Dennytown Camp 0.1W on paved road and 0.1W on dirt road.		

1374.7   NY 17
Southfields, NY 10975 (2.1E)

📬 M-F 8-12 & 1-5, Sa 8:30–11:30, 845-351-2628

🏨 ⚕ **Tuxedo Motel** 845-351-4747, $44.50S, 49.50D, $10EAP, no pets, accepts Visa/MC.

Harriman, NY (3.7W)

✗ **Corner Deli**

$ ATM located across the street from Southfields.

Lodging, groceries, restaurants, and laundromats.

1392.5   **Bear Mountain, NY**
(more services on map)

📬 M-F 8-10, 845-786-3747 Note limited hours before sending a maildrop.

1393.2   **Trailside Museum and Zoo**

10–4:30; no charge for hikers passing through. Dogs not allowed. Lowest elevation on the AT, 124 ft above sea level, is within the park. If you have a dog, or if the zoo is closed, use the bypass (see map).

Fort Montgomery, NY (1.8W)
(more services on map)

🏨 ⊠ **Bear Mountain Bridge Motel** 845-446-2472, $69S, $75D, no pets, accepts Visa/MC, shuttles back to trail with stay. Guest maildrops: PO Box 554, Fort Montgomery, NY 10922.

🏨 **Econo Lodge** 845-446-9400, $71.995, $99.99D, pets $10.

🏨 ⚕ ⊠ ⏚ **Holiday Inn Express** 845-446-4277, $110 standard room, includes continental breakfast, pool. Maildrops: 1106 Route 9 W, Fort Montgomery, NY 10922.

🏨 **Victorian Riverview Inn** 845-446-5479, $175/room.

🏨 **Overlook Lodge** 845-786-2731, $119/up, includes continental breakfast, no pets.

✗ **Bagel Café** ATM, **Tony's Pizzeria** 845-446-4000, **Dunkin' Donuts, Fox's Country Deli**

🛒 **Key Foods** (2.0N)

🛒 ✗ **$ M & R Market** deli, restaurant, hiker box.

🛒 **Food Mart**

⏚ **Highland Falls Library**

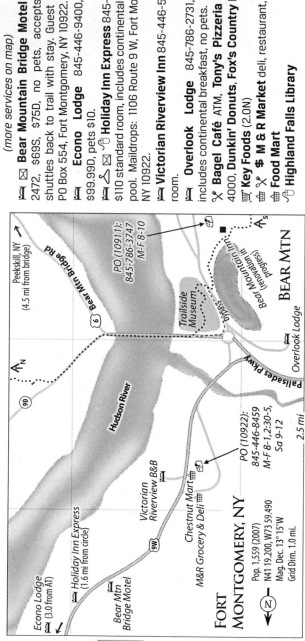

Econo Lodge
(3.0 from AT) 🏨

🏨 ⚕ Holiday Inn Express
(1.6 mi from circle)

Bear Mtn
Bridge Motel 🏨

Hudson River

Peekskill, NY
(4.5 mi from bridge) →

Bear Mtn Bridge Rd

PO (10911):
845-786-3747
M-F 8-10

Trailside
Museum

Ⓐₙ

⑨⓪

⑥

bypass

Beer Mountain Inn
(renovation in
progress)

BEAR MTN

Ⓐₛ

Overlook Lodge 🏨

Palisades Pkwy

9W

Victorian
Riverview B&B 🏨

Chestnut Mart 🛒
M&R Grocery & Deli 🛒

PO (10922):
845-446-8459
M-F 8-1, 2:30-5,
Sa 9-12

FORT
MONTGOMERY, NY

Ⓝ

Pop. 1,559 (2007)
N41 19.200, W73 59.490
Mag. Dec. 13° 15'W
Grid Dim. 1.0 mi.

2.5 mi

845-446-3113, M 10-5, Tu 10-7, W-F 10-5, Sa 10-2.

1399.1   US 9

🏛 **Appalachian Market** at trailhead

Peekskill, NY 10566 (4.5E) large town with all services

🖃 M-F 9-5, Sa 9-4, 914-737-6437

1399.7   Old West Point Road

Graymoor Spiritual Life Center (0.4E)
800-338-2620 Hikers permitted to sleep at monastery's ball field picnic shelter which has water, privy, and shower during warm months. Open all season and free. Follow signs and blue-blazes; stay to the left at both forks in the road.

1404.1   Canopus Hill Rd
🏛 (1.6E) **Putnam Valley Market** 845-528-8626
Directions: (0.3E) on Canopus Hill Rd, (0.1S) on Canopus Hollow Rd, (1.2W) on Sunset Hill Road. Pizza, hot food from the grill, phone, ATM, open M-Sa 6-9, Su 6-7.

770.6 **1408.5** Stream . . . . ♦ 794

769.7 **1409.4** Sunk Mine Rd 800
769.6 **1409.5** Bridge over stream . . . . ♦ 745

767.6 **1411.5** NY 301, **Clarence Fahnestock State Park** (1E) . . . . ▲ 🚿 🚻 (900
845-225-3998, Open 3rd Fri in Apr – 2nd Sun Sept, tent sites $15
766.7 **1412.4** Rocky stream . . . . ♦ 1101

765.4 **1413.7** Small stream . . . . ♦ 1021
764.8 **1414.3** Small stream . . . . ♦ 985

763.4 **1415.7** Shenandoah Mountain 1282
763.0 **1416.1** Long Hill Rd 1060
762.5 **1416.6** Stream, intermittent . . . . ♦ 999

761.9 **1417.2** Shenandoah Tenting Area (0.1W) , hand pump . . . . ♦▲ 905

760.8 **1418.3** Bridge over brook . . . . ♦ 355
760.6 **1418.5** Hortontown Rd, ... N41 30.843 W73 47.509 🅿 ☽ ♦ ⌐(6) 350
RPH Shelter (1982) 39.4◄34.1◄31.0◄►9.0►16.8►25.5
Shelter open Apr-mid-Nov, grounds available year-round. Iron water
pump to left of shelter (treatment recommended).
760.3 **1418.8** Taconic State Pkwy 540
759.0 **1420.1** Brook . . . . ♦ 900

757.1 **1422.0** Hosner Mountain Rd 400

755.5 **1423.6** NY 52, **Stormville, NY** (1.9W) . . . . **(pg.132)** 800

754.4 **1424.7** Stormville Mountain Rd (south end) over I-84 1050
754.3 **1424.8** Mountain Top Rd (south end) 972
754.1 **1425.0** Grape Hollow Rd 960

752.2 **1426.9** Stream . . . . ♦ 1210
751.7 **1427.4** Mt Egbert 1329
751.6 **1427.5** **Morgan Stewart Shelter** . . . . ☽ ♦ ⌐ (6) 1285
43.1◄40.0◄9.0◄►7.8►16.5►20.5

750.5 **1428.6** Depot Hill Rd . . . . N41 34.288 W73 40.840 🅿 1280

SoBo	NoBo			Elev
748.7	**1430.4**	Railroad track, Whakey Lake Stream	♦	684
748.6	**1430.5**	Old Route 55		750
748.3	**1430.8**	NY 55 .... N41 35.380 W73 39.551 **P** (0.1W) **(pg.132)**		720
		Poughquag, NY (3.1W)		
747.4	**1431.7**	Stream	♦	702
747.0	**1432.1**	Stream	♦	730
746.6	**1432.5**	Nuclear Lake		760
744.8	**1434.3**	Penny Rd		1080
744.3	**1434.8**	West Mountain		1200
743.8	**1435.3**	**Telephone Pioneers Shelter** (0.1E)	☾ ♦ ⊏ (6)	910
		47.8◄16.8◄7.8◄►8.7►12.7►21.1 ▷		
		Trail to shelter crosses stream. If dry, get water from residence 0.7N.		
743.1	**1436.0**	County Rd 20, West Dover Rd, **Pawling, NY** (3.1E)	♦ **(pg.132)**	600
		Dover Oak north side of road, largest oak tree on AT. Girth 20'4" and estimated to be over 300 years old. Spigot on fence post at the residence just east of the trail. Please help yourself, they would prefer that you do not interrupt them to ask permission.		
740.8	**1438.3**	**Appalachian Trail Railroad Station**	**(pg.132)**	480
740.7	**1438.4**	NY 22, **Wingdale, NY** (4.0W) ...... N41 35.629 W73 35.224 **P** **(pg.132)**		480
739.8	**1439.3**	Stream	♦	670
738.8	**1440.3**	Stream	♦	899
735.5	**1443.6**	Leather Hill Rd		750
735.1	**1444.0**	**Wiley Shelter**	☾ ♦ ⋏ ⊏ (6)	740
		25.5◄16.5◄8.7◄►4.0►12.4►19.7 Pump (0.1N), treat water.		
734.9	**1444.2**	Duell Hollow Rd and Brook 0.1 apart		600
733.9	**1445.2**	**NY-CT** border, Hoyt Rd .... N41 38.508 W73 31.248 **P**		400
		Campfires prohibited in CT. Camping only in designated sites.		
733.4	**1445.7**	Brook, reliable	♦	429
733.2	**1445.9**	CT 55, **Gaylordsville, CT** (2.5E) ..... N41 38.679 W73 31.155 **P** **(pg.133)**		490
		Wingdale, NY (3.3W)		
732.1	**1447.0**	Ten Mile Hil		1100
731.1	**1448.0**	**Ten Mile River Lean-to** (0.1E)	☾ ♦ ⋏ ⊏	290
		20.5◄12.7◄4.0◄►8.4►15.7►25.7 Well/pump to east at camping area by river. Group campsites across river and up trail to left.		
730.9	**1448.2**	Ten Mile River, Ned Anderson Memorial Bridge	♦ ⋏	280
730.2	**1448.9**	Bulls Bridge Rd	**(pg.133)**	350
729.5	**1449.6**	Schaghticoke Rd		350
728.9	**1450.2**	**CT-NY**		349
727.8	**1451.3**	Schaghticoke Mountain (in NY)		1330

1423.6   NY 52

🚰 ✕ ((0.4E) **Mountain Top Market Deli,**
Open daily 6–8, welcome to water from faucet on side of building.
✕ **Danny's Pizzeria**

Stormville, NY 12582 (1.9W)

📮 M–F 8:30–5, Sa 9–12, 845-226-2627
🏪 **Stormville Grocery**
✕ **Stormville Pizza**

1430.8   NY 55

✕ (0.2E) **The Elite Dog**
Mobile hot-dog stand parks at east intersection, open Apr–Dec.
🛒 ✕ ((1.5W) Pleasant Ridge Plaza with **Poughquag Central Market, Pleasant Ridge Pizza** L/D.
🅱 (1.2W) **CVS**
✕ **R's Gulf Quickmart & Deli** 845-452-4040.

Poughquag, NY 12570 (3.1W)

📮 M–F 8:30–5, Sa 8:30–12:30, 845-724-4763
🛏 **Pine Grove Motel** 845-724-5151, $65S $70D, no pets, accepts Visa/MC.
✕ **Great Wall, Clove Valley Deli & Café**
🐾 **Total Care Pharmacy , Beekman Pharmacy**
🐾 **Beekman Animal Hospital** 845-724-8387

1436.0   County Road 20, West Dover Road

Pawling, NY 12564 (3.1E)

📮 M–F 8:30–5, Sa 9–12, 845-855-2669
🏠 🛁 ⊠ **Sharadu B&B** 305-826-3198, hiker rate available, with continental breakfast, no pets, call ahead, closed during the winter. Guest maildrops: 107 East Main Street, Pawling, NY 12566.
⛺ 🚿 (**Edward R. Murrow Memorial Park** Town allows hikers to camp in park, 1 mile from the center of Main Street, park offers

lake swimming, no pets, two-night maximum.
✕ **Great Wall II Take Out Chinese** 845-855-9750
✕ **Hong Kong Chinese Kitchen**
✕ **Mama Pizza II** 845-855-9270
✕ **Vinny's Deli & Pasta**
✕ **Gaudino Pizzeria**
✕ **McKeever's Restaurant** L/D
🛒 🅱 **Hannaford Supermarket & Pharmacy** (2S) on NY 22.
🛒 🅱 **A&G Food Market** (3.4S) on NY 22.
🏪 **Family Quick Stop**
🅱 **CVS**
🧺 **Laundromat**
📖 **Pawling Free Library** Tu–Th 10-8, F-Sa 10-4.
🚆 **MTA Metro-North Railroad** 212-532-4900 Train service to NYC.

1438.3   **Appalachian Trail Railroad Station**
🚆 **Metro-North Railroad** 212-532-4900
⟨www.mta.info\mnr\index.html⟩ New York City commuter train runs in the afternoons and is a two hour ride in each direction. One way: Peak $21, Off Peak $12. Round Trip: Peak $31.50, Off Peak $24.

1438.4   NY 22

✕ ⊞ ☕ ⚹ (0.6E) **Tony's Deli** sandwiches, salads, soda machine outside. Open daily 5-midnight.

Wingdale, NY 12594 (4.0W)

⊞ M-F 8-5, Sa 8-12:30, 845-832-6147

🛏 ⚘ **Dutches Motor Inn** 845-832-6400, $65S/D, guest laundry $7, pets allowed.

✕ **Adam's Diner** 24 hrs, **Big W's Roadside Barbeque, Jacye's Bar & Grill, Peking Kitchen**

🍴 **Wingdale Supermarket**

⊞ **Ben's Store** deli, hot foods.

🔧 **Wingdale Hardware**

🏛 **Dover Plains Library** M-F 10-8, Sa 10-4.

1445.9   CT 55

Gaylordsville, CT 06755 (2.5E)

⊞ $ ☕ M-F 8-1 & 2-5, Sa 8-12, 860-354-9727

✕ $ ☕ **Gaylordsville Country Store** deli

✕ **Gaylordsville Diner, Alfredo's, White Peach.** W-Th 5:30-9, F-Sa 5:30-10, Su 12-9, Closed M-Tu.

Wingdale, NY (3.3W) listed above

✕ (2.5W) **Buttonwood Café** M/W 9-3, Th-F 9-5, Sa-Su 9-5, bakery serving B/L and ice cream.

1448.9   Bulls Bridge Rd (0.5E) to market and restaurant

⊞ $ **Country Market** fruit, Ben & Jerry's, water, ATM.

✕ **Bulls Bridge Inn**

Gary Monk (trail name "Blaze") counted every white blaze he passed during his 2002 northbound thru-hike. There were 80,900. I wouldn't tell anyone about getting lost.

SoBo	NoBo		1000	2000	3000	4000	5000	6000	Elev
726.6	**1452.5**	**NY-CT**							1250
726.5	**1452.6**	Stream						◊	1224
726.2	**1452.9**	Indian Rocks							1320
725.6	**1453.5**	Schaghticoke Mountain Campsite						◊▲	990
723.7	**1455.4**	Thayer Brook							950
722.7	**1456.4**	**Mt Algo Lean-to** . . . . ☽◊▲⌐							655
		21.1◄12.4◄8.4◄►7.3►17.3►29.6							
722.4	**1456.7**	CT 341, Schaghticoke Rd, **Kent, CT** (0.8E) . . . .**(pg.138-139)**							350
722.3	**1456.8**	Macedonia Brook							350
719.6	**1459.5**	Skiff Mountain Rd							780
718.9	**1460.2**	Calebs Peak							1160
718.2	**1460.9**	St. Johns Ledges, 91 stone steps down to Housatonic River.							895
717.7	**1461.4**	River Rd						🅿	425
717.1	**1462.0**	North Kent Brook						◊	378
715.4	**1463.7**	**Stewart Hollow Lean-to** . . . . ☽◊▲⌐(6)							400
		19.7◄15.7◄7.3◄►10.0►22.3►29.8							
715.0	**1464.1**	Stony Brook Campsite . . . . ◊▲							435
713.0	**1466.1**	River Rd . . . . N41 48.342 W73 23.697 🅿 ◊							439
712.2	**1466.9**	Silver Hill Campsite . . . . ☽◊▲							1000
		Water from pump							
711.3	**1467.8**	CT 4, **Cornwall Bridge, CT** (0.9E) . . . . **(pg.139)**							670
711.2	**1467.9**	Guinea Brook . . . . ◊							690
		High water bypass east on CT 4, unpaved Old Sharon Rd							
711.1	**1468.0**	Old Sharon Rd							700
709.9	**1469.2**	Hatch Brook							880
709.2	**1469.9**	Pine Knob Loop Trail							1170
708.8	**1470.3**	Caesar Rd, Caesar Brook Campsite . . . . ▲							800
706.6	**1472.5**	Carse Brook . . . . ◊							800
706.5	**1472.6**	West Cornwall Rd, **West Cornwall, CT** (2.2E), **Sharon, CT** (4.7W) **(pg.139)**							800
706.3	**1472.8**	Pass through cracked bolder similar to lemon squeezer..							840
705.4	**1473.7**	**Pine Swamp Brook Lean-to** . . . . ☽◊▲⌐(6)							1075
		25.7◄17.3◄10.0◄►12.3►19.8►21.0							

SoBo	NoBo			Elev
704.5	1474.6	Sharon Mountain Rd		1070
704.2	1474.9	Mt Easter		1350
703.0	1476.1	Sharon Mountain Campsite, stream nearby..	⚑▲	1210
700.2	1478.9	Belters Campsite	⚑▲	770
699.8	1479.3	US 7, CT 112 . . . . N41 55.928 W73 21.840	🅿	550
699.2	1479.9	US 7, Housatonic River (be attentive for possible reroute notice) . .	⛺✗	500
		Mountainside Café & Cottages 860-824-7886, cabin $75, B/L/D M-Th 6:30-2, F 6:30-9, Sa 7-9.		
699.1	1480.0	Mohawk Trail		550
697.3	1481.8	Hydro plant, shower	�🚿	550
697.2	1481.9	Iron Bridge, **Falls Village, CT**	(pg.139)	550
696.6	1482.5	Housatonic River Rd N41 57.736 W73 22.442	🅿	750
696.1	1483.0	Spring	⚑	860
693.8	1485.3	Prospect Mountain		1475
693.1	1486.0	**Limestone Spring Lean-to** (0.5W) . . . . ☽⚑▲⌐(6)		1200
		29.6◀22.3◀12.3◀▶7.5▶8.7▶17.5 Road 0.25 further. Follow stream to spring coming out of small limestone cave.		
693.0	1486.1	Rands View. No camping.		1375
692.6	1486.5	Giants Thumb		1260
692.2	1486.9	Billys View		1190
689.7	1489.4	US 44, **Salisbury, CT** (0.4W)	(pg.140)	700
689.0	1490.1	US 41, Undermountain Rd. N41 59.616 W73 25.588	🅿(pg.140)	680
		Salisbury, CT (0.8W)		
688.8	1490.3	Stream	⚑	700
687.2	1491.9	Stream	⚑	1150
686.3	1492.8	Lions Head		1738
685.6	1493.5	**Riga Lean-to** . . . . ☽⚑▲⌐(6)		1610
		29.8◀19.8◀7.5◀▶1.2▶10.0▶10.1 Tent platform behind shelter.		
685.0	1494.1	Ball Brook Campsite.	⚑▲	1705
684.4	1494.7	**Brassie Brook Lean-to**. . . . . ☽⚑▲⌐(6)		1705
		21.0◀8.7◀1.2◀▶8.8▶8.9▶23.2 Stream 20 yards north on AT.		
683.7	1495.4	Bear Mountain Rd		1900

SoBo	NoBo			Elev
			1000 2000 3000 4000 5000 6000	
683.0	1496.1	Bear Mountain		2316
682.3	1496.8	**CT-MA** border		1850
682.2	1496.9	Sages Ravine Brook Campsite	♦ ⛺	1380
		Tent platforms and campsites. No campfires.		
681.6	1497.5	Sages Ravine	♦	1340
680.4	1498.7	Spring	♦	1420
680.3	1498.8	Laurel Ridge Campsite	☽ ♦ ⛺	1650
		platforms, bear box. No fires.		
678.5	1500.6	Race Mountain		2430
677.4	1501.7	Race Brook Falls Trail	♦ ⛺ (0.4E)	1980
676.7	1502.4	Mt Everett, road		2602
676.0	1503.1	Guilder Pond Picnic Area, road	☽	2042
675.6	1503.5	**The Hemlocks Lean-to**	☽ ♦ ⌐ (10)	1880
		17.5◄10.0◄8.8◄►0.1►14.4►19.7 Bear box. Water on AT 0.1N.		
675.5	1503.6	**Glen Brook Lean-to**, 2 tent platforms.	☽ ♦ ⛺ ⌐ (6)	1885
		10.1◄8.9◄0.1◄►14.3►19.6►21.4 Bear box, Reliable stream to left.		
674.9	1504.2	Elbow Trail		1780
673.2	1505.9	Jug End		1750
672.1	1507.0	Jug End Rd, (Curtiss Rd)	N42 8.665 W73 25.893 🅿 ♦	850
		Reliable piped spring (0.2E).		
671.2	1507.9	MA 41	**(pg.140)**	620
		South Egremont, MA (1.2W)		
669.6	1509.5	Hubbard Brook	♦	672
669.4	1509.7	South Egremont Rd.	N42 8.809 W73 23.153 🅿	700
		Sheffield Rd, Shays Rebellion Monument.		
667.9	1511.2	West Rd		620
667.7	1511.4	Railroad tracks		673
667.6	1511.5	US Hwy 7, Main St, **Great Barrington, MA** (3.0W)	**(pg.140-141)**	620
		Sheffield, MA (3.3E)		
666.7	1512.4	Housatonic River, Kellogg Rd	N42 8.637 W73 21.572 🅿	610
666.3	1512.8	Broadman Street		700
664.7	1514.4	Homes Rd		1100
663.9	1515.2	Spring at bottom of cleft	♦	1605
663.3	1515.8	East Mountain	♦	1800
661.2	1517.9	Ice Gulch, **Tom Leonard Lean-to**	☽ ♦ ⛺ ⌐ (10)	1540
		23.2◄14.4◄14.3◄►5.3►7.1►21.1 Campsite overlooking ravine north of		
		lean-to. Stream 0.2 on path to left or 0.3 on path to right.		

660.1	**1519.0**	Lake Buel Rd, parking area with kiosk. . . . . N42 10.471 W73 17.639 🅿	1100
659.7	**1519.4**	Stream . . . . 💧	1000
659.2	**1519.9**	MA 23 . . . . N42 11.038 W73 17.436 🅿 **(pg.141)**	1000
		East Mountain Retreat Center (1.0W)	
658.7	**1520.4**	Stream, intermittent . . . . 💧	1350
658.0	**1521.1**	Blue Hill Rd, Stony Brook Rd	1500
657.2	**1521.9**	Benedict Pond, (0.5W) on blue-blazed trail to . . . . (💧 🛖	1610
		Beartown State Forest Beach, picnic area, phone, tent sites $10.	
656.6	**1522.5**	The Ledges	1813
656.0	**1523.1**	Stream, east of AT . . . . 💧	1813
655.9	**1523.2**	**Mt Wilcox South Lean-to** . . . . 🌙 💧 🛖 ⌐ (6)	1720
		19.7◄19.6◄5.3◄►1.8►15.8►24.6 Spring crossed en route to lean-to. 5 tent platforms. Privy downhill 0.2mi.	
654.7	**1524.4**	Swann Brook . . . . 💧	1800
654.1	**1525.0**	**Mt Wilcox North Lean-to** (0.3E) . . . . 🌙 💧 ⌐ (10)	2100
		21.4◄7.1◄1.8◄►14.0►22.8►31.6	
653.5	**1525.6**	Beartown Mountain Rd . . . . 💧	1805
653.0	**1526.1**	East Brook . . . . 💧	1700
650.3	**1528.8**	Fernside Rd . . . . 💧	1200
650.0	**1529.1**	Shaker Campsite; platforms, cables. Water north on AT. . . . . 🌙 🛖	995
649.9	**1529.2**	Hop Brook. . . . . 💧	875
648.2	**1530.9**	Jerusalem Rd . . . . 💧	1100
		West on road, before first house, look for sign and piped spring.	
647.1	**1532.0**	Main Rd, **Tyringham, MA 01264** (0.6W)	930
		📬 M–F 9–12:30 & 4–5:30, Sa 8:30–12:30, 413-243-1225	
		🛏 **Cobble View B&B** 413-243-2463, $110 and up, includes continental breakfast, no pets, no smoking, Visa/MC accepted.	
645.2	**1533.9**	Webster Rd . . . . 💧	1800
643.7	**1535.4**	Spring on unmarked side trail (0.1W) . . . . 💧	1734
642.8	**1536.3**	Goose Pond Rd. . . . . N42 16.459 W73 11.025 🅿 (0.1E)	1650
642.4	**1536.7**	Cooper Brook. . . . . 💧	1551
640.9	**1538.2**	Upper Goose Pond	1480
640.1	**1539.0**	**Upper Goose Pond Cabin** (0.5W) . . . . **(pg.141)**	1483
		21.1◄15.8◄14.0◄►8.8►17.6►34.3	

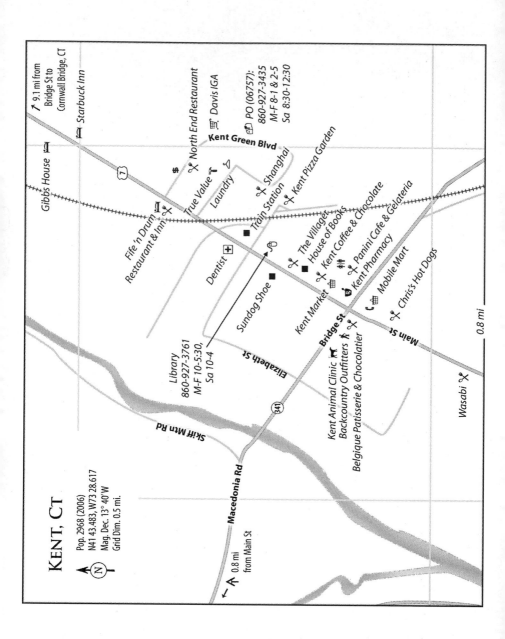

KENT, CT

Pop. 2968 (2006)
N41 43.483, W73 28.617
Mag. Dec. 13° 40'W
Grid Dim. 0.5 mi.

9.1 mi from
Bridge St to
Cornwall Bridge, CT

Starbuck Inn

Gibbs House

North End Restaurant

Davis IGA

PO (06757):
860-927-3435
M-F 8-1 & 2-5
Sa 8:30-12:30

Kent Green Blvd

True Value

Laundry

Shanghai

Kent Pizza Garden

Train Station

Fife 'n Drum
Restaurant & Inn

The Village
House of Books

Kent Coffee & Chocolate

Dentist

Panini Cafe & Gelateria

Sundog Shoe

Kent Market

Kent Pharmacy

Mobile Mart

Chris's Hot Dogs

Bridge St

Library
860-927-3761
M-F 10-5:30,
Sa 10-4

Elizabeth St

Kent Animal Clinic

Backcountry Outfitters

Belgique Patisserie & Chocolatier

Main St

Skiff Mtn Rd

Macedonia Rd

Wasabi

0.8 mi

0.8 mi
from Main St

1456.7 CT 341, Schaghticoke Road

Kent, CT 06757 (0.8E) *(more services on map)*

[icons] **Fife 'n Drum Inn & Restaurant** 860-927-3509 (www.fifendrum.com) rooms with hiker rates $95D wkdays, $121D wkends, $25 EAP + tax, no pets. Call for reservations, front desk closed Tu. Guest maildrops: for USPS P.O. Box 188, Kent, CT 06757, for FedEx/UPS 53 N Main Street, Kent, CT 06757.

[icons] **Gibbs House B&B** 860-927-1754 $145/up for single or double. Ask in advance about shuttles with stay.

[icons] **Cooper Creek B&B** 860-927-4334, $85 hiker rate. (2.5N) of town via US 7. Shuttles provided to/from trail head and town with stay. Maildrops: 230 Kent Cornwall Road, Kent, CT 06757.

[icons] **Starbuck Inn** 860-927-1788 $180/up for single or double. Sometimes discounted mid-week. Credit cards accepted, no pets.

[icons] **Backcountry Outfitters** 860-927-3377, 888-549-3377 (www.bcoutfitters.com) M-Sa 9-6, Su 10-4. In summer hours extended till 8:30 every day. Fuel/oz, iso-butane, backpacking gear and supplies. Ice cream & grill inside serving hot dogs, coffee and other snacks. Shuttles anywhere. Maildrops: 5 Bridge Street, Kent, CT 06757.

Also: House of Books UPS services, open daily 10-5:30.

1467.8 CT 4

Cornwall Bridge, CT 06754 (0.9E)

[icons] (1N) of town on US 7, **Housatonic Meadows State Park** campsite $13(1-4)/$2EAP, 6 per site, open mid-Apr to Sep, registration information at main cabin by gate, no alcohol, accessible from the AT via Pine Knob Loop Trail.

[icons] **Hitching Post Motel** 860-672-6219, $65S, $75D, wkends $95/up, pets $5, laundry $5, shuttle when available. Maildrops: 45 Kent Road, Cornwall Bridge, CT 06754.

[icons] **Baird's General Store** groceries, deli, ice cream.

[icons] **Housatonic River Outfitters** 860-672-1010 (www.dryflies.com) some hiker gear, white gas/alcohol/oz.
Housatonic Veterinary Care 860-672-4948, closed Su & W.
Also: Cornwall Package Store 860-672-6645, closed Su, water spigot outside. Stopping to sign their register can be refreshing.

1472.6 West Cornwall Road

West Cornwall, CT 06796 (2.2E)

[icons] M-F 8:30-1 & 2-4:30, Sa 9-12, 860-672-6791
Berkshire Country Store deli
Wandering Moose Café 860-672-0178

Sharon, CT 06069 (4.7W)

[icons] M-F 8:30-4:30, Sa 9:30-12:30, 860-364-5306
Sharon Motor Lodge 860-364-0036 (www.sharonmotorlodge.com) Su-Th $75S/D, small pets only.
Country Corner Restaurant
Trotta's Supermarket
Sharon Pharmacy
Sharon Hospital 860-364-4141
Queen B Cleaner 7 days 7-9.

1481.9 Iron Bridge (Housatonic River)

Falls Village, CT 06031

[icons] M-F 3:30-1 & 2-5, Sa 8:30-12, 860-824-7781, from where the Trail meets the parking lot at the end of the nature trail, it is 0.5 mile east on Water Road to the village center.
Toymakers Café 860-824-8168, B/L, Th-F 7-2, Sa-Su 7-4, free tent sites, hiker friendly, knock on upstairs door if closed.
Pizza Restaurant

$199S/D, all non-smoking, pet rooms available, includes continental breakfast.

✗ **Chaiwalla** 860-435-9758, W-Su 10-6. Hiker friendly tea room.

✗ **Country Bistro, Holly's Place, Roast** B/L, **Thyme-Enz Harvest** B/L, **Bev's Ice Cream**

📖 **Scoville Memorial Library**
Tu 10-7, W 10-5, Th 10-7, F 10-5, Sa 10-4, Su 1-4.

₿ **Salisbury Pharmacy**

1507.9   MA 41

South Egremont, MA 01258 (1.2W)

🏤 M-F 8:15-12 & 12:30-4, Sa 9-11:30, 413-528-1571

ⓘ **ATC New England Regional Office** 413-528-8002 in the Kellogg Conservation Center.

🛏✗✉ **The Egremont Inn** 413-528-2111
⟨www.egremontinn.com⟩
M-Th hiker rate $75S/D, includes breakfast, return ride to trail. Maildrops: 10 Sheffield Road, PO Box 418, South Egremont, MA 01258

🏪 **Country Market** deli

✗ **Mom's Restaurant** pizza, ice cream

1511.5   US 7, Main St.

🛒(1.5W) **Guido's** with organic produce, cold juices, and more.

Great Barrington, MA 01230 (3.0W)

🏤 M-F 8:30-4:30, Sa 8:30-12:30, 413-528-3670

🛏⛺✉ **Monument Mountain Motel**
413-528-3272, wkdays $50S $65D. Maildrops: 247 Stockbridge Road, Rt 7, Great Barrington, MA 01230

SALISBURY, CT

Pop. 3,958 (2008)
N41 59.010, W73 25.330
Mag. Dec. 13° 47'W
Grid Dim. 0.5 mi.

Under Mtn. Rd. — Cobble Rd. — Cemetery — 41 — 44 — Main St. — Maria McCabe — Grove St. — White Hart Inn — Salisbury Pharmacy — Chaiwalla — The Roast Coffee Shop (internet access) — Sweet Williams Bakery — Vanessa Breton — Country Bistro — LeBonnes Market

Town Hall 860-435-1287

Library 860-435-2838
Closed Mon.
Tu,Th 10-7
W,F 10-5
Sat 10-4
Sun 1-4

P.O. (06068):
860-435-5072
M-F 8-1 & 2-5, Sa 9-12

0.8 mi

1489.4   US 44, Lower Cobble Road (0.4W)
1490.1   US 41/Undermountain Road (0.8W)

Salisbury, CT 06068 (more services on map)

🛏 **Maria McCabe** offers rooms in her home, 860-435-0593, $35PP, includes shower, use of living room, shuttle to coin laundry/store, cash only, 4 Grove Street.

🛏⛺✉ **Vanessa Breton** offers rooms in her home, 860-435-9577, cell 860-318-1037 four beds $35PP. Maildrops for guests: 7 The Lock Up Road, Salisbury, CT 06068.

🛏✗ **White Hart Inn** 860-435-0030 Recently renovated to larger rooms and so there is no longer a hiker. Regular rates start at $299. Hikers welcome in the tap room and in the restaurant which serves B/L/D.

🛏 **Iron Masters Motor Inn** 860-435-9844, wkdays $130S, $140D $15EAP, wkend

🏨⛺ **Travel Lodge** 413-528-2340 hiker rate Su-Th $55
🏨 **Mountain View Motel** 413-528-0250, $50S, $65D, higher on weekends.
🏨⛺🐾✉ **Comfort Inn** 413-644-3200, $115/up, includes cont B, indoor heated pool and hot tub, no pets. Maildrops with advanced reservation: 249 Stockbridge Rd, Rt 7, Great Barrington, MA 01230.
🍴🐾 **Big Y Foods** 7days
🍴🐾 **Price Chopper**
➕ **Fairview Hospital** 413-528-0790
💊 **Bills Pharmacy**, cash only for bus tickets
🐾 **All Caring Animal Ctr** 413-528-8020
⛺ **Laundromat**, 24 hrs
🔧 **Auburchon Hardware**

Sheffield, MA 01257 (3.3E on US Hwy 7)

🏨✉ M-F 9-4:30, Sa 9-12, 413-229-8772
🏨✉ **Racebrook Lodge** 413-229-2916 ⟨www.rblodge.com⟩ Su-Th $85-$170, F-Sa $115-245, includes B, $20 pets, dinner Th-Su only, pool, accepts Visa/MC/Amex, open year-round. Maildrops for guest: 864 S Undermountain Road, Sheffield, MA 01257
🍴 **Sunrise Diner, The Bridge, Bogies Restaurant & Pub**
🛒 **Gretta's Market & Deli**
🔧 **Hardware store**

1519.9   MA 23
🏨⛺✉ (1W) **East Mountain Retreat Center** 413-528-6617 ⟨www.eastretreat.org⟩ left 1.0 mile, blue sign on left, $10PP donation suggested, shower, laundry $3, pizzeria delivers to hostel, 10pm curfew and 8:30am checkout, cash only, UPS/FedEx maildrops only: 8 Lake Buel Road, Great Barrington, MA 01230.
🍴 (2.7W) **Panda Garden** L/D, Chinese
Great Barrington, MA (4W) (see above)

1539.0   ***Upper Goose Pond Cabin*** (0.5W)
★📖(14) ▲) ◐ On side trail north of pond. Fireplace, covered porch, bunks with mattresses. Swimming and canoeing. Open daily Memorial Day-late-Sep & weekends late-Oct. During summer, caretaker brings water; otherwise, pond is water source. Tent platforms. When caretaker not in residence, hikers may camp on porch or tent platforms. Donations requested.

🚌 **BRTA** Commuter bus service connects the trail towns of **Great Barrington, Dalton, Cheshire, North Adams, Adams, Williamstown, Pittsfield** and **Lee** and the Berkshire Mall. Buses run M-F and Sa until 6pm. Fares $1.25/town up to $4.40. Drivers cannot make change. Flag a bus from anywhere on the route. For routes call: 800-292-2782.

SoBo	NoBo		Elev
638.9	**1540.2**	MA Turnpike I-90	1400
638.8	**1540.3**	Greenwater Brook . . . . ♦	1361
638.5	**1540.6**	US 20, **Lee, MA** (5.0W) . . . . N42 17.537 W73 9.579 🅿 (0.1W) **(pg.144)**	1400
637.7	**1541.4**	Tyne Rd / Becket Rd.	1500
637.2	**1541.9**	Becket Mountain	2180
636.2	**1542.9**	Walling Mountain, wooded summit	2220
635.7	**1543.4**	Finerty Pond south side . . . . ♦	1926
635.4	**1543.7**	Finerty Pond northwest side . . . . ♦	1900
634.1	**1545.0**	Washington Mountain Brook . . . . ♦	1820
633.1	**1546.0**	County Rd.	1850
632.9	**1546.2**	Bald Top	2040
631.3	**1547.8**	**October Mountain Lean-to** . . . . 🌙♦🏕️⛺ (12)	1950
		24.6◄22.8◄8.8◄▶8.8▶25.5▶32.1 Cables. Stream intermittent.	
630.6	**1548.5**	West Branch Rd, Left/west to Lenox	1950
629.1	**1550.0**	Washington Mountain Rd . . . . N42 22.635 W73 9.061 🅿 **(pg.144)**	2000
		Becket, MA 01223 (5.0E)	
627.1	**1552.0**	Stream . . . . ♦	1900
625.9	**1553.2**	Blotz Rd, small parking lot on north side . . . . . N42 24.561 W73 9.017 🅿	1800
625.2	**1553.9**	Warner Mountain	2050
622.6	**1556.5**	Power lines	1896
622.5	**1556.6**	**Kay Wood Lean-to** (0.2E) 31.6◄17.6◄8.8◄▶16.7▶23.3▶33.2 🌙♦⛺ (10)	1860
622.2	**1556.9**	Grange Hall Rd	1650
622.0	**1557.1**	Barton Brook . . . . ♦	1480
620.1	**1559.0**	Railroad tracks	1250
619.5	**1559.6**	MA 8 & 9, **Dalton, MA** . . . . **(pg.144)**	1200
618.5	**1560.6**	Gulf Rd/High Street . . . . 🅿	1176

SoBo	NoBo			Elev
615.8	**1563.3**	Power lines		1914
614.8	**1564.3**	Crystal Mountain Campsite, ...	☾ ♦ ⋀ (0.2E)	2100
		Five tent platforms. Water on AT just north of side trail.		
614.4	**1564.7**	Gore Brook, outlet of Gore Pond		2050
611.9	**1567.2**	The Cobbles Outcroppings of marble with view of Hoosic		1800
		River Valley, Mt Greylock , and the town of Cheshire.		
611.0	**1568.1**	Furnace Hill Rd (south end)		964
610.6	**1568.5**	Church St + School St, **Cheshire, MA**	**(pg.145)**	974
610.4	**1568.7**	School St (north end)		988
610.2	**1568.9**	MA 8, **Cheshire, MA, Adams, MA** (4.0E)	**(pg.145)**	1000
609.4	**1569.7**	Outlook Avenue		1300
609.0	**1570.1**	Power line		1355
606.7	**1572.4**	Old Adams Rd		2300
605.8	**1573.3**	**Mark Noepel Lean-to** (0.2E)	☾ ♦ ⋀ ⌁ (10)	2800
		34.3◄25.5◄16.7◄►6.6►16.5►23.7		
		Spring to right of lean-to, runs stronger the further you go.		
605.2	**1573.9**	Jones Nose Trail, Saddle Ball Mountain		3238
604.4	**1574.7**	Stream	♦	3100
603.3	**1575.8**	Rockwell Rd . . . . N42 37.864 W73 10.696 🅿		3119
603.0	**1576.1**	Notch Rd		3250
602.5	**1576.6**	Mt Greylock, highest peak in MA.	**(pg.146)**	3491
602.1	**1577.0**	Thunderbolt Ski trail		3114
600.2	**1578.9**	Mt Williams		2951
599.3	**1579.8**	Notch Rd	♦	2300
599.2	**1579.9**	**Wilbur Clearing Lean-to** (0.3W)	☾ ♦ ⌁ (8)	2300
		32.1◄23.3◄6.6◄►9.9►17.1►23.0 West on Money Brook Trail. Several tent		
		sites behind shelter. Intermittent stream to right.		
597.1	**1582.0**	Pattison Rd . . . . ♦ N42 41.256 W73 9.586 🅿		900
596.6	**1582.5**	Phelps Ave (south end)		633
596.2	**1582.9**	MA 2 . . . . N42 41.941 W73 9.208 🅿 (0.1E) **(pg.146-147)**		650
		Williamstown, MA (west), **North Adams, MA** (east)		
596.1	**1583.0**	Hoosic River, footbridge		618
596.0	**1583.1**	Massachusetts Ave		693

1540.6 US 20
Lee, MA 01238 (5W)

M-F 8:30-4:30, Sa 9-12, 413-243-1392

Americas Best Value Inn 413-243-0501 <www.bestvalueinn.com> Su-Th $60/up, F-Sa $110-$195, busy on weekends in Jul-Aug with Tanglewood Music Festival.

Roadway Inn 413-243-0813 Su-Th $79S $99D, F-Sa $159S $179D.

Pilgrim Inn 413-243-1328 Su-Th $95D, F-Sa $225D.

Athena's Pizza House, Friendly's, Joe's Diner, and many more.

Price Chopper Supermarket 413-528-2408

Rite Aid

Valley Veterinary Clinic 413-243-2414

Lee Coin-Op Laundry

1550.0 Washington Mountain Road
Becket, MA 01223 (5E)

M-F 8-4, Sa 9-11:30, 413-623-8845

(0.1E) Home of the **"Cookie Lady"** 413-623-5859, Water spigot near the garage door, please sign register on the steps. Homemade cookies are often available; pick your own blueberries at reasonable rates. Camping allowed; ask permission first. Shuttles, maildrops (call ahead to arrange): Roy and Marilyn Wiley, 47 Washington Mountain Road, Becket, MA 01223.

1559.6 MA Routes 8 & 9
Dalton, MA (more services on map)

Thomas Levardi 83 Depot Street, allows hikers to use water spigot outside his home and provides the hospitality of his front porch and back yard for tenting (get permission first).

Shamrock Village Inn 413-684-0860, pets allowed with $75 deposit, accepts Visa/MC/Amex, restaurant serves L/D and breakfast on weekends, closed Monday.

Duff & Dell's Variety B/L, closed Su. **Angelina's Subs** with veggie burgers, **Dalton Restaurant** serves D Th-Sa with live entertainment.

Dalton Laundry, closed Su, provides towel and wash cloth for clean-up in bathroom sink, coffee and TV while you wait.

LP Adams sells Coleman/denatured alcohol.

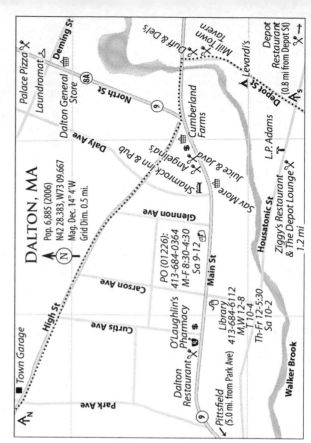

DALTON, MA

1568.5 Church St + School St
1568.9 MA 8

Cheshire, MA *(more services on map)*

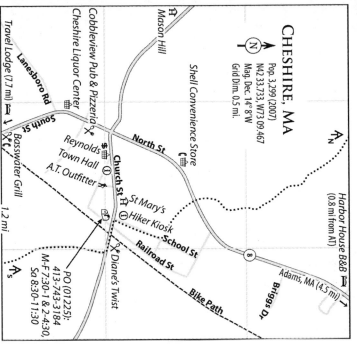

Mason Hill / Wayside Hiking Hostel
413-743-2492 Bunk $25 tent $15. Two 2-person private cabins; one for $40 and the other $50. Shower without stay $5, laundry $5, free internet. Shuttles covering all of MA.

CHESHIRE, MA
Pop. 3,299 (2007)
N42 33.733, W73 09.467
Mag. Dec. 14°8'W
Grid Dim. 0.5 mi.

Map labels:
Mason Hill
Shell Convenience Store
North St
Cobbleview Pub & Pizzeria
Cheshire Liquor Center
Lanesboro Rd
South St
Reynolds
Town Hall
A.T. Outfitter
Church St
St Mary's
Hiker Kiosk
School St
Basswater Grill
Travel Lodge (7.7 mi)
Diane's Twist
Railroad St
Briggs Dr
Bike Path
Adams, MA (4.5 mi)
Harbor House B&B (0.8 mi from AT)
1.2 mi
PO (01225): 413-743-3184 M-F 7:30-1 & 2-4:30, Sa 8:30-11:30

St. Mary of the Assumption Church Check in with Father David Raymond. Two hiker rooms, use of restrooms and outside cooking area. No laundry or showers. Welcome to attend service in hiker attire. Please donate. Maildrops: 159 Church Street, Cheshire, MA 01225.

Harbour House Bed & Breakfast 413-743-8959 ⟨www.harbourhouseinn.com⟩ $85 hiker rate, includes breakfast, no pets, no smoking, shuttle to trail with stay. Operated by Eva. Maildrops for guest: 725 North State Rd, Cheshire, MA 01225

AT Bicycle Works & Outfitters 413-822-5357 ⟨www.atbicycleworks.com⟩ Some hiker supplies, Coleman/alcohol by ounce and iso-butane, owner 2005 thru hiker Larry "Draggin' Dragon. No regular hours, call and he will open shop for you.

Cobbleview Pub, Bass Water Grill, Diane's Twist, M-Su 11:30-9, deli sandwiches, soda, ice cream

HD Reynolds a general store, hiker snacks and Coleman fuel.

BRTA stops across the street from the post office.

Adams, MA (4.0E)

M-F 8:30-4:30, Sa 10-12, Su 11-4, hiker supplies, Coleman/alcohol/oz, minor equipment repairs.

Mount Greylock Inn 413-743-2665 ⟨www.mountgreylock-inn.com⟩ $89-$159, includes breakfast, D $25, kitchen access, one load of laundry free with stay, accepts MC only, open year round

Big Y Foods supermarket

Berkshire Outfitters 413-743-5900 ⟨www.berkshireoutfitters.com⟩ M-Sa 10-5, Su 11-4, hiker supplies, Coleman/alcohol/oz, minor equipment repairs.

Rite Aid, Medicine Shop

Adams Veterinary Clinic 413-743-4000

Thrifty Bundle Laundromat, Waterworks, many fast-food outlets

1576.6　Summit Road, Mt Greylock
Mt Greylock is Massachusetts highest peak at 3,491 ft. On top of the mountain is Veterans War Memorial Tower and views of the Green, Catskill, and Taconic mountain ranges and surrounding towns. No camping or fires on summit.

🏠 Bascom Lodge on summit 413-743-1591 private rooms $100/up, bunkroom $35, shower w/towel $5, snacks, phone, restaurant serves B/L/D.

1582.9　MA 2
P Greylock Community Club 413-664-9020 Allows parking; ask first.

Williamstown, MA (2.6W) (more services on map)
Redwood Motel 413-664-4351 ⟨www.redwood-motel.com⟩ $69.99-119.99, major CC accepted.
Williamstown Motel 413-458-5202 $59 wkdays, $69 wkends, includes cont B. Will pickup at Route 2. Major CC accepted. Maildrops: 295 Main Street, Williamstown, MA 01267.
The Villager Motel 413-458-4046, 877-986-6835 ⟨www.williamstownvillager.com⟩ M-Th $45S $55D, weekends higher, pets $10. Maildrops: 953 Simonds Road, Williamstown, MA 01267.
Williams Inn 413-458-9371, at $180D and up, but $6 gets you a shower, swim and sauna, $1 towel.
Willow Motel 413-458-5768, $69-129, continental B, no pets. Maildrops: 480 Main Street, Williamstown, MA 01267.

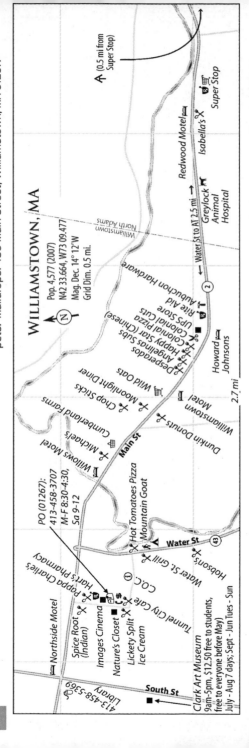

WILLIAMSTOWN, MA

N

Pop. 4,577 (2007)
N42 33.664, W73 09.477
Mag. Dec. 14° 12'W
Grid Dim. 0.5 mi.

Williamstown
North Adams

↑ Water St to AT 2.5 mi
Redwood Motel ↑
Isabella's ✗
Super Stop
↙ 0.5 mi from Super Stop

Greylock
Animal
Hospital

Audubon Hardware
Rite Aid
Colonial Pizza
UPS Store
Colonial Cuts
Happy Star (Chinese)
Angelinas Subs
Desperados

Howard
Johnsons

Wild Oats
Moonlight Diner
Chop Sticks
Cumberland Farms
Michael's
Willows Motel

Main St

Dunkin Donuts
Williamstown
Motel

2.7 mi

PO (01267):
413-458-3707
M-F 8:30-4:30,
Sa 9-12

Pappa Charlie's
Hart's Pharmacy

Hot Tomatoes Pizza
Mountain Goat
Water St
Water St Grill ✗
Hobson's ✗
C.O.C.
Tunnel City Café

Northside Motel
Spice Root (Indian) ✗
Images Cinema
Nature's Closet
Lickety Split ✗
Ice Cream

South St

Library 413-458-5369

Clark Art Museum
9am-5pm, $12.50 free to students,
free to everyone before May)
July - Aug 7 days; Sept - Jun Tues - Sun

E 🛏 ⊠ **Howard Johnson** 413-458-8158, $69-$119, 5% hiker discount, continental B. Maildrops: 213 Main Street, Williamstown, MA 01267.

🥾 ▲ **The Mountain Goat** 413-458-8445〈www.mountaingoat.com〉 open 7 days, backpacking gear and supplies, Coleman/alcohol by the once, no fire camping allowed behind the store with permission, for up to 5 people, 2 days maximum.

✕ **Spice Root Indian Cuisine** 10% hiker discount.

⊠ **Nature's Closet** Recently relocated from Bennington, apparel & footwear. Maildrops: 61 Spring St., Williamstown, MA 01267.

🖥 **Milne Public Library** M-F 10-5:30, W 10-8, Sa 10-4

🚌 **Greyhound Bus Service**

North Adams, MA *(east) (more services on map)*

✕ **Oriental Buffet,** AYCE L/D buffet

🏥 **North Adams Regional Hospital** 413-664-5000

✚ **Greylock Animal Hospital** 413-663-5365, M-Th 8-7, F 8-5, Sa 8-3, Su 9-1

🚌 **David Ackerson** 413-346-1033 daveackerson@yahoo.com Shuttles to trailheads ranging from Bear Mtn Bridge to Hanover, and to/from area airports.

NORTH ADAMS, MA
Pop. 13,617 (2007)
N42 41.919, W73 06.599
Grid Dim. 0.5 mi.

A N

A S
0.7 mi to Friendlys →
2.2 to State St.

Legacy Bank
Getty's
Thrifty Bundle
Friendly's
Price Chopper
Oriental Buffet (L/D)

YMCA

(2)

Massachusetts Ave

Main St.

2.8 mi

PO (01247):
413-664-4554
M-F 8:30-4:30,
Sa 10-12

Porches Inn
Family Dollar
Subway
China Buffet
Holiday Inn
Burger King
Olympic Sports
Movieplex
State St
(8)
Ashland St

Regional Hospital 🏥
Big Y
CVS
Rite Aid
Nassif's
Jack's Hot Dogs
Dunkin Donuts
McDonalds
Library
413-662-3133

147
MA

594.4 **1584.7** Sherman Brook Campsite . . . . ☽ ◊ ⋏ 1300
Tent platforms. Blue-blazed trail bypasses boulder field north of campsite.
Petes Spring at junction of AT and blue-blazed trail.

593.4 **1585.7** Pine Cobble Trail 2100

592.7 **1586.4** Ephs Lookout 2250

592.1 **1587.0** **MA-VT** border, southern end of Long Trail (LT) 2330
The AT and LT are concurrent northbound for the next 105.2 miles.

591.7 **1587.4** Brook . . . . ◊ 2105

589.3 **1589.8** **Seth Warner Shelter** (0.2W) . . . . ☽ ◊ ⋏ ⊏ (8) 2180
33.2◄16.5◄9.9◄►7.2►13.1►21.6
Brook 0.1 left of shelter, known to fail in dry years.

589.0 **1590.1** Mill Rd 2250

587.4 **1591.7** Power line 2868

586.3 **1592.8** Roaring Branch . . . . ◊ 2490

582.6 **1596.5** Stamford Stream . . . . ◊ 2115

582.1 **1597.0** **Congdon Shelter** . . . . ☽ ◊ ⋏ ⊏ (8) 2060
23.7◄17.1◄7.2◄►5.9►14.4►18.7

581.0 **1598.1** Brook . . . . ◊ 2250

579.6 **1599.5** Harmon Hill 2325

577.8 **1601.3** VT 9, **Bennington, VT** (5.1W) . . . . . . N42 53.104 W73 6.950 🅿 ◊ **(pg.152)** 1360

576.2 **1602.9** Brook, **Melville Nauheim Shelter** . . . . ◊ ⊏ (8) 2330
23.0◄13.1◄5.9◄►8.5►12.8►17.4 Stream north of trail to shelter.

575.7 **1603.4** Power line 2605

574.6 **1604.5** Hell Hollow Brook . . . . ◊ 2480

573.4 **1605.7** Porcupine Ridge 2815

SoBo	NoBo		Elev
572.0	**1607.1**	Little Pond Lookout	3060
570.2	**1608.9**	Glastenbury Lookout	2870
567.7	**1611.4**	**Goddard Shelter** . . . . ☽ ◊ ⊏ (12)	3540

21.6◄14.4◄8.5◄►4.3►8.9►19.3 Tent at least 80 yards from water source, which is piped spring 50 yards south on AT.

| 567.4 | **1611.7** | Glastenbury Mountain, observation tower . . . . | 3748 |
| 563.4 | **1615.7** | **Kid Gore Shelter** . . . . ☽ ◊ ⊏ (8) | 2795 |

18.7◄12.8◄4.3◄►4.6►15.0►19.9

563.0	**1616.1**	Several streams in area . . . . ◊	2690
559.7	**1619.4**	South Alder Brook . . . . ◊	2600
558.8	**1620.3**	**Story Spring Shelter** . . . . ☽ ◊ ▲ ⊏ (8)	2810

17.4◄8.9◄4.6◄►10.4►15.3►18.3
Spring 50 yards north on AT.

557.3	**1621.8**	USFS 71 . . . . N43 3.218 W72 59.428 🅿	2524
556.2	**1622.9**	Black Brook . . . . ◊	2222
555.2	**1623.9**	Stratton-Arlington Rd, Kelley Stand Rd . . . . . N43 3.663 W72 58.083 🅿 ◊	2330
555.1	**1624.0**	East Branch Deefield River . . . . ◊	2218
552.0	**1627.1**	Stream . . . . ◊	3500
551.4	**1627.7**	Stratton Mountain, fire tower open to hikers	3936

SoBo	NoBo			Elev
550.9	**1628.2**	Brook	◆	3520
549.5	**1629.6**	Unimproved road		2477
549.0	**1630.1**	Stream	◆	2493
548.4	**1630.7**	**Stratton Pond Shelter** (0.2W) Overnight fee . . . . ☽ ◆ ⫏ (16)		2565
		19.3◀15.0◀10.4◀▶4.9▶7.9▶12.7 No tenting, no fires.		
548.2	**1630.9**	Stratton Pond. . . . . ◆ ⛺ (0.5W)		2555
		North Shore Trail to North Shore Tenting Area.		
546.3	**1632.8**	Winhall River	◆	2300
543.5	**1635.6**	**William B. Douglas Shelter** (0.5W) . . . . ☽ ◆ ⫏ (10)		2210
		19.9◀15.3◀4.9◀▶3.0▶7.8▶15.9 Spring to left of shelter.		
543.4	**1635.7**	Stream	◆	2200
542.6	**1636.5**	Old Rootville Rd, Prospect Rock		2080
542.0	**1637.1**	Stream	◆	2380
541.6	**1637.5**	Stream	◆	2300
540.5	**1638.6**	**Spruce Peak Shelter** (0.1W) . . . . ☽ ◆ ⫏ (14)		2180
		18.3◀7.9◀3.0◀▶4.8▶12.9▶17.6		
540.1	**1639.0**	Spruce Peak		2060
537.7	**1641.4**	VT 11 & 30, ... N43 12.409 W72 58.243 🅿 (pg.153-155)		1800
		Manchester Center, VT (5.4W)		
537.6	**1641.5**	Stream	◆	1862
535.8	**1643.3**	Stream	◆	2550
535.7	**1643.4**	**Bromley Shelter** . . . . ◆ ⛺ ⫏ (12)		2560
		12.7◀7.8◀4.8◀▶8.1▶12.8▶14.3 Four tent platforms.		
534.7	**1644.4**	Bromley Mountain		3260
		View five states from observation tower. No tenting, no fires.		
532.2	**1646.9**	Mad Tom Notch, USFS 21, water from pump	◆	2446
530.6	**1648.5**	Styles Peak		3395

SoBo	NoBo			Elev

528.9 **1650.2** Peru Peak 3429

527.6 **1651.5** **Peru Peak Shelter** . . . . ☽ ♦ ⛺ ⌐ (10) 2605
15.9◄12.9◄8.1◄►4.7►6.2►6.4 Overnight fee, tent platforms.
527.1 **1652.0** Griffith Lake Tenting Area . . . . ♦ ⛺ 2500
Camping only at designated sites within 0.5 mile of Griffith Lake.
526.9 **1652.2** Griffith Lake north end . . . . ♦ 2613

524.9 **1654.2** Baker Peak; rocky summit. 2850

522.9 **1656.2** **Lost Pond Shelter**. . . . . ☽ ♦ ⛺ ⌐ (8) 2150
17.6◄12.8◄4.7◄►1.5►1.7►4.7 Overnight fee. Tent sites.
521.4 **1657.7** Old Job Trail to **Old Job Shelter** (1.0E). . . . . ☽ ♦ ⌐ (8) 1525
14.3◄6.2◄1.5◄►0.2►3.2►3.9 Lake Brook is water source.
521.2 **1657.9** **Big Branch Shelter** . . . . ☽ ♦ ⌐ (8) 1460
6.4◄1.7◄0.2◄►3.0►3.7►8.1 Close to road; receives heavy weekend use.
Water source is Big Branch. Privy uphill.
519.9 **1659.2** USFS 10, Brooklyn Rd, ... N43 22.362 W72 57.764 🅿 **(pg.155)** 1500
Danby, VT (3.5W)

518.2 **1660.9** **Lula Tye Shelter** 4.7◄3.2◄3.0◄►0.7►5.1►10.2 . . . . ☽ ⌐ (8) 1920
517.9 **1661.2** Little Rock Pond Tenting Area, spring 0.1 N . . . . ☽ ⛺ 1885
517.5 **1661.6** **Little Rock Pond Shelter** . . . . ☽ ⌐ (8) 1885
3.9◄3.7◄0.7◄►4.4►9.5►13.2
Water source for Lula Tye Shelter, Little Rock Pond Shelter, and LRP
tenting area is at the caretaker's platform between the two shelters. All 3
locations have an overnight fee. Tenting restricted to designated sites.

513.6 **1665.5** Trail to White Rocks Cliff 2400
513.1 **1666.0** **Greenwall Shelter** (0.2E) . . . . ☽ ♦ ⌐ 2025
8.1◄5.1◄4.4◄►5.1►8.8►14.6 Located on spur trail. Spring 0.1 mile on
side trail behind shelter, prone to fail in dry seasons.
512.5 **1666.6** Brook . . . . ♦ 1709
511.7 **1667.4** Sugar Hill Rd 1693
511.6 **1667.5** VT 140, ... N43 27.418 W72 55.907 (0.2E) 🅿 **(pg.155)** 1600
Wallingford, VT (2.8W)

509.0 **1670.1** Button Hill. 2010
508.0 **1671.1** **Minerva Hinchey Shelter**. . . . . ☽ ♦ ⛺ ⌐ (10) 1530
10.2◄9.5◄5.1◄►3.7►9.5►13.8
Swimming in nearby Spring Lake, spring 50 yards on side trail.

Bennington, VT 05201 (5.1W)
(more services on map)

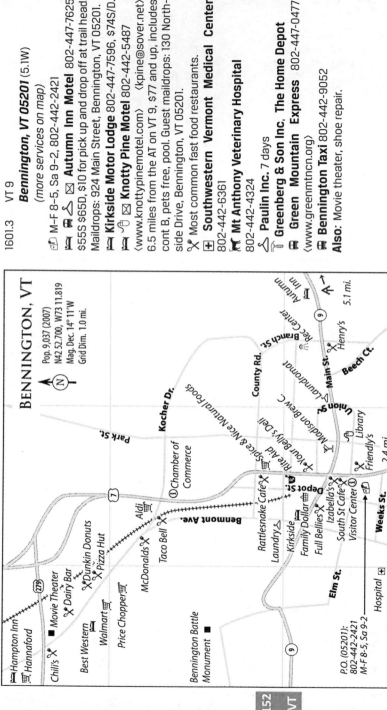

BENNINGTON, VT

Pop. 9,037 (2007)
N42 52.700, W73 11.819
Mag. Dec. 14° 11'W
Grid Dim. 1.0 mi.

Hampton Inn
Hannaford
Chili's
Movie Theater
Dairy Bar
Dunkin Donuts
Pizza Hut
Best Western
Walmart
Price Chopper
McDonalds
Taco Bell
Aldi
Bennington Battle Monument
Kocher Dr.
Park St.
Chamber of Commerce
Benmont Ave.
Spice & Nice Natural Foods
Your Belly's Deli
Rite Aid
Rattlesnake Cafe
Depot St.
Kirkside
Laundry
Family Dollar
Full Bellies
South St Cafe
Izabella's
Visitor Center
County Rd.
Branch St.
Rec Center
Madison Brew C.
Laundromat
Union St.
Main St.
Henry's
Beech Ct.
Library
Friendly's
2.4 mi.
5.1 mi.
Autumn Inn
Weeks St.
Elm St.
Hospital

P.O. (05201):
802-442-2421
M-F 8-5, Sa 9-2

M-F 8-5, Sa 9-2, 802-442-2421

Autumn Inn Motel 802-447-7625 $55S $65D, $10 for pick up and drop off at trail head. Maildrops: 924 Main Street, Bennington, VT 05201.

Kirkside Motor Lodge 802-447-7596, $74S/D.

Knotty Pine Motel 802-442-5487 ⟨www.knottypinemotel.com⟩ ⟨kpine@sover.net⟩ 6.5 miles from the AT on VT 9, $77 and up, includes cont B, pets free, pool. Guest maildrops: 130 Northside Drive, Bennington, VT 05201.

Most common fast food restaurants.

Southwestern Vermont Medical Center 802-442-6361

Mt Anthony Veterinary Hospital 802-442-4324

Paulin Inc. 7 days

Greenberg & Son Inc, The Home Depot

Green Mountain Express 802-447-0477 ⟨www.greenmtncn.org⟩

Bennington Taxi 802-442-9052

Also: Movie theater, shoe repair.

1641.4   VT 11 & 30

🛏 🍴 ⛺ ⚡ 🖂 **Bromley Sun Lodge** (2.1E) 800-722-2159 $70/up, pets $20, tavern, indoor pool, game room, shuttle to and from trail head with stay. Maildrops: 4216 VT 11, Peru, VT 05152., nonguests $5.

🏪 🖂 **Bromley Market** (2.5E) Maildrops: 3776 VT 11, Peru, VT 05152.

🛏 🍴 🍺 🌲 🖂 **Johnny Seesaw's Lodge** 802-824-5533 ⟨www.johnnyseesaw.com⟩ wkdays $50, wkends $100, pets $10, restaurant serves B/D, lounge, shuttle to trailhead with stay. Maildrops: 3574 VT 11, Peru, VT 05152.

★ 🛏 🖂 **Bromley View Inn** (3.0E) on VA 30, 877-633-0308 ⟨www.bromleyviewinn.com⟩ $85D and up, includes B, call for shuttle to and from VT 11/30 trailhead with stay. Maildrops: 522 VT 30, Bondville, VT 05340.

About the Author

David Miller (Awol) thru-hiked the AT in 2003, and is the author of *Awol on the Appalachian Trail.* David was coauthor of the guidebook *Appalachian Pages* in 2008 and 2009, and is a member of the Appalachian Trail Conservancy (ATC), American Long Distance Hiking Association (ALDHA), and American Hiking Society (AHS).

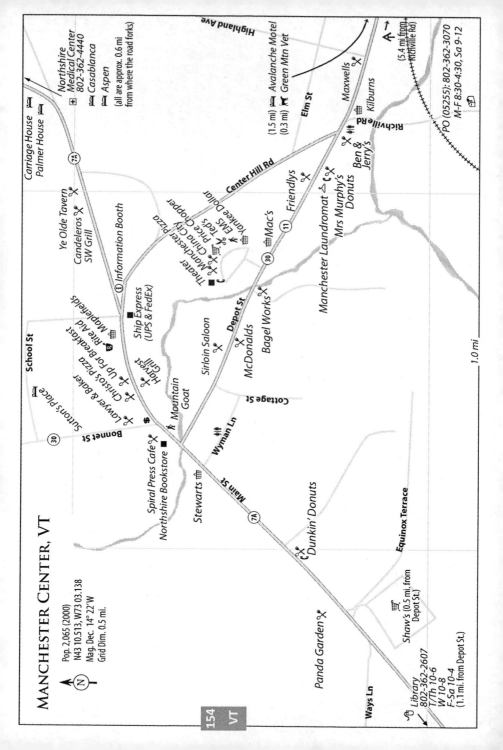

MANCHESTER CENTER, VT

Pop. 2,065 (2000)
N43 10.513, W73 03.138
Mag. Dec. 14° 22'W
Grid Dim. 0.5 mi.

Northshire
Medical Center
802-362-4440
Casablanca
Aspen
(all are approx. 0.6 mi
from where the road forks)

Carriage House
Palmer House

Ye Olde Tavern
Candeleros
SW Grill
Information Booth

Lawyer & Baker
Christo's Pizza
Up For Breakfast
Harvest Grill
Mountain Goat

Sutton's Place
Bonnet St
School St
Rite Aid
Maplefields

Ship Express
(UPS & FedEx)

Theater
Manchester Pizza
China City
Ted's
Price Chopper
EMS
Yankee Dollar
Mac's

Center Hill Rd

Friendlys

Sirloin Saloon
Depot St
Bagel Works
McDonalds

Cottage St

Wyman Ln

Spiral Press Cafe
Northshire Bookstore
Stewarts

Main St

Manchester Laundromat

Mrs Murphy's Donuts

Ben &
Jerry's
Kilburns
Richville Rd

Maxwells

Elm St
Highland Ave

(1.5 mi) Avalanche Motel
(0.3 mi) Green Mtn Vet

(5.4 mi from
Richville Rd)

PO (05255): 802-362-3070
M-F 8:30-4:30, Sa 9-12

1.0 mi

Dunkin' Donuts

Equinox Terrace

Panda Garden

Shaw's (0.5 mi. from
Depot St.)

Library
802-362-2607
T/Th 10-6
W 10-8
F-Sa 10-4
(1.1 mi. from Depot St.)

Ways Ln

154 VT

Manchester Center, VT (5.4W) *(more services on map)*

🏠✗♿✉ **Avalanche Motel** (3.5W) En-route to town, 802-362-2622, 10% discount. Well-behaved pets okay. Diner on-site. Maildrops: 2187 Depot St, Manchester Center, VT 05255.

✉ **Sutton's Place** 802-362-1165, $55S, $66D, $84(room for 3), no pets allowed but can stay on porch. USPS Maildrops: PO Box 142, or UPS Maildrops: 55 School St, Manchester Center, VT 05255.

✉ **Carriage House** 802-362-1706, no pets, call for pricing.

✉ **Palmer House** 802-362-3600, ask for hiker discount, no pets, indoor and outdoor pool.

🏠♿🍴 **Green Mountain House** 330-388-6478 Reservations required. Jeff & Regina Taussig host hikers at their residence. Open Jul 5 - Sep 7. They offer bed, shower with towel, laundry, high speed internet & full kitchen. Not a party place, no alcohol, no drugs. Shuttles from town and back to the trail in the morning. $15/night suggested donation.

🏃 ♿🍴 **Mountain Goat Outfitter** 802-362-5159, M-Sa 10-6, Su 11-5, ⟨www.mountaingoat.com⟩ full-service outfitter has information about alternative lodging choices for hikers. White Gas/alcohol/oz. Maildrops: 4886 Main St, Manchester, VT 05255.

🏃 **EMS** 802-366-8082, 7 days 10-6, full service outfitter, Coleman/alcohol/oz, maintains list of shuttle providers and places to stay.

♿ **Manchester Laundromat**

⚓ **Library** (see map) Call ahead to reserve internet time.

✚ **Northshire Medical Center** 802-362-4440

🏃 **Green Mountain Veterinary Clinic** 802-362-2620

Also: **Northshire Bookstore**

1659.2   USFS 10

Danby, VT 05739 (3.5W)

🍴 M-F 7:15-12 & :15-4, Sa 7:30-10:30, 802-293-5105

🏠✗🍴✉ **Silas Griffith Inn B&B** 802-293-5567 ⟨www.silasgriffith.com⟩ $99 and up, includes breakfast, no smoking, restaurant Th-Su by reservation. Shuttles to/from trail (USFS 10) with stay. Hiker friendly, family friendly, pet friendly. Maildrops for guest: 173 South Main St., Danby, VT 05739.

🏕🔥🏪🅿 ✉ **Otter Creek Campground** 802-293-5041 Two miles north of USFS 10 in Danby on US 7, tent sites $16, pets on leash, Coleman fuel, small selection of food items and camping supplies, shuttles and long-term parking for fee, no credit cards. USPS/UPS Maildrops: 1136 US 7, Danby, VT 05739.

🍴 **White Dog Tavern** with dinner menu.

🏪 **Mt. Tabor Country Store** 802-293-5641 M-Sa 5-8, Su 5-7

🏪 **Nichols Store & Deli**

⚓🍴 **Silas Griffith Library**

🔨 **Crosby Hardware**

1667.5   VT 140

Wallingford, VT 05773 (2.8W)

🍴 M-F 8-4:30, Sa 9-12, 802-446-2140

🍴 **Mom's Country Kitchen** 802-446-2606 B/L, closes at 2. **Sal's Italian Restaurant & Pizza**

🏪 **Wallingford Country Store & Deli, Cumberland Farms**

🔨 **Nail It Down Hardware**

🔨 **Gilbert Hart Hardware**

⚓🍴 **Gilbert Hart Library** 802-446-2685 Su-M closed, Tu 10-5, W 10-8, Th-F 10-5, Sa 9-12.

505.4 **1673.7** Clarendon Gorge, Mill River Bridge, no camping in gorge . . . . ♦ 860

505.3 **1673.8** VT 103 . . . . N43 31.286 W72 55.550 **P** (pg.158-159) 860
  North Clarendon, VT (4.2W) **Rutland, VT** (8.0W)

504.3 **1674.8** **Clarendon Shelter** (0.1E) . . . . ☽ ♦ ⴷ ⴷ (10) 1190
  13.2◄8.8◄3.7◄►5.8►10.1►14.5

503.4 **1675.7** Lottery Rd 1720

503.0 **1676.1** Hermit Spring (unreliable) . . . . ♦ 1700

501.7 **1677.4** Keiffer Rd 1516

501.4 **1677.7** Cold River Rd (Lower Road) . . . . 🧺 1450
  W.E. Pierce Groceries in N. Shrewsbury (2.4E)

500.6 **1678.5** Gould Brook . . . . Ⴟ ♦ 1480

499.9 **1679.2** Upper Cold River Rd 1670

498.6 **1680.5** Robinson Brook . . . . ♦ 1875

498.5 **1680.6** **Governor Clement Shelter** . . . . ☽ ♦ ⴷ (12) 1850
  14.6◄9.5◄5.8◄►4.3►8.7►11.6
  Shelter encircled by dirt road often used by dirt bikes, ATVs.

498.3 **1680.8** Stream . . . . ♦ 2500

497.4 **1681.7** Stream . . . . ♦ 3000

494.2 **1684.9** **Cooper Lodge Shelter**, Killington Peak Trail . . . . ☽ ♦ ⴷ (16) 3850
  13.8◄10.1◄4.3◄►4.4►7.3►16.3 Spring on opposite side of AT. Trail
  behind shelter to top of Killington 0.2 mile.

491.7 **1687.4** Sherburne Pass Trail, Pico Camp (0.5E) . . . . ♦ ⴷ 3400
  Camp on Sherburne Pass Trail where it leaves the Long Trail/AT south of
  Pico summit. Four bunks and table.

489.8 **1689.3** **Churchill Scott Shelter** . . . . ☽ ♦ Ⴟ ⴷ 2560
  14.5◄8.7◄4.4◄►2.9►11.9►21.8 Tent platform, composting privy,
  unreliable water source at southern spur from shelter, no fires.

489.3 **1689.8** Stream . . . . ♦ 2300

487.9 **1691.2** US 4, **Rutland, VT** (10.0W) . . . . . N43 39.996 W72 50.997 **P** (pg.158-159) 1880

486.9 **1692.2** **Tucker-Johnson Shelter** (0.4W), Maine Junction . . . . . . ☽ ♦ Ⴟ ⴷ (8) 2300
  11.6◄7.3◄2.9◄►9.0►18.9►30.5
  LT branches west from AT and ends at Canadian border.

486.0 **1693.1** Sherburne Pass Trail . . . . (pg.158-159) 2440
  0.5E to **Inn at Long Trail**

SoBo	NoBo			Elev
484.6	**1694.5**	VT 100, **Killington, VT** (0.6E) . . . . N43 40.455 W72 48.578 **P** (pg.159)		1690
		Gifford Woods State Park		
483.9	**1695.2**	Kent Pond . . . . **(pg.160)**		1685
482.7	**1696.4**	Thundering Brook Rd		1380
482.5	**1696.6**	Side trail to Thundering Falls		1260
482.4	**1696.7**	Boardwalk over Ottauquechee River	♦	1210
482.2	**1696.9**	River Rd		1220
481.7	**1697.4**	Stream	♦	2000
481.1	**1698.0**	Power line		2300
479.7	**1699.4**	Quimby Mountain		2650
477.9	**1701.2**	**Stony Brook Shelter** . . . . ☽ ♦ ▲ ⌐ (8)		1760
		16.3◄11.9◄9.0◄►9.9►21.5►30.3		
		Tent sites behind shelter. Water from Stony Brook (0.3N) on AT.		
477.3	**1701.8**	Stony Brook Rd, Stony Brook	♦	1358
477.2	**1701.9**	Mink Brook	♦	1369
473.2	**1705.9**	Chateauguay Rd		2000
472.8	**1706.3**	Locust Creek	♦	2023
470.4	**1708.7**	Side trail to lookout		2410
469.6	**1709.5**	Lookout Farm Rd		2220
468.0	**1711.1**	**Winturri Shelter** (0.2W) . . . . ☽ ♦ ⌐ (6)		1900
		21.8◄18.9◄9.9◄►11.6►20.4►27.7		
		Spring from stone surface in front of shelter.		
466.9	**1712.2**	Unpaved road		1756
464.2	**1714.9**	VT 12, **Woodstock, VT** (4.2E) . . . . . . N43 39.309 W72 33.972 **P** ♦ (pg.160)		882
		Gulf Stream south of road crossing.		

⊞ **Marble Valley Regional Transit District** "The Bus" 802-773-3244, ext 117 for dispatcher M-F. ⟨www.thebus.com⟩ Red and white bus can be flagged down; they will stop if there is a safe place to do so.

Manchester to Rutland: ($2PP) Loops from downtown Rutland to Mancester Center, passing through Clarendon, Wallingford, and Danby. Stops of note include Rutland Airport and Shaws in Manchester Center.

Within Rutland: Fixed routes $0.50 per boarding.

Rutland Killington Commuter (RKC) ($2PP) Continuous loop from downtown Rutland to Killington, crossing AT on US 4. Hikers can board eastbound (toward Killington) at the Pico Ski area 0.4E of AT or westbound at The Inn at Long Trail. Schedule subject to change; bus loops nearly every hour from 8am til 11pm.

Weekend of August 7, camping $5PP for the weekend. Rutland Hard Core Sunday and Monday.

⌂ X ⚲ ✉ **Simon the Tanner/Back Home Again Cafe** 802-775-9800 ⟨www.twelvetribes.com⟩ kitchenette, no pets, has information about local kennels with discount, no alcohol or smoking on property, suggested donation $20, ATM across the street, some hiking supplies at adjacent shop. Guest maildrops: Back Home Again Café, 23 Center Street, Rutland, VT 05701.

🎒 **Mountain Travelers Outdoor Shop** 802-775-0814, M-S 10-6, with backpacking equipment and supplies, Coleman/alcohol/oz.

🎒 **The Great Outdoors** 802-775-9989, M-Th 9:30-6, F 9:30-7, Sa 9-6, Su 9-5, backpacking supplies, fuels by container.

🐾 **Rutland Veterinary Clinic** 802-773-2779, 24/7.

🚂 **Amtrak** 800-872-7245 Provides daily train service from Rutland to New York and many other cities.

🚕 **Rutland Taxi** 802-236-3133

✈ **Rutland Airport** South of Rutland on US 7

1691.2   US 4 (0.8E to Inn)
1693.1   Sherburne Pass Trail (0.5E to Inn)

🛏 ▲ X ⚲ ✉ **The Inn at Long Trail** 802-775-7181 or 800-325-2540 ⟨www.innatlongtrail.com⟩ Hiker rooms and free camping across the street. One room in lodge for guest w/pet available on weekdays. Coin laundry, outside water spigot. Closed mid-April through mid-June. **McGrath's Irish Pub** serves L/D 11:30-9pm, live music Fri and Sat. UPS/FedEx Maildrops (no USPS): 709 US 4, Killington, VT 05751.

🛏 (0.9W) **Edelweiss Motel** 802-775-5577 ⟨www.killington-lodge.com⟩ $59S/D with breakfast, on bus route.

1673.8   VT 103

X (0.5W) **Whistle Stop Restaurant** 802-747-7070 Closed Mondays. Tu-Sa 6:30-7, Su 7-7, B/L/D, pizza, ice cream.

🐾 (0.5W) **Cold River Veterinary Center** 802-747-4076

🛒 ((1W) **East Clarendon General Store** 802-786-0948, M-Su 6:30-7, call ahead for maildrop information.

North Clarendon, VT 05759 (4.2W)
🏪 M-F 8-1 & 2-4:30, Sa 8-10, 802-773-7893
⊞ **Mike's Country Store** general store with snacks.

Rutland, VT (8.0W from VT 103) *(more services on map)*
Events: **Long Trail Festival** ⟨www.longtrailfestivalvt.com⟩

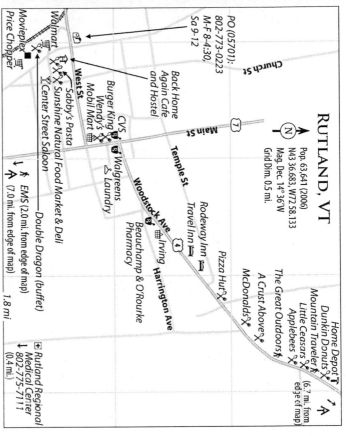

RUTLAND, VT

Pop. 63,641 (2006)
N43 36.683, W72 58.133
Mag. Dec. 14° 36'W
Grid Dim. 0.5 mi.

Home Depot
Dunkin Donuts
Mountain Traveler
Little Ceasars
Applebees
(6.7 mi. from edge of map)

Church St.

Back Home Again Cafe and Hostel

Burger King
Wendy's
Mobil Mart
CVS
Walgreens
Laundry

West St.

Sabby's Pasta
Sunshine Natural Food Market & Deli
Center Street Saloon

Main St.

Temple St.

Woodstock Ave.
Travel Inn
Rodeway Inn

Beauchamp & O'Rourke Pharmacy
Irving

A Crust Above
McDonalds
The Great Outdoors
Pizza Hut

Harrington Ave.

EMS (2.0 mi. from edge of map)
Double Dragon (buffet)
802-775-7111 (0.4 mi.)
1.8 mi.

Rutland Regional Medical Center
802-775-7111

PO (05701):
802-773-0223
M-F 8-4:30,
Sa 9-12

Walmart
Movieplex
Price Chopper

Mendon Mountain View Resort Lodge (1.5W) 802-773-4311 or 800-368-4311 (www.mendonmountainview.com) $49D and up, higher in fall, pet rooms available. Pool, game room, hot tub, saunas, laundry $6 per load, and restaurant serving B/D. On bus route. Maildrops: 78 US Route 4, Mendon VT 05701.

1E94.5   VT 100

Gifford Woods State Park with shelters, $21 tent sites for AT hikers in special hiker section, bath house, water spigot. Fills up quickly in fall. The AT passes thru

Killington, VT 05751 (0.6E)
M-F 8:30-4:30, Sa 8:30-12, 802-775-4247 Near deli.

Base Camp Outfitters 802-775-0166, M-F 9:30-5:30, Sa 9-6, Su 9-5, full service outfitter, Alcohol by ounce and iso-butane. Maildrops: 2363 Route 4, Killington VT 05751.

Killington Deli Marketplace

Wobbly Barn Steakhouse

Casey's Caboose Steakhouse

Pizza Jerks 802-422-4111

Peppino's Ristorante Italino.

Zorbas Mountain Mini Mart. Mac's

Sherburne Town Library, M & F 10-5:30, Tu & Tr 1-5:30, W 10-8, Sa 9-1.

Pittsfield, VT 05762 (7W) on VT 100
M-F 8-12, 2-4:30, Sa 8:30-11:30, 802-746-8953

Original General Store, B/L/D, daily special.

Pitt Stop Gas Station and Market, soft serve ice cream.

1695.2　Kent Pond

△▲✕△⌂ ⊠ **Mountain Meadows Lodge**
802-775-1010 〈www.mountainmeadowslodge.com〉 AT crosses property. Room $59 includes breakfast, Tent/hammock site $10/PP or work for stay. B/L $8.95, D $10, sodas available. No pets inside; barn & woodshed available. Outdoor pool, hot tub, and sauna. Open year round. Lodging not available during events (most weekends). Maildrops: 285 Thundering Brook Road, Killington, VT 05751.

1714.9　VT 12

　　　　Woodstock, VT 05091 (4.2E)

⌂ M-F 8:30-5, Sa 9-12, 802-457-1323
Tourist town with several motels and restaurants.
🏨 **Shire River View Motel** 802-457-2211 $138/up
🏨 **Braeside Motel** 802-457-1366, $98-118
🏨 **Pond Ridge Motel** 802-457-1667, $79S and up, $99D and up.
✕ **Bentley's, Pizza Chef**
⚰ **Cumberland Farms, Gillingham FH & Sons**
💊 **Woodstock Pharmacy**
🐾 **Woodstock Veterinary Hospital** 802-457-2229
📖 **Norman Williams Public Library** 802-457-2295 , M-F 10-5
Also: Movie theater, bookstore, salon.

Suggestions for Providing Trail Magic

Trail Magic, defined as an unexpected act of kindness, is a quintessential part of the Appalachian Trail experience for many long-distance hikers. The suggestions below incorporate Leave No Trace practices (www.LNT.org) to help those providing trail magic have the most positive impact on hikers, the Trail, its plants and wildlife, and the volunteers who maintain and preserve it. The Appalachian Trail Conservancy and the Appalachian Long Distance Hikers Association endorse these suggestions.

Help conserve and maintain the Trail. The most essential service you can perform is to volunteer to maintain the Trail and overnight sites, or to monitor boundaries and resource conditions. Visit www.appalachiantrail.org for more information, or check with your local trail-maintaining club to find out how or where you may assist.

Locate events in developed areas on durable surfaces. Large gatherings in the backcountry can lead to trampling of plants, soil compaction, and disturbance of wildlife habitat. Trail towns and local parks are better locations. Keep events small. Consider whether your event may be contributing to an overabundance of trail feeds in the local area or region. Some hikers come to the Trail to seek solitude and contemplation.

Prepare and serve food safely. If you will be cooking or preparing food, check with the landowner to find an appropriate area and learn what food-safety or other regulations apply. Permits may be required. Charging a fee or asking for donations may not be allowed.

Be present if you provide food or drink. Unattended items—including their packaging—can harm wildlife that consume them, or hikers, when unrefrigerated products grow bacteria or become contaminated. Unattended items are considered litter and their presence detracts from the wildland character of backcountry environments. Dispense food and drink in person, and carry out any trash or leftovers.

Restore the site. Leave the site as you found it—don't create a burden for Trail volunteers whose time is better spent in other activities.

Advertise off-trail. Advertising—even noncommercial—is prohibited on the A.T. Publicizing a "feed" in advance can lead to clumping of long distance hikers, causing overcrowded conditions and avoidable impacts at shelters and campsites.

Forgo alcoholic beverages. Don't risk the legality and liability associated with serving minors, over-serving adults, or the safety issues associated with intoxicated hikers.

Be hospitable to all. While many long-distance hikers will likely appreciate trail magic, be sure to make all trail users and volunteers feel welcome.

For more information, visit ATC's Web site at www.appalachiantrail.org/trailmagic.

SoBo	NoBo		Elev
462.7	**1716.4**	Woodstock Stage Rd, Barnard Brook	770
		(1.0E) **South Pomfret, VT** 05067 M-F 8-1, 2-4:40, Sa 8:30-11:30	
		Teago's General Store 802-457-1626, 7 days, PO inside store.	
461.9	**1717.2**	Totman Hill Rd	998
461.2	**1717.9**	Bartlett Brook Rd, stream.	982
460.5	**1718.6**	Pomfret Rd, South Pomfret	990
		Pomfret Brook south of road crossing.	
458.7	**1720.4**	Cloudland Rd	1480
		Previous AT shelter (Cloudland) now on private land (0.5W). Facility available at landowner's discretion.	
456.7	**1722.4**	Thistle Hill	1950
456.4	**1722.7**	**Thistle Hill Shelter** (0.1E) ♫ ♦ ⌐ (8)	1740
		30.5◄21.5◄11.6◄►8.8►16.1►25.6 Stream near shelter.	
455.0	**1724.1**	Dimick Brook	1282
454.9	**1724.2**	Joe Ranger Rd	1360
454.6	**1724.5**	Bunker Hill Rd	1387
452.5	**1726.6**	Quechee West Hartford Rd (south end)	469
451.6	**1727.5**	VT 14, White River, **West Hartford, VT** (0.3W) **(pg.167)**	400
451.2	**1727.9**	Tigertown Rd	415
451.0	**1728.1**	I-89 underpass N43 43.250 W72 24.793 🅿	500
450.2	**1728.9**	Podunk Rd, Podunk Brook N43 43.006 W72 24.013 🅿 ♦	851
448.4	**1730.7**	Griggs Mtn	1600
448.0	**1731.1**	Stream	1437
447.6	**1731.5**	**Happy Hill Shelter** (0.1E) ♫ ♦ ⌐ (8)	1400
		30.3◄20.4◄8.8◄►7.3►16.8►22.5 Brook near shelter.	
444.8	**1734.3**	Power line	1175
444.2	**1734.9**	Elm Street (south intersection, AT follows road)	762
443.3	**1735.8**	Elm St + Main St, **Norwich, VT** **(pg.167)**	400
442.3	**1736.8**	**VT-NH** border, Connecticut River	400
441.8	**1737.3**	**Hanover, NH** N43 42.391 W72 16.656 🅿 **(pg.166-167)**	531
		Dartmouth College	
441.1	**1738.0**	NH 120	530

440.3 **1738.8** **Velvet Rocks Shelter** (0.2W) . . . . ☽ ♦ ⌐ (6) 1040
27.7◄16.1◄7.3◄►9.5►15.2►21.9
Spring on northern access to shelter.
439.8 **1739.3** Ledyard Spring. . . . . ♦ (0.2W) 1220

438.1 **1741.0** Pond . . . . ♦ 856

437.3 **1741.8** Trescott Rd 880

435.9 **1743.2** Etna-Hanover Center Rd, **Etna, NH** (0.8E) . . . . **(pg.168)** 880

433.4 **1745.7** Three Mile Rd. N43 43.077 W72 10.559 **P** 1390
433.2 **1745.9** Mink Brook . . . . ♦ 1320

431.6 **1747.5** Moose Mountain south peak. 2290
430.8 **1748.3** **Moose Mountain Shelter** (0.1E) . . . . ☽ ⋏ ⌐ (8) 1850
25.6◄16.8◄9.5◄►5.7►12.4►17.7 Loop trail to shelter, water at AT and
northern leg intersection, tenting on northern leg of loop.
429.6 **1749.5** Moose Mountain north peak 2300

428.9 **1750.2** South fork of Hewes Brook 2000

427.6 **1751.5** Goose Pond Rd, Hewes Brook . . . . ♦ 952

425.6 **1753.5** Holts Ledge. 2100
425.1 **1754.0** **Trapper John Shelter** (0.2W) . . . . ☽ ♦ ⋏ ⌐ (6) 1345
22.5◄15.2◄5.7◄►6.7►12.0►19.1 Privy behind shelter 0.1 mile.

424.2 **1754.9** Lyme-Dorchester Rd, Dartmouth Skiway . . . . **(pg.168)** 880
Lyme Center, NH (1.3W), **Lyme, NH** (3.2W)

422.3 **1756.8** Grant Brook. . . . . ♦ 1108
422.2 **1756.9** Lyme-Dorchester Rd . . . . N43 47.556 W72 6.176 **P** 1080

420.4 **1758.7** Perking Brook . . . . ♦ 2321

SoBo	NoBo		NH 164	1000	2000	3000	4000	5000	6000	Elev

418.5 **1760.6** Smarts Mountain, abandoned fire tower sleeps two . . . . ▲ 3220
Tenting south of summit near spring.
418.4 **1760.7** **Fire Wardens Cabin**. . . . . ☽ ◦ ⌐ (12) 3240
21.9◄12.4◄6.7◄►5.3►12.4►21.0
Spring in front of shelter and down side trail 0.1 mile.

414.5 **1764.6** South Jacobs Brook. . . . . ◦ 1450

413.4 **1765.7** North Jacobs Brook. . . . . ◦ 1800
413.1 **1766.0** **Hexacuba Shelter** (0.3E) . . . . ☽ ◦ ▲ ⌐ (8) 1980
17.7◄12.0◄5.3◄►7.1►15.7►22.6 Shelter on steep side trail, 2 tent sites
nearby, unreliable stream at intersection with side trail.

411.5 **1767.6** Side trail to Mt Cube north summit 2911

410.0 **1769.1** Brackett Brook . . . . ◦ 1434

408.2 **1770.9** NH 25A. . . . . N43 54.078 W71 59.029 🅿 (pg.169) 900
Wentworth, NH (4.8E)
406.6 **1772.5** Cape Moonshine Rd . . . . N43 54.950 W71 57.876 🅿 1500

406.0 **1773.1** **Ore Hill Shelter** (2000) . . . . ☽ ◦ ▲ ⌐ (8) 1720
19.1◄12.4◄7.1◄►8.6►15.5►24.5
Spring in front of shelter 100 yds down path.

--*Wachipauka Trail* - See page 173 for an explanation of alternate trail names.

403.4 **1775.7** NH 25C, **Warren, NH** (4.0E) . . . . ◦ (pg.169) 1500
Ore Hill Brook north of road.

400.9 **1778.2** Mt Mist. 2200

--*Town Line Trail*

398.5 **1780.6** NH 25 . . . . N43 59.395 W71 53.971 🅿 (pg.169) 1140
Glencliff, NH (0.5E), **Warren, NH** (5.0E)
397.4 **1781.7** **Jeffers Brook Shelter** . . . . ☽ ◦ ⌐ (10) 1350
21.0◄15.7◄8.6◄►6.9►15.9►19.9 Jeffers Brook in front of shelter.
397.2 **1781.9** USFS 19 1326

397.1 **1782.0** Sanitarium Rd 1440

396.6 **1782.5** Stream . . . . ⏾ 2005

--*Glencliff Trail*

392.8 **1786.3** Mt Moosilauke 4802
North side of Mt Moosilauke is steep and often slick.

--*Beaver Brook Trail*

390.5 **1788.6** **Beaver Brook Shelter** . . . . ☾ ⏾ ⛺ ⌐ (10) 3650
22.6◄15.5◄6.9◄►9.0►13.0►28.1
Shelter on Beaver Brook trail. Beaver Brook on way to shelter.
389.2 **1789.9** Beaver Brook . . . . ⏾ 1911
389.0 **1790.1** NH 112 . . . . N44 2.389 W71 47.525 🅿 **(pg.169)** 1812
Kinsman Notch
North Woodstock, NH (5.0E)
Lincoln, NH (6.0E)

--*Kinsman Ridge Trail*

385.7 **1793.4** Gordon Pond Trail 2806
385.4 **1793.7** Brook . . . . ⏾ 2735

384.4 **1794.7** Mt Wolf east peak 3478

382.5 **1796.6** Reel Brook Trail 2511

381.5 **1797.6** **Eliza Brook Shelter** . . . . ☾ ⏾ ⛺ ⌐ (8) 2500
24.5◄15.9◄9.0◄►4.0►19.1►24.6 Two tent pads.
380.7 **1798.4** Eliza Brook . . . . ⏾ 2861
380.2 **1798.9** Stream . . . . ⏾ 3455

379.0 **1800.1** South Kinsman Mountain 4358

378.1 **1801.0** North Kinsman Mountain 4293

377.5 **1801.6** **Kinsman Pond Shelter** . . . . ☾ ⏾ ⛺ ⌐ (14) 3750
19.9◄13.0◄4.0◄►15.1►20.6►29.6
--*Fishin' Jimmy* Overnight fee $8PP, caretaker, five tent platforms.
Trail Pond water treatment recommended.
375.6 **1803.5** Lonesome Lake Hut. . . . . ☾ ⏾ 🛏 **(see AMC notes, pg.172-173)** 2760
Cascade Bunkhouses sleep 46 guests. Kitchen in main building. Self-service
--*Brook Trail* midMay-MemDay, full-service Jun-midOct.

| SoBo | NoBo | | | | 1000 | 2000 | 3000 | 4000 | 5000 | 6000 | Elev |

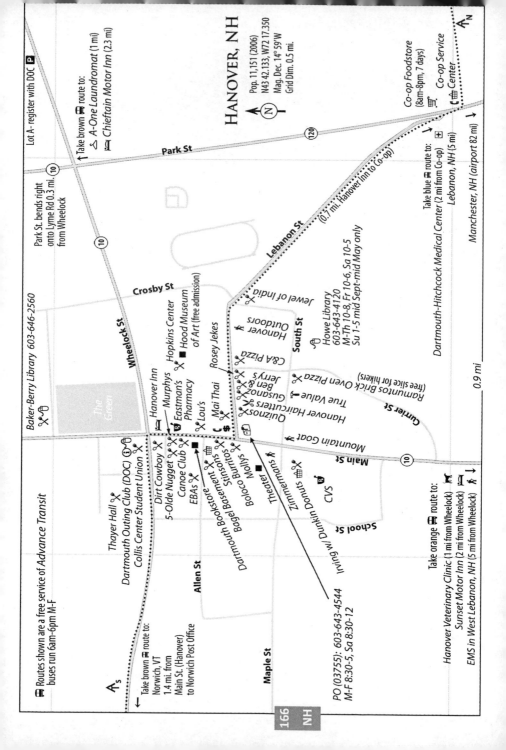

1727.5 VT 14 (White River)

West Hartford, VT 05084 (0.3W)

Ask at general store or library about places to stay.

✉ ✗ M-F 7:30-4:30, Sa 7:30-10, 802-295-6293

West Hartford Village Store Open until 7pm.

Twin State Taxi 802-295-7878

West Hartford Public Library 802-295-7992, M, Tu & W 2-7, till 7:30insummer,F12-7,Sa9-2,closedTh&Su.Fridaynightmovies7-9pm.

1735.8 Main St + Elm St

Norwich, VT 05055 (0.2E)

✉ ✗ M-F 8:30-5, Sa 9-12, **Norwich Inn** 802-649-1143 <www.norwichinn.com> innkeeper@norwichinn.com $94-$239 Rooms for pets, no smoking, reservations recommended. Restaurant Tu-Su B/L/D, pub serves dinner on M, brewery. Maildrops for guests: PO Box 908, Norwich, VT 04055.

Dan & Whits General Store 7 days 7-9, one block west on Main St.

Norwich Library 802-649-1184, M 1-8, Tu-W-F 10-5:30, Th 10-8, Sa10-3.

1737.3 *Hanover, NH*, Dartmouth College

(more services on map)

ⓘ **Dartmouth Outing Club (DOC)** 603-646-2428 In Robinson Hall. Not available during Dartmouth orientation 8/30-9/15/2010. Unsecured room in basement for hikers to store gear while in town, cannot be left overnight. Two computers for free internet use. There are no hiker accommodations on campus; ask about those nearby. Also see Tigger's Tree House listed at Etna-Hanover Center Road. Camping may be available where AT re-enters woods northbound; check with DOC.

P Overnight parking on Wheelock Street (Lot A), register with DOC. No parking near bridge over Connecticut River.

Sunset Motor Lodge 603-298-8721, open 8-11, Call ahead. Will shuttle when bus is not running, free laundry before 6pm, Quiet after 10pm, No pets. Maildrops: 305 N Main Street, West Lebanon, NH 03874.

Chieftain Motor Inn 603-643-2550, 2 miles north on NH 10, $75-$100, no pets, CATV, continental breakfast, shuttle may be available.

Hanover Inn 603-643-4300 High-priced rooms, discount sometimes available.

EBA's $6.99 buffet 7 days 11:00-2:30

Jewel of India buffet Su 11:30-2:30

Hanover Food Co-op open daily, large selection of produce & beverages.

Stinson's Convenience store that also sells deli sandwiches.

Hanover Outdoors 603-643-1263 M-Sa 9-6, Su 10-4.

Mountain Goat 603-676-7240 Full line of backpacking gear, fuel/oz. Maildrops: 17 1/2 Lebanon St, Hanover, NH 03755.

True Value Hardware Coleman/alcohol/oz

Advance Transit, 3-6 M-F, offers FREE bus service throughout Hanover, to medical center listed below, White River Junction, Lebanon and West Lebanon.

Apex Transportation 603-252-8294 Steve "Stray Kat" Lake '96-'06, Shuttle by reservation to/from anywhere originating/ending in Hanover. Airport pickups. Insured.

Hanover Veterinary 603-643-3313

A-One Laundromat 603-643-1514 (1.0N) on Lyme Road. Can take Advance Bus, get off at police station. M-F 7-8, Sa-Su 8-5.

(See wide-area map on next page)

White River Junction, VT

Amtrak 800-872-7245 Vermonter line travels north as far as St. Albans, Vt, and south through New York, Philadelphia, Baltimore and Washington, DC. There is no ticket office at this station, but you can reserve on the phone and pay when you board.

West Lebanon, NH

EMS 603-298-7716

Shaw's 603-298-0388 7am-10pm, 7-9 Sunday

Price Chopper 603-298-9670 24hrs

Lebanon, NH

Price Chopper 603-448-3970

1743.2   Etna-Hanover Center Road

Etna, NH 03750 (0.8E)

Tiggers Tree House 603-643-9213 Private home: not a party place. Call from trailhead, Etna General Store (they will let you use their phone) or Dartmouth Outing Club for pickup, pets allowed, donations accepted or buy laundry soap or work for stay. Advance notice ensures a place to stay. Can arrange rides to grocery store, Walmart, EMS.

(0.8E) **Etna General Store** 603-643-1655, M-F 6-7, Sa, Su 8-7. Deli, hot meals, open 7 days. Denatured alcohol/oz.

1754.9   Lyme-Dorchester Rd (Dartmouth Skiway)

Lyme Center, NH 03769 (1.3W)

(1.2W) Lyme Center M-F 8-12 & 2:30-5, Sa 8-11:30, 603-795-2688

Lyme, NH 03768 (3.2W)

M-F 7:45-12 & 1:30-5:15, Sa 7:45-12, 603-795-4421

Stella's Italian Kitchen & Market 603-795-4302 〈www.stellaslyme.com〉, M-Th 10-9, F-Sa 10-10, Su closed.

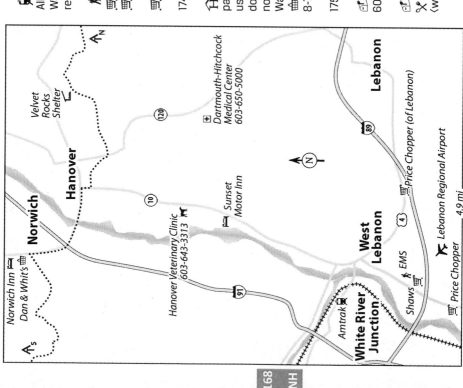

Norwich Inn
Dan & Whit's
Norwich
Velvet Rocks Shelter
Hanover
120
Dartmouth-Hitchcock Medical Center 603-650-5000
Hanover Veterinary Clinic 603-643-3313
Sunset Motor Inn
10
N
91
Amtrak
White River Junction
West Lebanon
Shaws
EMS
Price Chopper
89
Lebanon
Price Chopper (of Lebanon)
4
Lebanon Regional Airport
Price Chopper
4.9 mi

[icon] **Dowd's Country Inn B&B** 603-795-4712 (www.dowdscountryinn.com) starting at $85S $100D mid week through Sep, breakfast and afternoon tea included. Pets allowed in some rooms. Call in advance; pickup sometimes available.

[icon] **Lyme Country Store** (3.3W) ice cream, produce, deli, open 7 days.

[icon] **Lyme Veterinary Hospital** (2.8W) bear right onto High St and hospital is 50 yrds up on the left, 603-795-2747.

1770.9   NH 25A

Wentworth, NH 03282 East 4.3 on NH 25A, then right on NH 25 0.5 mile.

[icon] M-F 7-1 & 3-5, Sa 7:15-12, 603-764-9444

[icon] **Shawnee's General Store** 603-764-5553, Su-Th 6-9, F-S 6-9.

[icon] **Mt Cube Sugar Farm** (1.9W) 603-353-4709, owned and operated by the Thomson family. The fruit stand, open 8:30-dusk, offers homemade snacks, maple products, seasonal fruits and vegetables. Hikers may be allowed to stay in the hay barn, known as the Governor's Mansion, or tent outside, check on availability. No cooking or open flames allowed in the hay barn.

1775.7   NH 25C

Warren, NH 03279 (4E)

[icon] M-F 7:30-1 2:30-5, Sa 7:30-11:30, 603-764-5288, M-Su 6-8.

[icon] **Calamity Jane's Restaurant** 603-764-5733

[icon] **Sticky Fingers** ice cream M-Su 12-8

[icon] **Greenhouse Restaurant** 603-764-5708

[icon] **Warren Village Market** produce/deli.

[icon] **Laundry** M-Su 8:30-8:30.

[icon] **Trust Worthy Hardware**

[icon] **Mt Moosilauke Health Center** 603-764-5704, M, 8-6, Tu-Th 8-5, F 8-4, located past the Warren Village Market on the right.

1780.6   NH 25

Glencliff, NH 03238 (0.5E)

[icon] M-F 7-1 2:30-5, Sa 7-10 & 2-5, 603-989-5154

[icon] **Hikers Welcome Hostel** 603-989-0040 Bunk ($15) and camping ($10) includes shower. Shower only w/towel $2.50, laundry $5. Snacks, sodas, and ice cream. Slackpacking & shuttles (5mi to resupply in Warren). Coleman/alcohol/oz. Tools to help with gear repair, and selection of used gear available, particularly winter wear.

Warren, NH (5.0E) see entry above

1790.1   NH 112/Kinsman Notch

[icon] **Lost River Gorge** (0.5E) 603-745-8031 A tourist attraction featuring a boulder jumble similar to Mahoosuc Notch. Has a grill serving short-order lunch menu and a gift store with snacks.

[icon] **Lost River Valley Campground** (3.0E) 603-745-8321, 300-370-5678 (www.lostriver.com) cabin $50S, 65D, camping primitive sites $19, all other sites $25, pets allowed but not in cabins, showers, coin laundry, pay phone, open mid-May to Columbus Day 8-9, quiet 10pm-8am, owner Jim Kelly. Maildrops: 951 Lost River Road, North Woodstock, NH 03262.

North Woodstock, NH (5.0E), **Lincoln, NH** (6.0E)

(See page 174)

SoBo	NoBo		Elev
374.8	1804.3	Kinsman Pond Trail	2300
374.3	1804.8	Cascade Brook . . . . ♦	2094

--*Cascade Brook Trail*

372.9	1806.2	Whitehouse Brook . . . . ♦	1509
372.7	1806.4	US 3, I-93, AT passes under highways	1450

Hikers can bushwhack to road and hitch east to town (compass south), but it's better to take side trail (see next entry).

| 372.6 | 1806.5 | Franconia Notch, Trail to parking (0.8E) . . . . . . .N44 6.014 W71 40.952 **P** | 1450 |

--*Liberty* **North Woodstock, NH** (4.8S) left from parking area on US 3 .**(pg.173-175)**
Springs Trail **Lincoln, NH** (1.0E) of North Woodstock.

| 370.1 | 1809.0 | Liberty Spring tent site . . . . ♦ ⚠ | 3800 |

Overnight fee $8PP, caretaker, 7 single and 3 double platforms.

--*Franconia Ridge Trail*

368.0	1811.1	Little Haystack Mountain	4760
367.3	1811.8	Mt Lincoln, Franconia Ridge	5089
366.3	1812.8	Mt Lafayette, Greenleaf Hut (1.1W) . . . . ☾ ♦ (0.2W) ⇌	5249

Greenleaf Hut visible from summit of Mt Lafayette. Located down steep Greenleaf Trail. Bunkhouse sleeps 48 with a croo of 5. Self-service midMay-MemDay, full-service Jun-midOct.

--*Garfield Ridge Trail*

363.5	1815.6	Garfield Pond . . . . ♦	3884
362.8	1816.3	Mt Garfield	4488
362.4	1816.7	**Garfield Ridge Shelter/Campsite** . . . . ☾ ♦ ⚠ ⌐ (12)	3500

28.1◄19.1◄15.1◄►5.5►14.5►56.5 Overnight fee $8PP, caretaker, 2S and 5D platforms, dishwashing area, reliable water source.

| 361.9 | 1817.2 | Franconia Brook Trail goes steeply down to 13 Falls Campsite. . . . . | 3420 |
| 359.7 | 1819.4 | Galehead Hut, sleeps 38. Self-service mid May-Memorial Day, . . . ☾ ♦ ⇌ | 3800 |

full-service Jun-mid Oct.

| 358.9 | 1820.2 | South Twin Mountain, North Twin Spur . . . . | 4902 |

--*Twinway Trail*

| 356.9 | 1822.2 | Mt Guyot, **Guyot Shelter** (0.7E) . . . . ☾ ♦ ⚠ ⌐ (12) | 4560 |

24.6◄20.6◄5.5◄►9.0►51.0►57.1
Overnight fee $8PP, caretaker, 4 single and 2 double platforms, unreliable spring.

| 354.4 | 1824.7 | Trail to Zeacliff Pond . . . . | 3850 |
| 353.9 | 1825.2 | Zeacliff, Zeacliff Trail . . . . | 3600 |

SoBo	NoBo			Elev

352.8 **1826.3** Whitewall Brook . . . . ▲ 2691
352.7 **1826.4** Zealand Falls Hut . . . . ☽ ▲ ⇌ 2450
Next to falls, just off AT. Bunkhouse sleeps 36. Self-service midMay-
MemDay, full-service Jun-Oct. Nice stretch of level trail between hut and
Ethan Pond Campsite.

349.6 **1829.5** Kedron Brook . . . . ▲ 2591

--*Ethan Pond Trail*

347.9 **1831.2** **Ethan Pond Campsite** . . . . ☽ ▲ Λ ⊏ (10) 2950
29.6◄14.5◄9.0◄►42.0►48.1►61.8
Overnight fee $8PP, caretaker, 2 single and 2 double platforms,
dishwashing area next to Ethan Pond, inlet brook to pond.

345.4 **1833.7** Railroad track 1459
345.0 **1834.1** Crawford Notch, US 302 . . . . N44 10.236 W71 23.232 🅿 **(pg.175)** 1277
344.9 **1834.2** Saco River, footbridge . . . . ▲ 1270

--*Webster Cliff Trail*

341.7 **1837.4** Mt Webster 3910

340.3 **1838.8** Mt Jackson 4052

338.6 **1840.5** Mizpah Spring Hut, Nauman Campsite . . . . ▲ Λ ⇌ 3800
Bunkhouse sleeps 60. Self-service May 9-27, full-service Jun-midSep.
Tent site next to hut, overnight fee $8PP
337.8 **1841.3** Mt Pierce (Mt Clinton) 4310

336.9 **1842.2** Spring . . . . ▲ 4117

--*Crawford Path*

335.6 **1843.5** Spring . . . . ▲ 4700
335.0 **1844.1** Mt Franklin 5004

333.9 **1845.2** Lakes of the Clouds Hut . . . . ☽ ▲ ⇌ 5020
Open Jun 1–Sep 13, no self-service operation.

332.5 **1846.6** Mt Washington . . . . **(pg.175)** 6288
332.2 **1846.9** Cog Railroad 5971

--*GulfsideTrail*

SoBo	NoBo				1000	2000	3000	4000	5000	6000	Elev

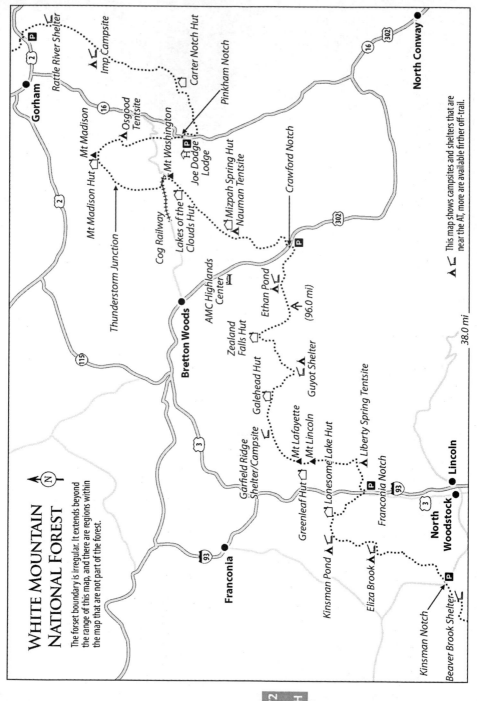

WHITE MOUNTAIN NATIONAL FOREST

The forset boundary is irregular. It extends beyond the range of this map, and there are regions within the map that are not part of the forest.

N

This map shows campsites and shelters that are near the AT, more are available firther off-trail.

38.0 mi

North Conway

302
16

Gorham

2

Rattle River Shelter

Imp Campsite

Carter Notch Hut

Pinkham Notch

16

Osgood Tentsite

Mt Madison

Mt Madison Hut

Joe Dodge Lodge

Mt Washington

Mizpah Spring Hut

Nauman Tentsite

Crawford Notch

Thunderstorm Junction

Cog Railway

Lakes of the Clouds Hut

302

2

115

Bretton Woods

AMC Highlands Center

Ethan Pond

(96.0 mi)

Zealand Falls Hut

Galehead Hut

Guyot Shelter

3

Garfield Ridge Shelter/Campsite

Mt Lafayette

Mt Lincoln

Liberty Spring Tentsite

Lonesome Lake Hut

Franconia Notch

93

Greenleaf Hut

Kinsman Pond

Eliza Brook

Franconia Notch

93

3

Lincoln

North Woodstock

Kinsman Notch

Beaver Brook Shelter

Franconia

93

White Mountain National Forest (the "Whites")

Passage through the Whites should be planned carefully. It is one of the more heavily visited sections of the AT, and campsites are limited. The trail is rugged, so your pace may be slowed. Weather is dynamic, adding to the dangers of hiking on stretches of trail above treeline.

Take adequate cold-weather gear, check weather reports whenever possible, carry maps, and know your options for overnighting. The Appalachian Mountain Club (AMC) and Randolph Mountain Club (RMC) maintain camps, which are detailed in the following pages. Most of these have fees. Have cash on hand even if you do not plan to use them; your plans may change.

There are many trails in the Whites. The AT is the only white-blazed trail, but blazes are further apart than they are elsewhere on the AT. The AT is almost always coincident with another named trail, and the other trail name may be the one you see on signs. Also note that mileages on trail signs may be outdated. The data section of this book is annotated with all trails with which the AT is coincident. There are line segments to the left of the mileage column, labeled with alternate trail names in italics.

The area within a quarter mile of all AMC and RMC facilities and everything above treeline (trees 8' or less) are part of the Forest Protection Area (FPA). Trails are often marked where they enter or leave the FPA. Do not camp within a FPA, and camp at least 200' from water and trails. Rocks aligned to form a trail boundary (scree walls) are an indication that you should not leave the treadway. Doing so damages fragile plant life.

Appalachian Mountain Club (AMC) 603-466-2727
The club maintains the AT from Kinsman Notch, NH to Grafton Notch, ME. AMC offers hikers overnight accommodations at eight huts, 14 shelters and tentsites, Joe Dodge Lodge at Pinkham Notch and the Highland Center at Crawford Notch.

Huts have bunk space for 30-90 people. There is no road access, no heat, and no showers. They use alternative energy sources and composting toilets. Overnight stay includes a bunk, dinner and breakfast, and the per-person cost starts at $85, and reservations are recommended. There is a discount for AMC members. Enviable work-for-stay is available to the first 2 thru-hikers; 4 at Lakes of the Clouds Hut. Work-for-stay hikers get floor space for sleeping and feast on leftovers. Do not count on hut stays without reservations, and camping is not allowed near most of the huts.

🚐 **AMC Hiker Shuttle** operates June 2 - Sept 12 with stops at Crawford Notch, Pinkham Notch, and Gorham.

1806.5　US 3, Franconia Notch
✕ ($ ⊠ (0.7E) **Flume Visitor Center** with snack bar, restaurant open daily early May-late Oct., 9-5. Maildrops: Flume Gorge, 9 Franconia Notch State Park, Franconia, NH 03580.

▲ ⚡ (🍴 ⊠ (2.1W) **Lafayette Campground** 603-823-9513, tent sites $25, limited store, no pets, quiet 10pm. Open mid-May-mid-Oct. Maildrops: Franconia State Park, Lafayette Campground, Franconia, NH 03580.

🛏 ⊠ (1.2E) **Profile Motel & Cottages** 603-745-2759 (www.profilemotel.com) weekday $59S $69D, weekend $72S $79D, fridge and microwave in room, grills and tables outside, open 7-10. Maildrops: 391 US 3, Lincoln, NH 03251.

🛏 ⛾ ⊠ (1.5E) **Mt. Liberty Motel** 603-745-3600 (MtLibertyMotel.com) $60D mid-May - mid-Oct, no pets, ask about shuttles. Maildrops: 10 Liberty Road, PO Box 422, Lincoln, NH 03251.

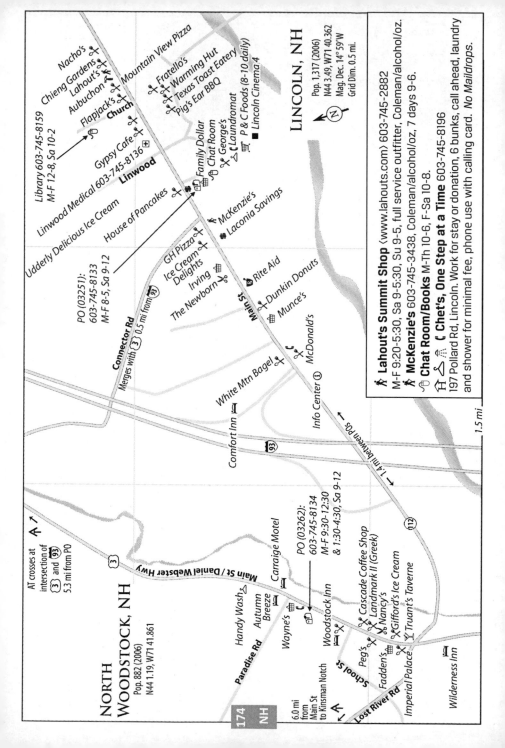

North Woodstock, NH (4.8S) *(more services on map)*

Woodstock Inn 603-745-3951, 800-321-3985 <www.woodstockinnnh.com> $94/up includes full breakfast, no pets. Two restaurants and a micro-brewery on-site.

Autumn Breeze 603-745-8549 <www.autumnbreezemotel.com> summer rates $70-78, rooms have kitchenettes, no pets.

The Carriage Motel 603-745-2416 <www.carriagemotel.com> $64D, $10EAP, no pets, game room, pool, and gas grills. Maildrops: 180 Main Street, North Woodstock, NH 03262.

Wilderness Inn B&B 603-745-3890, 888-777-7813 <www.thewildernessinn.com> $70S $80D and up. One four-person room. Includes full breakfast. No pets, no smoking. Free shuttle from Kinsman or Franconia Notch with stay as time permits. Maildrops: 50 Courtney Rd, North Woodstock, NH 03262.

Fadden's General Store ice cream, fudge shop.

The Shuttle Connection 603-745-3140 <www.shuttleconnection.com> Shuttles between town and trail or to bus terminals and airports ranging from Portland, ME to NY. Can handle large groups.

Franconia, NH 03580 (10.0W of Franconia notch)

Gale River Motel 603-823-5655, 800-255-7989 info@galerivermotel.com <www.galerivermotel.com> $50-$200, pets with approval, laundry wash $1, dry $1, Coleman/alcohol/oz., free return to trail with stay, call ahead, open year-round. Maildrops: 1 Main Street, Franconia, NH 03580.

M-F 8:30-1 & 2-5, Sa 9-12, 603-823-5611 **Gale River Motel**

Mac's Market

Franconia Village Store deli

Abbie Greenleaf Library

Also: AMC shuttle stop, Bus service, hardware.

1834.1 US 302 Crawford Notch

(1W) **Willey House** Snack bar, open daily mid-May to mid-Oct, 9-5.

(1.8E) **Dry River Campground** 603-374-2272 <www.nhstateparks.com/crawford.html> camping $23, pets allowed, coin laundry & showers, all major CC, quiet 10pm-7am.

(3.5W) **AMC's Highland Center** 603-278-4453 <www.outdoors.org> Lodge $75-90PP, includes B/D. Shapleigh Bunkhouse $38 for AMC members, $46 for non-members includes breakfast. No pets, no smoking. Short-order menu, coin shower for non-guests. Shuttles daily Jun-mid to Sep, afterwards only weekends and holidays until Oct. Maildrops: Route 302, Bretton Woods, NH 03574.

(E3.3) **Crawford Notch General Store & Campground** 603-374-2779 <www.crawfordnotchcamping.com> bunkhouse $22PP with shower and towel, pets allowed, free return ride, laundry for guests, Coleman/alcohol/oz and iso-butane, sandwiches, ice cream. Open daily mid-May to Columbus Day weekend, owners Marvin & Glenn Powell. Maildrops: 1138 US 302, Harts Location, NH 03812.

John Bartlett 508-330-4178 <jbclimbs@comcast.net> shuttle area between Crawford Notch and Gorham, NH, advance notice helpful.

1846.6 Mt. Washington
Second highest peak on the AT. **Summit House** open 8am-8pm Memorial Day-Columbus Day. Snack bar open 9am-6pm.

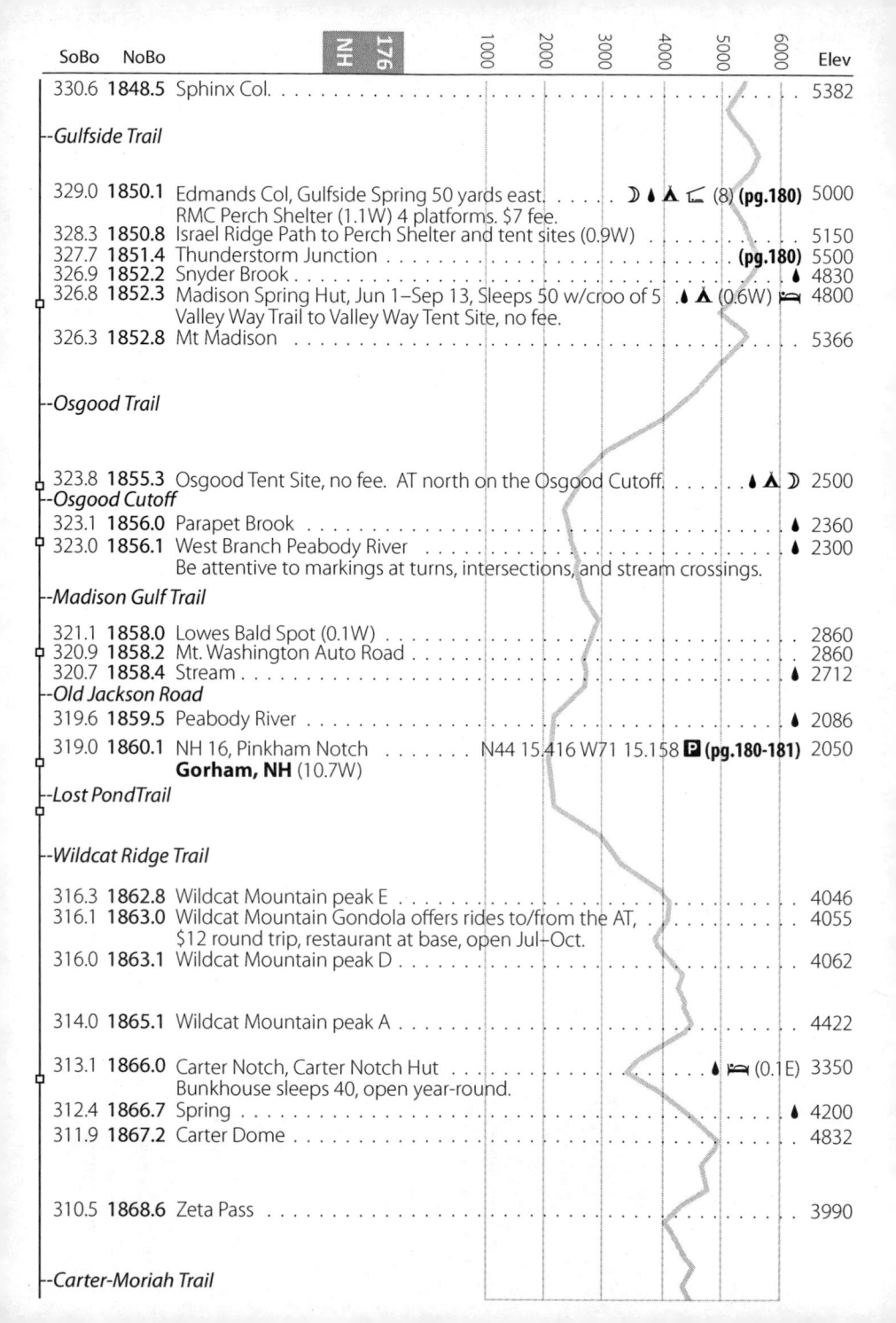

330.6 **1848.5** Sphinx Col. 5382

--Gulfside Trail

329.0 **1850.1** Edmands Col, Gulfside Spring 50 yards east. . . . . . ☽ ♦ ⛺ ⌂ (8) **(pg.180)** 5000
RMC Perch Shelter (1.1W) 4 platforms. $7 fee.
328.3 **1850.8** Israel Ridge Path to Perch Shelter and tent sites (0.9W) 5150
327.7 **1851.4** Thunderstorm Junction . . . . **(pg.180)** 5500
326.9 **1852.2** Snyder Brook . . . . ♦ 4830
326.8 **1852.3** Madison Spring Hut, Jun 1–Sep 13, Sleeps 50 w/croo of 5 ♦ ⛺ (0.6W) 🛏 4800
Valley Way Trail to Valley Way Tent Site, no fee.
326.3 **1852.8** Mt Madison 5366

--Osgood Trail

323.8 **1855.3** Osgood Tent Site, no fee. AT north on the Osgood Cutoff. . . . . . . ♦ ⛺ ☽ 2500
--Osgood Cutoff
323.1 **1856.0** Parapet Brook . . . . ♦ 2360
323.0 **1856.1** West Branch Peabody River . . . . ♦ 2300
Be attentive to markings at turns, intersections, and stream crossings.

--Madison Gulf Trail

321.1 **1858.0** Lowes Bald Spot (0.1W) 2860
320.9 **1858.2** Mt. Washington Auto Road 2860
320.7 **1858.4** Stream . . . . ♦ 2712
--Old Jackson Road
319.6 **1859.5** Peabody River . . . . ♦ 2086

319.0 **1860.1** NH 16, Pinkham Notch . . . . . . N44 15.416 W71 15.158 🅿 **(pg.180-181)** 2050
Gorham, NH (10.7W)
--Lost PondTrail

--Wildcat Ridge Trail

316.3 **1862.8** Wildcat Mountain peak E 4046
316.1 **1863.0** Wildcat Mountain Gondola offers rides to/from the AT, ... 4055
$12 round trip, restaurant at base, open Jul–Oct.
316.0 **1863.1** Wildcat Mountain peak D 4062

314.0 **1865.1** Wildcat Mountain peak A 4422

313.1 **1866.0** Carter Notch, Carter Notch Hut . . . . ♦ 🛏 (0.1E) 3350
Bunkhouse sleeps 40, open year-round.
312.4 **1866.7** Spring . . . . ♦ 4200
311.9 **1867.2** Carter Dome 4832

310.5 **1868.6** Zeta Pass 3990

--Carter-Moriah Trail

308.4	**1870.7**	Middle Carter Mountain		4600
307.4	**1871.7**	North Carter Trail		4483
305.9	**1873.2**	**Imp Campsite** (0.1W) . . . . ♦ ⟩ ⋏ ⊏ (10)		3250

56.5◀51.0◀42.0◀▶6.1▶19.8▶25.0
Overnight fee $8PP, caretaker, 5 platforms, composting privy.

| 305.2 | **1873.9** | Stony Brook Trail junction . . . . | | 2968 |
| 303.8 | **1875.3** | Mt Moriah . . . . | | 4049 |

--*Kenduskeag Trail*

| 301.3 | **1877.8** | Carter-Moriah + Kenduskeag Trail intersection . . . . ♦ | | 3350 |

--*Rattle River Trail*

301.3	**1877.8**	Rattle River . . . . ♦		2000
300.2	**1878.9**	East Rattle River . . . . ♦		1300
299.8	**1879.3**	**Rattle River Shelter** . . . . ⟩ ♦ ⊏ (8)		1260

57.1◀48.1◀6.1◀▶13.7▶18.9▶23.3 Many tent sites. No fee. Water source is
Rattle River. Gently sloping trail from shelter to US 2.

| 297.9 | **1881.2** | US 2 . . . . N44 24.048 W71 6.589 🅿 **(pg.180-181)** | | 760 |

Gorham, NH (3.6W) Nobo, AT 0.1W on US 2, then east on North Rd.

297.6	**1881.5**	Androscoggin River, road		750
297.4	**1881.7**	North Road parking area . . . . N44 24.386 W71 7.009 🅿		750
297.1	**1882.0**	Hogan Rd, unpaved		773
296.4	**1882.7**	Brook . . . . ♦		1485
296.0	**1883.1**	Mt Hayes		2555
292.1	**1887.0**	Cascade Mountain		2631
291.0	**1888.1**	Trident Col Tentsite . . . . ⟩ ♦ ⋏		2020

No Fee. Four tent pads. Spring on side trail.

| 290.0 | **1889.1** | Page Pond . . . . ♦ | | 2169 |
| 288.3 | **1890.8** | Dream Lake . . . . ♦ | | 2650 |

286.8 **1892.3** Moss Pond . . . . ◊ 2100

286.1 **1893.0** **Gentian Pond Shelter/Campsite** . . . ▸ . . . . ☽ ◊ ▲ ⌐ (14) 2166
61.8◄19.8◄13.7◄▸5.2▸9.6▸14.7
Located at junction of Mahoosuc Trail (AT) and Austin Brook Trail, 3S and
1D platform, inlet brook of Gentian Pond.

284.7 **1894.4** Stream 2510

283.3 **1895.8** Mt Success 3565

282.7 **1896.4** Success Trail 3188

281.4 **1897.7** **NH-ME** border 2972

280.9 **1898.2** **Carlo Col Shelter and Campsite** (0.3W) . . . . ☽ ◊ ⌐ (8) 2945
25.0◄18.9◄5.2◄▸4.4▸9.5▸16.4
On Carlo Col Trail, 3S and 2D platforms, bear box, no fee.

280.5 **1898.6** Mt Carlo 3565

278.7 **1900.4** Goose Eye Mountain east peak 3790

277.5 **1901.6** Goose Eye Mountain north peak 3675

276.5 **1902.6** **Full Goose Shelter and Campsite** . . . . ☽ ◊ ⌐ (12) 3030
23.3◄9.6◄4.4◄▸5.1▸12.0▸15.5 No Fee, stream behind shelter.

276.0 **1903.1** Fulling Mill Mountain south peak 3395

275.0 **1904.1** Mahoosuc Notch west end, Mahoosuc Notch Trail . . . . ◊ 2480
Most difficult or most fun mile of the AT? Make your way through a
jumbled pit of giant boulders.

273.9 **1905.2** Mahoosuc Notch east end, Mahoosuc Notch . . . . ◊ 2150

273.4 **1905.7** Brook . . . . ◊ 2610

272.3 **1906.8** Mahoosuc Arm (summit) 3770

271.7 **1907.4** Speck Pond brook . . . . ◊ 3700

271.4 **1907.7** **Speck Pond Shelter & Campsite** . . . . ☽ ◊ ▲ ⌐ (8) 3500
14.7◄9.5◄5.1◄▸6.9▸10.4▸20.9 Overnight fee $8PP, caretaker, tent sites.
Spring down Speck Pond Trail just beyond caretaker's yurt.

270.3 **1908.8** Grafton Loop Trail, Old Speck Trail to Old Speck Mtn 3985
with small observation tower.

267.9 **1911.2** Brook . . . . ◊ 2505

266.8 **1912.3** Grafton Notch, ME 26 . . . . N44 35.382 W70 56.803 **P** ☽ **(pg.182)** 1495
Bethel, ME (17.0E)

264.5	**1914.6**	**Baldpate Lean-to**	☽ ♦ ⌐ (8)	2660
		16.4◄12.0◄6.9◄►3.5►14.0►26.8 Brook next to lean-to.		
263.7	**1915.4**	Baldpate Mountain west peak, Grafton Loop Trail		3662
262.8	**1916.3**	Baldpate Mountain east peak		3810
261.0	**1918.1**	**Frye Notch Lean-to** . . . . ► . . .	☽ ♦ ⌐ (6)	2280
		15.5◄10.4◄3.5◄►10.5►23.3►31.6 Frye Brook in front of lean-to.		
257.3	**1921.8**	Dunn Notch and Falls	♦	1286
256.5	**1922.6**	East B Hill Rd . . . . N44 40.096 W70 53.594 **P** **(pg.183)**		1485
		Andover, ME (8.0E)		
254.7	**1924.4**	Surplus Pond outlet	♦	2050
254.6	**1924.5**	Gravel road		2077
251.8	**1927.3**	Wyman Mountain		2920
250.9	**1928.2**	Small brook	♦	2592
250.5	**1928.6**	**Hall Mountain Lean-to** . . . . ► . .	☽ ♦ ⌐ (6)	2650
		20.9◄14.0◄10.5◄►12.8►21.1►32.3 Spring south of lean-to on AT.		
249.2	**1929.9**	Small brook	♦	1250
249.1	**1930.0**	Sawyer Notch, Sawyer Brook (ford)	♦	1095
248.2	**1930.9**	Moody Mountain		2440
247.1	**1932.0**	Small brook	♦	1986
246.4	**1932.7**	South Arm Rd, Black Brook on south side of road	♦ **(pg.183)**	1410
		Andover, ME (9.0E)		
243.6	**1935.5**	Old Blue Mountain		3600

| SoBo | NoBo | | ME 179 | 1000 2000 3000 4000 5000 6000 | Elev |

Randolph Mountain Club (RMC)

The Randolph Mountain Club maintains four shelters in the Northern Presidentials. Per-person fees are: Gray Knob - $12.00, Crag Camp - $12.00, The Perch - $7.00, and Log Cabin - $7.00. Fees must be paid in cash for stays at Gray Knob, Crag Camp and The Perch. Persons without cash will be directed to stay at the Log Cabin and will receive a receipt to mail in their fee. There is a caretaker year-round at Gray Knob if you need assistance or have questions. During the summer months, a second caretaker is in residence at Crag Camp. A caretaker visits Crag Camp and The Perch every evening, throughout the year.

All are open year-round. The camps are busy on weekends. Reservations are not accepted at any of the shelters; usage is first-come, first-served. If space is not available, be prepared to camp. Camping is not permitted within a quarter mile of RMC shelters.

There is no trash disposal; carry in, carry out. Please keep noise to a minimum after 10pm. The use of cell phones and portable TVs is not permitted. Group size is limited to ten. There is no smoking inside RMC facilities. When a camp is full, all guests are asked to limit their stay to two consecutive nights. Outdoor wood campfires are not allowed at any of the camps. Dogs are allowed at RMC's facilities, but they should be under voice control at all times.

1850.1   Edmands Col

1851.4   Thunderstorm Junction
Ⓗ **Crag Camp Cabin** (1.1W) on Spur Trail, **Gray Knob Cabin** (1.2W) on Lowe Path. Camp at least 0.25 from either cabin.

1860.1   NH 16/Pinkham Notch

Ⓗ🛏✕🚿📷✉📞 **Pinkham Notch Visitor Center** 603-466-2721 Open year round. Cafeteria with B/L/D buffets. Coin shower. UPS Maildrops: AMC Visitor Center, c/o Front Desk, NH 16, Gorham, NH 03581.

Ⓗ✕🚿📷🏠 **Joe Dodge Lodge** 603-466-2721 〈www.outdoors.org〉 Thru-hikers get AMC rates here for the lodge, meals, and shuttle.   Bunks $65.66 June 4 - Oct 23, include B/D. No pets. Meals without stay $10B/$20D, a la carte lunch. Vending machines, Coleman/alcohol/iso-butane/oz. Shuttle 8am daily $17. Accepts major credit cards.

🛏⛺ (4W) on NH 16 to **Camp Dodge**, 603-466-3301 Headquarters for AMC's trail crew. Work for stay sometimes available. Call ahead (may take many rings before phone is answered). Open May to mid-Sep.

Gorham, NH (10.7W from Pinkham Notch)
(more services on map and page 182)

1881.2   US 2

🛏 **The Wildberry Inn** 603-466-5049 〈www.thewildberryinn.com〉 bed and breakfast $95D and up, phone on porch to call into town for rides, located on west side of the AT at the intersection with US 2.

Ⓗ🛏⛺🚿🏠📞 (1.8W) **White Birches Camping Park** 603-466-2022 〈www.whitebirchescampingpark.com〉 bunks $15, tent sites $11PP, pool, pets allowed, Coleman/alcohol/iso-butane, free shuttle from/to trail and town with stay, open May-Oct. Maildrops for guests: 218 US 2, Shelburne, NH 03581.

🛏✕🍴 (2.9W) **Town and Country Inn** 603-466-3315 〈www.townandcountryinn.com〉 $54-90, pets $6. Breakfast 6-10:30, dinner 5-10, cocktails. Indoor pool.

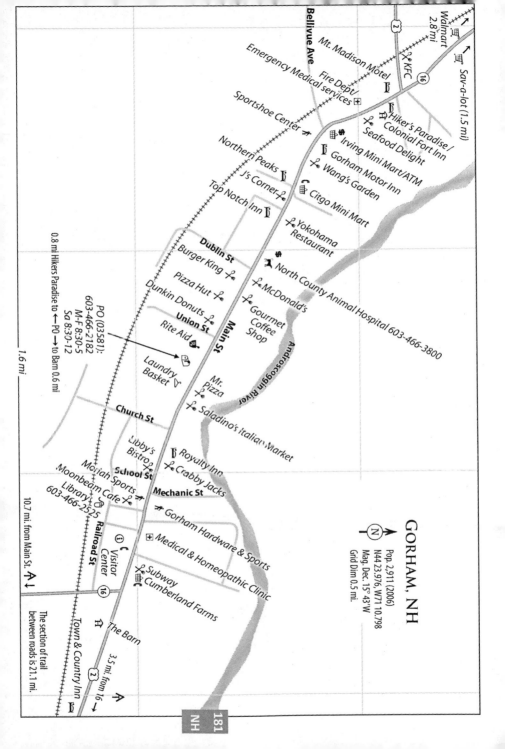

GORHAM, NH

N

Pop. 2,911 (2006)
N44 23.976, W71 10.798
Mag. Dec. 15° 43'W
Grid Dim 0.5 mi.

Walmart 2.8 mi

Sav-a-lot (1.5 mi)

Mt. Madison Motel

Bellivue Ave

Emergency Medical services

Fire Dept/

KFC

Sportshoe Center

Hiker's Paradise/
Colonial Fort Inn

Seafood Delight

Irving Mini Mart/ATM

Gorham Motor Inn

Wang's Garden

Citgo Mini Mart

Northern Peaks

J's Corner

Top Notch Inn

Yokohama
Restaurant

North County Animal Hospital 603-466-3800

Dublin St

Burger King

McDonald's

Pizza Hut

Gourmet
Coffee
Shop

Dunkin Donuts

Union St

Rite Aid

Main St

Androscoggin River

PO (03581):
603-466-2182
M-F 8-30-5
Sa 8:30-12

0.8 mi Hikers Paradise to ← P0 → to Barn 0.6 mi

Laundry
Basket

Mr.
Pizza

Church St

Saladino's Italian Market

Libby's
Bistro

Royulty Inn

Crabby Jacks

Moriah Sports

School St

Moonbeam Cafe

Mechanic St

Library
603-466-2525

Gorham Hardware & Sports

Visitor
Center

Medical & Homeopathic Clinic

Railroad St

Subway

Cumberland Farms

The Barn

Town & Country Inn

1.6 mi

10.7 mi. from Main St.

3.5 mi. from 16

The section of trail
between roads is 21.1 mi.

Gorham, NH (3.6W from US 2) *(more services on map)*

ID required; all packages should include your legal name.

Hiker's Paradise at Colonial Fort Inn 603-466-2732, 800-470-4224 ⟨www.hikersparadise.com⟩ bunks $20 with linen, tub/shower, kitchen. Private rooms available. No pets or maildrops. Coin laundry for guests. Restaurant serves breakfast. Coleman/alcohol/oz. Free shuttle with stay from/to Route 2, other limited shuttles.

★ **The Barn** also the **Libby House B&B** 603-466-2271, bunks $20, Coleman/alcohol/oz, kitchen, stove microwave, refrigerator for use, no pets, laundry $5, Visa MC accepted, shuttles as time permits. Maildrops for guests: 55 Main Street, Gorham, NH 03581

Royalty Inn 603-466-3312 ⟨www.royaltyinn.com⟩ $49-150, a/c, pool. **Crabby Jacks Restaurant** serves B/L/D.

Top Notch Inn 603-466-5496 ⟨www.topnotchinn.com⟩ Pool, a/c, pets allowed, no smoking, all major credit cards accepted.

Northern Peaks Motor Inn 603-466-3374 ⟨www.northernpeaksmotorinn.com⟩, a/c, pool, pets $5, no smoking, all major credit cards accepted, hiker friendly.

Gorham Hardware and Sports 603-466-2312 Open 8-5:30. Gear, hiking food, Coleman/alcohol/oz and iso-butane. Accepts Visa/MC/Discover.

Altitude 6288 Sport-Ski 603-466-2127 Short and long distance shuttles anywhere from VT through Katahdin and off-trail locations like Leki pole repair. Ships UPS.

Arthur Jolin 603-466-2127 Short and long distance shuttles anywhere from VT through Katahdin and off-trail locations like Boston or Portland airports.

John Bartlett (see Crawford Notch, page 175)

Concord Coach Bus service stops daily at Irving store. Routes to Pinkham Notch NH, Manchester NH, and many other cities.

Library M-F 10-6

Rite Aid 603-466-5636 M-F 8-8, Sa 8-6, Su 8-5.

North County Animal Hospital 603-466-3800

Laundry Basket 7 days 5:30-11.

Berlin, NH 03570

Androscoggin Valley Hospital 603-752-2200

1912.3   ME 26/Grafton Notch

(4.5E) **Mahoosuc Guide Service** 207-824-2073 ⟨www.mahoosuc.com⟩ bunkrooms $35PP with towel, linen extra. Full kitchen, will cook B/L/D. No dogs. Laundry $5, Coleman/alcohol/oz. Shuttles $10, call from top of Old Speck for shuttle from parking lot. Shuttles to town possible. Maildrops: 1513 Bear River Rd, Newry, ME 04261.

(12.8E) **Stony Brook Recreation and Camping** 207-824-2836, 207-824-2789, ⟨www.stonybrookrec.com⟩ tent site $25 for 4, lean-to $28 for 4, $4EAP, offer shuttles from Grafton Notch. Pool, miniature golf, rec room, convenience store, Coleman fuel. Located 12 miles east on Hwy 26, then left 0.8 miles on Route 2. Maildrops: 42 Powell Place, Hanover, ME 04237.

Bethel, ME 04217 12E to Rt 2, right for 5 miles on Rt 2

M-F 9-5, Sa 10-12:30, Su 207-824-2668

Chapman Inn 207-824-2657 ⟨www.chapmaninn.com⟩ Bunk space $25 in hiker dorm with shower. Rooms $59/up includes breakfast. Kitchen privileges, $4 laundry. Maildrops: PO Box 1067, Bethel, ME 04217.

Pat's Pizza 7 days 11-9, **Sudbury Inn Restaurant & Pub**, Tu-Su 5:30-9, pub 7 days 4:30-9.

Bethel Shop'n Save

True North Adventurewear 207-824-2201 Full service outfitter, open 7 days 10-6. Shuttles by appointment. Leki repair, Coleman/alcohol/oz and iso-butane.

Bethel Animal Hospital 207-824-2212

Also: Casablanca Cinema 4

1922.6   East B Hill Road
Andover, ME 04216 (8.0E)

⊕ M-F 8:30-1:30 & 2-4:30, Sa 8:30-11:30, 207-392-4571

⇔ ⇧ ⚑ △ ⊠ **Pine Ellis Lodging** 207-392-4161 ⟨www.pineellislodging.com⟩ private room $35S, $50D, bunks $20PP, free pickup from trailhead with reservation. Kitchen privileges. Laundry $3. Many shuttles services available. USPS/UPS Maildrops for guests: PO Box 12 or 20 Pine Street, Andover, ME 04216.

⇧ △ ⊠ ⚑ **The Cabin** (3E) 207-392-1333 ⟨www.thecabininmaine. com⟩ $20PP includes linens, kitchen use. Shuttles available. Meals by arrangement. Guest maildrops: PO Box 55 or 497 East Andover Rd, East Andover, ME 04226.

⊞ (✗ $ **Andover General Store** 207-392-4172   Deli serves short-order food and pizza, open 7 days 5-9.

⊞ (✗ **Mill's Market** 7 days 4-8, both have a

✗ **Little Red Hen**

Also: Massage therapist, Donna Gifford, 207-357-5686, call for rates. Free pickup/return to Andover.

1932.7   South Arm Road
★ ▲ ⊞ △ ⚶ ⊠ (3.5W) **South Arm Campground** 207-364-5155 ⟨www.southarm.com⟩ Tent site $15 up to 4, camp store, no credit cards, open May 1–Oct 1. Maildrops: PO Box 310, Andover, ME 04216.
Andover, ME (9.0E) (see above)

240.4 **1938.7** Bemis Stream Trail 3320

239.4 **1939.7** Bemis Range west peak 3580

237.7 **1941.4** **Bemis Mountain Lean-to** . . . . ☽ ◗ ⌐ (8) 2800
26.8◄23.3◄12.8◄►8.3►19.5►28.4 Small spring to left of lean-to.

234.2 **1944.9** Small spring . . . . ◗ 1837
234.1 **1945.0** Gravel road 1563
233.9 **1945.2** Bemis Stream (ford) . . . . ◗ 1495

233.1 **1946.0** ME 17. . . . . N44 50.181 W70 42.602 🅿 (pg.188) 2200
Oquossoc, ME (11.0W)

231.5 **1947.6** Moxie Pond . . . . ◗ 2420

229.7 **1949.4** Long Pond (sand beach) . . . . ◗ 2330
229.4 **1949.7** **Sabbath Day Pond Lean-to** . . . . ☽ ◗ Ⓐ ⌐ (8) 2390
31.6◄21.1◄8.3◄►11.2►20.1►28.1
Pond in front of lean-to. Sandy beach (0.3S) on AT (swimming).
228.9 **1950.2** Fire road 2372

227.7 **1951.4** Powerline 2850

224.8 **1954.3** Little Swift River Pond Campsite . . . . ◗Ⓐ 2460
Spring house next to pond.

223.6 **1955.5** Chandler Mill Stream . . . . ◗ 2193

222.1 **1957.0** South Pond . . . . ◗ 2174

SoBo	NoBo			Elev
220.0	**1959.1**	ME 4, **Rangeley, ME** (9.0W) . . . . N44 53.213 W70 32.431 **P(pg.188)**		1600
219.9	**1959.2**	Sandy River . . . . ♦		1595
219.3	**1959.8**	Gravel road		1957
218.8	**1960.3**	Old haul road		1980
218.5	**1960.6**	Small Brook . . . . ♦		2045
218.2	**1960.9**	**Piazza Rock Lean-to** . . . . ☽ ♦ ⊏ (8)		2065

32.3◄19.5◄11.2◄►8.9►16.9►35.5 Two-seat privy and cribbage board.
Stream passes through campsite, tent platforms.

217.5	**1961.6**	Ethel Pond . . . . ♦		2360
217.1	**1962.0**	Saddleback Stream . . . . ♦		2375
216.3	**1962.8**	Eddy Pond . . . . ♦		2680
216.1	**1963.0**	Gravel road		2662
214.3	**1964.8**	Saddleback Mountain		4120
212.7	**1966.4**	The Horn		4040
212.0	**1967.1**	Redington Stream Campsite . . . . ♦ Δ		3600
211.9	**1967.2**	Reddington Campsite . . . . ☽ ♦ Δ		3034

Four tent pads, water 0.2W on side trail.

210.7	**1968.4**	Saddleback Junior		3655
210.3	**1968.8**	Stream . . . . ♦		3190
209.3	**1969.8**	**Poplar Ridge Lean-to** (1961) . . . . ☽ ♦ Δ ⊏ (6)		2960

28.4◄20.1◄8.9◄►8.0►26.6►36.8
Some tenting at lean-to, more on knoll to the north. Stream in front.

206.6	**1972.5**	Orbeton Stream (ford) . . . . ♦		1550
206.5	**1972.6**	Gravel road		1870
205.8	**1973.3**	Sluice Brook . . . . ♦		2255
205.1	**1974.0**	Logging road		2260
204.6	**1974.5**	Logging road, Perham Stream nearby . . . . ♦		2275
203.5	**1975.6**	Lone Mountain		3260
202.4	**1976.7**	Mt Abraham Trail, summit 1.7E		3370
201.3	**1977.8**	**Spaulding Mountain Lean-to** . . . . ☽ ♦ ⊏ (8)		3140

28.1◄16.9◄8.0◄►18.6►28.8►36.1 Small spring to right.

200.5	**1978.6**	Crest NW shoulder of Spaulding Mountain		4000
		Side trail to summit 0.1E		
199.8	**1979.3**	Bronze plaque		3394
		Completion of the last section of the AT from GA-ME.		

SoBo   NoBo   ME 185   1000 2000 3000 4000 5000 6000   Elev

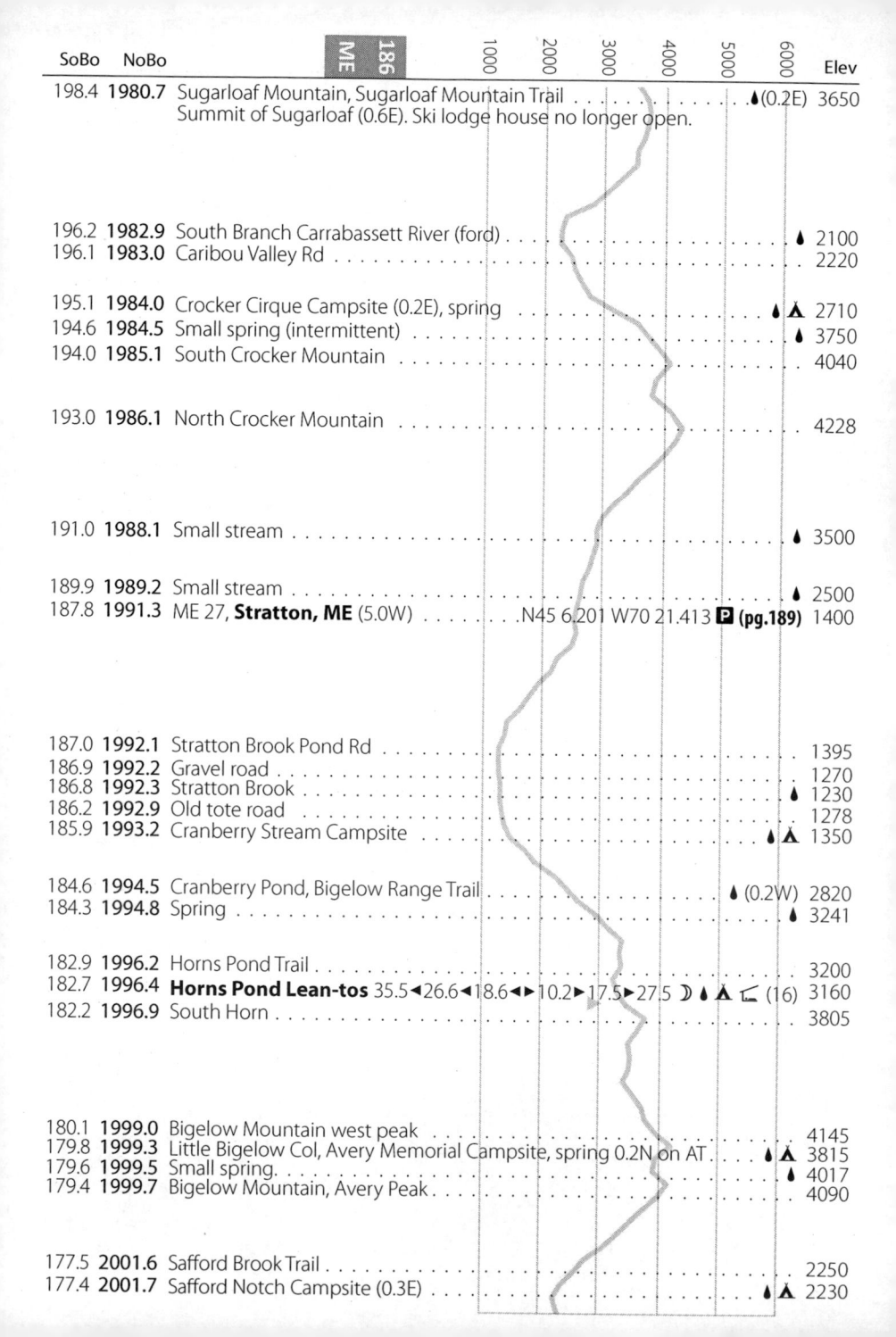

SoBo	NoBo		1000	2000	3000	4000	5000	6000	Elev

ME 186

SoBo	NoBo		Elev
198.4	**1980.7**	Sugarloaf Mountain, Sugarloaf Mountain Trail . . . . ♦(0.2E)	3650
		Summit of Sugarloaf (0.6E). Ski lodge house no longer open.	
196.2	**1982.9**	South Branch Carrabassett River (ford) . . . . ♦	2100
196.1	**1983.0**	Caribou Valley Rd	2220
195.1	**1984.0**	Crocker Cirque Campsite (0.2E), spring . . . . ♦▲	2710
194.6	**1984.5**	Small spring (intermittent) . . . . ♦	3750
194.0	**1985.1**	South Crocker Mountain	4040
193.0	**1986.1**	North Crocker Mountain	4228
191.0	**1988.1**	Small stream . . . . ♦	3500
189.9	**1989.2**	Small stream . . . . ♦	2500
187.8	**1991.3**	ME 27, **Stratton, ME** (5.0W) . . . . N45 6.201 W70 21.413 🅿 (pg.189)	1400
187.0	**1992.1**	Stratton Brook Pond Rd	1395
186.9	**1992.2**	Gravel road	1270
186.8	**1992.3**	Stratton Brook . . . . ♦	1230
186.2	**1992.9**	Old tote road	1278
185.9	**1993.2**	Cranberry Stream Campsite . . . . ♦▲	1350
184.6	**1994.5**	Cranberry Pond, Bigelow Range Trail . . . . ♦ (0.2W)	2820
184.3	**1994.8**	Spring . . . . ♦	3241
182.9	**1996.2**	Horns Pond Trail	3200
182.7	**1996.4**	**Horns Pond Lean-tos** 35.5◄26.6◄18.6◄▸10.2▸17.5▸27.5 ☽♦▲◸ (16)	3160
182.2	**1996.9**	South Horn	3805
180.1	**1999.0**	Bigelow Mountain west peak	4145
179.8	**1999.3**	Little Bigelow Col, Avery Memorial Campsite, spring 0.2N on AT . . . . ♦▲	3815
179.6	**1999.5**	Small spring. . . . . ♦	4017
179.4	**1999.7**	Bigelow Mountain, Avery Peak	4090
177.5	**2001.6**	Safford Brook Trail	2250
177.4	**2001.7**	Safford Notch Campsite (0.3E) . . . . ♦▲	2230

174.2 **2004.9** Little Bigelow Mountain east end 3010

172.5 **2006.6** **Little Bigelow Lean-to** . . . . ☽ ♦ ▲ ⊏ (8) 1760
36.8◄28.8◄10.2◄►7.3►17.3►27.0
Plenty of tent sites at lean-to. Swimming in "the Tubs" along AT.

171.1 **2008.0** East Flagstaff Rd . . . . N45 8.073 W70 10.283 🅿 (0.1W) 1200
171.0 **2008.1** Bog Brook Rd, Flagstaff Lake outlet . . . . ♦ 1200

169.3 **2009.8** Jerome Brook . . . . ♦ 1265
168.7 **2010.4** Long Falls Dam Rd . . . . ♦ 1225

167.0 **2012.1** Roundtop Mountain 1980
166.2 **2012.9** Brook . . . . ♦ 1326

165.9 **2013.2** West Carry Pond . . . . ♦ 1320

165.2 **2013.9** **West Carry Pond Lean-to** . . . . ☽ ♦ ⊏ (8) 1340
36.1◄17.5◄7.3◄►10.0►19.7►28.7 Swimming in pond. Spring house to
left of lean-to or West Carry Pond are water sources.
164.5 **2014.6** West Carry Pond east side . . . . ♦ 1324

162.6 **2016.5** Sandy Stream, Middle Carry Pond inlet . . . . ♦ 1340
161.8 **2017.3** Gravel road 1260

161.1 **2018.0** East Carry Pond north end . . . . ♦ 1238

159.4 **2019.7** Logging road 1130

158.7 **2020.4** North Branch of Carrying Place Stream . . . . ♦ 1150

158.2 **2020.9** Spring . . . . ♦ 1163

155.2 **2023.9** **Pierce Pond Lean-to**, east bank of Pierce Pond. . . . . ☽ ♦ ⊏ (6) 1160
27.5◄17.3◄10.0◄►9.7►18.7►22.8 ►

✕ **Four Seasons Café** 7 days 11-9 L/D vegetarian specialties.

1959.1   ME 4

Rangeley, ME (9.0W)
(more services on map)

⛺ 🏨 ⬧ ✉ **Gull Pond Lodge** 207-864-5563, $20PP bunk, private room $30S, $45D, includes shower, hiker box, kitchen/grill, TV, slackpacking. Will pick up from town (not the trailhead) free with stay. Maildrops: PO Box 1177, Rangeley, ME 04970.

🏨 **Town & Lake Motel** 207-864-3755 $85S $99D $10EAP, pets $5.

🏨 **Saddleback Motor Inn** 207-864-3434 $90, pets $10, pool.

🏨 ✕ **Rangeley Inn** 207-864-3341 〈www.rangeleyinn.com〉 High-end resort may give discount on low-demand nights. **Sunset Grill** on-site serves lunch & dinner, closed M&Tu.

✕ **Sarge's Sports Pub & Grub,** L/D and bar, seven days 11-1, house bands on Friday and Saturday.

🏪 **IGA Supermarket** ATM 7 days 7-8.

🏦 **Ecopelagicon** 207-864-2771 Hiker friendly nature store has white gas/alcohol/oz, cannister fuel, small gear items and books.

🥾 **Alpine Shop** 〈www.alpineshoprangeley.com〉 207-864-3741 Full range of gear, Coleman/alcohol/oz & iso-butane, M-S 9-7:30, Su 10-4.

🥾 **Back Woods** 207-864-2335 Gear, clothes.

➕ **Rangeley Health Center** 207-864-4397

℞ **Rangeley Pharmacy** 207-864-3984, M-F 9-5.

⬧ **Village Scrub Board** 7 days 7-7

Oquossoc, ME (7.0W) from Rangeley

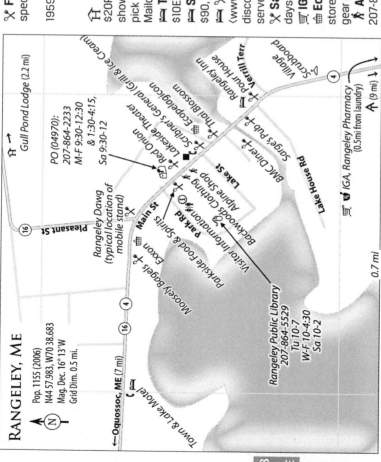

RANGELEY, ME

Pop. 1155 (2006)
N44 57.983, W70 38.683
Mag. Dec. 16° 13'W
Grid Dim. 0.5 mi.

→ Oquossoc, ME (7 mi)
Town & Lake Motel →

Gull Pond Lodge (2.2 mi)

PO (04970):
207-864-2233
M-F 9:30-12:30
& 1:30-4:15,
Sa 9:30-12

Rangeley Dawg
(typical location of
mobile stand)

Pleasant St

Main St

Moosely Bagels
Exxon

Parkside Food & Spirits

Park Rd

Visitor Information

Backwoods Clothing
Alpine Shop

Lake St

Red Onion

Lakeside Theater

Scribner's General (Grill & Ice Cream)

Ecopelagicon

Thai Blossom

Rangeley Inn

Pour House

Verrill Terr

BMC Diner

Sarge's Pub

Village
Scrubboard

Rangeley Public Library
207-864-5529
Tu 10-7
W-F 10-4:30
Sa 10-2

Lake House Rd

🏪 ℞ IGA, Rangeley Pharmacy
(0.5mi from laundry)

↑ (9 mi)

0.7 mi

1946.0   ME 17

Oquossoc, ME 04964 (11.0W)

📮 M-F 8-1 & 1:30-4:30, Sa 9-12, 207-864-3685

🍺 **Oquossoc Grocery** deli, bakery, Coleman fuel

🏦 **Gingerbread House** serves B/L/D, vegetarian specials.

✕ **Gingerbread House** serves B/L/D, vegetarian specials.

🍴 (2E) **Mountainside Grocers** 207-237-2248, open 8-6 May-1 Nov, 8-8 in winter.

Stratton, ME (5.0W) (more services on map)

🛏🍴🚻⛺🏕 **Stratton Motel** 207-246-4171 <www.thestrattonmotel.com> $20 bunk, $50 private room, $5 laundry, free long distance calling, all credit cards accepted. Shuttles as far as Bangor, Portland, or Monson. Maildrops for both the Motel and Maine Roadhouse: PO Box 284, Stratton, ME 04982.

🛏🏕🛁🚶 **Maine Roadhouse** 207-246-2060 <www.maineroadhouse.com> (5W) on route 16. Bunkroom $20pp, semiprivate rooms $40S, $45D, free laundry, free long-distance, satellite TV, hiker kitchen and use of outdoor grill. Free shuttles to and from Route 27 and PO. Maildrops same as Stratton Motel.

🛏✕🖂 **White Wolf Inn** 207-246-2922, $40S, $45D, pets $10, restaurant serves L/D closed Tu, W is Spaghetti, F is Fish fry, does not accept Amex. Maildrops: Main Street, PO Box 590, Stratton, ME 04982.

🛏✕🖂 **Spillover Motel** 207-246-6571, $55S, $72D, pets okay for a $20 deposit and $5 charge, continental breakfast. Full kitchen available for use by guests. Maildrops: PO Box 427, Stratton, ME 04982.

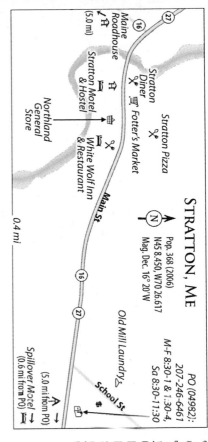

STRATTON, ME

Pop. 368 (2006)
N45 8.450, W70 26.617
Mag. Dec. 16° 20'W

PO (04982): 207-246-6461
M-F 8:30-1 & 1:30-4,
Sa 8:30-11:30

Maine Roadhouse (5.0 mi)

Stratton Diner ✕ — Stratton Pizza ✕ — 🖂 Fotter's Market

Stratton Motel & Hostel 🏠 — White Wolf Inn & Restaurant ✕

Northland General Store

Main St.

Old Mill Laundry 🛁

School St. 💲

Spillover Motel (0.6 mi from PO) 🛏↓

(5.0 mi from PO) 🛏↓

0.4 mi

✕ **Stratton Diner** B/L/D, daily specials, M-Tu 6-8, W 6-11am (only breakfast), Th-F 6-8, Sa Su 7-8.

✕🖂 **Stratton Pizza** L/D Tu-Sa 11-10.

🍴 **Northland Cash Supply** 207-246-2376, Open 7 days 5-10, pizza, hiker box, Coleman/alcohol by ounce. Hiker friendly owner (Mark) provides rides back to the trail for free. Maildrops: 152 Main Street, Stratton, ME 04982.

🍴 **Fotter's Market** 207-246-2401 ATM, Deli, Coleman/alcohol/oz, M-Sa 8-8, Su 9-5.

SoBo	NoBo		Elev
155.1	2024.0	Trail to Harrisons Pierce Pond Camps . . . . **(pg.196)**	1151
155.0	2024.1	Wooden dam, outlet of Pierce Pond . . . . ♦	1140
154.8	2024.3	Trail junction. East to Harrison's, west to boat landing . . . . **(pg.196)**	1097
154.0	2025.1	For the next mile (north), multiple side trails to waterfalls	1050
153.4	2025.7	Otter Pond Stream . . . . ♦	803
152.8	2026.3	Reach ledge overlooking several high waterfalls	825
151.5	2027.6	Kennebec River. Do not ford, use ferry service . . . . ♦ **(pg.196)**	490
151.2	2027.9	US 201, **Caratunk, ME** (0.3E) . . . . N45 14.302 W69 59.777 **P** **(pg.196)**	523
150.4	2028.7	Holly Brook . . . . ♦	907
148.5	2030.6	Holly Brook . . . . ♦	920
145.9	2033.2	Boise-Cascade Logging Rd	1390
145.7	2033.4	Old logging road . . . . N45 16.376 W69 55.319 **P**	1389
145.5	2033.6	**Pleasant Pond Lean-to** . . . . ☽ ♦ ⌐ (6)	1320
		27.0◄19.7◄9.7◄►9.0►13.1►22.0 Stream on path to lean-to and pond are water sources. Beach 0.2 on side trail beyond lean-to.	
144.2	2034.9	Pleasant Pond Mountain	2470
139.8	2039.3	Brook . . . . ♦	1100
139.5	2039.6	Power line	989
139.3	2039.8	Moxie Pond south end (ford), road . . . . . . ♦ N45 14.984 W69 49.857 **P**	970
139.0	2040.1	Power line	1029
136.7	2042.4	Bald Mountain Brook Campsite . . . . ♦ ▲	1292
136.5	2042.6	**Bald Mountain Brook Lean-to** . . . . ☽ ♦ ⌐ (8)	1300
		28.7◄18.7◄9.0◄►4.1►13.0►25.0 Bald Mountain Brook in front of lean-to.	
134.5	2044.6	Moxie Bald Mountain	2629

| 132.4 | **2046.7** | **Moxie Bald Mountain Lean-to** . . . . ☾ ♦ ⊑ (8) | 1220 |

22.8◄13.1◄4.1◄►8.9►20.9►28.3
Bald Mountain Pond in front of lean-to.

130.9 **2048.2** Gravel road 1276

130.3 **2048.8** Bald Mountain Pond outlet . . . . ♦ 1250

128.4 **2050.7** Gravel road 1125

126.9 **2052.2** Marble Brook and jeep road . . . . ♦ 975

126.6 **2052.5** West Branch of Piscataquis River (ford) . . . . ♦ 940
River normally knee-deep. During periods of heavy rain, fording can be
dangerous.

123.5 **2055.6** **Horseshoe Canyon Lean-to** . . . . ☾ ♦ ⊑ (8) 870

22.0◄13.0◄8.9◄►12.0►19.4►24.1
Lean-to on blue-blazed trail. Water source is stream at northern AT
junction or river in front of and below lean-to.

121.2 **2057.9** East Branch of Piscataquis River (ford) . . . . ♦ 650

120.8 **2058.3** Shirley-Blanchard Rd . . . . .N45 17. 072 W69 35.223 🅿 900

117.8 **2061.3** Blue-blaze to Monson . . . . N45 17.442 W69 31.995 🅿 900
Near Lake Hebron go east on old road bed 0.3 mile to Pleasant Rd and
parking, then left 1.7 miles to town.

115.9 **2063.2** Side trail to Doughty Ponds (0.1W) . . . . ♦ 1000

114.5 **2064.6** ME 15, **Monson, ME** (4.0E) . . . . . N45 19.856 W69 32.122 🅿 **(pg.196-197)** 1215
South end of 100-Mile Wilderness.

114.4 **2064.7** Spectacle Pond outlet . . . . ♦ 1230

113.3 **2065.8** Bell Pond . . . . ♦ 1250

112.6 **2066.5** Lily Pond . . . . ♦ 1150

111.5 **2067.6** **Leeman Brook Lean-to** . . . . ☾ ♦ ⊑ (6) 1060
25.0◄20.9◄12.0◄►7.4►12.1►16.1 Stream in front of lean-to.

| --- | --- | --- | --- | --- | --- | --- | --- | --- | --- | --- |
110.7	2068.4	North Pond outlet							♦	1100
110.3	2068.8	North Pond tote road							.	1065
108.4	2070.7	James Brook							♦	994
108.2	2070.9	Gravel haul road							.	1133
107.9	2071.2	Little Wilson Falls, west 30 yards . . .							♦	840
107.7	2071.4	Little Wilson Stream (ford)							♦	750
107.3	2071.8	Follow gravel road for 100 yards . .							.	1025
105.4	2073.7	Big Wilson tote road							.	587
105.3	2073.8	Thompson Brook							♦	596
104.8	2074.3	Big Wilson Stream (ford)							♦	600
104.5	2074.6	Railroad							.	900
104.1	2075.0	**Wilson Valley Lean-to** (1993) ▶						⟩♦⊏	(6)	1045
		28.3◀19.4◀7.4◀▶4.7▶8.7▶15.6 Spring on opposite side of AT.								
103.5	2075.6	Logging road							.	1210
100.9	2078.2	Wilber Brook (ford)							♦	626
100.8	2078.3	Vaughn Stream							♦	616
100.3	2078.8	Bodfish Farm, Long Pond tote road . .							.	622
100.2	2078.9	Long Pond Stream (ford)							♦	642
		Long pond stream can be quite difficult to ford at high water.								
99.4	2079.7	**Long Pond Stream Lean-to** . . . . ▶						⟩♦⊏	(8)	940
		24.1◀12.1◀4.7◀▶4.0▶10.9▶20.8								
98.1	2081.0	Barren Ledges							.	2005
96.3	2082.8	Barren Mountain							.	2660
95.4	2083.7	Side trail to **Cloud Pond Lean-to** (0.4E) . . ▶						⟩♦⊏	(6)	2420
		16.1◀8.7◀4.0◀▶6.9▶16.8▶24.0 Cloud Pond is water source.								
93.6	2085.5	Small stream							♦	1944
93.3	2085.8	Fourth Mountain							.	2380
91.2	2087.9	Stream at bottom of sag (intermittent) . . .							♦	1759
90.8	2088.3	Third Mountain, Monument Cliff							.	1920
90.2	2088.9	West Chairback Pond Trail							♦	1770

88.9	2090.2	Columbus Mountain, outlet stream from West Chairback Pond . . . . ♦	2325
88.5	2090.6	**Chairback Gap Lean-to** 15.6◄10.9◄6.9◄►9.9►17.1►20.7. . . ☽ ♦ ⊏ (6)	1930
		Unreliable small spring 13 yrds downhill and 25 yrds north.	
88.0	2091.1	Chairback Mountain, Long Pond from Barren-Chairback	2180
85.8	2093.3	East Chairback Pond Trail . . . . ♦ (0.2W) ▲	1630
85.3	2093.8	Small stream and spring . . . . ♦	1240
84.6	2094.5	Logging road . . . . N45 28.632 W69 17.107 ☐ (0.4E)	750
84.1	2095.0	West Branch Pleasant River (ford) . . . . ♦	630
		Wide ford with slick rocky bottom. No camping/fires for 2.0N.	
83.8	2095.3	The Hermitage, white pine reserve (0.7E) . . . . ♦	695
82.8	2096.3	Gulf Hagas Trail . . . . ♦	915
		5.2 mile loop trail whose ends intersect the AT 0.7 miles apart. Features narrow, deep gorge with many waterfalls.	
82.1	2097.0	Gulf Hagas Trail . . . . ♦	1100
78.6	2100.5	**Carl A. Newhall Lean-to** . . . . ☽ ♦ ⊏ (6)	1860
		20.8◄16.8◄9.9◄►7.2►10.8►18.9	
77.7	2101.4	Gulf Hagas Mountain	2680
76.8	2102.3	Sidney Tappan Campsite (0.1E) . . . . ♦ ▲	2425
76.1	2103.0	West Peak	3178
74.5	2104.6	Hay Mountain	3245
73.9	2105.2	White Brook Trail	3100
72.8	2106.3	White Cap Mountain	3650
		View of Katahdin from north side of mountain.	
71.4	2107.7	**Logan Brook Lean-to** . . . . ☽ ♦ ▲ ⊏ (6)	2480
		24.0◄17.1◄7.2◄►3.6►11.7►23.1 Some tent sites. Better sites (0.1N) on AT. Logan Brook behind lean-to; cascades upstream.	
69.8	2109.3	West Branch Pond Rd, French Town Rd	1625
69.3	2109.8	B Inlet Brook . . . . ♦	1218
67.8	2111.3	**East Branch Lean-to** . . . . ☽ ♦ ⊏ (6)	1225
		20.7◄10.8◄3.6◄►8.1►19.5►29.6 Pleasant River in front.	
67.5	2111.6	East branch of Pleasant River (ford) . . . . ♦	1210

SoBo	NoBo		Elev
65.9	**2113.2**	Mountain View Pond outlet . . . . ⬥	1640
65.6	**2113.5**	Short side trail to spring . . . . ⬥	1630
64.3	**2114.8**	Side trail 100 yards to Little Boardman Mountain (wooded).	1980
62.9	**2116.2**	Kokadjo-B Pond Rd	1390
62.0	**2117.1**	Crawford Pond outlet . . . . ⬥	1270
		Stealth camp near sand beach. Water source 70 yards away.	
59.7	**2119.4**	**Cooper Brook Falls Lean-to** . . . . ☽ ⬥ ⛺ ⌐ (6)	880
		18.9◄11.7◄8.1◄►11.4►21.5►29.6 Brook, falls, swimming hole in front of lean-to. Tent sites, privy across trail and up hill.	
59.5	**2119.6**	Large tributary to Cooper Brook . . . . ⬥	821
56.0	**2123.1**	Jo-Mary Rd . . . . N45 39.087 W69 1.900 🅿 ⬥ (pg.197)	655
55.3	**2123.8**	Side trail to north shore of Cooper Pond 0.2 . . . . ⬥	585
55.1	**2124.0**	Side trail to intermittent spring . . . . ⬥	567
54.0	**2125.1**	Logging road, near snowmobile bridge	525
53.1	**2126.0**	Mud Pond outlet . . . . ⬥	585
52.5	**2126.6**	Old logging road	500
51.8	**2127.3**	Antlers Campsite . . . . ⬥ ⛺ ☽	500
		Campsites on edge of Jo-Mary Lake. Unique privy west of AT.	
50.6	**2128.5**	Inlet brook . . . . ⬥	536
50.3	**2128.8**	Side trail to Potaywadjo Ridge (1.0W)	530
50.1	**2129.0**	Sand Beach, lower Jo-Mary Lake . . . . ⬥	520
48.8	**2130.3**	Branch of Nahmakanta Stream (ford) . . . . ⬥	513
48.3	**2130.8**	**Potaywadjo Spring Lean-to** (1995) . . . . ☽ ⬥ ⌐ (8)	710
		23.1◄19.5◄11.4◄►10.1►18.2►29.7 Potaywadjo Spring to right.	
48.2	**2130.9**	Twitchell Brook on bridge . . . . ⬥	510
47.7	**2131.4**	Side trail 75 feet to Pemadumcook Lake southwest shore . . . . . . ⬥	530
46.9	**2132.2**	Deer Brook . . . . ⬥	537
46.0	**2133.1**	Gravel road	525
45.9	**2133.2**	Mahar Tote Road (woods road) . . . . (pg.197)	520
		Blue-blazed trail to White House Landing boat dock (0.9E).	

SoBo	NoBo		Elev
44.5	**2134.6**	Tumbledown Dick Stream (ford) . . . . ♦	512
44.0	**2135.1**	Nahmakanta Stream Campsite . . . . ♦ ▲	575
		Stream in front of campsite.	
42.5	**2136.6**	Tumbledown Dick Trail	625
41.4	**2137.7**	Wood Rats spring . . . . ♦	801
41.1	**2138.0**	Gravel road . . . . N45 44.153 W69 6.247 🅿	575
40.8	**2138.3**	Nahmakanta Lake south end, campsite . . . . ♦ ▲	650
39.8	**2139.3**	Prentiss Brook . . . . ♦	752
38.5	**2140.6**	Side trail to sand beach on shore of Nahmakanta Lake. . . . ♦	682
38.3	**2140.8**	Wadleigh Stream . . . . ♦	682
38.2	**2140.9**	**Wadleigh Stream Lean-to** . . . . ☽ ♦ ⌐ (6)	685
		29.6◄21.5◄10.1◄►8.1►19.6►33.0	
		Stream can be dry during summer.	
36.3	**2142.8**	Nesuntabunt Mountain	1520
35.1	**2144.0**	Gravel logging road.	1020
33.9	**2145.2**	Crescent Pond west end. . . . . ♦	1035
33.5	**2145.6**	Pollywog Gorge, side trail overlooking gorge.	822
32.5	**2146.6**	Pollywog Stream. . . . . N45 46.//4 W69 10.320 🅿 ♦	682
		Cross stream on logging road bridge.	
30.5	**2148.6**	Outlet stream from Murphy Pond . . . . ♦	979
30.1	**2149.0**	**Rainbow Stream Lean-to** . . . . ☽ ♦ ▲ ⌐ (6)	1020
		29.6◄18.2◄8.1◄►11.5►24.9►0.0 Tenting on hill behind lean-to. Excellent	
		swimming hole upstream. Baseball bat floor.	
28.1	**2151.0**	Rainbow Lake west end . . . . ♦	1100
26.3	**2152.8**	Rainbow Spring Campsite. . . . . ♦ ▲ ☽	1120
24.8	**2154.3**	Unmarked trail leads to Rainbow Lake Camps (private) (0.2W)	1230
24.6	**2154.5**	Rainbow Mountain Trail (0.7E)	1202
22.9	**2156.2**	Rainbow Lake east end . . . . ♦	1100
22.8	**2156.3**	Side trail to Little Beaver Pond (0.1E) . . . . ♦	1079

2024.0 & 2024.3 Trails to:

★ ⌂ ⤬ **Harrison's Pierce Pond Camps**
207-672-3625 Reservations required. Offers cabins or can stop in just for breakfast.

2027.6 *Kennebec River*

Do not ford this river; the current is strong and unpredictable due to an upstream dam. The ferry is the official AT route. Ferry is in service 7 days:

Before May 1	No service
May 1 - May 27	time & weather permitting, call in advance
May 28 - July 15	9am-11am
July 16 - Sept 30	9am-11am and 2pm-4pm
Oct 1 - Oct 11	9am-11am
Oct 12 - Oct 31	time & weather permitting, call in advance
After Oct 31	No service

⌂ **Fletcher Mountain Outfitters** 207-672-4879 David Corrigan provides ferry service. Shuttles service available when not operating ferry. Some resupply on-hand.

2027.9 US 201

Caratunk, ME 04925 (0.3E)

✉ ℂ (1E) **The Sterling Inn** 207-672-3333 〈www.mainesterlinginn.com〉 $45-$72 includes breakfast and free pick up from trailhead or from P0. Kids under 12 stay free with parents. 1041 Route 201, Caratunk Maine 04920.

⌂ ▲ ⤬ △ ⌂ ℂ ⤬ (2W) **Northern Outdoors** 800-765-7238 〈www.northernoutdoors.com〉 Lodge rooms $40/up, Cabin tents $15 for 2 or $20 for 4. Coin laundry, hot tub. No pets allowed in campsites, cabin tents or lodging rooms. B/L/D, free shuttle to and from trail coinciding with ferry schedule. Also offers rafting trips (class IV), food and ale in Kennebec River Pub & Brewery. Maildrops: 1771 US 201, The Forks, ME 04985

🛒 **Berry's General Store** (7.5W) 207-663-4461 Food, and some hardware. 5am-7pm 7 days.

2064.6 ME 15

Monson, ME (4.0E) *(more services on map)*

⌂ ⤬ ▲ ⤬ △ ≋ ⌂ ⌂ ✉ **Lake Shore House Pub & Laundromat** 207-997-7069 〈www.lakeshorehouse-house.com〉 thelakeshorehouse@yahoo.com Pub open for lunch and dinner. Bunkroom $25PP, private rooms $40S, $55D, includes shared bath, common area, pets allowed. Tenting $8. WFS possible. Accepts credit cards. Coin operated shower and laundromat open 24 hrs. With stay: free pick up and return, use of kayak and paddleboats. For-fee shuttles all of Maine. Wifi and one computer for internet access. Maildrops for guests: P0 Box 215, Monson, ME 04464.

⌂ ⌂ ⤬ △ ≋ ⌂ ⌂ ✉ **Shaw's Lodging** 207-997-3597 〈www.shawslodging.com〉 Mid-May-mid-Oct, $23 bunks, private room $35 single or $28 each double occupancy. $12 tenting, $7 AYCE breakfast, $12 AYCE dinner on Mondays, $3 laundry, $5 shower and towel, internet available. With stay: free pick up and return. Slackpacking and shuttles all over Maine, Coleman/alcohol/oz and small gear selection. No credit cards. Maildrops (non guests $5): P0 Box 72 or 17 Pleasant St, Monson, ME 04464.

🛒 **Buddy Ward** 207-343-2564 shuttling anywhere in state of Maine and into NH, voicemail available.

🛒 **Sydney Pratt** 207-997-3221 pielady13@myfairpoint.net known as "The Pie Lady", will shuttle from Rangeley to Katahdin.

🛒 **Monson General Store** deli, grill serving B/L, Coleman/alcohol/oz. Friday night jams held in the store.

⤬ **Spring Creek Bar-B-Q** 207-997-7025 Th-Sa 10am-8pm, Su 9am-5pm or when food runs out, F&S ribs.

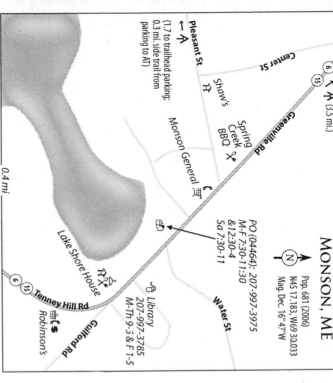

MONSON, ME

Pop. 681 (2006)
N45 17.183, W69 30.033
Mag. Dec. 16° 47'W

PO (04464): 207-997-3975
M-F 7:30-11:30
& 12:30-4
Sa 7:30-11

Library
207-997-3785
M-Th 9-5 & F 1-5

Greenville Rd

Center St

Shaw's

Spring Creek BBQ

Monson General

Pleasant St
(1.7 to trailhead parking; 0.3 mi. side trail from parking to AT)

0.4 mi

Lake Shore House

Tenney Hill Rd

Robinson's

Water St

Guilford Rd

(3.5 mi.)

Greenville, ME (14.0W from ME 15)

Kelly's Landing 207-695-4438, 7 days 7-9, AYCE breakfast on Sunday

Charles Dean Memorial Hospital 207-695-5200

Northwoods Outfitters <www.maineoutfitter.com> 2C7-695-3288, internet and café inside, 7 days, 8-5.

2123.1   J3-Mary Road
Light traffic on road, connects with ME 11 (12.0E).
(0.9E) **Jo-Mary Campground** 207-723-8117
Campsites $10, pets welcome. Campstore and grill, coin operated showers.

2133.2   Mahar Tote Road
(0.9E) **White House Landing Wilderness Camps** 207-745-5116 Mid-May-mid-Oct. Use air horn to be picked up by boat; no pickups after dark. In the morning you will be returned to a point closer to the trail. $39PP bunk, sleeps 18, $49PP private, includes AYCE breakfast. Meals available only during meal hours (breakfast 8am, lunch 11-1, dinner 5-6). Very adequate items for resupply; hiker foods, Coleman/alcohol/oz and cannister fuel. Visa MC cards accepted for small fee, shuttles can be arranged.

Kathy Preble 207-965-8464 chair_back_mt@yahoo.com Food drops and shuttles in the 100 mile wilderness, make arrangements well in advance. Maildrops: (USPS) PO Box 284, (UPS) 191 Main Rd, Brownville, ME 04414

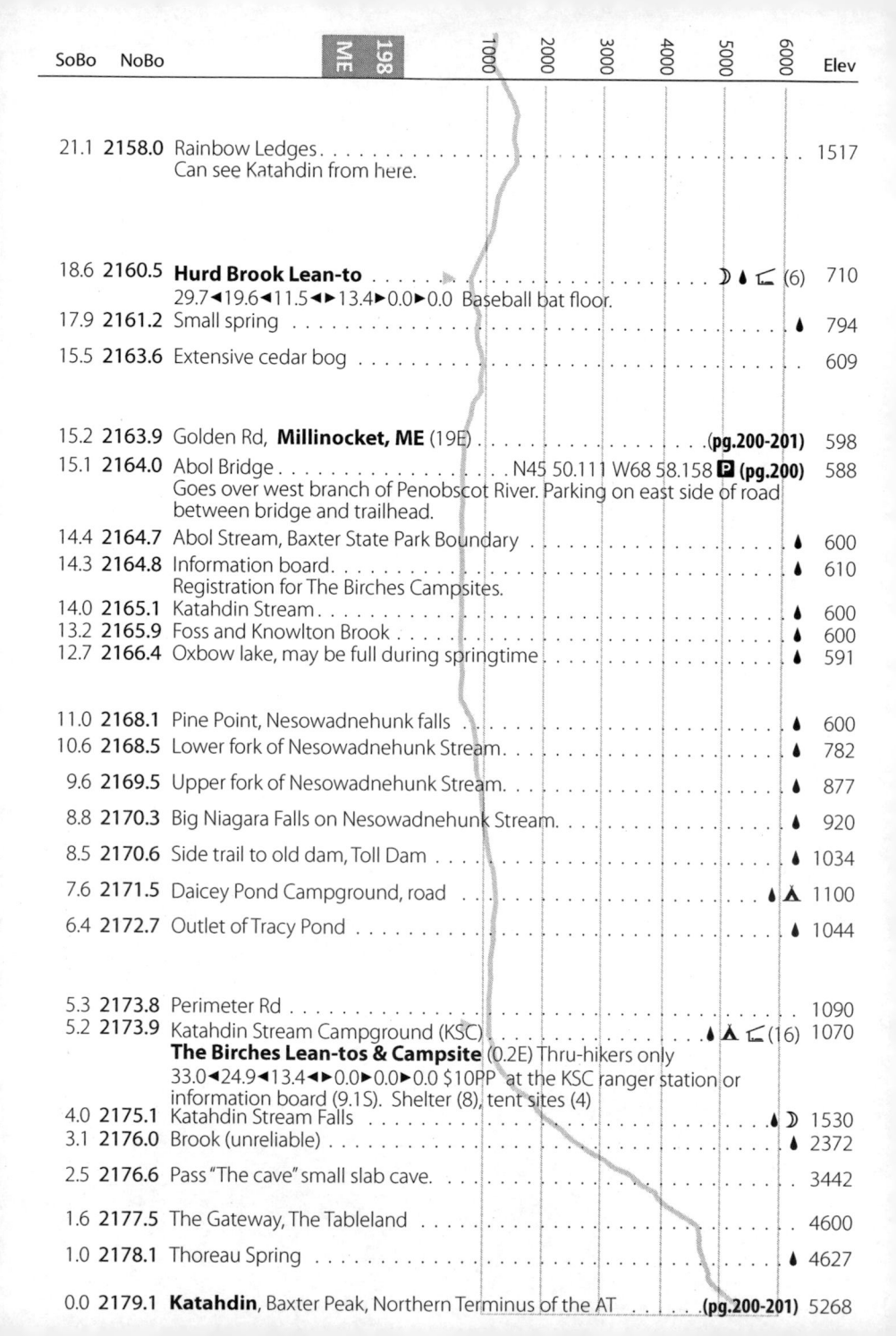

21.1	**2158.0**	Rainbow Ledges.	1517
		Can see Katahdin from here.	
18.6	**2160.5**	**Hurd Brook Lean-to** . . . . ☽ ♦ ⊏ (6)	710
		29.7◄19.6◄11.5◄►13.4►0.0►0.0 Baseball bat floor.	
17.9	**2161.2**	Small spring . . . . ♦	794
15.5	**2163.6**	Extensive cedar bog	609
15.2	**2163.9**	Golden Rd, **Millinocket, ME** (19E) . . . .**(pg.200-201)**	598
15.1	**2164.0**	Abol Bridge . . . . N45 50.111 W68 58.158 🅿 **(pg.200)**	588
		Goes over west branch of Penobscot River. Parking on east side of road	
		between bridge and trailhead.	
14.4	**2164.7**	Abol Stream, Baxter State Park Boundary . . . . ♦	600
14.3	**2164.8**	Information board. . . . . ♦	610
		Registration for The Birches Campsites.	
14.0	**2165.1**	Katahdin Stream. . . . . ♦	600
13.2	**2165.9**	Foss and Knowlton Brook . . . . ♦	600
12.7	**2166.4**	Oxbow lake, may be full during springtime. . . . . ♦	591
11.0	**2168.1**	Pine Point, Nesowadnehunk falls . . . . ♦	600
10.6	**2168.5**	Lower fork of Nesowadnehunk Stream. . . . . ♦	782
9.6	**2169.5**	Upper fork of Nesowadnehunk Stream. . . . . ♦	877
8.8	**2170.3**	Big Niagara Falls on Nesowadnehunk Stream. . . . . ♦	920
8.5	**2170.6**	Side trail to old dam, Toll Dam . . . . ♦	1034
7.6	**2171.5**	Daicey Pond Campground, road . . . . ♦Ⓐ	1100
6.4	**2172.7**	Outlet of Tracy Pond . . . . ♦	1044
5.3	**2173.8**	Perimeter Rd	1090
5.2	**2173.9**	Katahdin Stream Campground (KSC). . . . . ♦Ⓐ⊏(16)	1070
		The Birches Lean-tos & Campsite (0.2E) Thru-hikers only	
		33.0◄24.9◄13.4◄►0.0►0.0►0.0 $10PP at the KSC ranger station or	
		information board (9.1S). Shelter (8), tent sites (4)	
4.0	**2175.1**	Katahdin Stream Falls . . . . ♦☽	1530
3.1	**2176.0**	Brook (unreliable) . . . . ♦	2372
2.5	**2176.6**	Pass "The cave" small slab cave.	3442
1.6	**2177.5**	The Gateway, The Tableland	4600
1.0	**2178.1**	Thoreau Spring . . . . ♦	4627
0.0	**2179.1**	**Katahdin**, Baxter Peak, Northern Terminus of the AT . . . . .**(pg.200-201)**	5268

Baxter State Park

ⓘ For information and reservations, call 207-723-5140. When you are in the area, even as far as Medway, you can tune to AM 1610 for the most recent reports. On the web: ⟨http://www.baxterstateparkauthority.com/hiking/thru-hiking.html⟩

The hiking season is approximately May 15 through October 15. Dates vary based on weather, and the park can be closed any day of the year due to weather. Katahdin ascents may be disallowed even when the park is open. Weather reports are posted at **Katahdin Stream Campground** (KSC) at 7:00am every morning, along with one of these ratings:

Class 1: Open, conditions favorable for day use and climbing.
Class 2: Open, but hiking above treeline not recommended.
Class 3: Hiking above treeline not recommended; specified trails closed.
Class 4: Mandatory closure of all trails.

Consequences for hiking when the trail is closed includes fines, equipment seizure and loss of park visitation privileges.

All hikers intending to climb Katahdin must sign in at KSC and sign out when leaving. Hikes to Baxter Peak must be started by noon in June and July, 11am in August, 10am in September, and 9am in October. All AT hikers are welcome to leave their backpack at KSC. Loaner daypacks are available at no charge from the KSC ranger's station. Northbound thru-hikers completing their hike in late summer or early fall usually have an easy time hitching from KSC into Millinocket.

There are fees for entering the park by car, and for use of campsites. Fees must be paid in cash; no credit cards and no work-for-stay.

◣▲ There are 2 shelters at **The Birches** near KSC that are open only to northbound hikers who have hiked, at a minimum, continuously from the south end of the 100-mile wilderness. Stay is limited to a single night. The fee is $10 per person.

All other AT hikers who wish to overnight in the park should make reservations in advance. Common options, listed in order of their proximity to Katahdin, are **KSC, Abol Campground, Daicey Pond Campground,** and **Roaring Brook Campground** (north of Katahdin). Note that Abol Campground, Abol Pines and the privately run Abol Bridge Campground are three distinct entities.

🅿 If you are driving to Baxter: gates open 6am weekdays, 5am weekends. Maine residents enter for free; $13 per vehicle for non-residents. KSC parking is limited to 25 cars. This limit is often reached on weekends. NEW in 2010: parking can be reserved at KSC, Abol Campground or Roaring Brook Campground by calling up to two weeks in advance, for a $5 fee. There is no long-term parking in Baxter.

Cell phone reception is unlikely anywhere in the park other than on Katahdin, so do not count on calling for a ride from KSC. Even where there is reception, do not place calls from the summit or with n earshot of other hikers. Please use a cell phone only if there is an emergency.

Pets are not allowed in the park.

🐾 **Connie McManus** 207-723-6795 Privately run kennel service; pick up/drop off at Abol Bridge.

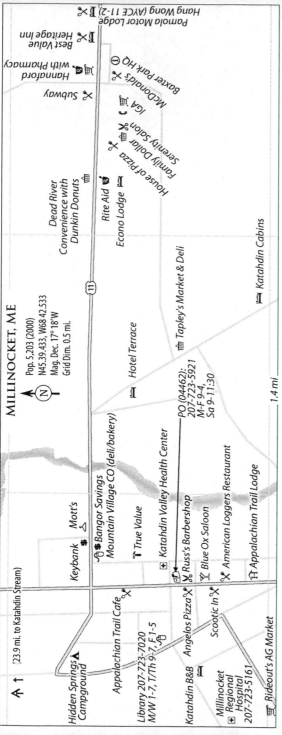

MILLINOCKET, ME

Pop. 5,203 (2000)
N45.39.433, W68 42.533
Mag. Dec. 17°18'W
Grid Dim. 0.5 mi.

2164.0 Abol Bridge over West Branch of Penobscot River – junction with International AT "Golden Road"/Abol Bridge

★ ⚑ ⛺ 🍴 **Abol Bridge Campground & Campstore,** open May –Sep, 7am-7pm, campsites $10PP, coin-op showers for those guests. Linda's Store at Abol Bridge, subs, sandwiches, microwave foods, ice cream, accepts Visa/MC.

⚑ **Abol Pines** $7 self-register tent sites and shelters across the street from Abol Bridge Campstore, south of Golden Road. Provided by Maine Department of Conservation.

2179.1 Katahdin, Baxter Peak, Northern Terminus of the AT
Millinocket, ME (20.0E) *(more services on map)*
Trails End Festival September 11-12, 2010

🏠 ⚑ 🛏 🍴 🏧 🏦 **P** ✉ **The Appalachian Trail Lodge and Cafe**
207-723-4321 ⟨www.appalachiantraillodge.com⟩, your one-stop hiker service, owners Paul (OleMan) & Jaime (NaviGator) Renaud, $25 bunkroom, $35s, $55d, furnished apartment call for rates; parking $1/day; showers for nonguests $3; WiFi, fuel, some hiking supplies; licensed and insured shuttle service to and from bus in Medway, into 100-mile wilderness or Monson, free daily shuttle from Baxter park, from Sept 1, till Oct 15, between 3pm – 4:30pm. food drops, slackpack in 100-mile wilderness; other shuttles by arrangement; one private room available for hikers with pets; credit cards accepted. SOBO special (pickup in Medway, bed in bunkroom, breakfast at AT Cafe', and shuttle to KSC. $70pp. By reservation.) Maildrops: 33 Penobscot Avenue, Millinocket, ME 04462.

**200
ME**

🛏️✕ **Hotel Terrace & Ruthie's Restaurant** 207-723-4545 $49.95S, $55.95D, $10EAP. Ruthie's serves B/L/D.

🛏️⛺ **Econo Lodge** 207-723-4555. Ask for hiker rate.

🛏️✕⊠ **Pamola Motor Lodge** 800-575-9746 $59S $69D includes cont B. Chinese restaurant on site with AYCE lunch buffet. Pets okay. Maildrops: 973 Central Street, Millinocket, ME 04462.

🛏️⊠ **Katahdin Cabins** 207-723-6305 <www.katahdincabins. com> $60 small cabin sleeps 2-3, $80 5-person cabin, includes continental breakfast, no smoking, cabins have TV, DVD, fridge & microwave, gas grill, bikes free for use, community room, 20% off for hikers and family, accepts Amex/cash/checks, owners Skip and Nicole Mohoff. Maildrops: 181 Medway Road, Millinocket, ME 04462.

🛏️⊠ **Best Value Heritage Motor Inn** 207-723-9777 $79S, $10EAP, pets $10, hot tub, pool. Maildrops: 935 Central Street, Millinocket, ME 04462.

🛏️✕ **Econo Lodge** 207-723-4555 $59.99/up includes cont breakfast. Pets allowed. Indoor heated pool, ping pong and pool tables. On site **Rooster's Restaurant and Lounge** serves dinner 4-10pm.

⛺ **Hidden Springs Campground** 207-723-6337, Tent sites $12PP, pool, shower.

✕ **Hang Wong** 207-723-6084 with AYCE lunch buffet.

🚌 **Town Taxi** 207-723-2000, 207-447-3474, shuttles from bus station in Medway to Millinocket $15, from Millinocket to Abol Bridge $45, Millinocket to Katahdin Stream (The Birches) $55.

🚌 **Maine Quest Adventures** 207-746-9615 <www.mainequestadventures.com> will pick up at Medway bus station and drop at Katahdin Stream or Abol Bridge $50, if late in the afternoon, stay at base camp and tent on lawn for free, shuttles to Monson and parts of the 100 Mile Wilderness.

✈️ **Katahdin Air** 866-359-6246 <www.KatahdinAir.com> One-way flights to a number of trailheads in Maine. $50 to $110 per person, includes shuttle from Abol Bridge to seaplane base.

Getting to Mount Katahdin

Most routes to Mount Katahdin lead through Bangor, Maine, a town with an airport and a bus terminal. Bangor is approximately 91 miles from Baxter State Park. Some shuttle services will pick you up in Bangor, but it is more economical to take **Cyr Bus Lines** to Medway 31 miles from Baxter State Park.

Bangor, ME - Medway, ME

🚌 **Cyr Bus Lines** 800-244-2335 <www.cyrbustours.com> Routes connecting Bangor and Medway. Most one-way routes are $11.50, cash only.

Mecway (station at Irving store) - Bangor departs 9:30am
Bangor (Greyhound hub) - Medway departs 6:00pm
Bangor (Concord Trailways hub) - Medway departs 6:30pm

🚌 **Concord Trailways** 207-945-4000 <www.concordtrailways.com> Hub near Bangor airport, service as far south as South Station in Massachusetts.

🚌 **Greyhound Bus Service** 800-231-2222 <www.greyhound. com> Bangor hub (207-945-3000) 158 Main St. (corner of Union and Main).

🚌 **The Appalachian Trail Lodge, Town Taxi, and Maine Quest Adventures** All listed in Millinocket, provide transportation from Medway to Millinocket and Katahdin.

There is an edition of this book made specifically for southbound hikers. The southbound edition, and other A.T. books and DVDs are sold on the website:

www.theATguide.com

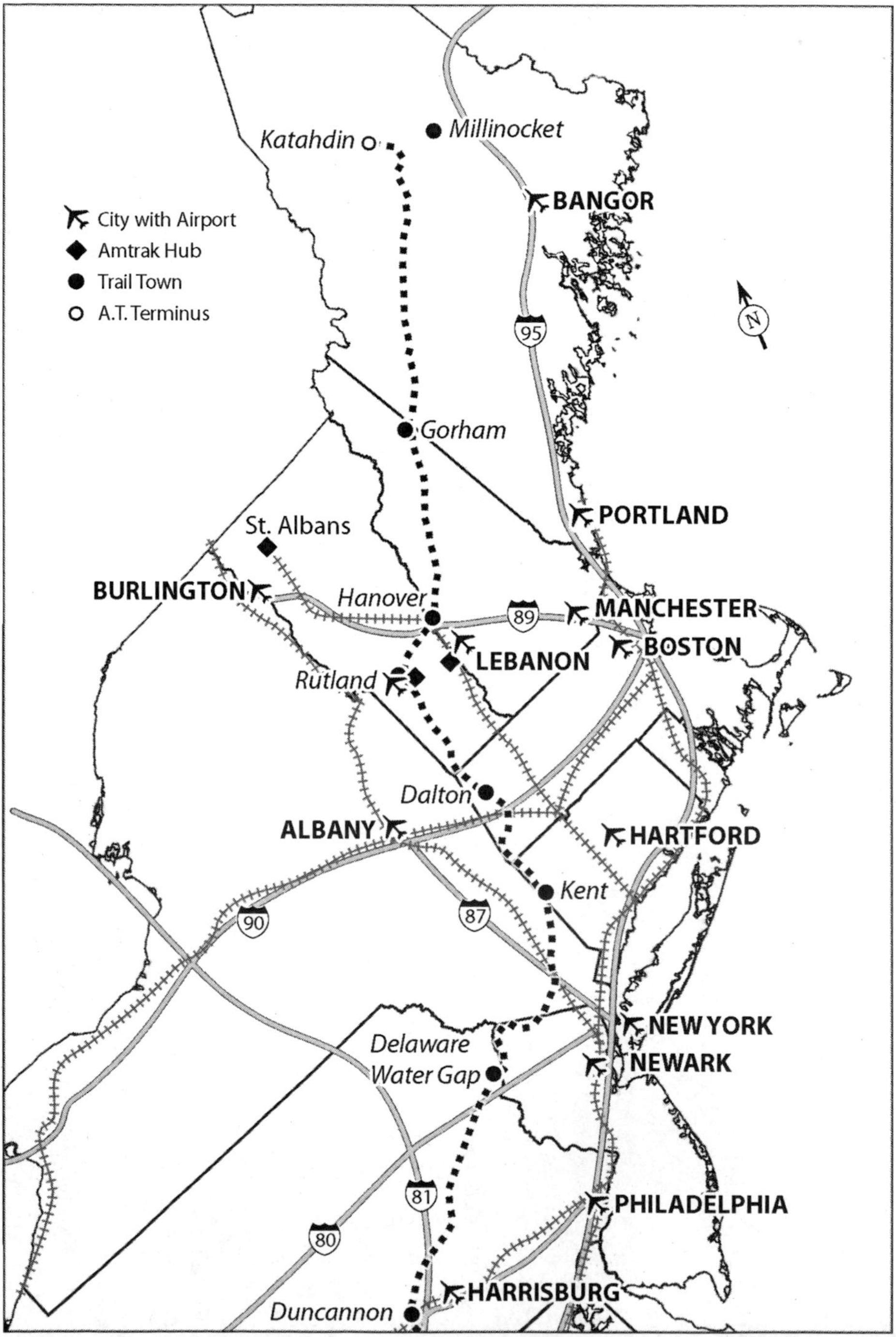

City with Airport
Amtrak Hub
Trail Town
A.T. Terminus
N
Katahdin
Millinocket
BANGOR
95
Gorham
PORTLAND
St. Albans
BURLINGTON
Hanover
89
MANCHESTER
BOSTON
LEBANON
Rutland
Dalton
ALBANY
HARTFORD
Kent
90
87
NEW YORK
NEWARK
Delaware
Water Gap
PHILADELPHIA
81
80
HARRISBURG
Duncannon

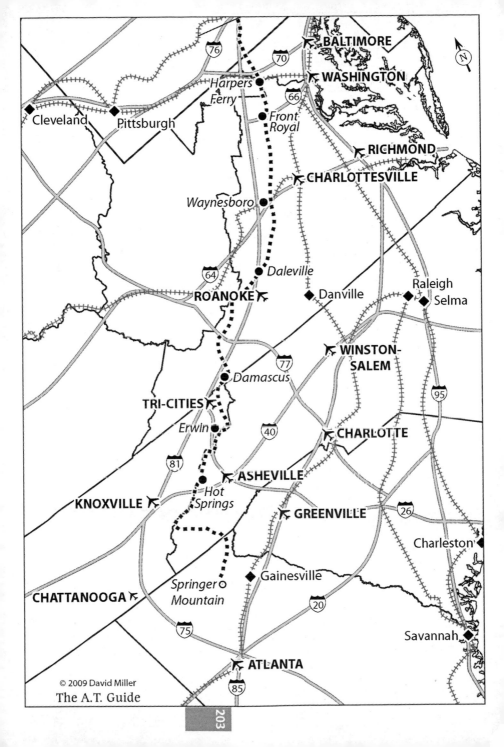

BALTIMORE

76

70

WASHINGTON

Harpers
Ferry

66

Cleveland

Pittsburgh

Front
Royal

RICHMOND

CHARLOTTESVILLE

Waynesboro

64

Daleville

ROANOKE

Danville

Raleigh
Selma

77

WINSTON-
SALEM

Damascus

95

TRI-CITIES

Erwin

40

CHARLOTTE

81

ASHEVILLE

KNOXVILLE

Hot
Springs

GREENVILLE

26

Charleston

CHATTANOOGA

Springer
Mountain

Gainesville

20

Savannah

75

© 2009 David Miller
The A.T. Guide

ATLANTA

85

N

2021 Calendar

JANUARY
Su	M	Tu	W	Th	F	Sa
					1	2
3	4	5	6	7	8	9
10	11	12	13	14	15	16
17	18	19	20	21	22	23
24	25	26	27	28	29	30
31						

Full Moon
1 New Year's Day
18 Martin Luther King Jr. Day

FEBRUARY
Su	M	Tu	W	Th	F	Sa
	1	2	3	4	5	6
7	8	9	10	11	12	13
14	15	16	17	18	19	20
21	22	23	24	25	26	27
28						

14 Valentine's Day
15 President's Day

MARCH
Su	M	Tu	W	Th	F	Sa
	1	2	3	4	5	6
7	8	9	10	11	12	13
14	15	16	17	18	19	20
21	22	23	24	25	26	27
28	29	30	31			

14 Daylight saving time starts
20 First day of Spring

APRIL
Su	M	Tu	W	Th	F	Sa
				1	2	3
4	5	6	7	8	9	10
11	12	13	14	15	16	17
18	19	20	21	22	23	24
25	26	27	28	29	30	

4 Easter

MAY
Su	M	Tu	W	Th	F	Sa
						1
2	3	4	5	6	7	8
9	10	11	12	13	14	15
16	17	18	19	20	21	22
23	24	25	26	27	28	29
30	31					

9 Mother's Day
31 Memorial Day

JUNE
Su	M	Tu	W	Th	F	Sa
		1	2	3	4	5
6	7	8	9	10	11	12
13	14	15	16	17	18	19
20	21	22	23	24	25	26
27	28	29	30			

20 Father's Day
21 Summer Begins

JULY
Su	M	Tu	W	Th	F	Sa
				1	2	3
4	5	6	7	8	9	10
11	12	13	14	15	16	17
18	19	20	21	22	23	24
25	26	27	28	29	30	31

4 Independence Day

AUGUST
Su	M	Tu	W	Th	F	Sa
1	2	3	4	5	6	7
8	9	10	11	12	13	14
15	16	17	18	19	20	21
22	23	24	25	26	27	28
29	30	31				

12-13 Perseids Meteor Shower

SEPTEMBER
Su	M	Tu	W	Th	F	Sa
			1	2	3	4
5	6	7	8	9	10	11
12	13	14	15	16	17	18
19	20	21	22	23	24	25
26	27	28	29	30		

6 Labor Day
23 First Day of Autumn

OCTOBER
Su	M	Tu	W	Th	F	Sa
					1	2
3	4	5	6	7	8	9
10	11	12	13	14	15	16
17	18	19	20	21	22	23
24	25	26	27	28	29	30
31						

11 Columbus Day

NOVEMBER
Su	M	Tu	W	Th	F	Sa
	1	2	3	4	5	6
7	8	9	10	11	12	13
14	15	16	17	18	19	20
21	22	23	24	25	26	27
28	29	30				

7 Daylight Saving time ends
11 Veteran's Day

DECEMBER
Su	M	Tu	W	Th	F	Sa
			1	2	3	4
5	6	7	8	9	10	11
12	13	14	15	16	17	18
19	20	21	22	23	24	25
26	27	28	29	30	31	

21 First day of Winter
25 Christmas

Jan 15-17   **Southern Ruck** Nantahala Outdoor Center (pg.20)
Jan 30-31   **PA Ruck** Ironmaster's Hostel, Pine Grove Furnace SP (pg.100)
Mar 6-7   **Backpacking Clinic & Celebration** Amicalola Falls SP (pg.1)
Apr 2-3   **Franklin Appalachian 100 Mile Event** Franklin, NC (pg.17)
Apr (TBD)   **White Blaze Day** Happy Hiker, Gatlinburg, TN (pg.25)
Apr 23-24   **Trailfest** Hot Springs, NC (pg.31)

May 14-16   **Trail Days** Damascus, VA (pg.47)
Jun 5   **National Trail Days®**, Everywhere - (AHS, pg.87)
Jun 5   **Hiker Fest** Waynesboro, VA (pg.76)
Aug 7-8   **Long Trail Festival** Vermont Fairgrounds, Rutland, VT (pg.158)
Sep 11-12   **Trail's End Festival** Millinocket, ME (pg.200)
Oct 15-17   **The Gathering** (ALDHA) Pipestem, WV

EYEWITNESS
ANIMAL

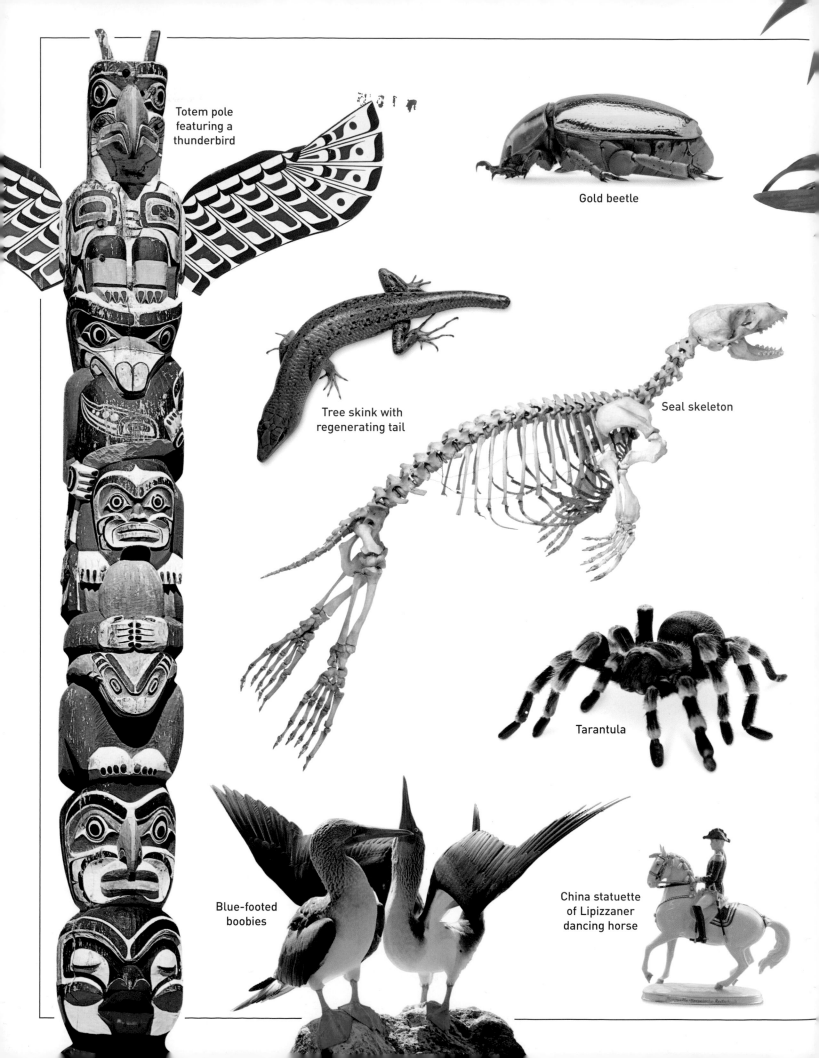

Totem pole featuring a thunderbird

Gold beetle

Tree skink with regenerating tail

Seal skeleton

Tarantula

Blue-footed boobies

China statuette of Lipizzaner dancing horse

Red-eyed
tree frog

Snake detecting
chemicals in
air with its
tongue

EYEWITNESS
ANIMAL

Written by
TOM JACKSON

Common octopus

Fisher's
lovebirds

Penguin
Random
House

Consultant Dr. Kim Dennis-Bryan

DK DELHI
Project editor Bharti Bedi
Project art editor Deep Shikha Walia
Senior editor Kingshuk Ghoshal
Senior art editor Govind Mittal
Senior DTP designer Tarun Sharma
DTP designer Neeraj Bhatia

DK LONDON
Senior editor Rob Houston
Senior art editor Philip Letsu
Publisher Andrew Macintyre
Picture researcher Myriam Mégharbi
Production editor Ben Marcus
Production controller Luca Frassinetti

RELAUNCH EDITION (DK UK)
Senior editor Chris Hawkes
Senior art editor Spencer Holbrook
US senior editor Margaret Parrish
Jacket editor Claire Gell
Jacket designer Laura Brim
Jacket design development manager Sophia MTT
Producer, pre-production Francesca Wardell
Producer Janis Griffith
Managing editor Linda Esposito
Managing art editor Philip Letsu
Publisher Andrew Macintyre
Publishing director Jonathan Metcalf
Associate publishing director Liz Wheeler
Design director Stuart Jackman

RELAUNCH EDITION (DK INDIA)
Project editor Bharti Bedi
Project art editor Nishesh Batnagar
DTP designer Pawan Kumar
Senior DTP designer Harish Aggarwal
Picture researcher Nishwan Rasool
Jacket designer Dhirendra Singh

European
common frog

Blue morpho
butterfly

Hamster

Homo habilis,
a human
ancestor

First American Edition, 2012
This American Edition, 2015

Published in the United States by DK Publishing
345 Hudson Street, New York, New York 10014

A Penguin Random House Company

15 16 17 18 19 10 9 8 7 6 5 4 3 2 1
001—183296—Jun/15

Published in Great Britain by Dorling Kindersley Limited.
A catalog record for this book is available from the Library of Congress.
ISBN 978-1-4654-3570-5 (Paperback)
ISBN 978-1-4654-3571-2 (ALB)

DK books are available at special discounts when purchased in bulk
for sales promotions, premiums, fund-raising, or educational use.
For details, contact: DK Publishing Special Markets, 345 Hudson
Street, New York, New York 10014 or SpecialSales@dk.com.

Printed by South China Printing Co. Ltd., China

A WORLD OF IDEAS:
SEE ALL THERE IS TO KNOW

www.dk.com

Penguin and chick

American
cockroaches

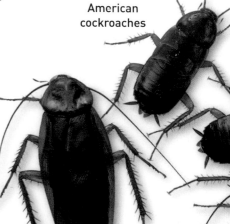

Contents

What is an animal?

To date, only about 1.3 million of Earth's animal species have been identified. They range from tigers to dust mites, and even sea anemones and sponges. Each is made up of millions, if not billions, of cells, performing specialized jobs in the body. What sets animals apart from other many-celled organisms is that they are more mobile and survive by eating other life-forms.

Belonging to a species

Every animal belongs to a species, the members of which look similar and share the same lifestyle and habitats. Members of a species can breed and produce young. The color, size, and body shape of this emerald tree boa help experts identify it.

Animal cell

All living bodies are formed of tiny units called cells. An animal cell is surrounded by a membrane made from a thin sheet of oily material. The flexible sheet can take any shape. Cells contain structures called organelles, which form their factories, power supply, and chemical transportation system.

Mitochondrion produces cell's energy

Nucleus houses cell's genes

Line of symmetry divides animal into equal halves

Liquid cytoplasm fills cell

Golgi body makes proteins

Going mobile

Animals are the only multicellular organisms (made from more than one cell) that can move from place to place. Most plants are rooted to something. Locomotion is usually as a response to changes in the environment. It is possible because an animal does not have rigid body cells. This helps it alter its body shape, so it can push against the ground or water to move.

Development plan

Every animal grows from a single cell that divides repeatedly, developing a body made of billions of cells. Most animals, such as this terrapin, develop bilaterally, with a mouth at one end and a rear opening at the other. Some simple animals, such as anemones, develop outward from a central point.

Red-eared terrapin

Line that divides animal into equal halves

Green sea anemone

Inside the animal kingdom

The system of organizing life into groups was developed by the Swede Carl Linnaeus in the 1750s. He split the animal kingdom into subgroups based on their shared features. Phylum is the largest subgroup, followed by class, order, family, genus, and then species. Every animal has a unique scientific name, which is formed by its genus and species.

Classification of some salamander species

Chordata	(Phylum)
Vertebrata	(Sub-phylum)
Amphibia	(Class)

(Order)	Caudata	Anura	Gymnophiona

(Family)	Cryptobranchidae	Ambystomatidae	Plethodontidae	Sirenidae

(Genus)	Plethodon

jordani	cinereus	glutinosus	(Species)

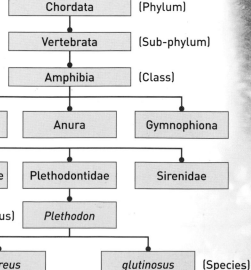

Plethodon jordani

Plethodon cinereus

Plethodon glutinosus

Ear and other sense organs give tiger information about its surroundings

Bamboo is low in nutrients, so giant pandas spend 16 hours a day eating

Eating food

Of all the multicellular life-forms—plants, fungi, and animals—only animals eat. An animal eats food through its mouth. The body then extracts the nutrients it needs—the body's fuels and building materials—from the food and expels the rest as dung. In scientific terms, an animal is a "heterotroph"—it survives by consuming the bodies of other life-forms. A fungus absorbs nutrients through its body, while a plant is powered by the energy in sunlight and absorbs raw materials from the ground.

Producers	Primary consumers	Secondary consumers	Tertiary consumers	Quaternary consumers

PHYTOPLANKTON • KRILL • WHALE • ALBATROSS • LEOPARD SEAL • RADIOLARIAN • ARROW WORM • PENGUIN • BLUE-GREEN BACTERIA • PELAGIC FISH • SQUID • DOLPHIN • COPEPOD • KILLER WHALE • SEAWEED • MARINE WORM • BOTTOM-FEEDING FISH

Webs of food

Living things in any environment are interconnected in food webs that link everything edible. It begins with producers, such as plants and bacteria—organisms that make their own food using energy from sunlight. Energy is then transferred to the primary consumers that feed on the producers, and so on.

Legs allow tiger to cross many different types of land surfaces efficiently

Almost an animal

Perhaps the closest life-forms to animals are a selection of microscopic, single-celled organisms, including amoeba. These organisms can surround their tiny prey, such as algae, until it is completely engulfed.

Invertebrates

An invertebrate is an animal without vertebrae, or spine bones. These were the first animals on Earth, appearing in the oceans at least 700 million years ago. More than 95 percent of animals alive today are invertebrates. There are more than 20 different groups, ranging from insects to jellyfish.

As simple as it gets

Today's sponges may be similar to the first invertebrates. Their simple bodies are made up of just a handful of cell types. Pore cells let water into the body, and cone cells sift food from it. Other cell types build the protein skeleton, including the spikes the sponge uses to fend off attack.

Blooming animals

Sea anemones are often mistaken for plants, and they are even named after a type of flower, but they are carnivorous animals. Anemones, jellyfish, and several other invertebrates have circular bodies with no heads at all.

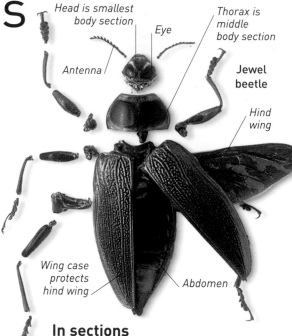

Head is smallest body section

Antenna

Eye

Thorax is middle body section

Jewel beetle

Hind wing

Wing case protects hind wing

Abdomen

Segment joins with others to make up leg

In sections

All arthropods have a body that is divided into segments. In insects—the world's biggest animal group with 1 million species—however, some segments have fused (joined) together during evolution to form body sections. Insect bodies are built in three main parts—the head, thorax, and abdomen.

Stinging tentacles look like petals

Many mollusks

The second largest invertebrate group are the mollusks, with 100,000 species. All mollusk bodies have one muscular "foot" to move, and the organs are held inside a mantle (a fleshy hood). Most mollusks have a hard shell made with a chalky mineral called calcium carbonate. Snails are some of the most common land mollusks. Several types, such as sea slugs and cephalopods, live without a shell.

Waterproof shell keeps body moist

Striped land snail

Mantle changes color to blend in with surroundings

Tentacle lined with suckers

Many-footed head

The largest invertebrates are the cephalopods—a group of mollusks that includes octopuses, squid, and cuttlefish. Most of the body is the bulging mantle, while the foot is divided into flexible tentacles covered in suckers. Octopuses have eight, while other cephalopods have up to 90.

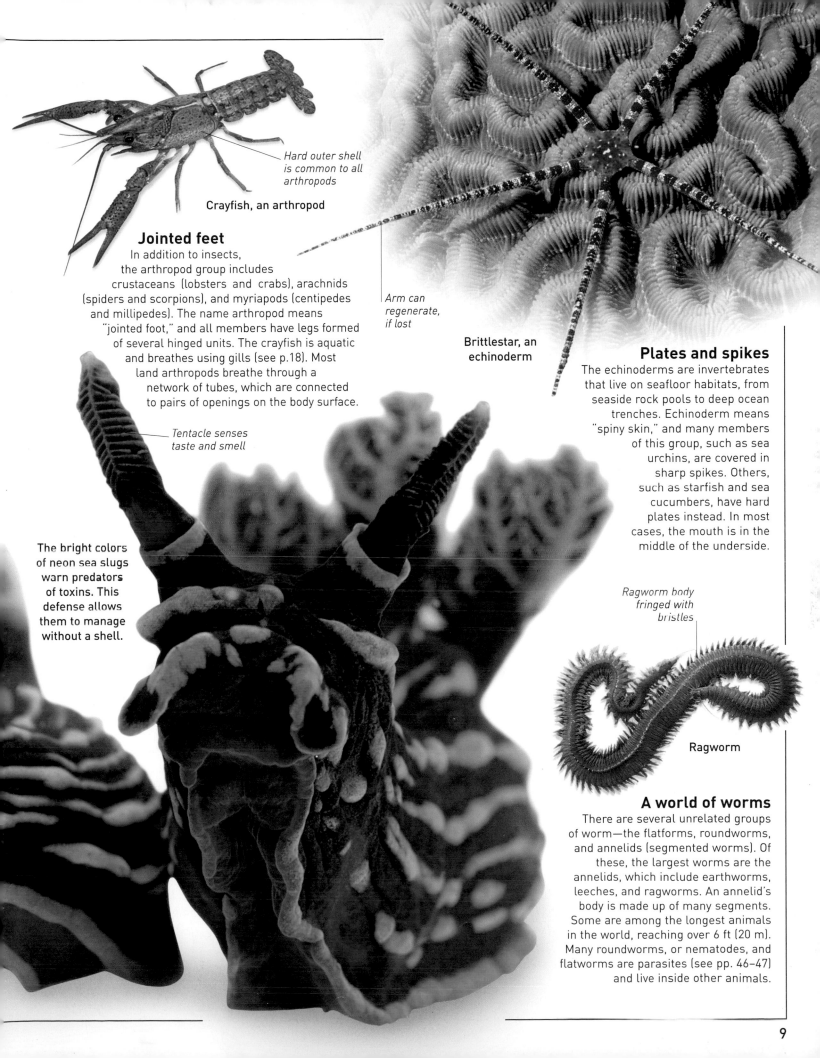

Crayfish, an arthropod

Hard outer shell is common to all arthropods

Jointed feet

In addition to insects, the arthropod group includes crustaceans (lobsters and crabs), arachnids (spiders and scorpions), and myriapods (centipedes and millipedes). The name arthropod means "jointed foot," and all members have legs formed of several hinged units. The crayfish is aquatic and breathes using gills (see p.18). Most land arthropods breathe through a network of tubes, which are connected to pairs of openings on the body surface.

Arm can regenerate, if lost

Brittlestar, an echinoderm

Tentacle senses taste and smell

The bright colors of neon sea slugs warn predators of toxins. This defense allows them to manage without a shell.

Plates and spikes

The echinoderms are invertebrates that live on seafloor habitats, from seaside rock pools to deep ocean trenches. Echinoderm means "spiny skin," and many members of this group, such as sea urchins, are covered in sharp spikes. Others, such as starfish and sea cucumbers, have hard plates instead. In most cases, the mouth is in the middle of the underside.

Ragworm body fringed with bristles

Ragworm

A world of worms

There are several unrelated groups of worm—the flatforms, roundworms, and annelids (segmented worms). Of these, the largest worms are the annelids, which include earthworms, leeches, and ragworms. An annelid's body is made up of many segments. Some are among the longest animals in the world, reaching over 6 ft (20 m). Many roundworms, or nematodes, and flatworms are parasites (see pp. 46–47) and live inside other animals.

Cold-blooded vertebrates

The vertebrates are animals with a chain of bony segments running down the middle of their backs, forming a backbone. Each spine bone is called a vertebra. Fish, amphibians, and reptiles are all ectothermic, or "cold-blooded," vertebrates. Ectotherms cannot maintain a constant body temperature, so they rely on their surroundings to keep them warm.

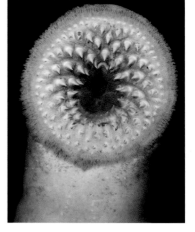

Eardrum on the outside of head

Throat pouch puffed out to make calls

Moist skin lets oxygen and water through

Not a vertebrate
The lancelet is not a vertebrate, since it has only a stiff cord supporting its back. With no skull, limbs, or side fins, it lives in the sea and grows to about the length of a finger. Biologists believe that vertebrates evolved from animals like the lancelet about 530 million years ago.

Without jaws
Most vertebrates have jaws. This lamprey, however, is jawless. It cannot bite its food. Instead, it twists its eel-like body to dig its spiral of teeth into the flesh of prey or to scrape food from rocks.

Tail carries a venomous sting

Without bone
A vertebrate's body gets its shape from its internal skeleton. In most cases, the skeleton is made of hard, mineralized bone. However, sharks, skates, and these stingrays have bones built of cartilage, which is made from flexible protein.

Rays of bone

Most fish have ray fins formed from skin stretched over slim shafts of bone. Ray fins are ideal for wafting water, but are too weak to hold a fish's weight. Land vertebrates evolved from another group called lobe-finned fish, which have fleshy fins and thick bones.

Large thigh muscle powers jump

Long leg bones lever frog forward

Spring king

Amphibians were the first land vertebrates. They are the ancestors of all tetrapods— animals with four limbs—including those with wings. Although early tetrapods also had short, rigid necks, they looked nothing like modern frogs. With their very long back legs, frogs are built to jump.

Pectoral fin used for fine control

Tail fin used for propulsion

Webbed feet to aid swimming

Frilly gill absorbs oxygen from water

Between two worlds

Most amphibians live two lives. They start out in water, hatching from eggs laid in pools. They breathe with gills and swim with fins like a fish. As they grow, amphibians develop legs for moving on land and switch to lungs for breathing. Some species, however, mix both ways of life. This mud puppy stays under water its whole life, but uses its legs to walk along riverbeds.

Life without legs

Not having legs makes it easier for snakes to slide through narrow burrows, twist and turn through tree branches, and slither over loose sand. Strong species, such as this cobra, can even rise up to stare into the eyes of taller animals. Snakes evolved from animals with legs. Some snake skeletons have hipbones where legs once attached to the body, and anacondas still have two tiny, clawlike legs.

High and dry

The reptiles were the first vertebrates to adopt a life away from water. They have waterproof scales to stop them from drying out, and their eggs have a hard shell. Reptiles are cold-blooded and cannot heat their own bodies, so most live in warm parts of the world and must spend time basking in the sun.

Pectoral fin flaps like a wing to move ray forward

Warm-blooded vertebrates

Birds and mammals are the only endothermic, or warm-blooded, animals. Endothermic means "heat within." Endotherms can regulate their body temperatures, and they often keep warmer than their surroundings by using fur, fat, or feathers to trap heat. Because of temperature controls like sweating, their bodies work in most environments.

Flexible feathers

A bird's plumage, or covering of feathers, has several functions. Fluffy down feathers close to the skin trap air, creating a blanket of warm air around the body. The long, stiff, and very light feathers are used for flight. These colored feathers also camouflage the bird and—for this macaw—attract mates.

Flight surface formed from overlapping feathers

Quill has tiny barbs that make it painful to pull out when stuck in skin

Flightless

The kiwi lives in New Zealand. Until humans arrived 750 years ago, it had no mammal predators, such as cats. The kiwi had no need to fly and did not develop a breastbone that could support strong flight muscles—making it a member of the flightless birds.

Flight feather extends back from bone at front of wing

Spikes and tufts

Mammal hair is sometimes put to unusual uses. For example, the defensive spikes, or quills, of a porcupine are very thick hairs. When threatened, a porcupine raises its quills, making itself appear larger than it is. Most of the quills point backward, so if a predator attacks from behind, it gets a sharp shock. Other animals use their hair to communicate. Bushy-tailed squirrels signal to each other by flicking their fluffy tails.

Feather versus hair

Hair and feathers are made of a waxy protein called keratin that grows out of the skin in strands. Mammal hairs are of different lengths. The short underfur insulates, while longer guard hairs keep water and dirt out. Feathers are more complex—the strands branch out from a central shaft, before dividing again to form thin fibers that hook together to make a flat surface.

Electron micrograph of fox fur (false color)

Electron micrograph of feather (false color)

Porcupine quills

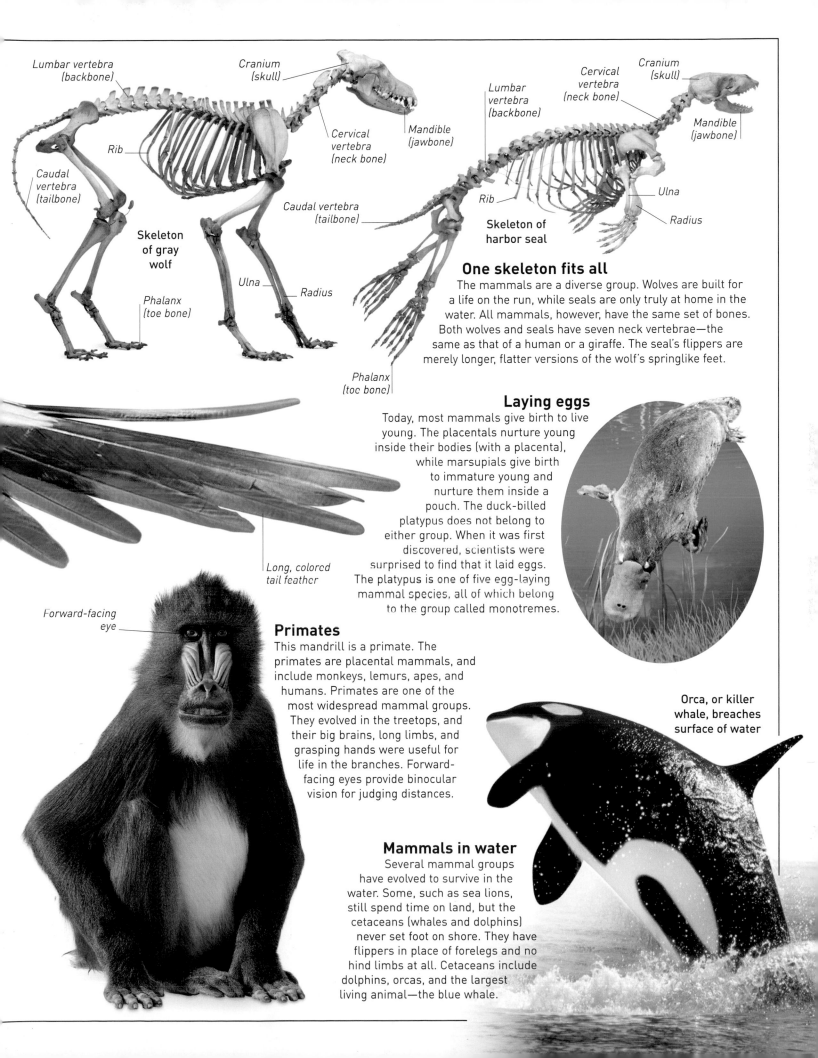

Skeleton of gray wolf

Lumbar vertebra (backbone)

Cranium (skull)

Rib

Cervical vertebra (neck bone)

Mandible (jawbone)

Caudal vertebra (tailbone)

Ulna

Radius

Phalanx (toe bone)

Skeleton of harbor seal

Lumbar vertebra (backbone)

Cervical vertebra (neck bone)

Cranium (skull)

Mandible (jawbone)

Rib

Ulna

Radius

Caudal vertebra (tailbone)

Phalanx (toe bone)

One skeleton fits all

The mammals are a diverse group. Wolves are built for a life on the run, while seals are only truly at home in the water. All mammals, however, have the same set of bones. Both wolves and seals have seven neck vertebrae—the same as that of a human or a giraffe. The seal's flippers are merely longer, flatter versions of the wolf's springlike feet.

Laying eggs

Today, most mammals give birth to live young. The placentals nurture young inside their bodies (with a placenta), while marsupials give birth to immature young and nurture them inside a pouch. The duck-billed platypus does not belong to either group. When it was first discovered, scientists were surprised to find that it laid eggs. The platypus is one of five egg-laying mammal species, all of which belong to the group called monotremes.

Long, colored tail feather

Forward-facing eye

Primates

This mandrill is a primate. The primates are placental mammals, and include monkeys, lemurs, apes, and humans. Primates are one of the most widespread mammal groups. They evolved in the treetops, and their big brains, long limbs, and grasping hands were useful for life in the branches. Forward-facing eyes provide binocular vision for judging distances.

Orca, or killer whale, breaches surface of water

Mammals in water

Several mammal groups have evolved to survive in the water. Some, such as sea lions, still spend time on land, but the cetaceans (whales and dolphins) never set foot on shore. They have flippers in place of forelegs and no hind limbs at all. Cetaceans include dolphins, orcas, and the largest living animal—the blue whale.

Evolution

Every species seems to be a perfect fit for its way of life. A sea snake has a flat, paddle-shaped tail that helps it swim, while a burrowing snake has a shovel-shaped snout suited to digging through soil. But both snakes have changed over time, evolving adaptations that better shape them to their environments. The driving force of this process is called natural selection.

Inherited features

The instructions for making a body are coded in an animal's genes—a set of chemicals called deoxyribonucleic acid (DNA) held in every cell. Genes are passed from parents to offspring and give the young traits of its parents, which can be an advantage or disadvantage. Those with desirable genes do well and have many offspring. As a result, their DNA becomes more common.

Thymine (T)

Guanine (G)

Adenine (A)

Cytosine (C)

Genes are strands of DNA coded with the chemical units, or bases, A, C, T, and G.

The backbone of DNA is made of sugar molecules

Long, toothy snout

Hind limb bones connect to the pelvis (hipbones)

Tall back bones anchor strong neck muscles

Hoofed foot

Wolflike *Pakicetus* evolved around 55 million years ago. It had hoofed feet but was a hunter that caught fish.

Powerful tail helps animal swim

Crocodile-like *Ambulocetus* lived 50 million years ago.

Legs used to swim and walk on land

Webbed foot

Jawbone picks up sounds like a modern whale

Extended body

Blind progress

Evolution is happening all the time. The process has no direction—an animal can even reverse its path. For example, mammals evolved from animals whose ancestors were fish. Much later, some mammals began pursuing a watery lifestyle. Their legs slowly evolved into flippers and their bodies became fish-shaped. The result was today's whales.

Hind limb is a small flipper

Bones of hind limb detached from pelvis

Tail has become a paddlelike "fluke"

Nostril halfway along snout

Dorudon lived in warm seas about 38 million years ago.

Large skull helps to break Arctic ice

Balaena—the modern bowhead whale—gulps tiny krill with the largest mouth in the animal kingdom.

Tiny hind limb bones

Flipper

The father of evolution

In 1859, the English scientist Charles Darwin put forward the idea of evolution by natural selection in a book called *On the Origin of Species*. Much later, scientists found more evidence to back up the theory. Francis Crick and James Watson showed how DNA's coded genes are responsible for the inheritance of traits, which is a crucial mechanism for evolution.

Co-evolution

Sometimes, different organisms evolve together in a process called co-evolution. These acacia ants have co-evolved with the bullhorn acacia shrub—the ants make nests in the shrub's hollow thorns and sting anything that tries to eat its leaves. They also chew through invading creepers. In return, the acacia provides nectar and grows an edible fatty nodule.

Small, spiked thorn

Ants on patrol

Never the same

Natural selection exists because no two animals are the same. Even members of the same species are at least slightly different because they have a unique set of genes. These two ladybugs belong to the same species. Despite their noticeable warning patterns, one of the bugs may get eaten. The other may survive and live to produce offspring.

Azara's agouti collects fruits and roots on rain forest floor

The gray squirrel harvests nuts from trees

The Arabian spiny mouse forages for seeds in grasses

Radiating species

These rodents evolved from a single ancestor that lived 65 million years ago, but the different descendants have evolved in different directions. This "adaptive radiation" gives rise to a whole range of new species that live in different habitats but share features, such as gnawing front teeth.

This wildebeest has reacted slower than its herd mates

Survival of the fittest

Darwin described animals that were able to survive and reproduce as being "fit." In these terms, a fit animal is not just strong and healthy, but its behavior also makes it successful at surviving and reproducing. This cheetah is "fit" because it has gotten within pouncing distance of a wildebeest.

Extinct animals

It is amazing to think that 99 percent of all species that have ever lived on Earth are now extinct. Over the last 700 million years, the animal kingdom has constantly changed, with new species taking the place of older ones. Extinction is a natural process. Animals may become extinct due to disasters. Species also die out when remaining members fail to reproduce or when a new species evolves and is more successful in the struggle for survival.

Echmatocrinus, a primitive echinoderm

An explosion of life

A great blooming of species—called the Cambrian Explosion—happened around 530 million years ago (mya). Almost all animals living today—from fish to fleas—had an ancestor that once swam in the ocean during this period. All of the Cambrian species, including the invertebrates seen here, are now extinct, but they paved the way for the animal diversity we see today.

Studying fossils

Everything we know about extinct animals comes from fossils, which are the remains of animals, their footprints, and droppings, preserved in rocks. It is rare for whole skeletons to be preserved—paleontologists (fossil scientists) build up a picture of how the animal looked and lived from fragments of bone. The large eye of this extinct sea reptile shows that it dived into dark waters.

Opabinia (possibly a giant ancestor of a tardigrade)

Haikouichthys, one of the earliest vertebrates

Marrella (thought to be a primitive arthropod)

Mass extinctions

Extinctions may occur due to a global catastrophe that kills thousands of species at once. Earth has witnessed at least five mass extinctions, the last of which occurred 65 mya, when the dinosaurs died out. The worst extinction of all was the one around 250 mya, which wiped out most life on Earth.

Corythosaurus, a dinosaur

Armor plates on a trilobite's back allowed it to roll up for protection

Extinct humans

Our species, *Homo sapiens,* is not the first human species, but it is the only one that has not died out. One of the earliest members was *Homo habilis,* or "handy man," which lived between 2.3 and 1.4 mya. The last one to become extinct was the tiny "Flores man"—*Homo floresiensis*—which died out about 17,000 years ago.

Homo habilis made cutting tools out of flakes of stone

Killed by humans

The thylacine, or marsupial tiger, became extinct in 1936, when the last one died in an Australian zoo. By then, all wild thylacines—predators more closely related to kangaroos than cats—had been shot because they were considered pests. Humans have wiped out hundreds of species, from the Cuban coney to the dodo—often by accident.

Dead end

An extinct species often leaves behind sister species, but some extinctions spell the end for an entire group of animal. Trilobites were one of the most common animals in the sea before they were all wiped out in the mass extinction around 250 mya.

Anomalocaris, a primitive arthropod

Hallucigenia (possibly a velvet worm)

Wiwaxia, a primitive annelid

Body systems

Just like a machine, an animal's body must be supplied with fuel and raw materials. It must also get rid of waste and repair itself when damaged. To perform these functions, most animals have a basic set of body systems, each of which manages one set of life processes: digesting food, transporting nutrients and waste, moving, and protecting the body. Different animal bodies perform the same jobs in different ways.

Skeletons

Rigid skeletons provide a framework for an animal's body. For land animals, this enables them to raise their body parts against the force of gravity. It also provides anchor points for muscles to pull on, allowing animals to move their bodies around. A vertebrate has an internal skeleton, but an insect, such as this beetle, has a hard exoskeleton (skeleton outside the body).

Hard wing case covers back

The flow of blood

Without a blood supply and the oxygen it contains an animal's body parts would soon start to die. In addition to cells carrying oxygen, blood carries a range of chemicals. These include hormones—chemical messengers that control different body systems. For many animals, such as this glass frog, blood travels inside special vessels that form the main chemical transportation network. In invertebrates, the blood sloshes through the whole body.

Heart pumps blood around body

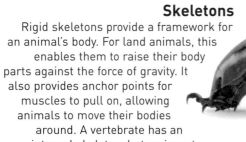

Crab spider drinks fleshy soup

Meat soup

Usually, after swallowing food, an animal must digest it, to break it down into sugars, fats, and proteins. It then uses these substances as fuel or to build up the body. Digestion is mostly done by powerful chemicals in the stomach and intestines called enzymes. A spider, however, pumps its stomach enzymes into its prey, turning the victim's insides into a fleshy soup, which it then sucks up.

Pouch is full of water so gills work even above water level

Gas exchange

Animals take in oxygen and give out carbon dioxide in a process called gas exchange. Oxygen chemically breaks down sugar, releasing energy and producing carbon dioxide as waste. Simple animals exchange gases through the surface of their bodies, but larger ones, like this mudskipper, use more complex systems like lungs and gills.

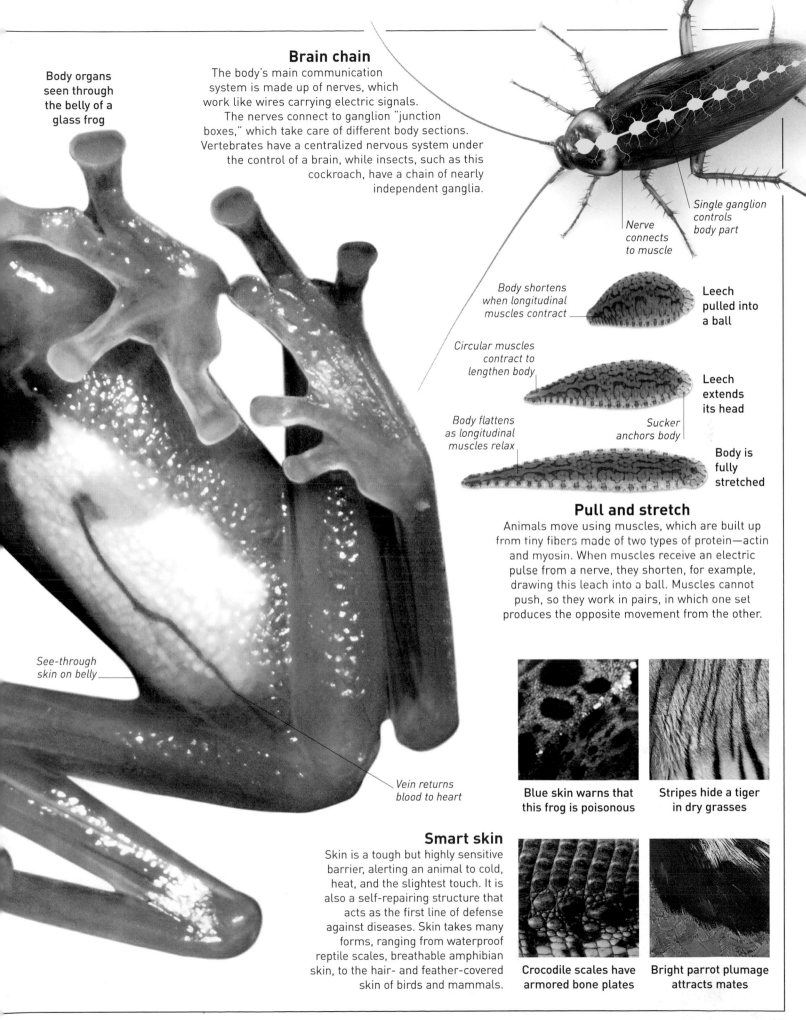

Body organs seen through the belly of a glass frog

Brain chain

The body's main communication system is made up of nerves, which work like wires carrying electric signals. The nerves connect to ganglion "junction boxes," which take care of different body sections. Vertebrates have a centralized nervous system under the control of a brain, while insects, such as this cockroach, have a chain of nearly independent ganglia.

Nerve connects to muscle

Single ganglion controls body part

Body shortens when longitudinal muscles contract

Leech pulled into a ball

Circular muscles contract to lengthen body

Leech extends its head

Body flattens as longitudinal muscles relax

Sucker anchors body

Body is fully stretched

Pull and stretch

Animals move using muscles, which are built up from tiny fibers made of two types of protein—actin and myosin. When muscles receive an electric pulse from a nerve, they shorten, for example, drawing this leach into a ball. Muscles cannot push, so they work in pairs, in which one set produces the opposite movement from the other.

See-through skin on belly

Vein returns blood to heart

Blue skin warns that this frog is poisonous

Stripes hide a tiger in dry grasses

Smart skin

Skin is a tough but highly sensitive barrier, alerting an animal to cold, heat, and the slightest touch. It is also a self-repairing structure that acts as the first line of defense against diseases. Skin takes many forms, ranging from waterproof reptile scales, breathable amphibian skin, to the hair- and feather-covered skin of birds and mammals.

Crocodile scales have armored bone plates

Bright parrot plumage attracts mates

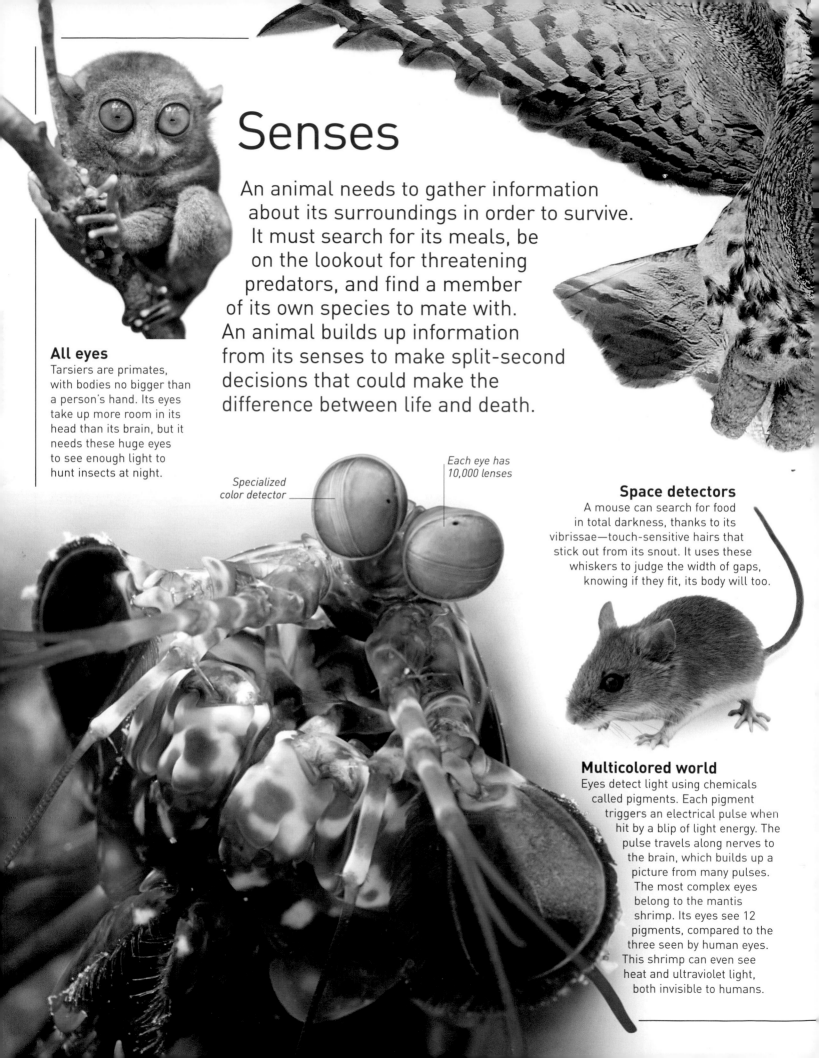

Senses

An animal needs to gather information about its surroundings in order to survive. It must search for its meals, be on the lookout for threatening predators, and find a member of its own species to mate with. An animal builds up information from its senses to make split-second decisions that could make the difference between life and death.

All eyes

Tarsiers are primates, with bodies no bigger than a person's hand. Its eyes take up more room in its head than its brain, but it needs these huge eyes to see enough light to hunt insects at night.

Specialized color detector

Each eye has 10,000 lenses

Space detectors

A mouse can search for food in total darkness, thanks to its vibrissae—touch-sensitive hairs that stick out from its snout. It uses these whiskers to judge the width of gaps, knowing if they fit, its body will too.

Multicolored world

Eyes detect light using chemicals called pigments. Each pigment triggers an electrical pulse when hit by a blip of light energy. The pulse travels along nerves to the brain, which builds up a picture from many pulses. The most complex eyes belong to the mantis shrimp. Its eyes see 12 pigments, compared to the three seen by human eyes. This shrimp can even see heat and ultraviolet light, both invisible to humans.

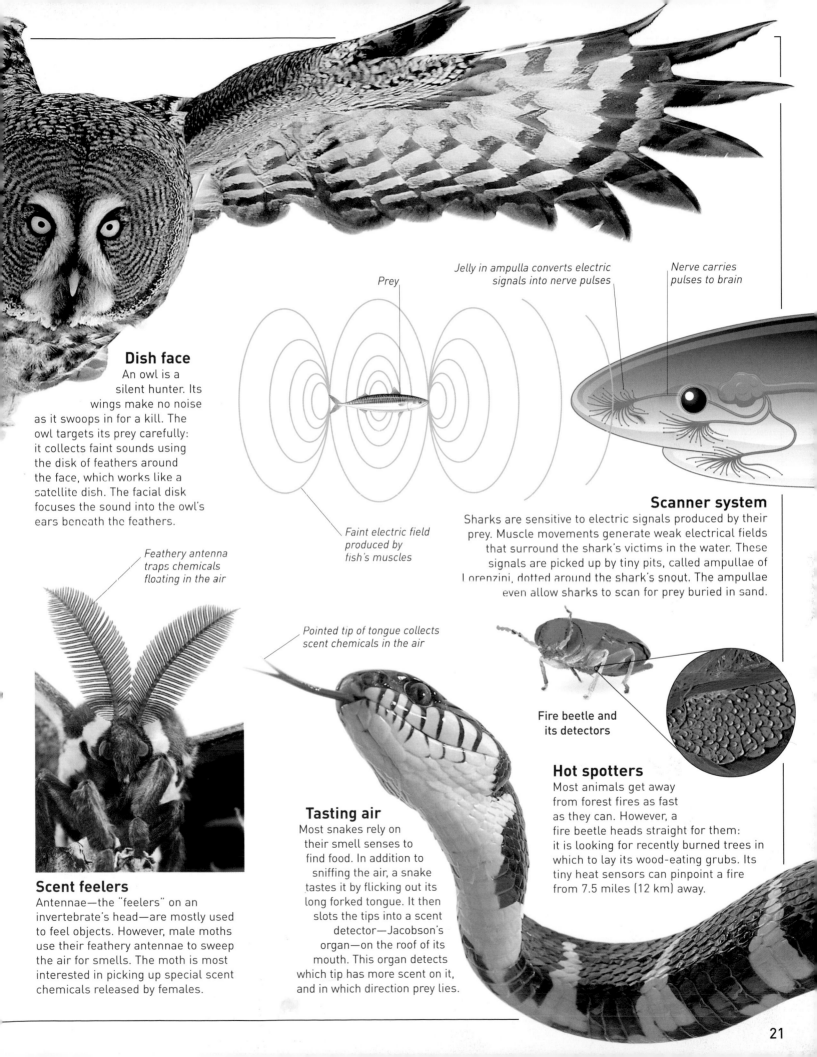

Dish face

An owl is a silent hunter. Its wings make no noise as it swoops in for a kill. The owl targets its prey carefully: it collects faint sounds using the disk of feathers around the face, which works like a satellite dish. The facial disk focuses the sound into the owl's ears beneath the feathers.

Prey

Jelly in ampulla converts electric signals into nerve pulses

Nerve carries pulses to brain

Faint electric field produced by fish's muscles

Scanner system

Sharks are sensitive to electric signals produced by their prey. Muscle movements generate weak electrical fields that surround the shark's victims in the water. These signals are picked up by tiny pits, called ampullae of Lorenzini, dotted around the shark's snout. The ampullae even allow sharks to scan for prey buried in sand.

Feathery antenna traps chemicals floating in the air

Pointed tip of tongue collects scent chemicals in the air

Fire beetle and its detectors

Scent feelers

Antennae—the "feelers" on an invertebrate's head—are mostly used to feel objects. However, male moths use their feathery antennae to sweep the air for smells. The moth is most interested in picking up special scent chemicals released by females.

Tasting air

Most snakes rely on their smell senses to find food. In addition to sniffing the air, a snake tastes it by flicking out its long forked tongue. It then slots the tips into a scent detector—Jacobson's organ—on the roof of its mouth. This organ detects which tip has more scent on it, and in which direction prey lies.

Hot spotters

Most animals get away from forest fires as fast as they can. However, a fire beetle heads straight for them: it is looking for recently burned trees in which to lay its wood-eating grubs. Its tiny heat sensors can pinpoint a fire from 7.5 miles (12 km) away.

Animal diets

Diet is a deciding factor in what an animal looks like and how it survives. Some species exploit one food source, while others survive on whatever comes their way. For instance, the snail kite is a little predatory bird that swoops over marshlands preying only on snails. In contrast, the Andean condor is an immense bird that glides for miles in search of a meal. It will eat anything, from the carcass of a beached whale to a nest full of eggs.

Esophagus carries food to crop

Gizzard grinds food

Intestines absorb nutrients

Crop stores food

Cloaca expels waste

Anatomy of a pigeon

Long neck helps giraffe access food out of reach of most browsers

Digesting seeds
Many small birds, such as pigeons, are seed-eaters. Seeds are packed with energy, but they have hard kernels. With no teeth, birds cannot chew. Instead, they grind the seeds in a muscular stomach pouch called the gizzard. Some birds peck grit to help grind the seeds more efficiently.

The ultimate browser
The giraffe is a browser—an animal that eats leaves. It strips away leaves from even the prickliest trees with its tough, long tongue. Browsers and grazers (animals that eat grasses) are herbivores and eat only plant food. Much of this diet is indigestible fiber and is low in nutrients. Herbivores must feed constantly to keep their bodies supplied with energy. They also rely on stomach bacteria to break down some of the fiber into useful sugars.

Seek and destroy
Animals that eat nothing but meat are known as carnivores. This diet is very nutritious, since flesh is full of the proteins and fats needed to build a strong body. However, carnivores must use a lot of energy to catch prey. This lioness is chasing a kudu calf—even a predator as powerful as this fails to kill in six out of seven hunts.

Cooperative farmers

Leaf-cutter ants grow their own food. Worker ants use their slicing mouthparts to cut slabs of leaves. They carry them back to the nest and pile them up in deep "garden" chambers. A species of fungus grows on the rotting leaves, and that is what the adult ants eat and feed to their young. The ants tend their crops, controlling bacteria by applying pesticide chemicals from their saliva.

Acacia tree leaves cluster out of reach of most browsers

Dung ball from herbivore, such as cattle

Long back leg used to roll dung

Everything is food

Herbivores can only extract a small proportion of nutrients from their food, so their dung is a useful source of food for other animals. Dung beetles collect the waste and roll it into balls, inside of which they lay their eggs—providing their grubs with a ready supply of dung to feast on.

Short head feathers do not get soaked with blood

Flesh of the dead

Animals that eat carrion—the flesh of dead animals—are called scavengers. A vulture is a top scavenger. It patrols the skies on wide wings and its hooked beak is ideal for ripping scraps of flesh from bones. The bird's stomach juices are highly acidic and kill any bacteria that may have infected the rotting carcasses.

Rüppell's vulture

Curiosity pays

Opportunist feeders never miss a chance to eat a meal. They are usually omnivores—animals that eat plant and animal food, dead or alive. The coati checks every nook and cranny with its long nose and sensitive forepaws. Its curiosity means it can find food almost anywhere—from a jungle to a junkyard.

Parenting

An animal that dies without reproducing cannot pass on its genes. In nature, the only animals that survive are those that are driven to reproduce. Most animals use sexual reproduction, in which a male and female pair up to mix both of their traits. This creates variation and increases the chances that some offspring will survive. After hatching or being born, young animals go through a period of growth.

Female   Male

Courting a mate

Strong and healthy animals make the best mates because it is likely that their offspring will be healthy too. The male blue-footed booby puts on a show for a potential mate by spreading his wings and stamping his feet. The deep blue color of the feet are a sign that this male might make a good mate.

Changing sex

Sexual reproduction requires a male sex cell (sperm) to fuse with a female one (ovum, or egg). Generally, an animal is either male or female—it produces sex cells of only one kind. The bluehead wrasse does things differently. A young female lives with other females and a large, mature "supermale" with a bright blue head. When this male dies, the largest adult female in the group changes sex to become the next supermale.

Young female produces eggs

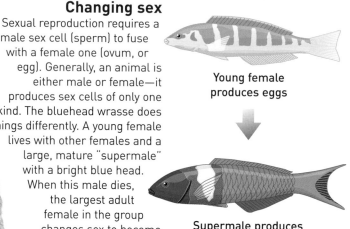

Supermale produces sperm instead of eggs

Precious cargo

Animals need to ensure that their offspring survive long enough to reproduce themselves. Most invertebrates lay eggs in large numbers so that at least a few survive to adulthood. Scorpions, however, produce only a few eggs. The offspring spend the first part of their lives on their mother's back. The mother protects her newborns so that they have a better chance of growing up and breeding.

Mothered by father

Seahorses have a unique breeding system—the female produces the eggs and transfers them to a brood pouch on the male's belly. The eggs hatch inside the pouch, but the young, called fry, stay for a while longer, adapting to increasingly salty water.

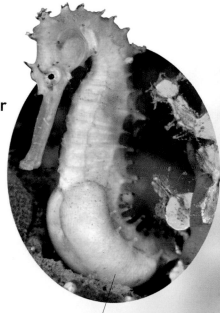

Pouch holds around 200 fry

Starter home

Most mammal babies develop inside their mother's womb, or uterus, where a structure called the placenta supplies them with oxygen and food. However, marsupial mammals, such as this kangaroo, give birth to immature offspring. This young kangaroo (left), called a joey, was born blind and hairless, and its hind legs were just little lumps. With its clawlike arms, it heaved itself into its mother's pouch, where it will complete its development.

Tail for swimming

Female aphid giving birth to young

Embryo in jelly

Gills Newly hatched tadpole

The cycle of life

A frog goes through several stages during its life. After hatching from eggs, the young—or larvae—begin to grow in water as tadpoles, froglets, and finally, frogs. As an adult, a frog devotes its energy to finding a mate and producing eggs of its own. This takes place mainly on land. Since the adults live on land and the larvae are in water, they do not compete for food.

Frog spawn

Half-tadpole, half-frog, 6–9 weeks

Mass production

Populations of aphids—also known as greenfly—grow very quickly using a form of asexual reproduction known as parthenogenesis. Females give birth to tiny clones (identical versions of themselves). These young aphids already have their own young developing inside them. In one summer, as many as 40 generations can hatch. However, all the offspring share the weaknesses—susceptibility to disease, for example—of the parent. Therefore, in fall, aphids lay eggs using sexual reproduction to ensure that a wide variety of individuals hatch the following spring.

Adult common frog

Froglet emerges from water after about 12 weeks

Tail slowly shrinks

Front legs now fully formed

Caring parents

Most invertebrates and fish produce many offspring and provide little parental care. Many mammals, however, have few young and devote a lot of time and energy to caring for them. Orangutans have one baby at a time, several years apart. The baby ape is almost helpless at birth. It also has a lot to learn— how to climb and where to find food—and needs its mother's help for its first five years or so.

Female orangutan with her babies

Patrolling the shore
The shoreline is a crowded habitat. Here, the tides sweep regularly over the shore before receding. Being covered by seawater and then exposed to the air is difficult for coastal animals, and many of them hide out in mud when the tide recedes. These animals make a rich food source for waders, such as these red knots.

Marine animals

Life began in the oceans more than 3.5 billion years ago, and the oceans are still home to every major type of animal. However, the oceans are not a single habitat. Marine environments are as different as rocky shores, mangrove swamps, and deep ocean trenches. Biologists estimate that there is 300 times more living space in the Earth's oceans than on dry land, and even in the open ocean there are variations in temperature, pressure, and saltiness that impact life.

Coastal raiders
Many sea mammals and birds live on the coast but raid the water for food. Terns snatch fish, seals chase down squid, and diving otters collect shellfish. Sea otters have highly buoyant bodies, which is partly due to their thick fur. With 1 million strands of hair per sq in (150,000 strands per sq cm), it traps a lot of air—these hunters can even sleep while floating.

Underwater jungles
Corals are colonies of organisms that are tiny relatives of jellyfish. Each animal is called a polyp and grows a tiny protective case made from calcium carbonate, which is left behind when it dies. Generations of these skeletons build up into limestone reefs that can be several miles long. The complex shapes, holes, and crevices created by the coral skeletons provide a lot of different niches where animals, such as these yellow butterflyfish, can live.

Schooling

There are few places to hide in the open ocean, and some fish swim in clusters called schools to stay safe from predators. Each fish here is trying to get into the middle of a school where it is safer. They dart around, making it difficult for a predator to pick out a single target.

Spotted skin camouflages shark against seabed

A docile shark

There are about 350 species of shark in the ocean. Some are fearsome, sharp-toothed predators that can prey on humans, but most sharks are harmless. This bullhead shark uses its sturdy fins to walk across the seabed at night, searching for urchins and crabs to eat.

Mantle (body covering)

Fin flaps up and down to propel squid

Devil in the dark

The deep-sea vampire squid spends its life in constant darkness, but its body produces light—a phenomenon called bioluminescence. The squid flashes its light to lure prey and attract mates. If this brings unwanted attention, it folds its webbed tentacles over the mantle and shuts out the light.

Webbed tentacle

Going flat

Flatfish, such as this flounder, go through an amazing change. A young flounder swims upright like other fish, but as it grows, its skull twists so that the right eye moves to the left side of the head. This way both eyes are on the same side of the head, and it can look for prey while lying camouflaged on the seabed.

Freshwater living

Inland water habitats can be as challenging to life as the oceans. Many aquatic animals rely on unpredictable little streams and ponds, which may freeze in winter and dry out in summer. Slow-flowing water loses oxygen and fish cannot use their gills effectively, while fast-flowing streams are a difficult environment in which to live. Plus, animal body tissues, which are full of salts, pull water in from freshwater, so freshwater animals must constantly produce watery urine to flush it out.

White plumage turned pink by diet

Thick skin resists chemicals in water

Mineral rich
Not every inland body of water is fresh. Flamingos live in desert lakes filled with salts and other chemicals. They survive by feeding on tough brine shrimp, which live on a diet of bacteria (small single-celled organisms).

Beak has plates that sift food from water

Bony scute protects body

Lurking in the shallows
This spectacled caiman, like other crocodilians, is superbly suited to hunting in shallow waters. It lies hidden under the water with only the eyes and nostrils above the surface, ready to surge up the bank to drag prey into the water. A crocodile's bite is 10 times stronger than that of a shark, and once its victim is in the water, death is almost certain. The caiman also eats large quantities of fish.

On their own
Freshwater lakes are isolated habitats with unique wildlife, in much the same way as remote islands far out at sea. Lake Baikal, the world's largest lake, in eastern Russia, is home to the only freshwater species of seal, known as the nerpa. The ancestors of the nerpa swam upriver from the sea about 80,000 years ago., but their route back to the ocean has since disappeared.

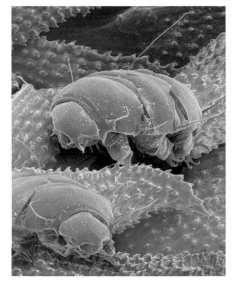

Survivors

Tardigrades, or water bears, are microscopic animals that live in all types of water—from hot springs to muddy puddles—and graze on bacteria. They are the toughest creatures alive. When the water dries out or becomes too salty, a tardigrade hauls up its eight legs and becomes dormant. Scientists have found that tardigrades can even survive in space.

Spider falls into water after being hit by water

Stream of droplets

Tree ponds

Freshwater habitats can be found in some unusual places. The leaves of succulent jungle plants called bromeliads form a cup that collects rainwater. These little ponds, high up in the trees, are used by many poison dart frogs to raise their young. If the baby outgrows its pool, the mother carries it to a larger one.

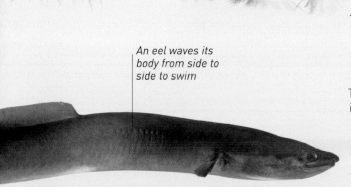

An eel waves its body from side to side to swim

Water cannon

The archerfish uses water as a weapon. It pokes its lips above the surface and fires a jet of water out of its mouth with a quick squeeze of its gill covers. The jet can travel up to 10 ft (3 m) into the air, knocking its prey from overhanging leaves into the water. The archerfish mostly hits its target at the first attempt, because its eyes and brain can adjust to the bending of light that happens when light moves from air to water.

A watery road

Most aquatic (water-dwelling) animals are adapted to one habitat, but the common eel has specialized kidneys that enable it to live in both salty and freshwater. This snake-shaped fish starts life in the Sargasso Sea. Baby eels, or elvers, head across the Atlantic Ocean to river mouths in Europe, where freshwater mixes with salty seawater. Some stay there, but most elvers head inland, even slithering over land to reach a suitable freshwater habitat. Once mature, the adult eels go back to sea to breed.

Hawker naiad spears a stickleback fish

Wet nursery

Very few insect species live in marine habitats, but many, such as the hawker dragonfly, start life in freshwater. This young dragonfly—known as a naiad—breathes with gills and uses a sharp mouthpart to spear prey with lightning speed. After several months of hunting in shallow pools, the naiad climbs up the stalk of a water plant and transforms into an adult.

Cold and ice

The coldest habitats on Earth are near the poles, where summers are too short to provide much warmth, and high up on mountains, where the air is too thin to retain heat. Most of the animals that live in cold places are warm-blooded, although a few cold-blooded species have evolved adaptations that enable them to survive in cold conditions. Some insects can freeze in winter, but still be alive and well when they thaw out in spring.

Found in plenty

The polar oceans are so cold that the surface of the water freezes over at times. The conditions under the water are less severe, however, and the polar seas thrive with life. Krill—tiny relatives of shrimp—swarm in their millions, providing an important food source for marine life.

Antarctic krill

Big is best

The bodies of large animals lose heat slowly in cold conditions, which is why animals in cold regions tend to be larger than those in warmer ones. The world's largest deer, the moose, lives in the cold north, as does the musk ox, the largest goat, and the gyrfalcon, the biggest falcon. Polar animals also tend to have shorter legs, ears, and tails, which also helps reduce heat loss.

Life in the Arctic

Earth's polar regions experience extreme seasonal changes. Most polar bears are active throughout the year, but pregnant females enter a hibernation-like state and sleep through the winter. Bear cubs are born at this time, growing strong on their mother's milk while she sleeps. Mother and cubs are ready to hunt as soon as summer arrives.

Pale fur camouflages bear among the ice

Wide feet do not sink into snow and help make bears strong swimmers

Wing is larger than those of other geese

High fliers

Bar-headed geese are some of the highest flying birds. They cross over the Himalayas while migrating from the wetlands in India to the Tibetan plateau. The temperature can drop to -22 °F (-30 °C), and the air is so thin that the geese breathe hundreds of times in a minute to get enough oxygen.

Happy feet

Body heat can cause problems in freezing conditions. Warm skin melts ice, but the ice freezes again almost instantly, bonding to the skin in the same way that a tongue sticks to an ice pop. Amazingly, emperor penguins can survive at -76 °F (-60 °C), the coldest conditions experienced by any animal. Warm blood pumping into the feet loses heat to cold blood flowing back to the heart, so the feet stay cold and never get warm enough to melt the ice.

Chick sits on father's feet to stay off cold ice

Best foot forward

This mountain goat lives on steep cliffs in British Columbia, Canada, where only the most sure-footed animals can survive. A mountain goat's hoof has two parts, which spread apart and grab the rough ground like a pincer. The sharp rim of the hoof digs into the ice, helping to grip the surface, while the base is covered in a spongy pad that prevents the animal from slipping.

Iceberg ahead

A beluga whale lives along the edge of the Arctic sea ice. Its white skin disguises it among the floating icebergs and helps it hide from orcas and polar bears. The beluga is hairless and keeps warm thanks to a 4-in- (10-cm-) thick layer of fatty blubber under its skin. It is nicknamed the sea canary because it communicates using whistles and chirps.

Small ear reduces heat loss

In the desert

About one-fifth of the Earth's land is very dry and receives less than 10 in (250 mm) of rain in a year—less than a bucketful. These regions are deserts, and they range from the Sahara and other searingly hot, tropical deserts to cold deserts, such as the Gobi in central Asia. Desert animals must cope with temperatures that plummet at night and long periods without food or water.

Wedge-shaped snout slices through sand

Leg held against body as lizard slithers like a snake

Swimming in the sand
A sandfish is actually a specialized skink—a type of lizard. Its strong, cylindrical body and short legs help it to slither through loose sand. The creature hunts on the sand, detecting tiny vibrations made by insects.

Thick fur keeps camel warm in cold, high desert

Bactrian camel has two humps

Fat reserves
Water drains through sandy desert soil quickly, so there are few places where plants can grow. Desert browsers, such as this Bactrian camel of central Asia, can go without water for 10 days and survive on the toughest desert shrubs. The camel carries a supply of food in its humps, in the form of oily fats.

Wing cases are fused shut, stopping the body from drying out

Drinking the fog
The huge sand dunes of Africa's Namib Desert rise up on the coast of the Atlantic Ocean. While rainfall is rare, dense banks of fog often roll in from the sea. Fog-basking beetles sit at the top of the dunes and literally drink the mist. Each beetle does a handstand, and tiny droplets condense on its body, running down grooves that lead to its mouth.

Following the rain

The Arabian oryx, a type of antelope, goes for weeks without drinking, getting all the water it needs from the plants it eats. It can smell rain from miles away and travels toward fresh plants that grow after rainfall. When not on the move, an oryx digs a cool pit in the sand and rests in the shade.

Surviving the heat

Frogs need to stay moist in the desert heat. The Australian water-holding frog keeps damp by digging deep into the ground and cocooning itself in a bag of mucus. The cocoon hardens and forms a water-tight barrier that locks in water around the frog's body. The amphibian stays underground until it rains again.

Keeping cool

Large mammals can get very hot under the Sun. Their body temperatures can rise above 105.8 °F (41 °C) to levels that would damage the brain of many mammals. A gazelle remains unaffected—its cooling system chills the blood entering its brain. This allows the gazelle to keep on running when being chased by a predator, while its pursuer must stop to keep from overheating.

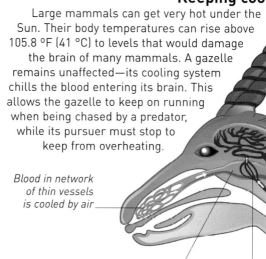

A gazelle's brain-cooling system

Some warm blood reaches brain directly

Blood in network of thin vessels is cooled by air

Cooled blood travels to rest of body

Sinus (chamber) filled with cooled blood

Warm blood to brain passes through cool sinus

Water in fog condenses on beetle's cold body

Sun spiders

Deserts are home to sun spiders, some of the fiercest predators in the animal kingdom. At about 6 in (15 cm) long, its large pincerlike mouthparts make up one-quarter of its body. It uses its huge pincers to slice beetles and other insects. A sun spider will even tackle desert mice.

Sun spider with prey

Fill the tank

Sandgrouse live in the dry parts of Europe, Africa, and Asia. They are seed-eaters and flock to deserts when flowering plants are in seed. The adult birds fly great distances to find watering holes. They then soak their belly feathers in water to airlift drinks to their chicks.

Open grassland

Pronghorn, a North American, hoofed grassland, mammal

Grasslands grow in areas that are too dry for forests to flourish, but not dry enough for deserts to form. There is sufficient rain for fast-growing grasses to grow, which provide enough food for the animals that live there. There are no specific food sources to defend, so plant-eating animals, such as bulky bulls, compete over other things, like the chance to mate.

Need for speed

There are no places to hide on grasslands, so when danger appears, hoofed animals, such as antelopes and pronghorns, run fast. The pronghorn is capable of reaching speeds of up to 60 mph (100 kph). Hoofed animals stand on their tiptoes. Their feet are long, and this helps them to lengthen their legs and increase their stride.

Snake in the grass

This reptile is not a snake, but a lizard that slithers along without legs. It lives in European and Asian grasslands, where it hunts slugs. It is named the glass lizard because it appears to break in two—like a piece of brittle glass—when picked up by the tail.

Termites

The most important grazers (grass-eaters) in some grasslands are tiny insects—termites. Like an ant's nest, a termite colony has a queen, but unlike an ant's nest, it also has a king. Millions of termites live in tall mounds made of mud reinforced with dried grass. A natural cooling system reduces the heat produced by the termites.

Ventilation shaft

Night hunter

It too easy to be spotted by prey during daylight, so many grassland predators spend their days lazing in the shade, waiting until dark. The serval, an African cat about twice the size of a house cat, uses its large ears to listen for rodents in the grass.

Worker termite

Chimney lets out rising hot air

Fungus grows on heaps of grass cuttings and provides food for nymphs

Follow the herd

Large herbivores, such as these wildebeest, gather in herds because it is safer for them to stay together. Every herd member looks out for danger, and when one reacts to a threat, the others follow suit. Predators usually pick off the weaker animals on the edges of a herd. Grazers form the biggest herds on the grassy plains.

Nursery chamber houses nymphs (young termites)

Underground cellar draws in cool air from outside mound

Queen lives in a royal chamber

Silent stalker

Unlike other birds of prey that swoop over grasslands, the secretary bird hunts on foot. Stalking slowly through short grass on its stiltlike legs, this gangle bird watches the ground intently, and when a lizard, locust, or other small animal comes out from a hiding place, it traps it with its foot. It kills its victim with a rip from its hooked beak.

Nesting underground

Temperate (cool) grasslands, such as the American prairies, have almost no trees at all. The American burrowing owl, therefore, nests underground. It usually does not dig the den, but sets up home in a hole vacated by another burrowing animal, such as a prairie dog. The burrow provides the owl with a shelter from predators.

Among the trees

More animals are found in forests than in any other habitat on Earth. Forests range from hot, damp jungles to cold conifer woodlands in the far north. A single tropical rain-forest tree can house more than a thousand species. In all cases, the tall trees provide hundreds of different habitats. As a result, forests are home to both noisy howler monkeys and quiet sloths.

Cuvier's toucan

Fruits and nuts

This toucan is a frugivore (fruit-eater). Frugivores live only in tropical forests in which warm temperatures allow year-round fruiting. The bird's colorful bill is long enough to reach fruits dangling from flimsy branches, and its jagged edge is strong enough to crack open nuts.

Target in sight

In the trees, a vine snake has only one chance to catch its prey before it has gone. The snake has a groove that runs from each eye to the tip of its snout that works like a gun sight. It lines up the grooves to zero in on mice and small birds.

Groove helps target prey

Hidden away

The jaguar is the biggest jungle cat in America. In the dappled light of the forest, the cat's distinctive pattern of blotchy rosettes (roselike markings) makes for perfect camouflage. This helps the predator hide in the foliage and sneak up on deer and other prey.

Foraging on the floor

Most of the time, this giant millipede remains hidden away among leaf litter—the thick layer of dead leaves that covers the floor of a forest. It grazes on dead plant material on the forest floor, which is also the hunting ground for predatory centipedes and blind snakes.

Up the tree

Moisture-loving frogs can easily survive high up in the branches of rain forests. Tree frogs crawl along leaves, using cup-shaped suckers on their toes to grip the flat surfaces. This red-eyed tree frog keeps its eyes shut tightly when hiding. If threatened by a predator, the frog stares squarely at it and flashes its startling blue and yellow body colors.

Vertical pupil tracks moving insects

Bright orange foot startles predators

Tail can support weight of monkey's body

Loose skin on sole of foot helps grip

Getting noticed

Sometimes animals need to get noticed to attract mates. When resting with its wings folded, the blue morpho butterfly may look drab among the leaves. When it flies, however, the tops of the wings are revealed, showing off a shimmering blue color.

Emergent tree
125 ft (38 m)

Canopy
92 ft (28 m)

Understory
56 ft (17 m)

Undergrowth
16 ft (5 m)

Forest floor

Hanging out

When living so high up, putting just one foot wrong could be fatal. The New World monkeys of South America get a helping hand from their prehensile tails, which can wrap around a branch. The tail has a hairless pad at the tip that also aids grip. This fuzzy monkey can hang from its tail alone.

The right fit

Jungle mammals tend to be smaller than those living in open habitats, such as grasslands. Being smaller helps this African forest elephant when pushing through thick foliage. Jungle birds, on the other hand, appear to have longer bills, or beaks, than their relatives living in cooler places. The birds might use a large beak as a radiator to give out heat, so their bodies do not overheat as they fly through the steamy forest.

Many levels

Tropical rain forests have layers, which function as habitats for different groups of animal. At the top are occasional giant trees called emergents. Emergents and canopy trees are out in the sunshine, but they block out the light, making the forest floor a gloomy place. The canopy forms a continuous layer that is home to most rain-forest animals.

Long fifth finger supports wing of skin

Taking to the air

Pterodactylus

In the history of life on Earth, four distinct groups of animal—insects, pterosaurs (flying reptiles), birds, and bats—evolved adaptations that enabled flight. Today, each flying animal combines a light body-weight with high muscle power. It is lifted off the ground by wings. As the wings cut through the air, they create a lift force that opposes gravity, and raises or holds the animal in the air.

Flying reptiles

The first flying vertebrates were the pterosaurs. These reptiles were closely related to dinosaurs and became extinct at the same time, around 65 million years ago. One of the first fossil pterosaurs discovered was *Pterodactylus*, meaning "wing finger"—its wing was mostly skin stretched behind a single long finger bone.

Small claw on thumb is used for gripping when bat is at rest

Primary flight feather

Handy wings

Bats, which appeared around 50 million years ago, were the last group of animal to take to the air. They are the only mammals that can fly. A bat's skin wing stretches between its finger bones. Although bats can see, many rely mostly on a system called echolocation to find their way. Bats emit high-pitched chirps that echo from objects around them. Based on the echoes, they then work out the distances to the objects, forming a sound picture of their surroundings.

Wing membrane stretches between thin finger bones

Secondary flight feather

Wing is a thin membrane running between stiff veins

Wing twists as it moves up, cutting through the air, but flattens again as it flaps down, pushing against the air

Wing is powered by muscles at its base

Four wings first

Insects were the first animals to fly. No other invertebrate group has taken to the air since. It is believed that the first flying insects, which appeared around 350 million years ago, had four wings and looked like today's dragonflies. Insect wings are not modified legs, like those of birds and bats, and may have evolved from gills of aquatic larvae.

Back wing moves in opposite direction to front wings in slow flight, to reduce speed while continuing to provide the lifting force for flight

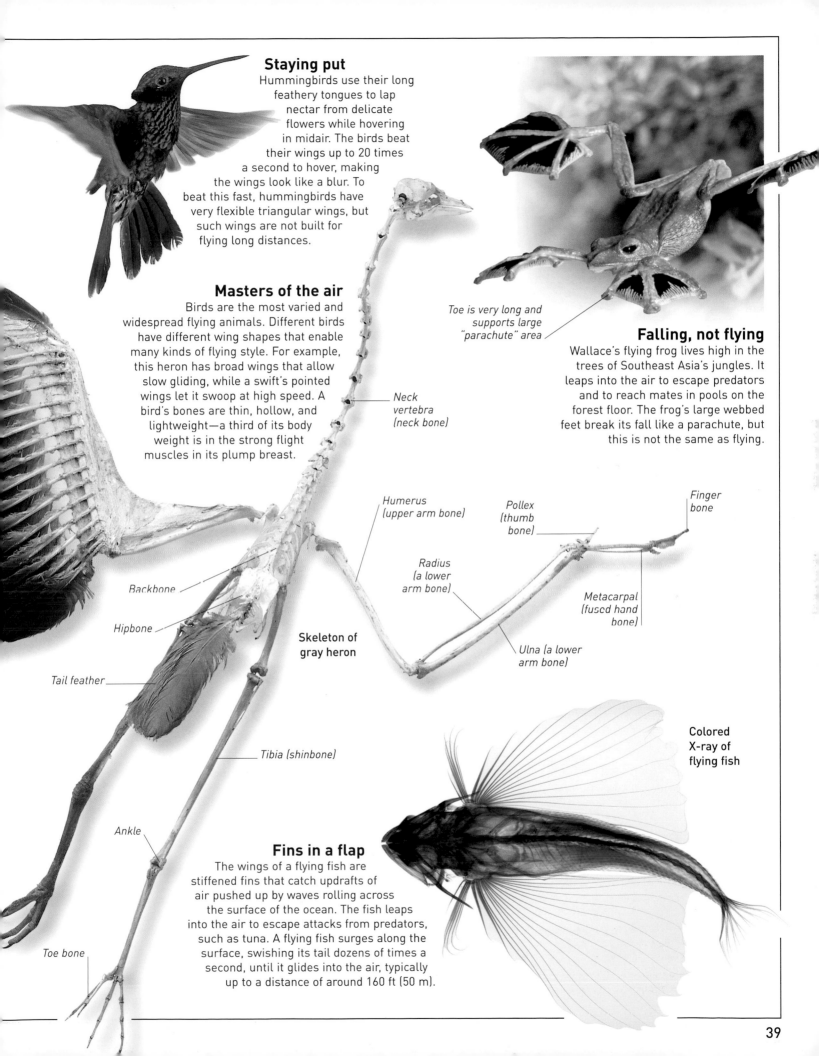

Staying put

Hummingbirds use their long feathery tongues to lap nectar from delicate flowers while hovering in midair. The birds beat their wings up to 20 times a second to hover, making the wings look like a blur. To beat this fast, hummingbirds have very flexible triangular wings, but such wings are not built for flying long distances.

Masters of the air

Birds are the most varied and widespread flying animals. Different birds have different wing shapes that enable many kinds of flying style. For example, this heron has broad wings that allow slow gliding, while a swift's pointed wings let it swoop at high speed. A bird's bones are thin, hollow, and lightweight—a third of its body weight is in the strong flight muscles in its plump breast.

Neck vertebra (neck bone)

Toe is very long and supports large "parachute" area

Falling, not flying

Wallace's flying frog lives high in the trees of Southeast Asia's jungles. It leaps into the air to escape predators and to reach mates in pools on the forest floor. The frog's large webbed feet break its fall like a parachute, but this is not the same as flying.

Humerus (upper arm bone)

Pollex (thumb bone)

Finger bone

Radius (a lower arm bone)

Backbone

Hipbone

Metacarpal (fused hand bone)

Skeleton of gray heron

Ulna (a lower arm bone)

Tail feather

Tibia (shinbone)

Colored X-ray of flying fish

Ankle

Fins in a flap

The wings of a flying fish are stiffened fins that catch updrafts of air pushed up by waves rolling across the surface of the ocean. The fish leaps into the air to escape attacks from predators, such as tuna. A flying fish surges along the surface, swishing its tail dozens of times a second, until it glides into the air, typically up to a distance of around 160 ft (50 m).

Toe bone

Animal homes

Some animals are always on the move, searching for food and mates. Others live in one area, defending their territory from other members of their species. Still others set up temporary homes to hibernate or raise their young. A bird's nest is perhaps the best known example of an animal's home, but even large mammals, such as gorillas, build nests.

Stitched homes

The masked weaver bird knits grass together to build a woven ball hanging from a tree. Only the male weavers create nests, and different males often build them in the same tree. When the nests are ready, female weavers inspect them. If a female likes a nest, she pairs with its builder because she considers him a good mate with which to raise chicks.

1 Best location

The male first chooses a small branch to hang the nest from. He prefers to locate it near the tops of trees, out of reach of climbing predators, such as snakes, and often near a source of water.

House of leaves

Weaver ants live in trees and they make their nests out of the material available. Teams of worker ants haul the edges of leaves together, while other adults bind the leaves together with a sticky silk produced by larvae. Adults hold larvae like tubes of glue to form a boxlike, green nest.

Silk produced by ant larvae glues together edges of leaves

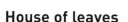

Diving bell

The web made by a water spider is not a sticky fly trap. Instead, it holds the spider's air supply during hunting dives. The spider retreats to its bubble home to digest food. Its web works like a gill, releasing waste carbon dioxide and taking in oxygen from the water. Every so often, the spider refills the web with fresh air at the surface.

Case made from plant stems and pebbles

Front end enlarges as larva grows inside

A bits-and-pieces home

Caddisfly larvae live in freshwater streams. Some species weave a silk tube to live in, which acts as a net to catch specks of food. Other caddisflies use their silk to glue bits of the riverbed into an armored case. This case is open at both ends and the insect draws in water, providing the animal with food and oxygen.

Size of spherical nest depends on the bird's reach

Fresh, flexible stalks are easier to weave

Hanging homes

With bodies that are adapted for flight, bats are not well adapted to life on the ground. They roost in high places, crawling into crevices and clinging to large leaves. This horseshoe bat hangs from the roof of a cave by its back legs. Its toes have a locking mechanism that grips tighter as the foot muscles are relaxed.

Entrance is at bottom of nest

2 In the loop

The nest starts out as a single loop of woven grasses and twigs. The bird adds more loops to build up the spherical shape of the nest.

3 Make or break

If a female likes the nest, she lines it with grass and feathers. If no female likes it, the male weaver breaks it apart.

Marking territory

This otter is marking its territory, leaving smelly droppings as scent marks—a sign that it controls the area. The otter finds its food within its territory and ensures that others stay away. When an otter smells another otter's scent, it knows an intruder is around. Other animals advertise their claims using sounds.

Lodge is a mound of logs and stones, sealed with mud

Sleeping chamber is above water's surface

Beavering builders

A beaver's lodge is one of the greatest feats of engineering in the animal kingdom. Beavers are hefty rodents that fell small trees with their large, gnawing teeth. They use the timbers to build dams on rivers, creating still-water ponds, which they stock with leafy branches.

Dam regularly repaired to keep water level steady

Entrance is underwater

Migrations

Birds take turns leading the flock

A migration is a journey that an animal undertakes, often along a set route. It is neither an aimless search for food nor simply a patrolling of territory. A migration has start and end points, and the animal always makes a return journey, or its descendants do. Animals migrate in response to changes in the seasons, which make it hard for them to survive. The sight of thousands of creatures on the move is one of nature's great spectacles.

Birthing site

Humpback whales spend the summer in the rich feeding grounds of polar seas. However, this water is too cold for newborn calves. They are born without the thick blubber that keeps the adults warm. Therefore, in winter, these whales migrate to warmer seas near the equator to give birth. The calves then return with their mothers.

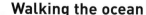

Head contains a mineral called magnetite, possibly helping the bird track Earth's magnetic field

Following the stream

The life cycle of each of these colorful sockeye salmon is one long migration. The fish start out in the headwaters of a river. As they grow, they head downstream, finally reaching the sea, where they mature over several years. The adult salmon travel all the way upriver to their birthplace to spawn, after which they die.

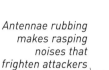

Antennae rubbing makes rasping noises that frighten attackers

Walking the ocean

These spiny lobsters march in line across the sandy seabed of the Caribbean during their fall migration to warmer waters. The lobsters also head for deeper waters, perhaps to escape the storms that disrupt their shallow summer territory.

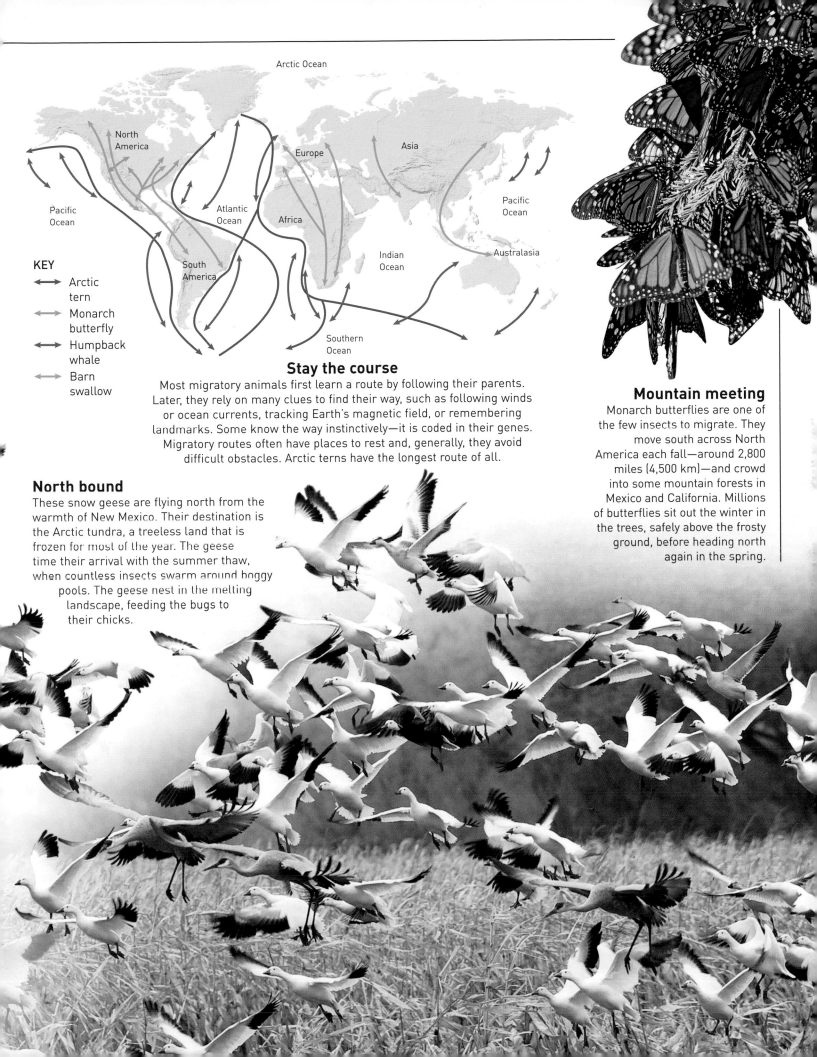

Arctic Ocean

North America

Europe

Asia

Pacific Ocean

Atlantic Ocean

Africa

Pacific Ocean

Indian Ocean

Australasia

South America

KEY

⟷ Arctic tern

⟷ Monarch butterfly

⟷ Humpback whale

⟷ Barn swallow

Southern Ocean

Stay the course

Most migratory animals first learn a route by following their parents. Later, they rely on many clues to find their way, such as following winds or ocean currents, tracking Earth's magnetic field, or remembering landmarks. Some know the way instinctively—it is coded in their genes. Migratory routes often have places to rest and, generally, they avoid difficult obstacles. Arctic terns have the longest route of all.

Mountain meeting

Monarch butterflies are one of the few insects to migrate. They move south across North America each fall—around 2,800 miles (4,500 km)—and crowd into some mountain forests in Mexico and California. Millions of butterflies sit out the winter in the trees, safely above the frosty ground, before heading north again in the spring.

North bound

These snow geese are flying north from the warmth of New Mexico. Their destination is the Arctic tundra, a treeless land that is frozen for most of the year. The geese time their arrival with the summer thaw, when countless insects swarm around boggy pools. The geese nest in the melting landscape, feeding the bugs to their chicks.

Staying alive

In the wild, animals face a constant struggle for survival. Predators must kill prey for food, while prey must always be ready to fend off a predator's attack. Both predator and prey are in a race to stay a step ahead of each other, each animal adapting constantly in the presence of an evolving foe. When a mouse evolves resistance to a snake's venom, the snake evolves in ways that make it more toxic—both predator and prey evolve constantly, but neither gains an advantage.

Hidden trickster

The Peringuey's adder lives in the deserts of southwest Africa. This snake is not easy to spot— its rough scales match the sand and it lies waiting to ambush prey, such as this gecko. The snake lures the lizard within biting distance by wiggling the dark tip of its tail. The adder's venom kills its prey in seconds.

Dry outer strand is held by spider

Traps of silk

The ogre-faced spider eats insects on the ground. These insects are sensitive to vibrations and are ready to scuttle for safety at the slightest scare. But this long-legged spider avoids detection by hanging motionless just above the ground, flexing a sticky net in its four front legs. It waits for an insect to walk to under the net, and then moves with lightning speed to snare it.

One whale dives to make bubble net

Fish "baitball" driven to surface

Waiting whale

Whale blowing bubbles

Waiting whale's calls scare fish into a tight school

Spiral path followed by whale

Bubbles rise to the surface

Eye spot looks like a large animal's eyes

Bubble nets

For humpback whales, eating a few fish at a time takes far too long to fill their stomachs. So they band together to herd fish into tight schools that are perfect for eating in gulps. The whales swim in a spiral, blowing a curtain of bubbles, and making the fish crowd together at the surface. Then, they surge up from below with their mouths gaping open.

Mimics

This owl butterfly would make an easy meal for a rain-forest tree frog. But the hungry frog stays away from it because when the butterfly opens its wings, two dark spots suddenly appear. This fools the frog into believing that it is looking into the eyes of a dangerous owl.

Diving down

A kingfisher has evolved eyes that allow it to spot fish before entering the water. Water bends light, so the bird has to adjust its eyes when targeting underwater prey. Each of the bird's eyes has two focus points—one for use out of the water and the other for after it dives in. The eyes of most animals have just one. The cells in a kingfisher's eyes also contain a pigmented oil that probably filters out the glare from water.

Spraying acid

In any colony, only the queen ant produces young, so it is common for worker ants to sacrifice themselves to protect her. To ward off predators, wood ants employ chemical weapons. They squirt formic acid from their abdomens—the same chemical that causes the burning pain of a beesting.

Transparent eyelid slides across eye to protect it

Tail regrows slowly

Two lives

The tree skink has a quick-release bone at the base of its tail that snaps off. If grabbed by the tail, the lizard can escape. The predator is left with a wriggling detached tail. The skink regenerates a new tail, but this one does not detach in the next attack.

Living together

Animals frequently rely on another animal species for their survival. Such a link is called symbiosis, which means "together living" in ancient Greek. There are three kinds of symbiosis. In parasitism, only one species benefits from the relationship, while the other—known as the host—is weakened by it. Mutualism is a relationship in which both species benefit, while in commensalism one animal benefits, while the other is completely unaffected.

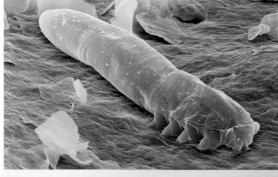

Tiny passenger
About 50 percent of people live in symbiosis with this microscopic eyelash mite. This mite sets up home in the follicle (a small sac or cavity from which a hair grows) of the human eyelash, eating oily flakes of skin.

Plaintive cuckoo chick

Cuckoo in the nest
This chick is being fed by a male sunbird, but this bird is not the chick's father. The chick is a cuckoo, and its mother laid the egg in the sunbird's nest. The cuckoo is a brood parasite—an animal that tricks another into raising its young. A cuckoo's egg looks a lot like a sunbird egg, so the sunbird fails to spot the interloper. Once the chick hatches, it ejects any sunbird chicks or unhatched sunbird eggs.

Wingless aphid sucks sap constantly

Aphid farms
Aphids are insects that drink plant sap. With a purely liquid diet, the little aphids produce a lot of sugary urine, known as honeydew. Some ants will stand guard over a herd of aphids, keeping away predators. The ants "milk" the aphids, stroking them to make them produce sweet droplets of honeydew. This relationship is an example of mutualism.

Male
mariqua
sunbird

Pecking to order

The oxpecker is a relative of
the starling. It lives among the
herds of grazing mammals,
such as this zebra, that
roam across the grasslands
of Africa. It slides its flat
beak between the hairs of
the host to pluck ticks and
lice from its host's skin. The
zebra gets a cleaning service,
while the bird is rewarded with
tasty, bloodsucking parasites. The
oxpecker may also act as a parasite,
feeding on blood from open wounds.

*Big eye gave watchman
goby its name*

Teaming up

The watchman goby and the pistol
shrimp team up on the sandy
seabed. The shrimp digs a burrow,
while the fish acts as the near-
sighted shrimp's lookout. If danger
approaches, the goby flicks the shrimp
with its tail, and the duo dash inside.

*Ridged sucker is
formed from a
flattened dorsal fin*

*Shrimp keeps the
burrow clean*

Remora

*Hyena stands
over its food in a
defensive posture*

Going with the flow

Commensalism is rare
compared to the other
forms of symbiosis. The
remora sticks itself to large
sharks, rays, and whales,
using a sucker on the top of
its head. The fish eats its
host's droppings or the
leftovers from the host's
meals. The larger animal
neither gains nor benefits.

*Black-backed
jackal—another
kleptoparasite—is
wary of the hyena*

Thieving carnivores

Spotted hyenas are scavengers that feast on the
carcasses of animals. Often a hyena gang will
chase a hunter, such as a big cat, away
from its kill. This behavior is called
kleptoparasitism. But the hyena's
meal is not safe either—other
thieves may try to snatch a bite.

Living in groups

Humans are not the only animals that live in societies. There are advantages and disadvantages to being a social animal. Group members have to share many things, such as food. Adult males may also have to compete for the same females in the group. Despite these problems, the members of a group stick together. In all cases, animal societies function in a delicate balance where the positives outweigh the negatives.

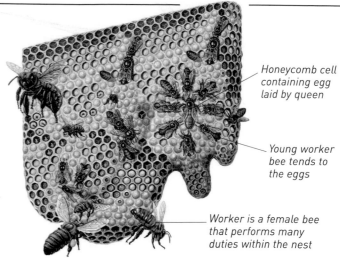

Honeycomb cell containing egg laid by queen

Young worker bee tends to the eggs

Worker is a female bee that performs many duties within the nest

Social bees

Honeybees have an advanced level of social organization that is also seen in ants, termites, some wasps, and even rodents. A single female—the queen bee—produces the offspring. The rest of the society is made up of her daughters, who work to raise their younger sisters—and occasionally brothers, or drones, who fly off to mate with young queens. The worker bees never produce young of their own. They collect nectar to make honey to feed the colony.

Pairing up

The smallest animal group is a breeding pair. In lovebirds—a small species of parrot—the male and a female pair up for life. Even if the two birds spend long periods apart, they meet and raise chicks together when the breeding season comes. This single-mate system is called monogamy. These pairs work together to protect their young and maximize their chances of survival.

Fisher's lovebirds

Superpods at sea

Dolphins and whales live in family groups called pods, which typically contain about 15 animals. They are made up of females, their calves, and a tight-knit gang of males. When several pods converge at one place to feed, a superpod forms.

Rank and file

Hamadryas baboons of East Africa and Arabia live in a highly ordered society. In a troop of around 400 monkeys, every monkey has a rank. Big adult males rule over a harem of females, and several harems band together as a clan—one of many per troop. Males frequently fight over females—young males are always ready to take over from an older, weakening male—but if a monkey steps out of line, it is punished with a bite.

Dominant male has tufts of gray fur

Baby travels with its mother

Young male is not allowed to mate

Female may be stolen by another harem

Hunting in a team

The wolf is one of the few animals that can kill prey that is bigger than it is. It does this by working in a team, or pack. Wolves can follow prey for hours without getting tired, so the pack chases prey, such as an injured deer, taking turns biting their victim until it crashes to the ground.

Wolves howl to warn other packs to stay away

Population explosion

Locust swarms are some of the largest animal groupings, containing billions of insects. These large grasshoppers normally live on their own, but crowd together in search of food. Increased levels of body contact cause the insects to create a different kind of young. When these transform into long-winged adults, they fly off as a swarm.

One of the crowd

Seabirds, such as these gannets, nest together in huge colonies, called rookeries. The cliffs are so inaccessible that egg-eaters, such as rats, cannot reach them. The parents take turns diving for food out at sea, bringing some back for the chicks. They tap beaks on returning to identify each other.

The human animal

The human species is called *Homo sapiens*, and it belongs to a group of mammals called the primates. The animals most closely related to humans are chimpanzees. These two species share 98 percent of their DNA (see p.14). However, the remaining bit of DNA is enough to make the two primates very different. Modern humans evolved around 150,000 years ago, several million years after chimpanzees.

Rounded skull on top of neck

Folds increase space for nerves

Human brain **Gorilla brain**

A complex brain

Humans have the largest brain in the animal kingdom, when compared to their body size. It is significantly larger than the brain of a gorilla—a close relative—and is incredibly complex. It has 120 billion nerve cells that communicate via a million billion connections.

S-shaped spine (backbone) helps absorb shocks while walking

Barrel-shaped rib cage allows arms to swing, helping body balance on two legs

Using medicine

Some mammals, such as dogs and non-human primates like chimpanzees, eat certain plants when they feel sick. This is called self-medication—something that humans also do. Many cultures have used willow and meadowsweet to make painkilling drinks. Humans isolate products from plants, such as aspirin, to make medicines and battle illnesses.

Painkilling tablets

Meadowsweet

Wide pelvis cradles and supports the soft organs

Growing food

For most of their history, humans have been hunters and gatherers. Early humans ate what they could find, killing some animals, but surviving mainly on seeds, roots, and fruits. About 10,000 years ago, humans learned to grow food plants, such as rice and wheat, and this was the birth of farming.

Thighbones are angled inward toward knees, keeping upper body over the hips

On two legs

These skeletons highlight some of the anatomical differences between humans and one of their closest relatives, the gorilla. The differences are a result of the varying ways in which these animals walk. Many primates, such as gorillas, walk mostly on all fours. Humans, however, are bipedal—mammals that walk upright on two feet. This mode of locomotion frees the hands and helps humans see distances.

Farmer working in rice field

Heel and toes of foot touch ground

Human skeleton

Global animal

Electric lights at night indicate where the human settlements cluster in different areas around the globe. Humans evolved in Africa, spreading across Europe, Asia, and Australia about 40,000 years ago, and reaching the Americas around 14,000 years ago. Humans are also the only vertebrates to stay in the frozen Antarctica all year round.

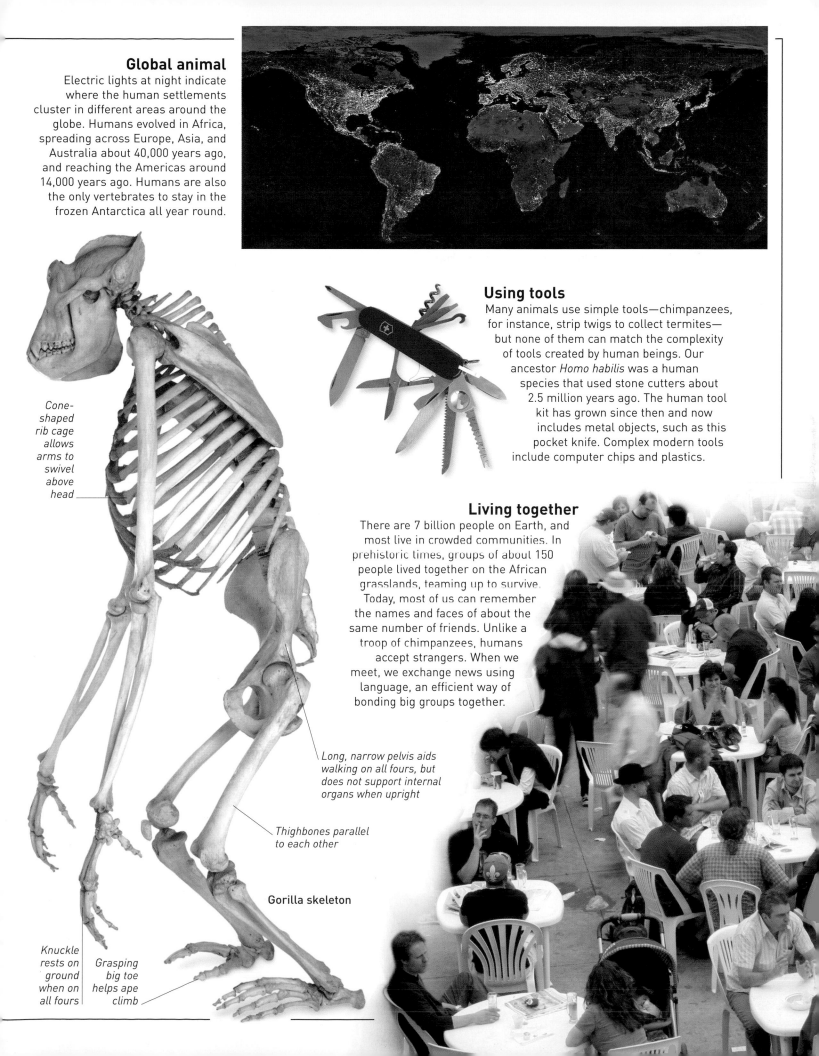

Using tools

Many animals use simple tools—chimpanzees, for instance, strip twigs to collect termites— but none of them can match the complexity of tools created by human beings. Our ancestor *Homo habilis* was a human species that used stone cutters about 2.5 million years ago. The human tool kit has grown since then and now includes metal objects, such as this pocket knife. Complex modern tools include computer chips and plastics.

Living together

There are 7 billion people on Earth, and most live in crowded communities. In prehistoric times, groups of about 150 people lived together on the African grasslands, teaming up to survive. Today, most of us can remember the names and faces of about the same number of friends. Unlike a troop of chimpanzees, humans accept strangers. When we meet, we exchange news using language, an efficient way of bonding big groups together.

Cone-shaped rib cage allows arms to swivel above head

Long, narrow pelvis aids walking on all fours, but does not support internal organs when upright

Thighbones parallel to each other

Gorilla skeleton

Knuckle rests on ground when on all fours

Grasping big toe helps ape climb

Livestock

Thousands of years ago, humans began to domesticate and rear useful animals, using them for their muscle power, products, and body parts. The first livestock (farm animals) were sheep and goats, which were probably domesticated around 8,000 years ago. Gradually, the list of livestock grew to include cattle, pigs, and chickens. Farmers bred animals so that their offspring would have the most useful traits, and, as a result, livestock is tame.

Owner's pride
The word cattle comes from the Old French word "chatel," meaning property. In several societies, cattle are symbols of wealth and status. These zebus (humped cattle), for instance, belong to the Dinka people of Southern Sudan. A single cow provides manure (used as fertilizer and fuel), milk, and even blood to drink. When a zebu dies, its skin is made into leather.

Aurochs—the ancestor of modern cattle

Scottish Aberdeen Angus is bred for good quality meat

Then and now
The domestic cow is a descendant of a grazer called the aurochs. Once spread across Europe and Asia, aurochs became extinct in 1627. Zebus (main picture) are descended from Indian aurochs, while beef cattle are related to European aurochs.

A living ancestor
Every domestic animal is a descendant of a wild ancestor. Many of these wild animals are extinct or have become very rare. However, red jungle fowl—believed to be the wild form of the chicken—are still widespread in Southeast Asia. Males display the same vibrant features of a barnyard rooster.

Red jungle fowl rooster

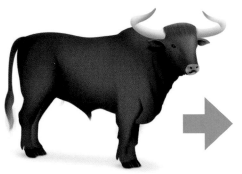

Wild inside
Despite centuries of captive breeding to shape domestic animals into tame and productive creatures, some still exhibit certain wild characteristics. For example, sheep dash uphill when frightened—just as their ancestor, the small and sturdy mouflon, would do when it needed to escape attackers in the rocky mountains of western Asia.

Wool sweater

For millennia, humans have used the fur of other mammals to stay warm in cold climates. Wool hairs can be spun into strands or yarn and used to weave warm clothing. Wool comes from sheep, alpacas, camels, and goats. Perhaps the softest wool comes from fluffy angora rabbits.

Bug to dye for

In the 16th century, red dyes in Europe were too expensive for all but the wealthiest families. Spanish settlers in South America were, therefore, intrigued by how the local people dyed their clothes deep red. Cochineal bugs, which live on cacti, produce a chemical that is used to make the dye.

Silk Route

The Silk Route—an ancient trade route that ran from China in the East to the Mediterranean in the West—was named after silk, the most lucrative product to be traded along it. In the West, the secret of the production of fine silk strands was unknown, but they are produced by silkworms—moth caterpillars that live on mulberry tree leaves. These silkworms are kept at a breeding base in Matou Town, China.

Animal workers

The first working animals may have acted as guards. These half-tamed wolves probably lived alongside humans about 15,000 years ago. They barked to warn humans of approaching danger. Before the invention of engines, many machines, such as wheeled carts and water pumps, were powered by animals. Today, humans use many animals for their natural abilities.

To the rescue
This search dog uses its sense of smell to find people buried in snow. A dog's sense of smell is far superior to a human's, because the odor-detecting part of its brain is 40 times bigger than the same section in a human brain. There are also about 195 million more smell receptors in a dog's wet nose.

Tracking device attached to flipper

Animal soldiers
This bottlenose dolphin works for the US Navy. The brain of a dolphin is larger than that of a human, but not as complex. Nevertheless, the dolphin is highly intelligent and can be trained to recognize enemy mines suspended in the water. Other navy dolphins are trained to search for injured human divers.

Hard worker
A mule's father (sire) is a donkey, but its mother (dam) is a horse. They cannot produce young of their own—they are born to work as beasts of burden. Mules have the best features of their parents. They are big and strong like a horse, but calm and sure-footed like a donkey.

Catching fish

The cormorant is an expert fish catcher, and Chinese fishermen have been using its skills for more than a thousand years. A loose snare around a cormorant's neck will allow it to swallow small fish, while bigger ones get stuck. When a bird returns to the boat, its owner gently eases the fish from the bird's throat.

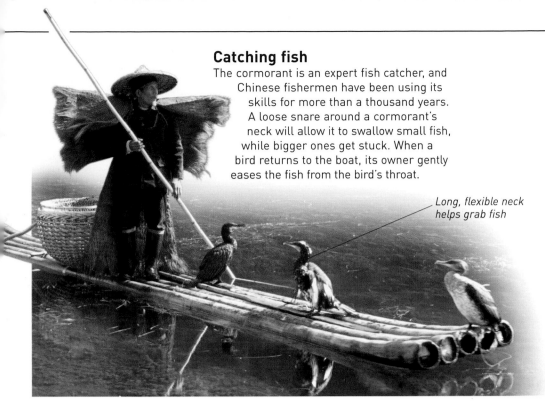

Long, flexible neck helps grab fish

China statuette of Lipizzaner dancing horse

Dancing horses

Lipizzaner horses come from Slovenia. These horses are descended from Spanish and North African varieties and were bred to be strong and agile. While adult Lipizzaners are white, foals are born much darker. Some stallions are trained to dance.

Easy to study

Scientists use the little fruit fly from the genus *Drosophila* to study the way genes work. They alter its genetic structure to see how it changes the way the insect grows. Genetic alteration has made this fly grow extra wings. *Drosophila* flies breed very quickly, taking just a few days to reach adulthood, so it is easy to study many generations.

Extra pair of wings

Fruit fly with modified genes

Pest controller

The mongoose is a small carnivore that lives in Asia and Africa. Many species are good at killing snakes, and in some countries they are used as pest controllers, clearing dangerous snakes from houses and gardens. A mongoose can tackle even a cobra, one of the most venomous snakes.

Hidden guard

This Pyrenean mountain dog is one of a breed of large dogs used to protect sheep from wolves, lynxes, and bears in the mountains between France and Spain. It has been bred to be a "dog in sheep's clothing"—its shaggy white fur helps it mingle with the flock, and the sheep soon grow used to it. The dog is ready to attack anything threatening the flock.

Shaggy white fur

Sheep remain calm in dog's presence

Animal friends

People often make room in their families for animals kept as companions. The most popular pets are cats and dogs—there are several hundred million of them, many more than their counterparts surviving in the wild. People also keep other animals as pets, from deadly snakes to tiny insects.

Border collie catches a toy in the air

Many breeds

Each dog breed has certain characteristics. For example, this border collie is intelligent and can follow instructions from its master. Collies are working dogs, commonly used as sheep dogs. The tiny chihuahua breed is the same species as a collie, but is 10 times smaller and was bred to be easy to carry, stroke, and cuddle.

The wolf within

All pet dogs are descended from wild wolves. Dogs and humans are both social species, which makes it easier for them to live together. Wolves began living alongside humans about 15,000 years ago. They scavenged on waste food and, once domesticated, may have teamed up with humans for hunting.

All in the family

Hamsters have pouches in their cheeks that store seeds, a useful feature in these desert rodents that allows them to go for days without finding food. These pouches give the hamsters cute rounded faces. In the 1930s, hamsters became fashionable pets. The craze began when a female hamster and her 12 offspring were taken from the wild in Syria and bred as pets.

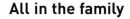

Skin has blue-gray patches

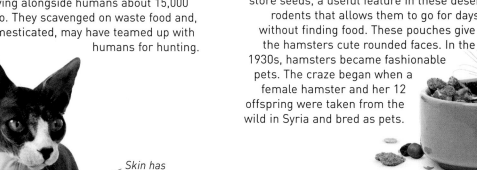

Creepy pets

Some people like to keep dangerous animals as pets. It was once believed that a tarantula's bite was deadly, and produced dangerous frenzies. The spider was named after a fast-paced Italian dance, the *tarantella*. However, a tarantula's bite is largely harmless to humans.

Mutant creatures

Some breeds of pet are mutants that could not survive in the wild. This strange-looking sphynx cat is descended from a single Canadian cat that was born hairless in 1966. Sphynx cats suffer in cold weather without a covering of hair and could not survive outside a warm house.

Winged companions

Parrots are famous for the way they can copy sounds, such as the ring of a telephone or the flush of a toilet. They even repeat the words people say, which is very enjoyable for their owners. Most parrots are too large to keep in a cage, but budgerigars—little parrots from Australia—make good pets. Parrots are good mimics because in the wild they learn a local set of calls by copying older parrots.

Color of feathers is created by selective breeding

Japanese children play with goldfish

Fish in a bowl

About 1,000 years ago—probably first in China—people began keeping carp as pets. Over the years, people created eye-catching breeds, such as goldfish and koi, which are now found in aquariums across the world. Fish use bright colors to attract mates, and many vibrant species from coral reefs and tropical rivers are also popular pets today.

The wild side

The dingo is one of Australia's most widespread animals. It was introduced to the continent about 4,000 years ago when people brought pet dogs over from Southeast Asia. These dogs escaped and became feral (reverted to a wild state). Now, dingoes living in packs are one of Australia's main predators.

Pests

In the wild there is no such thing as a pest, but humans label some animals "pests" when they damage crops, harm domestic animals, or spread diseases. Humans, meanwhile, have a very large impact on the environment—we turn wild land into fields and cities. While most animals lose areas of their habitat in this process, a few species benefit and thrive in these artificial landscapes.

City slackers

The pigeons living in cities are feral—they are descended from domestic pigeons that were once kept for food or for carrying messages. The wild relatives of pigeons, called rock doves, roost on steep cliffs. Tall stone buildings make an equally good habitat. City pigeons feed on a diet of waste food and breed four or five times a year.

Fruit killer

Helix aspersa, or garden snail, is a land snail native to Europe. It is usually seen grazing on leaves in vegetable patches and fruit trees. In the last 150 years, this snail has spread to many other regions of the world by hitching a ride on imported vegetables.

Pest at home

Cockroaches live wherever there is rotting waste, such as leftover food. These pests came from humid African jungles, but have set up home in basements and sewers across the world. Cockroaches are good at staying out of sight. They scavenge in the dark and scuttle quickly into cracks when lights are turned on. They can carry diseases.

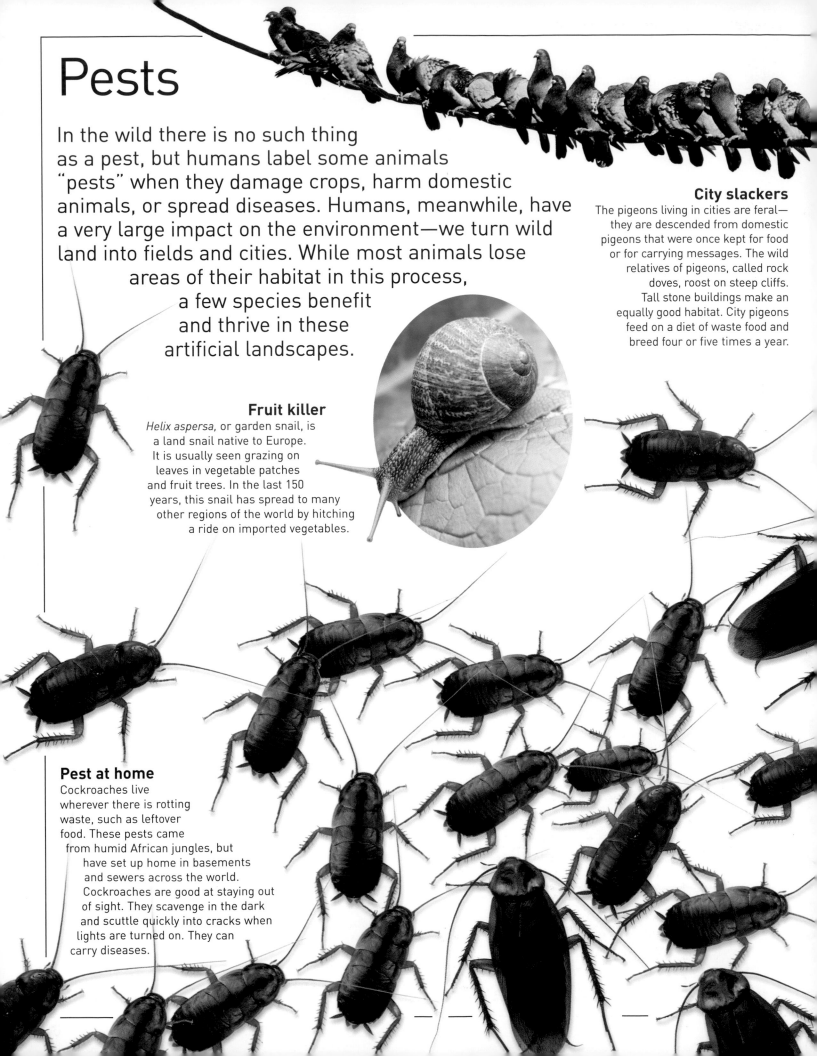

Accidental pest

In the 1930s, giant toads from South America were introduced to Australia, to eat up beetles that were ruining sugarcane crops. These ground-dwelling toads often could not reach the beetles high up in the canes. The plantations were also too dry, so these cane toads left the fields and spread in their millions across eastern Australia. They eventually became a bigger pest themselves—causing a decline in the numbers of many native predators.

Deadly bloodsucker

Female mosquitoes drink the blood of humans and other animals—to get the nutrients they need to grow eggs. When biting an animal, the mosquitoes secrete saliva into the blood of the animal. This saliva may carry germs that can cause deadly diseases, such as yellow fever, elephantiasis, and malaria.

Only the female has the bloodsucking mouthpart

Being a nuisance

Moles are seldom seen, but the hills of soil they produce when digging fresh tunnels ruin a neat lawn. The hills appear in lines as the mole pushes out excavated earth. Moles that dig under trees produce fewer molehills because the tree roots support the burrows.

Small hair on abdomen detects air currents created by an attacker from behind

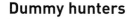

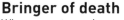

Dummy hunters

Animals become pests when they are taken out of their natural habitats and away from predators that keep their populations from getting too large. However, pests continue to be on the lookout for threats in human settlements. This lifelike model owl keeps crows, mice, and seed-eating birds away from fields and gardens.

Bringer of death

When a pest species arrives in a new area, it can cause devastation. When black rats spread from Asia on board trading ships, fleas living on the rats carried a disease called the plague. The worst outbreak of plague—termed the Black Death—was in the 14th century, when 100 million people were killed. The last major outbreak of the plague in England was in 1665.

Conservation

Human activities affect the natural environment, creating problems for wild animals. Humans continue to remove wild habitats, replacing them with farmland and settlements. Some animals, such as pests or farm animals, thrive under the changes, but most others find life much harder. They may face a shortage of food or places to raise their young, resulting in a drop in their numbers. Many wild animals have also been hunted to extinction by humans.

Pollution

These fish have died after crude oil was spilled into water, filling it with poisons. This is an example of pollution, which is the presence of harmful substances in the environment in unnatural amounts. Pollutants are most often chemicals released into water or air from homes or factories, but can also be excessive heat, or loud noises.

Hunting the hunter

Even this top predator has enemies. People hunt tigers for their skin, to sell body parts as traditional medicines, and sometimes just for sport. Despite their formidable strength, tigers are unable to protect themselves against hunting rifles. In the last 100 years alone, their number have fallen by 95 percent.

Damaged habitats

One of the ways in which humans endanger animals is by damaging their habitats or even wiping out the habitats completely. The 'ōhi'a tree is now the only tree from which the 'i'iwi bird of Hawaii, with its strange curved beak, can sip nectar. Without this tree, the bird could become extinct.

'I'iwi bird feeding on flowers of an 'ōhi'a tree

Changing fast

In the Arctic Ocean, walruses rest on ice floes (floating ice) after hunting for shellfish on the seabed. The area of sea ice in the Arctic has decreased in recent years. Climates and habitats are always changing, but natural changes are slow compared to the rapid changes caused by human activities.

Trade bans

Animals hunted in the wild are often protected by law. A ban on the trade of ivory makes it illegal to sell this elephant tusk anywhere in the world. With this trade ban, the world's governments hoped to reduce the number of elephants killed illegally for their tusks. Since the ban, elephant numbers have been rising.

Tag glued to seal transmits location data to a satellite

Studying animals

Sometimes animal numbers decrease without obvious reason. To understand why, scientists gather data about the environment. This harbor seal lives in an area polluted by an oil spill. It has been fitted with a tag that records where the seal goes to look for fish to eat, and this helps the experts build up a map of which areas of ocean have recovered and which are still polluted.

Walrus uses its tusks to climb on to ice floe

Children watch a penguin parade at Edinburgh Zoo, UK

Learning to care

Protecting endangered animals is called conservation, and one of the most important jobs of a conservationist is teaching people why it is important to look after animals in the wild. Zoos are one place where visitors can find out how they can help threatened animals.

Tourists view animals from safety of a van

Paying for protection

Tourists pay high prices for safaris, where they can see animals in the wild up close. Safari trucks are a common sight in East Africa's national parks. People also visit rain forests hoping to spot a tiger, or take boat trips to see whales. Parks and ecotourism schemes use the money from tourism to protect animals and their natural environments.

61

Animals and myths

Myths and legends from around the globe often feature animals that can do amazing things—not the least of which is the ability to talk to one another. Mythical monsters can have a basis in the natural world. For example, the mythical phoenix has a real-life counterpart—the Tongan megapode bird. The phoenix is a firebird that appears from the hot ashes of its burning mother, while the Tongan megapode bird incubates its eggs in the warm ash of a volcano.

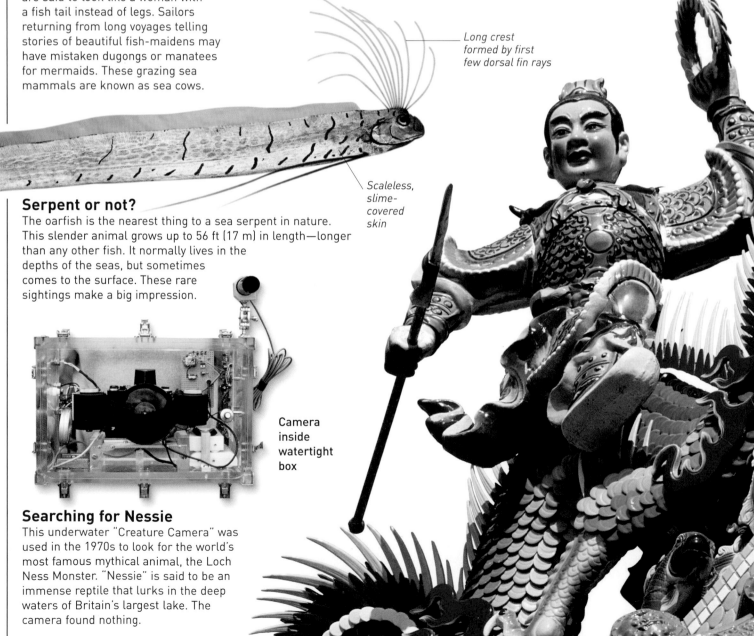

Long crest formed by first few dorsal fin rays

Scaleless, slime-covered skin

Camera inside watertight box

Something fishy

Mermaids are among the most familiar of mythical creatures. They are said to look like a woman with a fish tail instead of legs. Sailors returning from long voyages telling stories of beautiful fish-maidens may have mistaken dugongs or manatees for mermaids. These grazing sea mammals are known as sea cows.

Serpent or not?

The oarfish is the nearest thing to a sea serpent in nature. This slender animal grows up to 56 ft (17 m) in length—longer than any other fish. It normally lives in the depths of the seas, but sometimes comes to the surface. These rare sightings make a big impression.

Searching for Nessie

This underwater "Creature Camera" was used in the 1970s to look for the world's most famous mythical animal, the Loch Ness Monster. "Nessie" is said to be an immense reptile that lurks in the deep waters of Britain's largest lake. The camera found nothing.

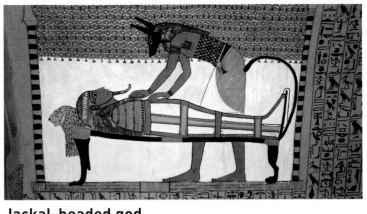

Jackal-headed god

The ancient Egyptians preserved the bodies of the dead as mummies, which were helped on their journey to the afterlife by the God Anubis. Because jackals were common in cemeteries, scavenging for human carrion, Anubis's human body and head of a jackal are not surprising.

Horns of a stag

Dragon statue at Tianhou Temple

Scales of a fish

Flaming pearl said to bestow great powers

Claws of an eagle

Wing resembles that of a large bird of prey

Birds of thunder

This Native American totem pole is topped with a thunderbird—a flying spirit that was believed to create thunder claps with its wing beats and light up the sky with lightning flashes from its eyes. With its hooked beak, this supernatural creature is most likely modeled on an eagle. Native Americans would have seen, and may have revered, this large bird of prey.

Dragon power

Dragons appear in almost all cultures. They may have been inspired by fossils of giant dinosaurs unearthed by ancient people. In Western traditions, dragons are thought to be brutal beasts that eat people. In eastern Asia, however, dragons are powerful spirits that live in water and under mountains and are usually associated with good luck. This statue of a dragon is dedicated to a sea goddess.

Tusk is a long front tooth grown by males and females

Skull of male narwhal

Only one horn

The unicorn is believed to be a white deer or horse with a single horn on its head. In the Middle Ages, Danish seamen hunted whales called narwhals for their long, spiraled tusks. These often fetched huge sums of money from wealthy collectors who believed they were unicorn horns. The narwhal is a 1-ton mammal with a 6½-ft- (2-m-) long spiked tooth sticking out of its head. It may be even more odd-looking than a unicorn.

Record breakers

Among the millions of species that make up the animal kingdom, there are many extraordinary creatures. For example, the blue whale, which is the largest living animal, or the cheetah, which can outrun every other animal on land. Biologists discover new record breakers all the time.

FASTEST ANIMAL IN WATER

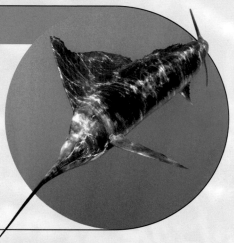

Sailfish
This predatory fish powers through the water with a rapid sweep of its tail and its sword-shaped bill. The sailfish raises its sail-like fin to frighten its prey.

Record: Can reach a speed of 68 mph (110 kph)

Group: Ray-finned fish

Habitat: Open oceans

LARGEST LAND INVERTEBRATE

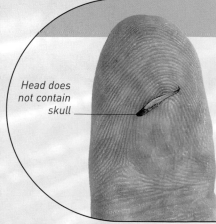

Coconut crab
Also known as the robber crab, this crustacean climbs on palm trees to eat fruits. Its large pincers are strong enough to crack coconuts.

Record: Legspan of 35 in (90 cm)

Group: Crustaceans

Habitat: Tropical islands

SMALLEST VERTEBRATE

Australian infantfish
This tiny fish is the smallest animal with a backbone. It lives in muddy swamps made acidic by peat. Being really small, the fish can survive in just a little puddle of water.

Head does not contain skull

Record: Length of 0.3 in (7.9 mm)

Group: Ray-finned fish

Habitat: Peat swamps

LARGEST COLONY

Argentinian ants
These little South American ants have spread to other parts of the world. A supercolony in Europe runs for 3,700 miles (6,000 km).

Record: Supercolony (billions of ants)

Group: Insects

Habitat: Coast of southern Europe

HOTTEST HABITAT

Pompeii worm
This sea worm lives in the Pacific Ocean in the hot water emerging from seafloor volcanic vents. The worm converts chemicals in the water into nutrients.

Record: Can survive at 176 °F (80 °C)

Group: Segmented worms

Habitat: Hydrothermal vents

LOUDEST ANIMAL

Pistol shrimp

The pistol shrimp stuns its prey with a shock wave created by its massive pincer snapping. The sound is so loud it superheats the water.

Record: Can produce sounds at 200 decibels

Group: Crustaceans

Habitat: Coral reefs

SLOWEST FISH

Seahorse

The seahorse can barely swim. A male seahorse spends its entire adult life in the same cubic metre.

Record: 0.0006 mph (0.001 kph)

Group: Ray-finned fish

Habitat: Seaweed

Tail coiled around seaweed anchors seahorse

FASTEST ANIMAL IN AIR

Peregrine falcon

The peregrine falcon preys on other birds in midair, plummeting toward them at high speed from far above. By the time the prey sees the falcon, it is too late.

Record: Max speed of 200 mph (325 kph)

Group: Birds

Habitat: Cliffs

LONGEST PREGNANCY

African elephant

The African elephant's pregnancy is the longest. Its calves weigh 220 lb (100 kg) and must be able to stand and walk soon after birth.

Record: Gestation period of 640 days

Group: Mammals

Habitat: African savanna

STRONGEST ANIMAL

Dung beetle

Dung beetles are able to shift dung balls weighing more than 1,000 times their own weight—the equivalent of a human moving six buses at a time.

Record: Pushes 1,141 times its body weight

Group: Insects

Habitat: Grasslands and forests

STRUCTURE BY A LIVING THING

Australian Great Barrier Reef

Over a period of about 7,000 years, countless generations of coral polyps have built Australia's Great Barrier Reef into a chain of hundreds of reefs and islands.

Record: Length of 1,615 miles (2,600 km)

Group: Cnidarians

Habitat: Warm, shallow waters

Tree of life

Biologists are still figuring out the relationships between different species and those between larger groups of animal. But they know enough to organize animals into a broad tree of life. Closely related animals are clustered together. Subgroups branch off. Distantly related animals are located far from each other. This tree begins with sponges, the simplest and, perhaps, oldest animal.

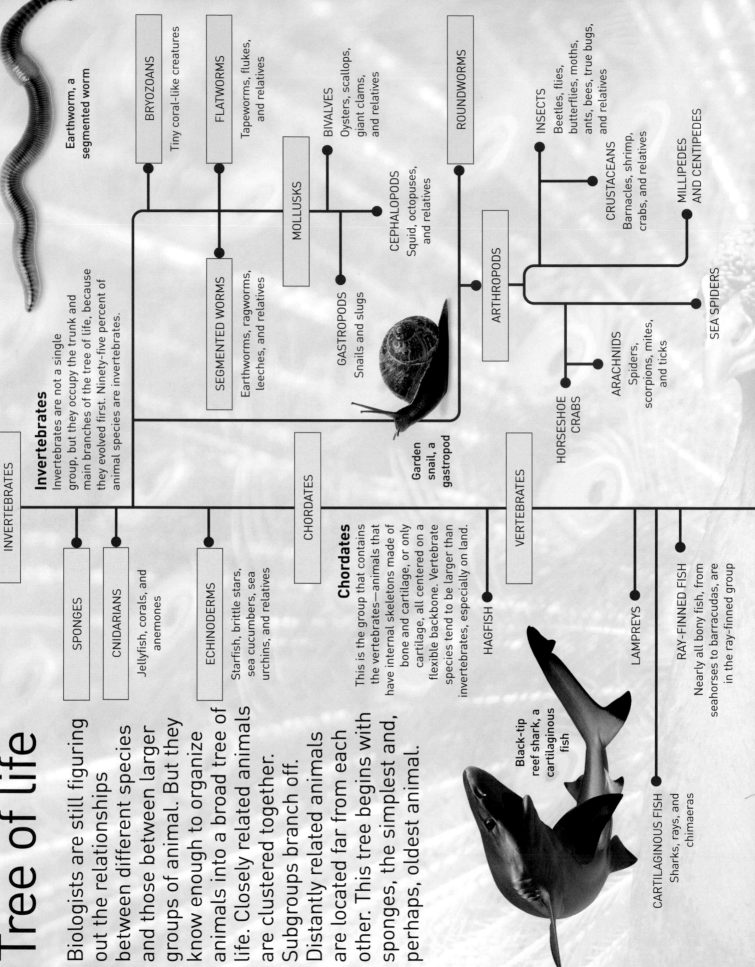

INVERTEBRATES

Invertebrates
Invertebrates are not a single group, but they occupy the trunk and main branches of the tree of life, because they evolved first. Ninety-five percent of animal species are invertebrates.

Earthworm, a segmented worm

BRYOZOANS
Tiny coral-like creatures

FLATWORMS
Tapeworms, flukes, and relatives

BIVALVES
Oysters, scallops, giant clams, and relatives

MOLLUSKS

CEPHALOPODS
Squid, octopuses, and relatives

SEGMENTED WORMS
Earthworms, ragworms, leeches, and relatives

GASTROPODS
Snails and slugs

Garden snail, a gastropod

ROUNDWORMS

INSECTS
Beetles, flies, butterflies, moths, ants, bees, true bugs, and relatives

CRUSTACEANS
Barnacles, shrimp, crabs, and relatives

MILLIPEDES AND CENTIPEDES

ARTHROPODS

ARACHNIDS
Spiders, scorpions, mites, and ticks

SEA SPIDERS

HORSESHOE CRABS

SPONGES

CNIDARIANS
Jellyfish, corals, and anemones

ECHINODERMS
Starfish, brittle stars, sea cucumbers, sea urchins, and relatives

CHORDATES

Chordates
This is the group that contains the vertebrates—animals that have internal skeletons made of bone and cartilage, or only cartilage, all centered on a flexible backbone. Vertebrate species tend to be larger than invertebrates, especially on land.

VERTEBRATES

HAGFISH

LAMPREYS

RAY-FINNED FISH
Nearly all bony fish, from seahorses to barracudas, are in the ray-finned group

Black-tip reef shark, a cartilaginous fish

CARTILAGINOUS FISH
Sharks, rays, and chimaeras

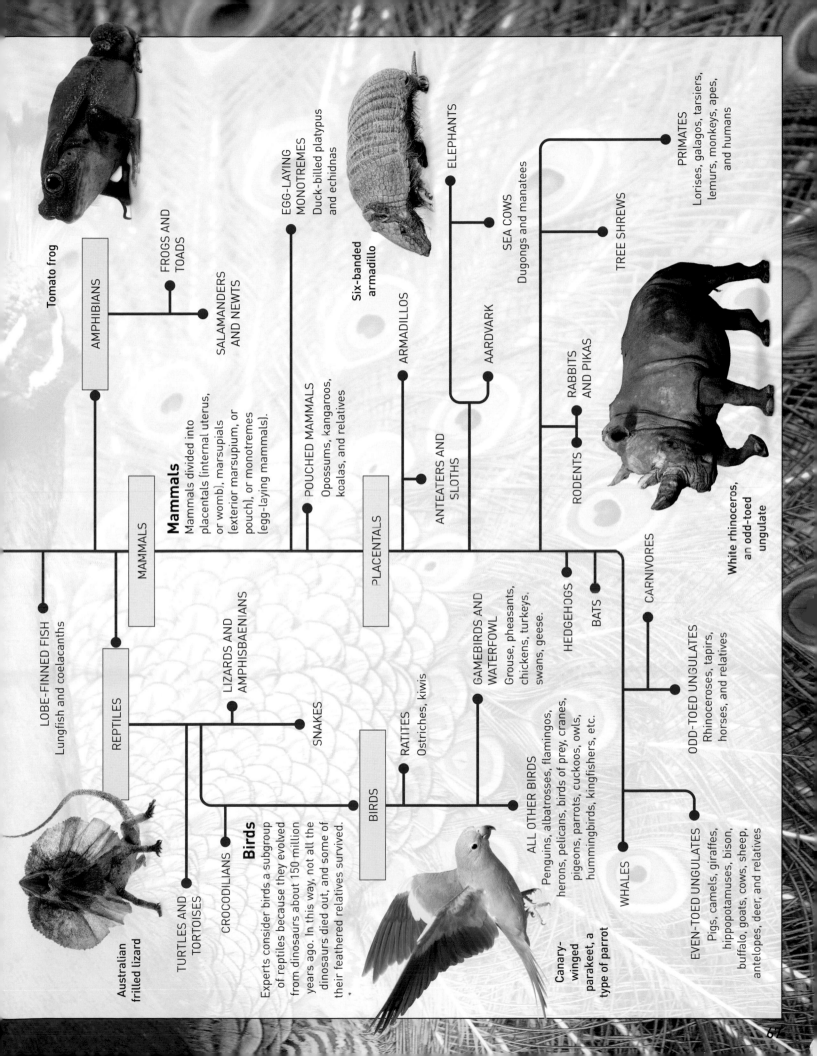

Tomato frog

Australian frilled lizard

Six-banded armadillo

White rhinoceros, an odd-toed ungulate

Canary-winged parakeet, a type of parrot

AMPHIBIANS
- FROGS AND TOADS
- SALAMANDERS AND NEWTS

MAMMALS

Mammals
Mammals divided into placentals (internal uterus, or womb), marsupials (exterior marsupium, or pouch), or monotremes (egg-laying mammals).

- EGG-LAYING MONOTREMES
  Duck-billed platypus and echidnas
- POUCHED MAMMALS
  Opossums, kangaroos, koalas, and relatives

PLACENTALS
- ARMADILLOS
- ANTEATERS AND SLOTHS
- ELEPHANTS
- SEA COWS
  Dugongs and manatees
- AARDVARK
- TREE SHREWS
- PRIMATES
  Lorises, galagos, tarsiers, lemurs, monkeys, apes, and humans
- RABBITS AND PIKAS
- RODENTS
- HEDGEHOGS
- BATS
- CARNIVORES
- ODD-TOED UNGULATES
  Rhinoceroses, tapirs, horses, and relatives
- WHALES
- EVEN-TOED UNGULATES
  Pigs, camels, giraffes, hippopotamuses, bison, buffalo, goats, cows, sheep, antelopes, deer, and relatives

LOBE-FINNED FISH
Lungfish and coelacanths

REPTILES
- LIZARDS AND AMPHISBAENIANS
- SNAKES
- TURTLES AND TORTOISES
- CROCODILIANS

Birds
Experts consider birds a subgroup of reptiles because they evolved from dinosaurs about 150 million years ago. In this way, not all the dinosaurs died out, and some of their feathered relatives survived.

BIRDS
- RATITES
  Ostriches, kiwis
- GAMEBIRDS AND WATERFOWL
  Grouse, pheasants, chickens, turkeys, swans, geese.
- ALL OTHER BIRDS
  Penguins, albatrosses, flamingos, herons, pelicans, birds of prey, cranes, pigeons, parrots, cuckoos, owls, hummingbirds, kingfishers, etc.

Animal watch

Observing animals requires a bit of skill and a lot of patience. Getting a good look at an animal in its natural habitat can be difficult. Wild animals are wary of anything unusual, but knowing when and where an animal will appear is crucial to studying them in the wild.

Blue tits are attracted to a nut-filled feeder

Magnifying glass helps study small invertebrates closely

Setting the scene

Animals are predictable and this works to a watcher's advantage. All animals need to eat and they often return to known feeding sites. For example, grizzly bears in Alaska gather near rivers in the fall to catch salmon migrating upstream. People also attract animals, such as blue tits, to a viewing spot by providing food.

A compact, weight-saving model

Notebook for sketching animals and noting location, time, and weather conditions of sightings

A grizzly bear catches a fish in Alaska

Binoculars allow watchers to see details at a distance

Walking boots keep feet warm and dry and are comfortable on long hikes

Getting ready

Wildlife watchers carry equipment for finding and viewing animals, recording the animals in their natural habitats, and perhaps even capturing a few. Nature lovers spend a lot of time outdoors in all kinds of weather. They need warm and dry clothing, that does not make rustling sounds, in muted colors to avoid standing out.

Sun hat provides shade and also breaks up the tell-tale shape of the head

Large grips reduce chances of slipping in mud and on loose stones

FOLLOWING THE SEASONS

As the weather of a region changes with the seasons, so does the behavior of animals living there. A good wildlife watcher will know where a species is likely to be at each time of year. For example, they do not look for European hedgehogs in winter but only in summer, when the ball-shaped nests of these animals can be seen in bushes and thickets.

Hide has a camouflage pattern to help it blend in with surroundings

These common cranes have arrived in northern Europe in early summer to breed. They perform distinctive courtship displays to attract mates.

This flock of pink-footed geese is leaving Greenland in fall for Europe, where many birdwatchers travel to watch them arrive.

User sucks shorter tube

Flask traps insects

A pooter is a suction device for collecting tiny insects

Insects sucked into longer tube

Large backpack to hold gear, water, and food

Camera to record interesting animals

Long lens also doubles up as a telescope

GPS device pinpoints its exact location, using satellite signals

Wildlife photographer spends hours in a portable hide, waiting for animals to appear

Wildlife experts can find animals from the signs they leave behind. Large animals leave distinctive footprints in snow and mud, in addition to broken twigs and flattened plants. Trackers keep an eye out for the signs that animals leave for each other, such as dung piles, smelly scents, and scratches in trees.

These marks are left by a red deer, known as an elk in North America, chewing on bark during winter. Fresh marks show that the deer may be nearby.

A black bear marks its territory by gouging deep scratches in soft tree bark with its claws and teeth. The height of the mark shows how tall the bear is.

This tree has been gnawed by a beaver as it collects logs for constructing its dam. This rodent will have dug a channel nearby leading to its pool.

These holes were made by a woodpecker looking for wood-boring insects under the bark. The noise made by this chiseling gives away the bird's position.

Glossary

ALGAE Organisms that photosynthesize like a plant, but are mostly single-celled. Algae often live in water or damp places.

AQUATIC To do with water. Aquatic animals spend most of their time in water.

ARTERY A blood vessel that carries oxygen-rich blood from the heart to other body organs.

BACTERIA Tiny, single-celled organisms that are not plant, animal, or fungus. Bacterial cells are at least 100 times smaller than an animal cell. Most bacteria are harmless, but some cause disease.

BRACKISH Water that is partly salty and partly fresh. Brackish water is found in coastal swamps and river mouths where freshwater mixes with seawater.

BIOLUMINESCENCE Ability of some animals to produce light using chemicals or specialized bacteria in their bodies. Bioluminescent animals generally live in the dark.

CARBON DIOXIDE A gas produced as a waste product by animals when they extract energy by processing sugars and other foods in their bodies. Animals take in oxygen and give out carbon dioxide when they breathe.

CARNIVORE An animal that mostly eats meat—the flesh of other animals. Carnivores are generally predators, often killing animals that they eat.

CHITIN A tough material in the outer body coverings of many invertebrates.

CHROMOSOME A microscopic structure in the cells of all animals that is used as a frame around which long strands of DNA are coiled.

COLD-BLOODED Also known as ectothermic, a cold-blooded animal is one that cannot maintain a constant body temperature. Instead, its body temperature varies with the environmental conditions.

CORPSE The body of a dead animal.

DNA Short for deoxyribonucleic acid, DNA is a complex chemical formed from a chain of four chemical units, or bases. The genetic code of an animal is stored in the way these four bases are ordered in its DNA chains.

DORSAL FIN The fin on the back of an aquatic animal, such as a shark or a dolphin. The fin stops the animal from rolling as it swims.

ECTOTHERM A cold-blooded animal. *Ecto* means "outside" and *therm* is "heat"—an ectotherm uses outside heat.

Chameleon, an ectotherm

ENDOTHERM A warm-blooded animal. *Endo* means "inside"; an endotherm uses its body heat to stay warm.

ENZYME A protein chemical with a specific job to do in an animal's body. Digestive enzymes break up certain foods into simpler ingredients, while other enzymes copy DNA. An enzyme's special shape helps it perform its task.

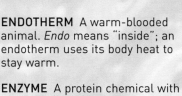

EVOLUTION A process by which organisms change over a period of time, and across many generations, as they adapt to changes in the environment. New species are often formed in this process.

Clownfish, a hermaphrodite—changes from male to female

Brown fungus growing on log

EXTINCT A species that has died out.

FUNGUS An organism that is neither an animal nor a plant. A fungus, such as a mushroom, grows into its food and digests it externally.

GENE A strand of DNA that carries the instructions for a characteristic of an organism—such as the color of a bird's feathers, or the shape of its wings.

GILL The organ used by many aquatic animals to absorb oxygen from water and give out carbon dioxide.

GIZZARD A muscular part of a bird's gut used to grind food.

HABITAT The place where an animal lives.

Toucan's bill contains keratin

HERBIVORE An animal that only eats plant food. It may eat leaves (folivore), fruits (frugivore), seeds (granivore), sap and juices (exudivore), or roots (radicivore).

HERMAPHRODITE An animal that has both male and female sex organs. Some hermaphrodites start life as one sex and change into the other as they grow. Other hermaphrodites have both sets of sex organs at the same time.

HYBRID A cross between two species or breeds. A mule is a hybrid of a horse and a donkey, while a mongrel is a hybrid between dog breeds.

INSULATOR A substance that stops heat escaping from an animal's body, keeping it warm. Blubber, feathers, and hair are the common insulators found in animals.

INVERTEBRATE Any animal that is not a member of the phylum Chordata. Most of the world's animals are invertebrates.

KERATIN A flexible protein present in the external body features of vertebrates, such as hair, feathers, claws, scales, horn sheaths, and fingernails.

KLEPTOPARASITE An animal that survives by stealing food from another hunter, generally of a different species.

LARVA The young form of an insect or other invertebrate that looks different from the adult form and also lives in a different way. A caterpillar is an example of a larva.

LIFT FORCE The force that pushes a flying animal off the ground.

MEMBRANE A thin layer or barrier that may allow some substances to pass through.

MICROSCOPIC When something is too small to see with the naked eye. A microscope is used to observe it.

NUTRIENTS The useful parts of food, such as sugars, proteins, fats, oils, vitamins, and minerals. An animal's digestive system extracts these from food.

NYMPH An early stage of development of an insect or other invertebrate that generally looks and lives in the same way as the organism's adult form.

OXYGEN A substance used by an animal's body in chemical reactions that release energy from sugars and other foods. It is taken in by breathing in air or absorbing it from water.

PARASITE An animal that lives on or in another animal of a different species.

Diving beetle nymph

PHYLUM The largest grouping used to organize, or classify, life. There are dozens of animal phyla. Some of the main ones are Arthropoda (insects and crabs), Mollusca (snails and squid), and Chordata (vertebrates).

PIGMENTS Chemicals that give color to an organism. Giving color may be the main function of the pigment or the coloration may be incidental. For example, the pigments in the eye are used as light detectors.

PREDATOR An animal that hunts and kills other animals for food.

PROTEIN A complex chemical found in all life forms, but most prominently in animals. Proteins help build body parts. Enzymes are examples of proteins.

SALIVA The liquid produced by salivary glands in the mouth of an animal to moisten food, making it easier to swallow and digest.

SCUTE An armored plate of bone covered in skin or horny keratin. A turtle shell is made up of interlocking scutes, while a crocodile's body is protected by ridges of scutes.

Turtle shell contains scutes

SPECIES A group of animals that look the same and live in the same way, and are also able to breed with each other to produce fertile offspring that will be able to reproduce themselves.

SYMBIOSIS A partnership between two animals of different species that live with each other. In most cases, each animal provides a service or benefit to the other in the relationship.

TERRITORY An area of land or water defended by an animal. Territory is used as a feeding space or as an area for mates to live and unwanted members of the same species are driven away.

TETRAPOD A vertebrate with four limbs.

URINE The liquid waste of mammals and other animals. While dung, or feces, is the undigested materials in food, urine is the waste removed from the blood and body tissues.

VEIN A blood vessel that carries oxygen-poor blood from the body organs toward the heart.

VENOM Poison that is produced by an animal and injected into another by a bite, scratch, or sting. Venom is used in hunting as well as in defense.

VERTEBRATE An animal with a backbone—a set of small vertebrae that connect to form a flexible spine. The vertebrate groups are fish, amphibians, reptiles, birds, and mammals.

WARM-BLOODED Also known as endothermic, a warm-blooded animal is one that controls its body temperature internally, using a lot of energy to heat or cool its body, so it stays at more or less the same temperature whatever the weather conditions at that time.

Leopard, a predator, with its kill

Index
ABC

Acknowledgments

Dorling Kindersley would like to thank: Caitlin Doyle for proofreading; Dr. Laurence Errington for the index; Aanchal Awasthi, Honlung Zach Ragui, and Nitu Singh for design assistance; and Dan Green for text editing.

The publishers would also like to thank the following for their kind permission to reproduce their photographs:
(Key: a-above; b-below/bottom; c-center; f-far; l-left; r-right; t-top)

Alamy Images: Amazon-Images 23tr, CML Images 59br. Mark Conlin / VWPICS / Visual&Written SL 42bl, Stephen Dalton / Photoshot Holdings Ltd 39tr, Chris Mattison 32tr, Mauritius images GmbH 32b, MicroScan / Phototake Inc. 12br, Todd Mintz 42crb, Mira 26tl, Richard Mittleman / Gon2Foto 11cr, V. Muthuraman / SuperStock 36clb, NaturePics 64cra, Matthew Oldfield 24br, Clément Philippe / Arterra Picture Library 49crb, Bjorn Svensson / Science Photo Library 69br, Duncan Usher 48–49bc, Dave Watts 13cr, 17ca; Ardea: Steve Downer 27bl, Ferrero-Labat 22–23c, François Gohier 48bl, Stefan Meyers 30cra; Corbis: Hinrich Baesemann / DPA 30-31b, Hal Beral 9tr, Carolina Biological / Visuals Unlimited 10cla, Nigel Cattlin / Visuals Unlimited 15clb, Ralph Clevenger 42–43, Dr. John D. Cunningham / Visuals Unlimited 69cr, Mark Downey 2bc, 24tl, Macduff Everton 53cra, Michael & Patricia Fogden 18–19, 36bl, Stephen Frink 10b, Tim Graham 68br, James Hager / Robert Harding World Imagery 23c, Dave

Hamman / Gallo Images 55crb, Martin Harvey 37br, Martin Harvey / Gallo Images 22bl, Eric & David Hosking 4tl, 48cl, Jason Isley - Scubazoo / Science Faction 42cl, Wolfgang Kaehler 28br, Karen Kasmauski / Science Faction 61tr, Thomas Kitchin & Victoria Hurst / First Light 13br, Peter Kneffel / DPA 54tl, Stephen J. Krasemann / All Canada Photos 34tl, Frans Lanting 4bl, 31cl, 33br, 60bc, Frans Lemmens 49cra, Wayne Lynch / All Canada Photos 31cb, John E. Marriott / All Canada Photos 31tr, Dan McCoy - Rainbow / Science Faction 50cla, Joe McDonald 11clb, 38cl, 68cl, Tim Mckulka / UNMIS / Reuters 52–53, Dong Naide / Xinhua Press 53tr, David A. Northcott 6tl, Michael Redmer / Visuals Unlimited 6bc (plethodon jordani), 9tl, Bryan Reynolds / Science Faction 59fcra, David Scharf / Science Faction 55cl, Shoot 60tl, David Spears / Clouds Hill Imaging Ltd. 65tc, Keren Su 55tl, Jeff Vanuga 58l, Carlos Villoch / Specialist Stock 26–27, Visuals Unlimited 7br, 44tl, Stuart Westmorland 8clb, 11tr, Ralph White 62bl, Lawson Wood 27br, Norbert Wu / Science Faction 20bl, 47c; Dorling Kindersley: ESPL— modelmaker 50r, Exmoor Zoo, Devon 15cra (Azara's Agouti), Hunterian Museum (University of Glasgow) 4cr, 17tr, Trustees of the National Museums Of Scotland 17cla, Natural History Museum, London 4br (larger cockroach), 8tr, 12fbr, 13tl, 16cra, 44br, 58br (two larger coackroaches), 58fcrb (larger cockroach), 59c (larger cockroach), 68ftr, Based on a photo by David Robinson / The Open University 33cr, Rough Guides 50bl, 51br, 61crb, Stanley Park,

Totem Park, Vancouver, British Columbia 2l, 63r, University College, London 51l, Whipsnade Zoo, Bedfordshire Barrie Watts 66ca, 67cra, Jerry Young 4tr, 4cra, 10–11tc, 24cra, 37ca, 56cla, 67tl; FLPA: Ingo Arndt / Minden Pictures 37tr, Flip De Nooyer / Minden 68bc, Michael Durham / Minden Pictures 19cra (leeches), Suzi Eszterhas / Minden Pictures 47br, John Holmes 30–31tc, Donald M. Jones / Minden Pictures 69cra, Mark Moffett / Minden Pictures 29tr, Jurgen & Christine Sohns 35tr, Konrad Wothe / Minden Pictures 45cr, 65cla, Norbert Wu / Minden Pictures 47clb; Fotolia: Eric Isselee 60cl; Getty Images: AFP 64bl, Gerry Bishop / Visuals Unlimited 46br, Tom Brakefield - The Stock Connection / Science Faction 15br, The Bridgeman Art Library 57cr, Stephen Dalton / Minden Pictures 29br, George Day / Gallo Images 8tl, David Doubilet / National Geographic 8-9bc, Georgette Douwma / Photographer's Choice 27tr, Richard du Toit / Gallo Images 47tr, Guy Edwardes / The Image Bank 59tl, Eurasia / Robert Harding World Imagery 62-63bc, George Grall / National Geographic 18clb, Louis-Laurent Grandadam / The Image Bank 55b, Jamie Grill 69ca, Henry Guttmann / Hulton Archive 15tl, Hulton Archive 59bl, David Maitland 44cra, Joe McDonald / Visuals Unlimited 46-47, Bruno Morandi / The Image Bank 20tl, Marwan Naamani / AFP 33tr, Piotr Naskrecki / Minden Pictures 33cb, Radius Images 65br, 71cra, David Silverman 23br, Keren Su 7tr, U.S. Navy 54bl, Mario Vazquez / AFP 43tr, Gary Vestal / Photographer's Choice 7l, 25b, Alex Wild / Visuals Unlimited, Inc. 65cb; imagequestmarine.com: 64br; NASA: GSFC / Craig Mayhew &Robert Simmon 51t; naturepl. com: Chris Gomersall 41tc, Rolf Nussbaumer 45l, Andy Rouse 36r, Kim Taylor 25tr, 38b (dragonflies), Dave Watts 40tc, 40tr, Wild

Wonders of Europe / Rautiainen 69bl; Photolibrary: Kathie Atkinson / Oxford Scientific (OSF) 40clb, Stefan Auth / Imagebroker.net 54br, Paulo de Oliveira / Oxford Scientific (OSF) 10cra, 62cla, David B. Fleetham / Oxford Scientific (OSF) 27cr, François Gilson / Bios 40bl, jspix jspix / Imagebroker.net 12tr, Steven Kazlowski / Alaskastock 60-61cc, Morales Morales / Age fotostock 64clb, Rolf Nussbaumer / Imagebroker.net 21clb, Frank Parker / Age fotostock 35 (main image), Jean-Paul Chatagnon / Bios 49tr, Gerhard Schultz / Oxford Scientific (OSF) 40crb, Gerhard Schulz / Bios 41crb, M. Varesvuo 20-21tc; Science Photo Library: Susumu Nishinaga 12bc, Power & Syred 29tl, 46tr, D. Roberts 39br, Volker Steger 21crb, 21fcrb; SuperStock: Minden Pictures 33cla.

Wall Chart Images: Corbis: Peter Kneffel / DPA (crb/rescue dog), Frans Lanting (cra/penguin), Norbert Wu / Science Faction (crb/spotted shrimp goby); Dorling Kindersley: Natural History Museum, London (br/larger cockroach); Getty Images: Georgette Douwma / Photographer's Choice (fcra/fish), Gary Vestal / Photographer's Choice (c); Photolibrary: jspix jspix / Imagebroker.net (tl/macaw).

Jacket images: Front: Ardea: M. Watson (main image); Dorling Kindersley: Natural History Museum, London tr/(skull); Getty Images: Don Farrall / Photographer's Choice tc/(butterfly); naturepl.com: Nick Garbutt ftr; Back: Photolibrary: Watt Jim / Pacific Stock bl, jspix jspix / Imagebroker.net tl.

All other images © Dorling Kindersley
For further information see: www.dkimages.com